IMPERIAL DIVAS:
THE VICEREINES OF INDIA

Pomp and circumstance in Calcutta. The family of the Viceroy, Lord Hardinge, are escorted from Government House to a Polo match in 1914

IMPERIAL DIVAS:
THE VICEREINES OF INDIA

Penny and Roger Beaumont

HAUS PUBLISHING
LONDON

Dwarfed by the Gates of India arch as they disembark in Bombay in 1926. Lord and Lady Irwin are given their first view of the viceregal fanfare that would be an integral part of their lives in Imperial India.

First published in Great Britain in 2010 by
Haus Publishing Ltd
70 Cadogan Place
London SW1 9AH
www.hauspublishing.com

A CIP catalogue record for this book
is available from the British Library

ISBN 978-1-906598-19-0

Typeset in Optima by MacGuru Ltd
info@macguru.org.uk
Printed and bound in the UK by CPI Mackays, Chatham ME5 8TD

Contents

To Maconda Brown O'Connor, Ph.D., veteran social worker, scholar, distinguished humanitarian and patron of the arts, cherished friend and supportive enthusiast of this project.

Introduction

While some vicereines' lives have been described at length by biographers and historians, they have not been surveyed as a whole. In studies of the Indian viceroyalty, aside from Charlotte Canning, Mary Curzon, Edith Lytton and Edwina Mountbatten, most vicereines have received a few paragraphs or incidental mention, with sparse reference to their charitable work, or involvement in the dynamics of the viceroyalty. Little is to be found in biographies of the viceroys, several of whom had long and distinguished careers of which their time in India was but one episode. Of those several vicereines wrote about their lives in India, perhaps most oustanding of those efforts, Hariot Dufferin's *Our Viceregal Life in India* reveals her deep fascination with India's people and culture, and eagerness to learn more and record her experience. Early drafts of Mary Minto's *India, Minto and Morley*, written to highlight her husband's his role in framing the Morley-Minto reforms of 1909, display a sparkle and texture which were substantially blunted in editing. Yvonne Fitzroy's diary of her service as secretary to Lady Reading offers insights into viceroyalty in the 1920s, including the prejudices and social slights endured by a Jewish viceroy and his wife. But none provide a comprehensive look at these "imperial divas" and the evolution of the role of the viceroy's wife through the 90 years of the *Raj*.

The diaries and oral histories of women who had spent years in India reflect extreme views they held of their experience – either as the most horrific or the most exhilarating and exciting of their lives – or both. Virtually none were ambivalent. Some left India regretfully, savouring an independence of mind and liberating experiences gained there as they returned to a world in which their talents would be far less appreciated, and where they would enjoy far less freedom than they did on the ramparts of empire. Others left joyfully, never looking back, delighted to leave the misery that being in India was for so many women. And a few realised only long afterward how much India "had seeped into their bones."[1]

Most vicereines' unpublished diaries, journals, and correspondence provide details of their experience, as do some of their husbands' papers, both public and private, or letters written home from India. While each viewed India from a unique perspective, some common themes are visible. The vicereines were all at once fascinated by the exotic environment of the East, filled with palaces and bejewelled princes and maharajahs, horrified by the glimpses of the "real" India and its pervasive eroticism, and confused by the unique blend of violence, poverty, ugliness, gross wealth, and sublime beauty. How their views of all that changed during their tour of duty is a common thread of their story. Despite the luxury of dwelling in palatial residences in Calcutta, Simla, and later Delhi, like other Englishwomen in India, vicereines dealt with sometimes appalling heat and humidity, intrusions by insects and animals, spoiled food, warm beverages, and such trivial but cumulatively wearing things as the decay of treasured books, clothing, and shoes. They often left children and elderly parents in England, and until the extension of the cable system, learned of deaths and illnesses only weeks or months after they occurred. And all of them saw death come close, often, and sometimes instantly, and without warning, from disease or terrorism, living with the fear, based on certain knowledge, that they, like the first vicereine, Charlotte Canning, or many loved ones or friends, might not live to return home.

Beyond all that, the public activities of the vicereines, as women at a particular time in history, reflected values and norms that shaped and constrained both British and Anglo-Indian upper class society. Although greatly sheltered from Indian poverty, kept at a distance from the rich texture of myriad subcultures, and cramped by British social pressures aimed at assuring "appropriate" behaviour, all vicereines found India a life-changing experience and none left the subcontinent unaffected. For many, their post-Indian lives provided an interesting coda to their experiences in South Asia. Some continued their social activism in Britain, others moved on to more comfortable diplomatic posts, while a few simply slipped back into their "normal" lives as gentry in the countryside. As a whole, the stories of the vicereines, as facets of the dusky diamond that was British India, are worth the telling.

1
Invisible Empresses:
The Vicereines of India

Since India gained independence in 1947, almost all of the viceroys and vicereines of India have been consigned to the margins of history. Few now recall any of their names or deeds, and the vicereines especially are seen as faded symbols of imperialist vanity, a step or two removed from the bride figure on a wedding cake, decorative mannequins, devoid of identity, the very well dressed and bejeweled wives of and helpmates to Britain's proconsuls in India. Ironically, the most enduring symbol of a vicereine is that of an American, the beauteous Lady Mary Curzon, whose jewel-encrusted "peacock" dress at the 1903 Durbar created a lasting image in British popular culture of a vicereine as a "great ornamental." It was not wholly fanciful. Drawings and photographs of viceregal life show elegant women, beautifully dressed and bejeweled – usually overdressed, given the climate – at ceremonial dinners, garden parties, or durbars, in hunting dress, or riding in a silver *howdah* atop an elephant during a state entrance into the city. A few are pictured in camp on tiger hunts – but only the most daring actually went on *shikar*.

The vicereines' lack of visibility in conventional histories is due in some measure to the harsh glare of post-imperialist judgments which place all that happened under the Raj in a kind of combination of prisoner's box and detention cell, to be castigated in perpetuity. Aside from such reflexive dismissal, the near-eclipse of vicereines also reflects the marginalising of most viceroys of various European imperial powers. The very few brief and distorted portrayals of viceroys of India in popularised history and film leave little sense that from the 1850s until India gained independence from Britain in 1947, they were martial leaders and powerful executives, the highest ranking surrogate monarchs on the globe during the great last phase of imperialism. The fact that they have been forgotten by the children of the former masters as much or more than those of the subjects is not surprising, since they were the most glaring symbols of authoritarian rule. Whether it be deemed schizoidal or hypocritical, they also represented the grand contradiction that many European imperial powers, and the United States as well, established increasingly liberal regimes at home while imposing rule by force over subject peoples.

Whether one looks back at that grand contradiction through literalist lenses, or through such surreal optics as those of post-modernist Subaltern Studies, or post-imperial perspectives, it remains hard to grasp how those elaborate systems of power functioned, and appreciate why the popular stereotype of viceregal marginality is off the mark. But it is also understandable, since few realize today how monarchies and aristocracies were the mainstay of governmental authority throughout most of the world until that elaborate Europe-centred network was mortally wounded by the First World War, leaving only scattered feeble vestiges, symbols and traditions. It means something quite different now to point out that almost all vicereines were aristocratic women than it would have a century ago when such rank and status had a powerful influence both in social circles and the realm of political power. Few now remember that until the middle to the 20th century, parents of *haut bourgeois* American debutantes strove to have their daughters "presented" at the court of St. James, including the Irish-American millionaire and Anglophobe Ambassador Joseph P. Kennedy. And some American luminaries – including the arch-Anglophobe Douglas MacArthur, with a dispensation from Congress to become a Knight of the Bath, since that was technically illegal – accepted British feudal awards of the kind that so offended many of the Founding Fathers, including Washington. And however absurd it may seem to compare pre-1918 nobles and monarchs to 21st Century athletes, film or rock stars, the aura of notoriety that surrounds such popular culture icons offers something of a crude analogy to the degree of celebrity and social leadership that noble and royal status connoted.

After most of the great royal houses of Europe and the Turkish Caliphate were swept away in the Great War, some glimpses of the old aura flashed into view here and there due to media hype, in such cases as Queen Marie of Rumania; the Crown Prince of Germany; Edward, Prince of Wales, who became Edward VIII and later Duke of Windsor; Princess Grace of Monaco; and Diana, Princess of Wales. Significantly, none of those exercised any substantial power, whatever romanticist nostalgia they inspired. Only the Emperor of Japan and monarchs of small and tiny regimes in Europe, most of them constitutional monarchies like Britain's, survived that great cataclysm. In a special paradox, for another generation after the Great War, the viceroys and vicereines of India loomed above that plain of wrecked authoritarian regimes, while many chips in the game of sovereignty were gathered in by dictators. From the vantage point of over a half-century of Indian independence, viceroyalty, depending on one's point of view, appears to have been a splendid feudalistic remnant, an anomaly, or an atavistic reminder of the time so recently past when much of the world was bound in networks of power under the sway of rulers whose status and privilege derived from hereditary succession.[1]

After the first traders of the Honourable East India Company arrived in India in the early 1600s, British influence expanded incrementally as the Mughal empire's power ebbed, so that by the mid-1800s, the basic foundations of what would later be known as the *Raj* were in place. From 1774 onward, the HEIC's chief executive in India was known as the Governor-General, a title retained after the bloody uprising known in Britain as the Great Mutiny of 1857–58, when Britain formally took control of roughly two-thirds of India, and indirect rule of some 600 princely states. Of the 33 Governors-General of India, from Warren Hastings, who took office in 1774 to Admiral of the Fleet Lord Louis Mountbatten, in 1947, the last 20 were also called viceroys, 19 of whose wives held the title of vicereine between 1858 and 1947.[2]

Until the 1920s, those who assumed the premier administrative and diplomatic position in the British Empire were hereditary aristocrats, since, early on, the British government chose its Indian proconsuls of sufficient noble rank to deal effectively with the hundreds of Indian rulers of the various states. British elites also saw the Indian caste system as something like their own social hierarchy, with potentates as "natural aristocrats" worthy of treatment as social equals – within limits. The Marquess of Wellesley's dictum that "India must be ruled from a palace, not a counting house; with the ideals of a prince, not those of a retail dealer in muslin and indigo" set the tone of viceroyalty which encompassed military and civil authority, diplomacy, elaborate court protocols, symbols of prestige, extravagant ceremonials and palaces evanescent of the Mughal dynasty. Beyond that, some hoped that "exporting" aristocrats to the colonies and dominions would replicate Britain's aristocratic hierarchy in those domains, and set proper social standards and tone among their imperial subjects.

Selecting the Viceroy and Governor General of India was highly political, like all major diplomatic appointments, but was further complicated by the requirement that the candidate pass muster with the monarchy, since the viceroy was the ruler's personal representative and the most prominent proconsul in the Empire, overlord of the largest and most populous domain in the empire. And his wife had to meet royal approval as well. While even the last viceroy, Lord Mountbatten, deemed it "The greatest office in the world,"[3] not all vicereines were enthusiastic about being required to "...play at being kings and queens," as Emily Lytton Lutyens put it.[4] The Viceroy of India was far more an autocrat than other Governors General in the empire, despite many constraints from the Home Government and the politics of India itself. Even after the telegraph link to London was completed in 1870, establishing instant communications between Calcutta and London, the viceroy retained significant powers, particularly in foreign affairs and local defense matters. His own foreign minister, the viceroy was also the crown's principal representative to some 600 princely states that included roughly two-fifths of the subcontinent's area. While his wife lacked formal authority, she had considerable influence and responsibilities as vice-queen, and had to be willing and able to bear the many burdens of the office, as well as basking in the fame and glory that came with the appointment.

The motives and attitudes of the 20 viceroys who served between 1858 and 1947 – and in several cases, desperately lobbied for the prestigious office – were as varied as their backgrounds. Although the first viceroy, Lord Canning, was the son of a former foreign secretary and Prime Minister, his performance in several early diplomatic posts did not suggest that he was well-suited for such a responsible role and London gossips attributed his being sent out to India as a way to separate him from his long-time mistress. His successor, Sir John Lawrence, was an old India "hand," with many years of service under his belt before being named viceroy, and had the additional cachet of being the brother of Sir Henry Lawrence, a hero of the Indian Mutiny. The Elgin, Minto, Hardinge, and Irwin families had historic links to India, while Dufferin and Lansdowne were highly respected diplomats for whom the viceroyalty was seen to be a reward for prior services. Lord Mayo, relatively unknown outside Ireland when appointed, saw India as a place to "do good," as did Lord Ripon, who was rewarded for his services to the Liberal Party in the 1880 election under the tortuous logic that his being made viceroy was less controversial, his being a Catholic, than filling a cabinet post. Lord Northbrook, one of whose forbears was Chairman of the East India Company, reluctantly accepted the viceroyalty at Prime Minister Gladstone's urging. So did his successor, the romantic and eccentric Robert Lytton, not eager to leave the sophisticated courts of Europe for the heat and danger of the East, but somewhat attracted by India's reputation for sensuality and opulence.

No viceroy sought the post more ardently than George Curzon. Highly and blatantly ambitious, and convinced he was destined for great things,

Curzon had visited the Dufferins in 1887. The similarity of Calcutta's Government House to Kedleston, his family residence, fed his resolve to become a ruler of India. On the other end of the spectrum, Lord Chelmsford's appointment was more a matter of fate. While he was serving as a captain in the Territorials in India in 1916, Prime Minister Asquith chose him on the basis of his being a Liberal and, like the PM, a Fellow of All Souls. That sudden and dramatic elevation startled many in British elite circles, although Chelmsford had been the governor of two Australian provinces and was nominated as governor of Bombay.

The appointment of Rufus Isaacs, Lord Reading, set up much greater shock-waves. Not only did he lack the Indian connections and aristocratic background of most viceroys, but he was a Jew. Lord Montagu, Secretary of State for India (SOSI) at the time Reading was appointed and also Jewish, reasoned that Reading being, in a sense, an Oriental, he would therefore provide a "natural bond" which would make him an effective viceroy.[5]

Lord Willingdon's lengthy services in India, including tours as the President of Bombay and Madras, were seen as sound credentials for the "top job." Both he and Lady Willingdon agreed, seeing the position as the appropriate capstone of his – or more accurately, their – career. Disappointed several times by having been passed over for the viceroyalty, the Willingdons returned in triumph in 1931, and fervidly played the roles of Lord and Lady Sahib.

Willingdon's successor, Lord Linlithgow, was an acknowledged expert on Indian affairs in the Conservative Party, having chaired a Parliamentary select committee which paved the way for the Government of India Act of 1935. The last two viceroys – Wavell and Mountbatten – were top echelon military commanders, and the latter was very closely connected – indeed, related – to the royal family. Twice a theater commander in the early years of World War II, and Commander-in-Chief India under Linlithgow, Wavell, in the role of viceroy, oversaw the last phase of the conflict in India, while Mountbatten, after heading Southeast Asia Command, 1943–45, shouldered the greatest and last burden born by a viceroy in orchestrating the demise of the *Raj*, partition, and the bloody and tragic transition to independence.

From the moment that vicereines-to-be learned that the viceroyalty was imminent, they approached their tenure in India with varying levels of enthusiasm and excitement, but with certain common fears. Beneath all the grand and glittering facades and the posturing of the *Raj* were layers of steel that reflected the essential insecurity of what Philip Mason called "the Guardians." As Mary Minto wrote in the first drafts of her book *India, Minto and Morley*, "we rule India by the sword." The list of grim contingencies which vicereines faced was long and intimidating. On the personal level, the viceregal family, like all Britons in India, faced the risks of disease, accident, and violence. A wide spectrum of threats, from the greatest of cataclysms to a household servant running amok, bedeviled most viceroys throughout their tours of service, and suffused the viceregal entourage with a constant sense of danger and alertness. Beyond the dimension of personal safety, as administrators, the viceroy had to cope with vast array of matters, including famine, plague, assassination, riots, terrorism, agitation, espionage, transport, agriculture, irrigation, the legal system, health care, education, forestry, police, public works, etc., leaving little time for family or social concerns, which became the vicereine's responsibility. Expectations for the vicereine were high. In 1905, the SOSI St. John Broderick bluntly told Mary Minto what was in store for her: "Remember your domestic life is at an end. A Viceroy is the hardest worked servant of the state: your part is to relieve him of his trivial worries and ease his burden to the best of your ability," a rather clear statement of what the government expected of a vicereine.

In the domain of security and defense, the grimmest prospects facing viceroys in the late 19th Century were another uprising like the Great Mutiny or a massive Russian invasion – or both. Thinking out and preparing for such grim contingencies was a main preoccupation of the Home government, the SOSI and his staff, the viceroy and his Council and staffs, and the senior British military officers in India. Although many worthies published articles in popular journals on the Russian threat, there could be no serious public discussion by pundits in periodicals of graver questions like the quandary of so many chips being at risk in sustaining the *Raj* that there seemed to be no clear advantage in maintaining it. The balance sheet, to the extent that imperialists were able to measure prospects on any kind of cost-benefit basis, did not justify Britain's holding onto India so tightly, especially if the proverbial balloon went up in the East. The "Great Game," the not-all-that covert game of push-and-shove between Britain and the Tsarist empire in Central Asia, was openly discussed by pundits and statesmen, and dramatised by Kipling's novel *Kim*. The threat of that erupting into a major war highlighted the tension between Mother Country's defense concerns and India's strategic interests.

The claim of the *Raj* serving a guardian or steward of India as it evolved under the philosopher kings of the Indian Civil Service rang hollow when Britain realigned its strategy after the humiliating and expensive Boer War of 1899–1901. Planners recognised that India's security needs did not mesh closely with the Mother Country's, especially the revised war plans that required Britain to deploy substantial forces to defend India while fielding large armies in Europe.[6] Some of those concerns could be discussed in public, with appropriate caution, of course, but other matters were restricted to the inner councils of power.

Although the vicereines were certainly aware of the diplomatic and military issues with which their husbands were grappling, their first and foremost concern remained their own and their family's health and safety. As they fulfilled their duties and dealt with family matters at the core of their life, like most women of their class and British women in India and elsewhere in the Empire, the vicereines' time abroad was a mix of pleasures and ordeals. Unlike most of the other *memsahibs*, however, their tours of duty were brief, from five to seven years, in which inconveniences, the lack of "civilised" comforts, and dangers endured to support their husbands' careers were buffered by omnipresent retainers and servants and the fact that they lived in huge palaces.

Despite their rank and privilege, vicereines shared many of the attitudes toward the Indian experience of other European women. The mid-19th century vicereines, especially those of childbearing age, lived with the perils associated with pregnancy and childbirth, and all European women, regardless of their status, were haunted by the memory of the Great Mutiny of 1857–58. They were well-acquainted with the massacres at Meerut, Cawnpore and Lucknow, and most had read the post-mutiny literature which often dwelt on the violence perpetrated by the rebels against women and children. The constant reminders of these horrors engendered a suspicion and fear of Indians – even trusted servants – which lasted for years and which coloured the behaviour of most, if not all, British women in India. In spite of that pervasive fear, as the memories of the uprising began to fade, some vicereines took advantage of their position to seize upon the unique opportunities to travel, study exotic cultures, sketch, paint or take photographs, ride to the hounds, and shoot big game, while maintaining their position atop an elaborate social hierarchy in some ways more feudal than the aristocratic-royal nexus in the Mother Country.

In addition to worries about the effect of viceroyalty on family well-being and finances, there were the more diffuse but no less burdensome prospects of being at the pinnacle of India's social firmament, and in the media spotlight as well. When Charles Canning's appointment was being debated in 1855, Charlotte wrote her sister:" I will not take any part in the decision, only be ready to follow like a dog." Her submissive words to the contrary, Charlotte would have endured any hardship for the chance to have her beloved and unfaithful "Carlo" all to herself and to rekindle the early passion of her marriage once his inamoratas were thousands of miles away.

Mary Louisa Elgin, Julia Mayo, and Harriette Lawrence were in their childbearing years during their husband's viceroyalty, and determined to be "good soldiers" for the *Raj*, balancing the dread of delivering and raising a young child in the dreaded Indian climate against their desire to be close to their husbands. Hariot Dufferin, Maud Lansdowne, and Mary Minto, experienced diplomatic wives (and past childbearing), were less intimidated by the prospect of viceroyalty. Each was fully aware of how important it was that their husbands performed well in filling the most powerful position in the Empire, and recognised their role in helping their spouses by publicly and privately demonstrating the solid Victorian "family values" so important to the *memsahibs* of the *Raj*. Their prior experience as well as their connections to the royal family gave them absolute self-assurance in conducting their vicereinal duties with aplomb and relative ease. Mary Curzon was less confident, both because of her American heritage and her relative youth. Ever deferential to her overbearing if devoted husband, she worried about her ability to handle the responsibilities of being vicereine. Nevertheless, she was determined to support her beloved husband by using her considerable charm to smooth the troubled waters often generated by a demanding and highly critical viceroy.

The mid-20th century vicereines also had mixed feelings about their position before heading off to India. Only the death of Alice Reading's mother in October 1920 enabled the Readings to go to India, since she and her mother had been inseparable. Reading would never have gone to India without his wife, and her health remained a consuming concern throughout his viceroyalty. He even obtained a letter signed by the Prime Minister Lloyd George and the SOSI, Lord Montagu, stating that if Alice's health should prove to be a serious problem, Reading could resign the viceroyalty at the end of his second year, "…however untimely and regrettable this might be for public reasons, there could be no cause of complaint."[7] Doreen Linlithgow shared her husband's reluctance to leave Scotland in 1936, and was desperately homesick during most of her tenure, as were her daughters. The luxuries and "perks" of their imperial lifestyle weighed for little, and beyond the usual concerns about family at home, personal safety in India, and family finances, the Linlithgows arrived in a nation striving for independence, and suffering from increasing ethnic and religious conflicts as Europe moved visibly closer to the brink of another general war. Like Lady Curzon, Lady Linlithgow was frequently ill, and she found herself caught in the role of buffer between her husband's dislike of ostentation and the customary routines and ceremonies of the viceregal court.

The last vicereine, Edwina Mountbatten, was probably the most reluctant to go to India yet arguably had one of the most impressive and successful reigns. Both Mountbattens were stunned when the call came from the Prime Minister: "Bombshell from the PM," was Edwina's reaction to the news, later noting in her diary her husband's possible appointment as "Possible new horror job."[8] She would have much preferred to keep on with her post-war relief work in Britain and Europe. Nevertheless, Edwina had already played a major role in her husband's campaign to acquire a higher rank – a viscountancy rather than the proposed baronetcy as thanks for his war service – working under his direction behind the scenes to apply "quiet pressure" (including a personal visit to the Palace) to gain her husband the rank he thought he deserved.[9] Mountbatten battled for the peerage more directly, writing briefing papers rationalising his elevation that "somehow" found their way to the King. A master at self-promotion, Mountbatten did not doubt Edwina's suitability for the position, having once told her that if the viceroyalty "ever became unavoidable, I know you would make the world's ideal vicereine!"[10] As she warmed to the task, Edwina told a friend "Isn't it delicious? Some of the old hands around here refer to me as the Vice Queen. It makes me feel like Mrs. Meyrick," a reference to a lady who ran "clubs" in London that were regularly raided by the police.[11]

And while all the vicereines knew the importance of their role, some – Mary Curzon, Constance Elgin, Frances Chelmsford and Marie Willingdon – had watched their husbands aggressively maneuver and lobby for the viceregal appointment, and knew that a wife's concerns or fears would not keep their husbands from going out to India. Those like Harriette Lawrence and Marie Willingdon who attained the viceroyalty after long service in India, were more prepared for some of the particular aspects of the position. Alice Reading was keenly aware that she and her husband would be under close scrutiny and before leaving England both she and Reading prepared by improving those skills traditionally associated with the aristocracy, such as riding and ballroom dancing. Her husband's many successes capped by his being the only commoner since the Duke of Wellington to rise to an earldom (later marquessate), and her rank of countess did not compensate for their faith being a debit in the eyes of many in British and Anglo-Indian society.

There was, of course, no real job description for aristocrats, let alone viceroys and vicereines. The feudal system in which most of them were nurtured was originally based on granting holdings of land in exchange for obligations to provide military service to one's liege lord, a complex system which over time became hereditary. In keeping with that duality of duty and pedigree, almost all the vicereines were seen as doing their duty by just being there, well-turned out and gracious, and standing alongside the viceroy. But as grand, powerful and glittering as the viceregal couples appeared to be, especially when photographs began to appear in the mass media, they were human, and vulnerable to many dangers, from disease and financial difficulties, to accidents and a chronic threat of assault by terrorists. Indebtedness had dogged aristocratic families over the centuries, as the host-parasite relationship between nobility and *bourgeoisie* led to fusion through marriage, and ultimately the triumph of wealth over feudal honour. The exasperation of tradesmen with aristocrats ignoring duns and skipping out on debts became a major sub-theme in European literature, and from the late Renaissance onward, the spectacle of foreclosure, seizure, and fleeing creditors was omnipresent in towns, cities, and sometimes on the great estates.

Indeed, for nearly all the viceroys, financial concerns were paramount in the decision to accept the viceroyalty. Even though gaining great wealth did not guarantee status and respectability in higher social circles, nor were they necessarily lost with impoverishment, many looking at the upper strata from a distance assumed that those in the very highest tiers of the upper classes were boundlessly rich. In fact, many prominent British aristocratic families were chronically indebted or land-poor, and being in parlous financial straits drove several viceroys to seek or accept the job. The eighth Earl of Elgin, for example, reluctantly decided to go to India to earn money to improve his Scottish estate of Broomhall, while Lord Lansdowne, who labelled his time in India as a "term of banishment," was brought back from the financial brink by his viceroy's income and the ability to lease out Lansdowne House, the family's mansion in London, during his absence. In 1910, when Lord Hardinge was considering the offer to become viceroy, Lord Kitchener, who desperately coveted the viceregal appointment, advised Hardinge that an annual income of at least £8,000 was the minimum necessary for maintaining proper standards of dress and entertaining. Lansdowne, however, rebutted Kitchener's negative analysis, telling Hardinge that he had managed to save £20,000 during his tenure, the equivalent of several million early 21st century dollars. Hardinge, buoyed up by Lansdowne's more encouraging counsel, took the job, inadvertently putting an end to Kitchener's viceregal hopes. At the opposite end of the financial spectrum, Mary Curzon's and Edwina Mountbatten's personal wealth enabled their husbands to take on the job with few financial worries and to maintain the viceregal households in a manner both Curzon and Mountbatten found appropriate – and expensive.[12]

Despite the financial effects of Indian service – beneficial or draining – on any particular viceregal family, and the vicereines' lack of formal authority in the Indian government structure, most showed substantial skill in managing their many responsibilities and imposing their will while playing the role of a symbolic queen. Even though most viceroys served a term of roughly five years, with no prospect of continuance, vicereines exercised more power during that tenure than the wives of most presidents and prime ministers, and even the consorts of most European sovereigns, aside from the empresses of the Hapsburg and Romanov imperial houses and the consorts of Windsor male monarchs. But their status, like the viceroy's, was a constitutional anomaly, in keeping with H. G. Wells' view of British presence in India as an accident, "like a man who has fallen off a ladder on to the back of an elephant and doesn't know what to do or how to get down. Until something happens he remains." The Indian government's organizational chart, for example, included no deputy viceroy. Although the occasion never arose, if a viceroy was rendered unable to govern at a time when communications with the home government were impaired, as in a Great Mutiny II scenario, a vicereine – and certainly some more than others – might well have taken an active hand in the process of governance *a la* Woodrow Wilson's wife until the Home government named a proper successor. The most notable example of a vicereine assuming governmental authority, albeit temporarily, is that of Winifred Hardinge, who in the immediate aftermath of the terrorist bomb which severely wounded her husband, assumed responsibility for communicating with Indian officials as well as the monarch and the home government. Frances Chelmsford was also involved in governmental affairs. At her husband's request, she discussed the appointment of her husband's Military Secretary, Ralph Verney, with Austen Chamberlain, the SOSI, and then with the man himself. Flattered by the new vicereine's personal attention, Verney accepted the appointment; he could not have predicted the misery Lady Chelmsford would create for him and his wife during her reign.[13]

How much any of the other vicereines took on similar authority or responsibility behind the scenes remains unclear. Like many wives of politicians in England they often exercised substantial influence behind the scenes, and their involvement in the actual governance of India as informal advisors to their husbands is well-documented, such as the role of Lady Curzon in attempting to mediate the bitter dispute between the viceroy and Lord Kitchener which ultimately led to Curzon's resignation. Most vicereines also played prominent roles within their families and on the stage of British politics, as well as in the government of India, and despite their formally powerless and anomalous role, several vicereines used their sometimes considerable charm to influence or gather information from people important to the viceroy. Military officials discussed strategy and upcoming operations with them, sometimes at length in correspondence. On visits home, vicereines served as unofficial channels between the viceroy and the India Office, government officials and members of Parliament, pressing their husbands' policies and talking with politicians.

Like the viceroys, almost all vicereines were the offspring of English, Scottish, or Irish landed nobility. While their feelings about India ranged from excitement and enthusiasm to reluctance and horror, most vicereines were upper class British women imbued with a sense of duty, with their primary focus on husband and family. Most came from prominent, usually aristocratic families, with their fathers, brothers, and/or sons in politics, the diplomatic service, or the military. Often, their own family's rank, relationships, and wealth aided their husband's career.

Charlotte Canning, a former lady-in-waiting and a favourite of the Queen, was never in personal danger during the Mutiny, but her detailed accounts of its progress, atrocities, and horrors – including notations about the difficulty of telling truth from rumour – which she sent directly to Queen Victoria had a significant impact on the monarch's perception of the grim events unfolding. The monarch asked Charlotte to confirm and expand upon the official and media reports of British women being "defiled" by native rebels, and as the months passed, Victoria told Charlotte that she had come to depend more upon her than her ministers or accurate and specific information about the mutiny.[14]

Mary Minto also had significant political and royal connections as daughter of Sir Charles Grey, private secretary to Prince Albert, and later, to Queen Victoria. She had been raised at Windsor Castle, and was a close friend with several of the Queen's daughters as well as Queen Alexandra. Although not as close to the royals as Lady Minto, Maud Lansdowne was arguably the most aristocratic vicereine and a renowned political hostess. The daughter of the first duke of Abercorn, Maud's aristocratic pedigree was further enhanced by her marriage, as was that of her sister Albertha who married the heir to the Duke of Marlborough.[15]

Winifred Hardinge's family connections and social skills helped her husband achieve his goal of becoming viceroy and following in the footsteps of his grandfather, the 1st Viscount Hardinge who had served as Governor General of India from 1844–1848. She once jokingly attributed her husband's success in the diplomatic service to the fact that "My family knows Lord Salisbury [then Prime Minister] well," she said, "and as everyone knows, Lord Salisbury cannot remember names. So each time there's a new post to be filled, Lord Salisbury says to one of his staff: 'What's the name of that diplomat Winifred Sturt married?' – and it's still Charlie Hardinge, so he gets the post."[16]

For all vicereines – but particularly for those not as well-connected or personally known to the royal family – there was a quiet, behind-the-scenes review process before the appointment was formalised, similar to the vetting of corporate, political, and military spouses in the modern world. Discreet inquiries were made regarding the suitability of a viceregal candidate's wife, not only because she would represent the Crown, but because it was understood – but rarely discussed specifically, in the open, at least – that she would influence her husband's policies as well as his world-view, and have a powerful role in shaping the tone and substance of Anglo-Indian high society. Those with close links to the royal family like Charlotte Canning, Winfred Hardinge, Mary Minto, Dorothy Irwin, and Edwina Mountbatten, usually passed official and royal scrutiny easily, as did those whose husbands held high-level positions in the government, or in major diplomatic posts, like Hariot Dufferin, Maud Lansdowne, and Marie Willingdon.

For a few, the going was tougher. Mary Curzon's beauty, charm, and enormous wealth weighed for little among her critics. Most such barbs were aimed privately, but even the Queen, when Lord Salisbury brought Curzon's appointment before her asked: "Would Mrs. Curzon who is an American do to represent a Vice Queen?"[17] Both Salisbury and the American ambassador, John Hay, hastened to assure the Queen that Mary was more than suitable, and the latter wrote encouragingly to Mary that "No Vicereine has ever gone to India with so full an equipment of knowledge and capacity. No Vicereine with such resources of radiance and charm."[18]

Alice Reading probably faced the greatest scrutiny, both at home and in India. Although her husband was a famous lawyer and well-known in the councils of power, Alice had not moved in the same aristocratic and political circles as her predecessors, and due to her poor health, did not entertain her husband's friends and allies with the same energy and regularity as other political hostesses of the day. To further complicate matters, the Readings were not only *bourgeois* but Jewish, which placed them in an elite social milieu in which both class-snobbery and anti-Semitism were pervasive, and, like the fins of sharks, only fleetingly and momentarily visible, just often enough to maintain the sense of menace. While many doubted the Readings' suitability for viceroyalty, none dared openly display their intolerance.

A similar scrutiny of the new vicereine was conducted – albeit usually via the newspapers and "reports" from those who had met the new appointee – by the leaders of Anglo-Indian society. The British community in India felt that it was imperative that the rank, social skills, and bearing of the wife of the man holding the exalted position of viceroy needed to match her role as "vice-queen" and they were quite prepared to prejudge the new vicereine, or at least to form an immediate opinion when she arrived. The vicereine sat atop an incredibly rigid and elaborate social system set forth in a Warrant of Precedence listing all positions in British India and relative rank. Being first lady of the *Raj* to whom all others looked for social guidance exposed her to close scrutiny and criticism, with every dress, hat, and jewel she wore, every conversational gambit, whim, and gesture a potential subject for gossip and journalistic reportage. So were her actions as hostess, especially if she changed any complex ritual, for such details and procedures were seen as a vital part of the fabric of prestige and the tone of the Anglo-Indian social scene by Britons who lived most of their adult lives in that social network

The vicereines were equally judgmental – at least initially – about Anglo-Indian society. Many, if not most were accustomed to the relatively lively and informal social life of the British aristocracy, and they found the Indian regimen stilted, and the people they had to entertain rather boring. Charlotte Canning wrote her mother about the dullness of Calcutta society and feeling isolated, for no one would speak to her "voluntarily" because of protocol and rank. Others, like Hariot Dufferin, were more comfortable in the rigid social ambiance, where formal social interactions were carefully planned and specified. And like it or not, every vicereine knew she was bound to uphold certain standards, and that any deviation would be criticised.

Some vicereines tried to put a personal stamp on that highly cohesive and reactionary inner circle by increasing or decreasing the formality of the viceregal court ritual, or trying to inspire more productive behaviour by engaging in charitable works, an increasingly popular activity among aristocratic and *haute bourgeois* women in England and elsewhere from the mid-19th century onward. As a result, several vicereines made significant contributions to the welfare of India and to imperial imagery. Despite the onus that has accrued to the label "imperial," they warrant some recognition for attempting, as intelligent, caring women, to seek improvements in health and well-being in India on a then unprecedented scale. From Lady Hariot Dufferin in 1885 to Lady Edwina Mountbatten in 1947, viceroys' wives strove, to varying degrees of effort, to provide improved medical care in India, especially to women and children. While a few plunged into this work eagerly and energetically, others were less enthusiastic, preferring the comforts of Government House and chairing committees and overseeing fund-raising social events to visiting dispensaries and *zenanah* hospitals.

Like aristocratic women in Britain, the vicereines' grinding routine of cutting ribbons, giving prizes, chairing committees, and overseeing large households were familiar duties, but obviously not to such a degree. Far more energy and attention was required to oversee viceregal residences and social schedules, and large staffs than for even the grandest London mansion or country estate. Like its counterpart in England, the viceregal court had an annual calendar, but one dictated far more by the weather than by events: winter in Calcutta (later New Delhi), late spring through summer in the hills at Simla, fall tours of various princely states and a return in late fall to Calcutta to begin the cycle again. The viceregal social calendar was complicated by a constant flow of visitors from home – royalty, politicians, or just friends of someone who knew the viceroy.

Departure and arrival

A new vicereine, once her husband's appointment was announced, faced a myriad of decisions and planning. Would the children go or stay home under the care of relatives? What family silver and plate and other entertaining necessities would be taken to India? Then there was the tricky question of which family servants would accompany the family and which would remain to help maintain estates or London homes. The Readings intended to use the appointment as a reason to pension off Alice's devoted maid and former nanny, Squires, whose age and health had long since kept her from active service. It fell to Lord Reading to give Squires the bad news, which he began by announcing that he had accepted the viceroyalty and that they would soon be embarking for India. "That will be very nice," Squires replied, "I have always wanted to see India." Somehow the new viceroy couldn't bring himself to burst her bubble of anticipation, so Squires accompanied the Readings to India and stayed for the full five years.[19]

Another major concern was the vicereine-designate's wardrobe which had to be significantly expanded, to include appropriate day dresses and elaborate evening gowns ordered and fitted before departure. In the nineteenth century, that often meant a stop in Paris at Mr. Worth's emporium. Lord Dufferin gave Hariot and her daughter free rein as they prepared for India: "[I have] imagined two wild women being turned loose w/unlimited credit at the family's bankers... . . you are welcome to any amount of tea gowns, morning toilettes and evening costumes, especially as I hope to arrive in time to see you wear them."[20] In addition to her new wardrobe from Worth, Mary Curzon employed a seamstress for two months to sew her "simpler" garments as well as clothes for her small daughter and an expected new baby. Charlotte Canning also ordered gowns from Worth, but she also ordered large numbers of simpler white muslin dresses, albeit trimmed in Valenciennes lace, in preparation for the heat of India. Mindful of the post-war constraints most women were suffering, Edwina Mountbatten had old garments altered before going to India, but she also had new ones made by her dressmaker, including a simple gown of ivory brocade for her first major appearance as vicereine, the swearing-in ceremony to take place in Delhi, the better to show off her decorations – the Crown of India, the Conspicuous Service Medal, the Grand Cross of the Order of St. John – and her tiara and jewels.

The jewels posed a special dilemma. The vice-queen could not be outshone by any European woman in India, and should be able to at least hold her own in the face of diamonds and emeralds as large as pigeon's eggs worn by maharajahs and maharanis at official events. Charlotte Canning took along her grandmother's ropes of pearls, fully expecting to return with even more, larger ones. Even the Liberal Lord Ripon, who came to India determined to reduce the "swagger" of the viceregal court in the wake of Lytton's extravagances, wrote to his wife that he was considering spending £2,000 on a necklace for her to wear as vicereine. In addition to a large pre-departure cash gift to her husband, Mary Curzon's father provided his daughter with a magnificent tiara and other jewels to ensure that she would not arrive lacking the requisite magnificence. While Maud Lansdowne lacked Mary Curzon's enormous personal fortune she was able to flaunt a five-row necklace of what were popularly known as "the Lansdowne pearls," on formal viceregal occasions. Rivalling any of those worn by an Indian potentate, the Lansdowne pearls earned praise from the Maharajah of Holkar, who was struck not so much by their size, but their "light."

Whatever their financial status, once the announcement was made, the full fiscal impact of the decision became immediately apparent to viceroys and vicereines as they were apprised of the substantial pre-arrival expenses. The incoming viceroy was required to purchase his predecessor's silverware and plate, horses, carriages and contents of the wine cellar, as well as paying for his own and his entourage's passage to India. For the Curzons, in 1898, that required an outlay of roughly £9,700, as well as £1,000 for Mary's new Worth wardrobe – all chosen by George – plus his new uniforms, and new jewels for the vicereine – equal to roughly a million 21st century American dollars. Arrangements also had to be made regarding the family homes (renting them out gave several viceroys a sizable windfall), and accommodations arranged for the vicereine's expected home visits. If the family's London residence was not available, a vicereine could usually count on family or friends to provide temporary lodgings, often an entire mansion which provided appropriate viceregal status.

In addition to the financial complications attendant to the viceroyalty was the social turbulence which began with announcement of the appointment to the most important post in the Empire. Whether abroad or at home, that brought a wave of media attention and a literal flood of invitations. For most of the appointees, the most, the most important of those was to "dine and sleep" at Windsor with the monarch. After 1878, during that visit a vicereine-designate would be invested with the Imperial Order of the Crown of India, which had been established that year by Queen Victoria, following her assumption of the title of Empress of India,[21] and which continued well into the 20th century, even as India came ever closer to independence from the crown. The pre-departure social turmoil continued as the newly elevated viceregal couple was honoured at banquets and balls, and at numerous "small" parties given by their friends. For example, while preparing to depart for India in 1898, the Curzons were given the Freedom of the City of London, and honoured at a Court ball at Buckingham Palace, in addition to dinners in Oxford and Southport, and a gala ball given by the Duke of Portland at Welbeck Abbey. Things hadn't changed much; the society press described a similar round of grand entertainments that marked the imminent departure of the Willingdons in 1931 as "the Willingdon Season." A reporter deemed the viceroy-to-be "the most charming man in London society..." and his wife a woman who "possesses intense energy...and both seem extraordinarily young" – an interesting comment since Willingdon, at 64, was the oldest man to assume the viceroyalty, and his wife was 55.[22] Nor was her fascination with the colour mauve overlooked, with one story describing Lady Willingdon's creation of a "Blue Gallery" in her home, stocked with Chinese art, furniture and cushions in her favourite colour. In the month they had to prepare for departure in 1946, the Mountbattens were feted by the cream of London society, including their royal relations, with every event reported in detail in the society press. One farewell cocktail party for some 700 guests included the Duke of Gloucester, Marina, the recently widowed Duchess of Kent, Queen Ena of Spain and a host of friends and co-workers. By the time she boarded the plane for India, Edwina was exhausted by a recent minor surgery, the closing of her house, and the constant entertainments.

In the midst of all the social events, the new vicereine had to supervise the packing, and make decisions regarding what would be needed during the long voyage, and at stops along the way, and what could be stowed until arrival in India. While her husband was briefed on official matters, the new vicereine usually received some helpful advice from her predecessor on wardrobe, household and entertaining needs, as well as family matters, including children's nurses and schooling. In addition to previous vicereines, others, even government officials, were often eager to give advice.

Although the viceroy-designate did not assume his office officially until arriving in India, or in some cases, at Aden, leaving London offered the first glimpse the impending formality and ceremony, with guards of honour and bands at Victoria station, and official farewells from representatives of the government and the royal family. Any thrill that accrued from being the centre of attention was diluted by sadness as they said goodbye to family and friends, but any show of untoward emotion was eschewed, no matter how great the strain. When Mary Minto's sister, Louisa, Countess of Antrim, went to see the Prince and Princess of Wales off to India a few weeks before the Mintos left, she suffered in advance anticipating her sister's departure. "It gave me a lump in my throat, thinking of Mary in a fortnight," Louisa wrote. On November 2, 1905, after tearfully parting with their school-age sons who were remaining in England, Lord and Lady

The State procession from the Apollo Bunder in Bombay, marking the arrival of Lord and Lady Chelmsford in India in April 1916. The Golden parasol is visible above the viceregal carriage.

Minto left from Victoria Station after what Louisa described as "a tremendous send off, and all so well behaved."[23] The Mintos' experience was a typical bittersweet departure – the beginning of a great adventure, but tinged with sadness as well as triumph, presaging the harder realities of going east of Suez, and then encountering life in India.

Whatever the inner turmoil or personal discomfort, outward appearances counted most. The vicereines were always described in the press as enthusiastic about their journey. "Lady Willingdon," a journalist noted, "could not have looked more smiling or happy if she had been starting on her honeymoon instead of leaving for a disturbed country to help her husband in a mission of extreme delicacy and difficult." While that was probably all too true in Lady Willingdon's case, Mary Curzon's departure was opposite in tone and mood. Immediately after a farewell dinner at the Cecil Hotel, accompanied by only her children and their nanny, she left London on the midnight train to Plymouth to join her husband in Marseilles. As she boarded *S.S. Arabia* the next morning, there was no band or official ceremony, and the new vicereine was overcome by the realization that she was moving several thousand miles farther from her American family.

"Going out" was not an easy journey for the early vicereines despite their VIP status, and the opening of the Suez Canal in 1869 which smoothed the way and eliminated several embarkations and disembarkations. And although ships grew larger and faster, and creature comforts improved, things did not improve all that much in the later years of the *Raj*. For the earlier vicereines, depending upon the number of stops, trips out and back could take as long as two months. Sometimes, of course, that leisurely pace was the product of choice. The Cannings, for example, embarked in November, 1855, and did some sightseeing in Paris, Alexandria, and Cairo while progressing toward India. The Lyttons made much the same journey in 1876, stopping in Paris so that Lady Lytton could order clothes from Worth, then moving on to the British Embassy in Rome, embarking from Naples on a troopship for Alexandria, and eventually arriving in Bombay. In Edith Lytton's case, the long journey proved all the more difficult when pregnancy added to her misery from seasickness.

Despite all the inconveniences – rough weather and seasickness, boring company aboard ship, state functions along the way, and ever-increasing heat on the way out in an age without air conditioning – most vicereines saw the sea voyage as the real beginning of their great adventure. As Alice Reading wrote home to her family: "The fairy tale has begun in earnest," even though some things hadn't changed since Edith Lytton's time, even with faster and larger ships. Three days later, a seasick Alice wrote that she was "...hanging on by my eyelashes to the table."[24] When the seas calmed, viceregal couples passed the time by reading books about India, and a few tried to learn Hindustani in preparation for their new positions.

Official ceremonies, smaller in scale than those which marked the departure from London, marked the welcome stops along the ocean journey. However novel and fascinating, they were mere hints of what was to come. Landing in Aden, the first outpost of their new empire, vicereines gained the first view of the elaborate stagecraft that would henceforth accompany their every arrival and departure. It was here that the viceroy assumed all the "attributes" of his new position, including the hoisting of his viceregal flag on board the ship. Once it was moored in the harbour, the couple boarded a State barge manned by scarlet liveried attendants, and went ashore to be greeted by the British Resident, government and military officials, and crowds of curious locals. This was the vicereine's first official ceremony in the tropics, standing under a large umbrella or a tent, listening to lengthy speeches while perspiration soaked through her elegant and usually clothing too heavy for the climate, and longing for a cool drink. At each stop, the vicereines were housed in palaces whose luxury and magnificence were unlike anything most of them had ever seen, bolstering their hope that life in India would be lived in similar

A painting by William Simpson of Lord Canning's visit to the Maharaja of Kashmir, in 1867. Gives an indication of how crowded and formal a viceroy's life could be.

surroundings. The proverbial opulence of the East was pervasive, even in so mundane a matter as bath furnishings. Charlotte Canning wrote home that the towels in Said Pasha's Alexandria palace had "...gold embroidery six inches deep around them – it is like wiping one's face on a Field Marshal's uniform."[25]

For vicereines who went to India during the era of the "high *Raj*" from the 1870s until the advent of World War II, arrival on the subcontinent provided the first real perspective on the complex matrix of the ceremony and protocol that would surround them while they were in India, although most were familiar and even comfortable with aristocratic social norms, including the more demanding protocol of royalty. As the ship neared Bombay, the new vicereine waited anxiously for her first close-up view of the Indian subcontinent that was to be her home for at least the next five years.[26] Even though she had already felt the mounting heat while crossing the Indian Ocean, only landing in India brought full understanding of what lay in store. She found that her delicate parasol offered little shelter from the burning sun, that her carefully chosen arrival gown was clinging to her skin and that she was literally drenched in perspiration by the cloying humidity. Now she realised that this overpowering climate would influence everything she did, no matter what she wore, or what special accommodations were made for her. She also began to fully appreciate the scale and intricacy of the official ceremonies, and accompanying personal isolation that her role in the dynamic of viceroyalty entailed. "We might as well be Monarchs," Mary Curzon wrote to her family,[27] describing their welcome in Bombay.

As the ship bearing the viceregal party drew closer to the shore, she saw the red carpet on the landing stage, the glittering buttons, buckles and medals on the guard of honour's uniforms – turbaned and gloved lancers, with gleaming jackboots, and wide cummerbunds, band instruments glistening in the sunlight, and the elegantly attired welcoming committee, awaiting their first glimpse of the viceregal couple. Local Indian rulers whose domains lay within the Bombay presidency stood with luminaries of Anglo-Indian society around a stage engulfed in masses of sweet-smelling flowers to mask the various stenches wafting from the harbour and the city.

Once ashore, the vicereine was caught up in that human tide which surpassed any prior experience. Suddenly she was the focus of everyone's attention, her every move and gesture of vital intense interest to Europeans and Indians alike. Now she stood at the top of the subcontinent's social pyramid, lonely and vulnerable, despite the luxury of the viceregal establishment, and the vast forces deployed to provide her and the viceroy with as much security as was possible under those difficult circumstances. From that moment on, her every public act – and especially her wardrobe – would be watched closely, analysed and reported to millions in India, Britain and throughout the world. In 1898, an Indian correspondent wrote ecstatically of Mary Curzon in the *Bangabasi*, the leading Hindu daily of Bengal: "Her colour is like that of molten gold, its whiteness having already assumed a tinge of red in the warm climate of this country. Her teeth are like a set of pearls, her waist is beautifully slender. Her raven tresses, setting off the whiteness of her white complexion, make her look like the very image of Saraswati [the Hindu goddess of knowledge and the arts]… Lady Curzon bears in her handsome person all the auspicious marks of prosperity."

With that kind of scrutiny now routine, the vicereine was compelled to be aware of every nuance of the *Raj*'s complicated and rigid social protocol for the slightest gaffe was seized upon by gossips among the Anglo-Indian community, and might even be reported in the press, and could damage her husband's reputation and notionally, his ability to govern. Sometimes things went awry literally at the vicereine's first step on shore, as it did with Maud Lansdowne in 1888, whose crisp embroidered white linen dress was covered by a mixture of coal dust and steam on the launch during her trip ashore, forcing her to greet her new subjects in a soggy gown flecked with soot. Little wonder then that she eagerly stripped the gown off at her first opportunity, and exhausted by the ceremony and overcome by the heat, flung herself onto a sofa, only to be told by an Indian woman waiting on her that she was far too thin.

After the dockside ceremonies, welcoming speeches, and replies by the new viceroy, as the vicereine stood still, hoping her dress was not sweat-streaked, and patting her face delicately with a linen hankie, the viceregal couple went for a seven-mile carriage drive through the city to the Governor's house where they stayed until going on to Calcutta (and later Delhi), or Simla.

The scene along the route was a mix of order in the procession and chaos in the crowds, as the viceregal party moved steadily through masses of Indian spectators who shouted and strained to gain a view of their new rulers, despite the best efforts of uniformed troops along the avenues to hold them back. The gaudy diversity of the crowd, some of the Indians nearly naked, shiny with sweat, and the raucous shouting and deafening din heightened the British overlords' underlying fear of the populace. The rough choruses of "God Save the Queen" ringing out here and there along the way reinforced the strangeness of becoming a ruler over this vast and exotic land, and the chasm that lay between ruler and ruled. Those vicereines for whom this brief journey was their first contact with the "real" India were usually overwhelmed if not dizzied by roar of the masses and the fugue of scents and stenches. As the carriage moved slowly along, Indian footmen shaded them with the Golden Umbrella, one of India's ancient symbols of royalty, projecting the image of the British viceroy as legitimate successor to the Mughal dynasty. Whatever its symbolic value, the umbrella did not protect them from the billows of dust stirred up by the trotting cavalry and carriages in the procession. But however great the discomforts and shocks to the senses the vicereine could display no sign of her discomfort or unease. "Stiff upper lip" was the rule of this day, and would be for all the others to follow as she acted out her role as vice-queen over the next half-decade.

As the procession reached the Governor's residence in the suburb of Parell, the viceregal couple found themselves in a more verdant and tranquil setting, the "bubble" of the sumptuous elegance and formality that surrounded British India's ruling class. Within the compound, things were made to seem as much like home as possible. Neatly tended gardens surrounded large houses modelled after English mansions, but modified to blunt the heat and dampness. Finally, once inside the grand residence, the vicereine was able to remove her sodden clothes, rest briefly, then bathe and prepare for evening as she was introduced to the British elite of Bombay. That included, as the evening cooled, another official drive through the streets, also accompanied by the full honour guard, and after returning to the Governor's residence, a change into an elegant evening gown followed by dinner for several hundred. A reception followed during which she and the viceroy greeted, while standing, more than 1,000 people who bowed but did not stop to speak, in keeping with protocol required.

Alice Reading's most lasting impression of the formal arrival ceremonies in 1921 was the absence of her family at this most momentous of occasions. She was suddenly overcome with loneliness, and like vicereines before her, realised how completely her elevation to vicereine separated her from all other British women in India. Coming out of the Convocation Hall in Bombay where Reading had been sworn in, Alice felt absolutely friendless. "Not a soul I knew to give me a hug and wish me well, only strange, strange faces everywhere." No one could understand what the position is and what demands it makes upon individuals, she wrote. "Buckingham Palace, Windsor, everything simple in comparison with the show and glitter (necessary, I understand, to impress with power)."[28]

The newspaper accounts on the following day would confirm for the vicereine that being stared by large numbers of strangers was one of the less pleasant aspects of her role, and that her every movement, gesture, and change of costume would be painstakingly recounted in the local press, albeit in glowing terms. Thus did the *Advocate of India* describe Mary Curzon: "As she leaned with crossed hands on the twisted silver handle of a parasol that matched her dress one could detect no suggestion of nervousness in a single twitch of her fingers," and went on to praise her beauty extravagantly, as well as her self-possessed demeanour and charming smile [29] Such detailed and almost always laudatory reportage of the vicereine's demeanour and deportment was a staple of the Anglo-Indian press throughout the era of the *Raj* – even, on occasion, at the expense of the viceroy. Newspapers cited Lady Willingdon's ability "to inspire effort everywhere," while observing that the " [viceroy's] strength is of a lesser standard."[30]

While the transfer of power between viceroys was usually cordial, ceremony and public civility did not always effectively disguise tension between departing and arriving proconsuls, which, naturally enough, affected the behaviour and attitude of the respective vicereines, as they strove to maintain appropriate *sang-froid*. Technically, the new viceroy succeeded rather than replaced his predecessor, and both arrival and departure ceremonies were designed to reflect that distinction. That meant that there was usually a brief interval, rarely more than a couple of days, when both were in the country, and even living in the same residence. In perhaps the most discordant episode in viceregal succession, George Curzon displayed his displeasure at what he saw as being shabbily treated by the home government by cancelling the traditional dockside arrival ceremony for the Mintos. He then chose not to welcome them at the steps of the viceregal residence in Bombay, and added insult to injury a few days later by later driving to the dock with a full viceregal escort of two cavalry regiments and a battery of the Royal Horse Artillery. That studied rudeness reverberated throughout India and back to London.

There was also some discomfiture, although short of overt hostility, when the Hardinges arrived to succeed the Mintos in 1910. In that case, a two-day overlap in Calcutta between the arrival and departure of the two viceroys placed Hardinge in the awkward position of waiting to take possession of a throne not yet vacated. Despite the Mintos' widespread popularity in the Anglo-Indian establishment, the officials of the *Raj* recognised who was in charge, and for whom they would be working for the next five years. As a result, as Hardinge noted, he was "…[treated] as the rising and not the setting sun."

As well-bred aristocrats, most vicereines were excruciatingly polite to each other during the transition, despite an occasional tense moment. Alice Reading concluded that the cool reception she and her husband received from the Chelmsfords (especially Lady Chelmsford) was due to Reading being named an earl before coming to India, while Chelmsford was only raised to a viscount as a reward for his Indian service, when both he and Frances felt he deserved the traditional earldom. The animus arising from that discrepancy made Alice unsure how much the Chelmsfords' *hauteur* was due to that rather than a reaction to the Readings being Jewish. Five years later, Alice's successor, Dorothy Irwin, maintained a discreet silence during their first meeting as Alice expressed her regret at leaving India, and described the exciting future that lay ahead for her as vicereine. Despite her poor health and initial isolation, Alice had very much warmed to being vice-queen, especially the ceremonies and rituals that Dorothy founding repellent. "I felt very sorry for them," Dorothy noted after the meeting, "but I wondered whether it could be possible, if and when the day came for E[dward] and me to leave, that we should not be skipping down the steps trying to hide our obvious delight."[31]

As impressive as the official welcoming ceremonies and festivities were in Bombay, the viceroy was most often officially sworn in at yet another elaborate ceremony, held at the principal seat of government, Calcutta (later Delhi) or Simla, for those who arrived during the government's annual retreat to the hills. Travelling across India from Bombay was the couple's introduction to the viceregal train, which exceeded in the splendour of its appointments the monarch's royal train, and some averred, even that of the Russian Tsar's. Until the Willingdons initiated the practice of viceregal air travel, rail remained the primary means of transport for the vicereines. Wherever it went in India, the train – "as long as the New York Limited" as Mary Curzon described it – was instantly recognizable with its white-and gold carriages. The viceregal couple each occupied their own carriage which included a saloon or sitting room, a bedroom, bathroom, maid's or valet's room, and a place to store trunks so that dresses and wardrobes could be easily accessed. Other equally comfortable carriages were assigned to senior staff and servants who traveled with the viceroy. Until the advent of mechanical air-conditioning, electric fans blowing over beds of ice placed in the centre of each sitting room were the only means of cooling. With the train taking on ice every eighty miles or so, water from the melting ice drained away rapidly along the rain's route.

The effectiveness of this system depended on the weather, the perceptions of various passengers, and the state of cooling technology. Once air-conditioned, the viceregal train would become a very comfortable way to travel in the hot weather, but until that time, the vicereines found little comfort aboard. Mary Minto complained that since the ice melted so quickly, it had little effect in chilling the carriage. (Her opinion may have been influenced by her railway car having caught fire, requiring her rescue from the burning carriage.) Even without air-conditioning, Alice Reading found the train a marvel: "The moving of a Viceroy in India is a wonderful piece of management. You go to bed in the train, several of your [motor] cars go on in advance and meet you at the station, your servants are there behind your chair for a four-course breakfast and even your favourite chair and cushion come along."[32] Her secretary, Yvonne Fitzroy, differed, noting that although the viceroy's train was certainly luxurious, it "could not defeat this climate." No screen or filter could keep out the dust, fans merely circulated hot air, door handles were too hot to touch, and beds too hot to lie on. The high temperatures made clothes "a literally painful necessity…and…water from the cold tap [was]… nicely boiled."[33] Each trip was planned with military precision, and arrivals at each stop for meals or baths were timed down to the minute to assure each stationmaster had all in order when the viceregal train pulled in. Alice Reading described arriving at one of the stations as "like a scene in Ruritania."[34] Part of the planning encompassed elaborate military and security provisions, including the stationing of soldiers every 100 yards along the tracks. At night, each man held a torch, and the flickering lights could be seen for miles.[35]

The splendour and intricacy of the ceremonies attending the viceregal arrival in Calcutta – and in later years, New Delhi – exceeded those in Bombay. The viceregal couple was escorted from the train station to Government House by large cavalry and infantry units, and the 120 lancers of the Viceroy's Bodyguard, and here again thousands of Indians lined the route, and vicereines were often struck by the sharp imbalance between rulers and ruled. Since this arrival was "official" India's first chance to see a new vicereine in person, she strove to make the very best impression as she sat, stood, walked sedately, or bowed, listened calmly during speeches, looked admiringly at her husband as he responded to the official welcome, and gracefully accepted bouquets offered by shy Indian children.

That ceremony remained almost unchanged until the advent of the last viceroy, Lord Mountbatten. No viceroy and his consort since the Curzons had strode onto the stage of India so boldly, nor been so empowered to get great things done quickly, if not hastily. Nor had any stirred such public and private curiosity and apprehension, for both Edwina and Louis had become major public figures before stepping into the spotlight of the viceroyal publicity, he as a World War II naval hero, head of Combined Operations, and finally Allied Supreme Commander in southeast Asia, she as a wealthy socialite and major leader of private charities, renowned for her forceful wartime leadership in the Red Cross and the St. John Ambulance Brigade. Beyond their status as international celebrities, they had a reputation for very liberal if not radical political views, and had raised an almost prurient curiosity in the media and among British elites regarding their links to the royal family, and rumours of a highly unorthodox social lives. Edwina's beauty and personal wealth evoked memories of Mary Curzon among older British-Indians, who waited eagerly to see how (or if) she would change the social ambiance at the Viceroy's House in what were now clearly seen to be the final days of the *Raj*. Her wartime reputation and engaging personality were assets in the end game in which the Mountbattens now found themselves key players.

From the moment he took office, the degree of change the Mountbattens were to introduce to the viceroyalty was evident, as was their awareness of the importance of public perception. For the first (and last) time, still and movie photographers were allowed to take pictures of the swearing-in ceremony from a platform high up in the Durbar Hall (personally designed by Mountbatten). He also broke with tradition by giving a brief address after the formal ceremony, and had his staff provide a press release with all the salient details of the ceremony and his remarks, displaying once again his understanding of the importance of first impressions. It was as if he was "letting in daylight upon the magic" that had been the viceroyalty for nearly 90 years, an action first proclaimed and decried by Walter Bagehot, the 19th century journalist, in relation to the British monarchy.

Once the welcoming ceremony was over, the viceregal couple proceeded to Government House (or later, Viceroy's House) their home for the next five years. There, the new viceroy and vicereine alighted from their carriage at the bottom of wide marble steps, covered in red carpet for the occasion. They slowly ascended past ranks of soldiers standing at attention, and were greeted at the top by their predecessors, several maharajahs and their entourages, and senior government officials in military or civil full dress. After a round of introductions, with appropriate bows and curtseys, and several more speeches, the two couples withdrew for a private visit over tea. With some exceptions, the welcoming at the capital was the first time the incoming and outgoing vicereines had met on Indian soil. And usually, both couples were in residence for a few days as the outgoing family turned over to their successors, in sequence, their private quarters, and then the state rooms. As the former viceroy departed, his successor accompanied him to the station or the docks, where yet another elaborate ritual much like that which had greeted the new viceroy honoured the departing viceroy and his wife – and they left. Only then could the new vicereine fully take possession of her domestic domain, explore the palace's public and private rooms at her leisure, make decisions about which space she would occupy, and begin her reign.

Gilded Cages –
Viceregal Residences

Within their viceregal households, the vicereines presided over little empires of their own, domains whose scale and intricacy surpassed even the British royal domestic establishment. As aristocratic women, most had substantial experience in managing estates, some with several residences, but all were – at least initially – overwhelmed by the viceregal domestic enterprise. Until the 1820s when Governors-General began the annual trek to Simla, their wives had only Government House in Calcutta and a retreat at Barrackpore to be concerned with – a relatively manageable domestic establishment. However, over the years of the *Raj*, the viceregal enterprise steadily expanded to the point that, in the final days of 1947, some 7,000 people were employed in its upkeep throughout India, including staff, families, and servants of all classes, but not including military and security forces.

The vicereines' domestic duties were eased substantially by the Military Secretary to the viceroy and his large staff who oversaw day-to-day operations of the residences, gardens, trains, carriages, and, from the early 20th century onward, motor cars and later airplanes. However, as in any aristocratic or domestic establishment, the "vice-queens" themselves were held responsible for the general tone of life in all the official residences – Government House in Calcutta, and later, the Viceroy's House in Delhi; Peterhof, then Viceregal Lodge in Simla, as well as retreats at Barrackpore and Mashobra, and – to a lesser extent – the temporary viceregal camps they occupied on the annual tours. All were required to reflect her taste in interior design and social organization, insofar as that was possible, both financially and administratively. In her role as social overseer, a vicereine struggled to create a comfortable environment for her family without disturbing the status quo and all the ritual, routine, and protocol that made up the viceregal lifestyle. Beyond all the formal rules and constraints, changes in interior design, ceremonies, or social customs were closely scrutinised by Anglo-Indian society. Vicereines were often criticised, usually in whispers, behind fans or gloved hands, or behind closed doors, for making changes that they saw as incidental or vitally necessary, but which lay outside what India's polite society saw as acceptable. Although only temporary residents, the vicereines were not shy about proposing changes, nor criticising their predecessors' interior design sense. One of the most visible of such cases was Lady Willingdon's dramatically kitschy architectural changes to the Viceroy's House in New Delhi in the 1930s, and her successor Lady Linlithgow's subsequent invitation to the palace's original architect, Edwin Lutyens, to return it to his original elegant vision.

The viceregal domestic routine also included extensive travel within India and sometimes elsewhere in South Asia. As a result, vicereines grappled with administrative challenges, discomforts, and sometimes very real danger of those journeys, in addition to voyages back and forth to England. Lady Minto noted that prior to her arrival, it was customary to haul all the furniture – huge bed, dressing tables, chairs and wardrobes – from the Viceregal Lodge in Simla to each camp during the fall tour. She ordered portable camp furniture, and soon found that even this seemingly sensible change was criticised. "In the viceregal establishment there is an unwritten law that everything must continue on the lines initiated years ago," she wrote. "Nothing gives me more pleasure than to discard these antiquated methods and introduce a modern system."[1]

Managing the massive support provided by staffs and servants, viceregal homes, palaces, and camps was daunting, and sometimes bewildering and oppressive. As the vicereine tried to make her family feel at home in the huge residences, she dealt with servant problems, and strove to smooth relations among the viceregal staff, strove to maintain a diplomatic mien before visitors, and, increasingly, endure the scrutiny of the media in the age of photography. At a more mundane level, the vast gardens at each residence needed planning and oversight, an area of greater interest to some vicereines than others. Travel arrangements seemed endless, including trips to the princely states aboard viceregal trains, barges, and atop elephants, hunting trips and visits to outlying military posts in carts and on horseback. In her domestic relationships, the vicereine dealt closely with a formidable mini-bureaucracy, and each residence provided unique challenges to family as well as official life.

Several vicereines had personal secretaries to assist them, but most relied on the staff network headed by the Military Secretary and a band of aides-de-camp to the viceroy. Each ADC administered a different department – household, kitchen and cook, invitations, and stables and transport – each of which had a number of Indian servants. These ranged from *jemadars,* the private servants to members of the household, to the *khitmagars* who waited at table. Sentries were omnipresent in all the halls, even standing outside bedroom doors, and the residences had a veritable army of cleaners, often seven or eight to a room. However discreet and unseeing their eyes, the result of all the constant presence of so many servants was, as Lord Northbrook wrote, like being "a gold fish in a glass bowl under a dinner table…"[2]

Government House – the first palace

Until the 1930s, depending upon the time of year they arrived in India, the vicereines travelled from their disembarking in Bombay to Calcutta, or to Simla, the summer capital in the foothills of the Himalayas, but most vicereines' introduction to their domestic responsibilities usually began in Calcutta. After a formal greeting, the vicereine had her first glimpse of her new home – Government House, the first great palace built in India by the British. The Company's early Governors-General and their families lived in various rented quarters, and later in Belvedere House on the outskirts of Calcutta, which had been built by Warren Hastings in 1763 as a venue for official entertaining, although he preferred to live at nearby Hastings House. An imposing Italianate mansion surrounded by spacious grounds, Belvedere was purchased by the East India Company in 1854 as the official residence of the Governor of Bengal. When the capital was transferred from Calcutta to Delhi in 1912, Government House became the Governor's residence, and Belvedere was reserved for the viceroy's use when in Calcutta.

When Hastings' successor, Richard Wellesley, brother of the future Duke of Wellington, arrived in 1798 he quickly decided that he needed a residence more suited to what he saw as his exalted position as Governor General. Wellesley's young admirer, Lord Valentia, during a visit to Calcutta, reinforced Wellesley's assessment, and agreed that India should be ruled from a palace, not a counting house, and certainly not with the ideas of "a retail trader in muslin and indigo." India was a country of splendor, and "the Head of a mighty Empire ought to conform himself to the prejudices of the country, he rules over," he concluded.[3] The classical structure that would be known as Government House was modeled after Kedleston Hall, the Derbyshire seat of the Scarsdales, the family of a future viceroy, George Curzon. Long considered one of the finest examples of English country houses, Kedleston's simple yet elegant layout appealed to

the young man commissioned to design Wellesley's new palace – Lieutenant Charles Wyatt of the Bengal Engineers, a lesser-known, but nonetheless talented member of the Wyatt architectural family.

Wyatt had recognised that Kedleston's design with its central block
and four detached wings linked to the centre by curving corridors enabled
good air circulation, and thus was an excellent choice for a tropical
climate. However, he modified the basic design, building a much larger
house, with two more wings and one more storey more than Kedleston.
Government House was constructed of brick and covered with white
plaster – not built from stone like Kedleston. The plaster was rewashed
every year, which while it gave the building a luminous quality evident
in early paintings, also changed its colour. Curzon had the plaster hue
changed to "wedding cake white" when he arrived, finding the "dirty
yellow" incompatible with his vision of how his ancestral home should
look in India. The building was constructed with a large central block on
three floors, connected by "spider-like...long curving corridors"[4] to four
symmetrical wings each of which was virtually a separate house. The Ionic
portico, which was reached by a wide staircase, faced north, toward the
centre of Calcutta. On the other side was a softer, domed front topped by
a large figure of Britannia, overlooking the gardens. Impressive gateways
marked the entrance to the compound; Adam-esque in design, they were
topped by lions and sphinxes, again reinforcing the British Imperial vision.

Government House in Calcutta was the seat of British rule in India until the capital was moved to New Delhi in 1911.

A stylised view of Governor General Wellesley's original house at Barrackpore, with sentries guarding the bridge and an elephant making its slow progress towards the house. 1808

Until the carefully sited trees grew, the building dominated not only the immediate grounds, but the city itself.

The central block contained the huge State apartments: the grand Marble Hall with its Doric columns, huge crystal chandeliers, the busts of twelve Caesars along the walls, and a ceiling so high palm trees could be used for decoration, could comfortably seat 100 for dinner. There was also a grand drawing room, a breakfast room and a supper room, each of which was more than 100 feet long. The throne room where the viceroy received Indian princes and other distinguished guests, seated on Tipu Sultan's silver throne – was a "must-see" stop on any house tour by European visitors. There were two ballrooms in this central core, while in the wings of the house space was allotted for the viceroy's offices and private apartments, guest bedrooms with connecting bathrooms and the council chamber. Designed to catch any available breeze, the building had smooth, cool marble floors, and high ceilings of polished oak. The addition of gas lighting in 1863 and hot and cold running water in 1872 added considerably to its comfort, and over the years, the house maintained its dignity, and as the gardens matured, it acquired an "unexpected charm."[5]

The mammoth white building stood close to the river, and dominated the Calcutta scene, overlooking the *maidan*, a huge open space used for military and other spectacles of empire. As with all British official residences in India, Government House's site, design style, and interior decoration were intended as much a political statement as a home for a proconsul and his family. The Indian elites, whatever their real power and status in comparison to their British rulers, lived in huge palaces. How could those Westerners who came to rule and exploit the country's riches hope to maintain influence and control if their dwellings were not at least equal in size and grandeur? Wellesley's new building would not only demonstrate British style and influence, but would also serve as a reminder, albeit modified to fit the unique needs of India, of the aristocratic country life that was the experience – or expectation – of most of the viceroys. Despite its location, Government House, like all official residences of British India, was "unmistakably English." Visitors were always aware that whatever concessions were made to the Indian environment – such as uniformed lancers welcoming guests to dinner and turbaned servants standing behind each chair – "these were the domestic arrangements of English gentlefolk, temporarily transferred."[6] From the day they arrived, the vicereines knew approximately how long their stay in India would be – barring political change – so it was logical that they would try to recreate within this great palace the domestic and social environment with which they were most comfortable, with some allowance for the very un-English setting in which they were now living.

The final cost for construction was £63,291 – not to mention the over £3,000 for fireworks and illuminations at the opening ball celebrating the Treaty of Amiens – a figure deemed excessive by the Company, as were other expenditures by Wellesley that dramatically increased the pomp and circumstance surrounding with the position of Governor General – far beyond anything done by his predecessors. By 1805, the Company directors had enough and recalled Wellesley, sending the aging Lord Cornwallis to replace him and to scale down the level of expenditures and pomp which Wellesley believed so essential to the Governor Generalship. Always frugal and disdainful of ceremony, Cornwallis did just that in his short tenure, even dismissing most of the Government House servants. Still, as with any house, costs continued to accrue: the first Lord Minto tried to strike a balance between Wellesley's extravagance and Cornwallis's frugality, while the Marquess of Hastings (no relation to the first and more famous Lord Hastings) and his aristocratic wife brought back the excesses of the Wellesley era, even considering completing Wellesley's unfinished palace at Barrackpore.

A parade by British troops in the mid-19th century on the Esplanade in Calcutta.

Sir John and Lady Lawrence, more restrained in their lifestyle, were criticised by Anglo-Indian society, who felt that they were not quite grand enough for the house or the position, since they preferred family prayers and croquet games on the lawn to formal social events. The pendulum swung again with the Mayos, who revived the viceregal reputation for glamour, gaiety, and splendid hospitality. Lady Mayo oversaw the expenditure of significant sums on furniture and draperies and improvements to the gardens in the 1860s, and dramatically improved the quality of the wine served at social events – a fact not unnoticed by Calcutta society. A significant portion of the outlay was made in preparation for a visit of the Queen's son, Prince Alfred (The Duke of Edinburgh). In preparation for the royal visitor, Lady Mayo ordered gilt French furniture from Paris for the state rooms, and even secured mistletoe from Simla to further enhance the Prince's Christmas. Lord Northbrook continued the Mayo tradition, spending his own money to ensure that there was no reduction in viceregal hospitality or in the maintenance of Government House. Still, reviews were mixed on Government House in the Northbrook era: Edward Lear, visiting in 1873, was not enthusiastic about the house or the complex social order associated with it, writing of his "artificial life in dark rooms and *Punkah* air," and complaining that there was never any rest in the world he called "Hustlefussabad," a statement about the almost constant activity that was the hallmark of the viceregal household.[7] A more positive view was expressed later by George Curzon during his visit in 1887. The similarity between Government House and his ancestral home in Derbyshire only added to Curzon's determination to one day rule India and exchange "Kedleston in England for Kedleston in India"[8]

In contrast to the clean Palladian lines of its exterior, for most of its life, Government House's interior featured the dark paneling, heavy draperies, mahogany furniture, and clutter of photographs and potted palms of early and mid-Victorian England, along with polished cotton chintz on comfortable chairs in the private quarters. The furniture in the public rooms was solid walnut or mahogany, upholstered in plush velvets, while the marble audience halls contained more traditional eighteenth century French-style settees and chairs with needle-pointed or satin cushions placed strategically around the large, columned drawing and reception rooms. The house was well-suited for imperial social and political events, but less than welcoming as a family home, despite its size and elegant rooms. There was no private dining area, and when they were on their own, the family took their meals in the Marble Hall or the Throne Room. For all its size, the house was remarkably short of bedrooms. There were spacious rooms in the northwest wing for one or two honoured guests, and a few more could be squeezed into the family wing. When there was a large party, however, guests were housed in tents on the lawn, as was the custom in India.

Lady Charlotte Canning, finding Government House not nearly luxurious enough and impossible to manage, was despondent at the thought that this huge building would be her responsibility for the next five years. She complained about the lack of privacy from the "gliding people" – the omnipresent Indian servants, as well as the highly inefficient location of kitchens 200 yards from the house, which meant that soufflés collapsed between kitchen and table as they were carried in boxes on poles on men's shoulders. The situation did not improve over time: "The kitchen is somewhere in Calcutta, but not in this house," noted Hariot Dufferin correctly in 1884, as the kitchens were still located outside the grounds on a filthy, narrow street to the north of the residence.

In the early days there were no toilets in the entire house, but commodes that were emptied by a native sweeper after use. Like all vicereines who assumed responsibility for this palace, Lady Canning spent many weeks rearranging the furniture to her own taste and comfort – placing comfortable seating under the essential *punkahs* since no one would sit elsewhere. Finding that her private apartments were too isolated from her husband's, Charlotte took over a first floor room in the southeast wing that she transformed into an English drawing room with chintz on the overstuffed chairs, blue Sevres china in the cabinets, and portraits of the royal children on all the tables. Since the room had nine doors, eight of which were always open, arranging the room was no small task. Proud of her ability to avoid the stereotypical Indian furniture arrangement of

The first Vicereine, Charlotte Canning, was a talented and energetic artist. Her drawing-table was among her most treasured possessions.

"round tables in the middle, chairs all around and an ottoman on each side,"[9] she wrote to her family: "I flatter myself it is the most civilised room in India."[10] Chintz was also in evidence in her own sitting room where Charlotte used a white fabric printed with lily-of-the-valley and installed white *punkahs*. She also noted the distinct lack of both plate and linen for formal entertaining, which she put down to her predecessor Lady Dalhousie's death[11] some three years earlier and the failure of her daughter to keep things "up to snuff." With no children to care for, and a husband who was consumed by his work, Charlotte found that she was relegated to the roles of household manager and social organizer, both of which she found tremendously boring. 'Putting dimity in a drawing room or a new mat, is about the principal event I can look forward to: or choosing

30 names out of a list for dinner, and ditto two days later, and so on three times a week."[12]

While indoor plumbing and other comforts were added over the years, isolation, loneliness, and the sheer size of Government House continued to plague viceregal families. The last viceroy to live in Government House, Lord Hardinge, complained in 1910 that he had to walk some 250 yards to get from his bedroom to that of his young daughter, Diamond. Even Lady Dufferin, who had lived in diplomatic residences all over the world, was daunted somewhat by the size of the palace and the condition in which she found it. Writing to Queen Victoria shortly after her arrival in December 1884, the vicereine tactfully reported that while she wasn't directly criticising Lady Ripon, nonetheless, "all small matters have been quite neglected…and furniture and plate are at the very lowest ebb possible." When Lady Dufferin assured the Queen that she was bending every effort to have things in good order before the Duke and Duchess of Connaught (the Queen's son and daughter-in-law) arrived,[13] she also told the Queen about her effort to create a more homelike atmosphere for her family in the enormous palace. Hariot disliked the fact that her sitting room and bedroom were in opposite wings of the house, separated by two long corridors and the vast open spaces of the State apartments, so she and Lord Dufferin moved out of the traditional viceregal bedrooms and into the wing that contained her sitting room. This placed Dufferin's living quarters a long walk away from his office, which some took as another indication of his indolence and lack of real interest in the detailed work of a viceroy. In fact, Dufferin took his job very seriously, and enjoyed the ceremonial aspects of his position, as did his wife, both of whom understood and appreciated the significance of their roles, and saw India through romantic eyes, taking pleasure in living in Wellesley's historic palace. When Dufferin added to its magnificence in 1886 installing huge gilt mirrors taken from the palace of King Thibaw after the British conquest of Mandalay, Hariot did some redecorating of her own, reupholstering furniture in her sitting room in pink silk, and adding tables, screens, plants and photographs of her children.

Changing living spaces and redecoration did not alleviate one of the vicereines' chief discomforts, the constant invasion of wild creatures and insects. During one monsoon, Lady Canning reported that her dinner table in Calcutta "was covered w/creatures as thickly as a drawer of them in a museum." The problem was exacerbated as the heat increased, when she began to see huge cockroaches ("as big as mice." she wrote) in her bedroom, "some moving away, side by side, like pairs of coach horses…" Saucers of water beneath the legs of tables kept the ants from climbing up, and lids were essential to keep bugs out of glasses on the table. Spiders, earwigs, and various other specimens were regular visitors throughout the house,[14] and the rains only increased the insect population as crickets, grasshoppers, black beetles, and huge cockroaches came inside. Insects were only one of the natural threats: snakes slithered in through the constantly open doors and windows, and bats were a common sight from beneath mosquito netting at night. Things hadn't improved much by the 20th century: Mary Curzon awoke one night to find a civet cat sipping water from her bedside carafe, a terrifying event that reinforced her view of India as a dangerous, if not fatal, venue for women and children, no matter what their status.

Coping with the weather was a dominant element of British life in India, no matter where one lived. For much of the year, life was, as Hariot Dufferin noted, "entirely ruled by the sun, and schedules adjusted accordingly." On Sundays, she reported, the family went to church before breakfast, and stayed indoors the rest of the day, keeping doors and window shut, only venturing out for a walk just before sundown. The constant hot wind of the plains blew gritty dust everywhere, even in a palace, banging doors, and flying curtains. "This is the way the hot season begins," Lady Dufferin wrote, "and day by day the wind gets hotter and hotter till it scorches you as though it came out of an oven. The sound of a strong wind on a warm day is very depressing – there is something unnatural about it."[15] Alice Reading described her reaction to the climate in a letter home shortly after her arrival in India in 1921: "I have been baked and roasted, grilled and blistered. I am so hot the ink is mixed with water," i.e., sweat, adding that she is living on milk and cream.[16]

Following the model of all English residences in India, the vicereines employed traditional Indian technologies to keep the suffocating heat at bay, shutting up all windows by 7:30 a.m. and hanging *tatis*, large screens made from fragrant grasses that were kept wetted, against the outer doors and over large windows. Those measures, plus the ceaseless, soft whisper of the *punkahs* made the inside rooms bearable, but opening a door or window let in air so hot it seemed to come from an oven. At 6 p.m. the shutters and windows could be opened, which often brought gales of wind that blew papers off tables and desks, lifted tablecloth corners and made the chandeliers swing. No matter the temporary inconvenience, the evening wind offered the only hope of cool air in the evening.[17]

The *punkahs* in Government House were panels created from heavy fabric that hung from the ceiling and moved slowly back and forth to circulate the air, and they could be small and situated throughout a room, or very large, requiring complicated pulley arrangements to keep them moving, operated by the *punkah-wallah*, a man whose sole job was to keep the fan moving and the air circulating. Originally, the *punkah-wallah*

stood behind the chair of his master, but later he was moved outside the room, where he operated the *punkah* by means of a string slotted through the wall, sometimes tied to a toe, so that little real effort was required, and which incidentally also eliminated the need to see the person whose labour provided one's comfort. When she first arrived in India, Lady Canning was determined to do without *punkahs*, at least at night, feeling guilty that one man's sole job was to keep her comfortable by pulling on a rope. She coped by moving from room to room during the day so that the various *punkah-wallahs* could have some rest. Eventually, the heat won: the vicereine gave in completely, even having a *punkah* at night so she could get a decent night's sleep. "I am completely vanquished on the *punkah* point,' she wrote to her family, having reached the point where she gave the *punkah-wallah* no thought at all – survival and an acceptance of the reality that was India overcame Victorian guilt.

The *punkahs* continued to be a challenge well after Lady Canning's time. In the 1890s, Lady Elgin described a particularly frightening experience

Charlotte Canning seated on her elephant together with her escorts, sets off on a painting expedition.

with the *punkah* over her bed underneath the mosquito netting, which was pulled by a man in the hall outside her room. One night a huge storm blew in, with winds so strong that glass covering the candles was toppled and there was a real danger that the netting or curtains would be set on fire. Lady Elgin rang a bell to call the *punkah-wallah* and have him stop pulling, so that the fire danger would not be exacerbated by the breeze created by the *punkah*. Because none of the servants were of high enough caste to enter the vicereine's bedroom and see what she wanted, they assumed she wanted more air, and simply pulled the *punkah* faster! The *punkah-wallah* eventually became unnecessary in Government House when electric motors powered the huge fabric fans and the *punkahs* themselves were replaced later by electric fans throughout the house, except in the state rooms where they were kept for the sake of tradition.

An unusual counterpoint to the heat was the fact that cold weather and rain could sometimes be a problem for viceregal families in Calcutta, as well as in Simla. The elegant living quarters with their tall ceilings, wide verandahs, and folding doors which seldom closed tightly were designed to capture any possible breeze and to allow for the free flow of any moving air. Those same qualities meant that they were difficult, if not impossible to heat and to make draft-free. Government House, like most British houses in India was far from snug, which was what its inhabitants longed for when the cooler weather came. In 1885, Hariot Dufferin wrote that she was sitting "in not one, but twenty draughts at a time"[18] in her room in Government House. The architecture could not align the two extremes, so houses (and viceregal palaces) built to catch whatever cool air might be stirring, could not easily be converted into cozy homes where a roaring fire might warm the dampness during the monsoon.

Although the basic architecture was not significantly modified, over the years Government House was improved with the addition of indoor plumbing, elevators (the first steam-operated lift in India), electric bells to call servants, and eventually, some air conditioning. Still, its grandeur failed to impress some viceroys: Lord Lansdowne, to the manner born and used to the luxuries of his ancestral homes, Bowood and Lansdowne House in London, commented on the "utter absence of anything like homely comfort."[19]

Perhaps no viceroy appreciated Government House more than George Curzon, although he saw more differences than similarities between the model, Kedleston and its twin in Calcutta. The lack of Adam detailing inside disturbed him most, and he made no secret of his belief in the superiority of his ancestral home. Whatever he thought about its architectural insufficiencies, Curzon was captivated by the great palace. He appreciated it as a great work of architecture, and throughout his reign, tried to restore and maintain its original character, modernize it where possible, and fill in any gaps in the collection of portraits of former grandees. Curzon paid for several major upgrades out of his own pocket – or more correctly, out of the fortune his wife Mary brought to their marriage. In 1898, finding that smoky gas lighting didn't provide adequate light for dressing and doing her hair, Lady Curzon urged her husband to install electric lights throughout the private quarters. The viceroy quickly ordered lighting fixtures and many electric fans to ensure the comfort of his wife and daughters. He also added fixed baths, replacing the old wooden tubs that were painted a sickly green, and maintained an interest in the house long after he had returned to England.

Curzon strongly opposed the move of the capital to Delhi, and was particularly indignant at the thought of what would happen to Government House and its contents. The slide from viceregal grandeur to relatively democratic simplicity was gradual between 1912 and 1947. Most of the house's contents went to Delhi to furnish the new viceregal palace, and Government House became the residence of the Governors of Bengal. Today, the Governor of West Bengal lives in what is now known as the *Raj Bhavan*. There are still smartly uniformed sentries guarding its entrances, and *khitmagars* stand at attention in the hallways, but most of the rooms are now either empty or filled with furnishings under dust-covers. There are no viceregal or colonial portraits on the walls, and the enormous rooms overwhelm the scale of present entertainments. Still, the social constraints of the vicereines seem to live on in the current restrictions on entry to the great palace. A current website describing the building includes the following caveat: "The hoi-polloi are prohibited to enter this building. In order to get in, one has to show some reasonable excuse and seek permission from the concerned authorities."[20]

Barrackpore – the escape

One palace wasn't going to be enough for a man like Wellesley. Like any English country gentleman, he felt the need for a country retreat, and planned to revamp Barrackpore, a military station fourteen miles up the Hooghly River, into yet another magnificent residence, joining the two with a long, perfectly straight avenue. However, he was recalled to London to answer for his overspending in Calcutta before his grand design for a complex of official residences could become a reality. On learning that the Barrackpore project was estimated at £50,000, the Company's directors stopped all progress. Wellesley's partially built mansion stood unfinished for years, and was ultimately pulled down by Lord Hastings, who decided to build an imposing, albeit more modest, mansion at another location at

*In a
contemporary
painting,
elephants and
cavalry officers
stride through
the grounds at
the entrance
to Barrackpore
Park in 1848.*

Barrackpore, designed by Captain Thomas Anbury of the Bengal Engineers. It quickly became and remained the favourite residence of all viceregal families, and as the first Lord Minto said, it "took the sting out of India."[21] Although it was only fourteen miles outside of Calcutta, Barrackpore was in effect the viceroy's country house, a place of refuge and ease for viceregal families, since it could be easily reached easily by boat. The viceroy and his party would travel upriver quite comfortably, first in a houseboat initially pulled by coolies walking along the bank, and later towed by a steamer.

Emily Eden, sister of an early Governor General, Lord Auckland (1836–1842), was apparently unaware of the complex arrangements and support systems needed at Barrackpore, observing that going to the retreat was "such a simple way of going to pass two nights in the country."[22] In fact, the move was anything but simple, given that their progress to Barrackpore was aboard the magnificent houseboat "Golden Face" or *Sonamukhi*. Built originally for Lord Hastings, the houseboat contained a drawing room, a bedroom, and two dressing rooms, each elegantly appointed in luxurious fabrics of white and gold, with green Moroccan leather furniture. The houseboat even had marble baths while Barrackpore itself lacked indoor plumbing until the 1930s. The viceroy and his family were accompanied upriver by a flotilla of state barges or *feelchehras* bearing some 400 servants from Government House, as well as tow-boats, cook-boats, and even boats for the viceregal band – everything that might be needed for a weekend retreat. On their first trip upriver, Lord Auckland and his sisters were amazed to see that all their personal possessions, even a pianoforte, had been transported upriver for the weekend. Three days later, everything was back in place in Calcutta. For viceregal families, the short trip to the retreat was an escape in itself. George and Mary Curzon remembered the restful journey upriver in the fading twilight, the hand-carried lanterns twinkling a welcome as they walked from the river to the house, having landed by the "glimmering tomb" of Lady Canning.

Barrackpore offered the viceroy and his family an escape from the searing heat of Calcutta and a modicum of privacy, even though they sometimes entertained official guests and senior members of the government. The house itself was a large, comfortable yet classic Georgian mansion, with a deep entrance portico in front and wide colonnaded verandahs on the other three sides. The house was actually only one storey high, set atop an arcaded basement. An enormous drawing room was in the centre of the house, with a dining room and billiard room on the sides; the viceroy and his family also had their private apartments on this floor, while the servants lived in the basement. High ceilings added to the charm of the rooms, which were separated by jalousies (blinds or shutters designed with horizontal slats to let in light but keep out wind and rain) but no doors. Six of the jalousies opened onto a deep verandah which also had a high ceiling, with the Tuscan columns draped in fragrant vines. This openness was welcome most of the year, but during cooler weather could make the house quite cold and drafty. The openness also allowed insects, snakes and even jackals easy entry to the house, to the discomfort of the vicereines and their guests. Nevertheless, in 1903 the journalist Pearl Craigie described it as "the most delightful house in India...for Europeans."

Despite the vicereines' best efforts, Barrackpore could not entirely replicate an English country house, although Hariot Dufferin said it reminded her of Cliveden and nearly every vicereine added something to the house or grounds in an attempt to increase its Englishness. In the early and mid-19th century, the floors were covered in date-leaf matting said to deter ants – but which failed to do so – topped with blue and white cotton mats. Furniture and rugs were placed away from the walls to prevent insects and other creatures from invading. Here as in Calcutta, *tatties* helped to keep out the dust and heat, and interior doorways were

hung with blinds of bamboo or muslin to allow as much air circulation as possible.

The walls were covered with "Chunam," a lime made from seashells, waxed to a high sheen that resembled marble, which was especially lovely in the soft glow of candlelight. The house did not have electricity until the late 19th century, so in the large main living area, hundreds of candles and painted lamps, protected by glass shades from the breezes stirred by the *punkahs* as well as those coming through opened shutters, created a romantic environment, with shadows flickering along the highly polished walls as the family and their guests enjoyed whatever cool air was available.

Despite the house's discomforts, every viceregal family fell in love with the grounds – the garden, large park, and the walkway along the broad river. The house itself was situated in the middle of an "official hamlet" of smaller, thatched bungalows for staff and guests (rebuilt in 1863 of more substantial materials), guard rooms for soldiers, and kitchen quarters. Barrackpore and its environs presented a comforting reminder of England, and allowed viceregal families to break away from the rigors of duty and protocol for a few hours or days. Wellesley had enlarged the park around the house to some 350 acres, and like so many English aristocrats, literally remade the landscape, clearing the jungle and draining swamps to create hills and hollows and even a waterway, over which he placed a bridge in the classical style. The view of the steeple of the church at Serampore from across the river added to the illusion of being in an English country village. Over the years, the Barrackpore compound was expanded and enhanced with the addition of a "Temple of Fame," built by the first Lord Minto to honour the twenty-four officers who died in the conquest of Java and the Ile de France in Mauritius in 1810–11, the "inevitable" artificial Gothic ruin, a monument to a Lord William Beresford's famous racehorse, and thanks to Lady Canning and other vicereines, everywhere gardens, walks, and terraces, filled with ferns, white lilies, and a magnificent grove of banyan trees.

Charlotte, smitten with Barrackpore on her first visit, spent many hours updating the interior decorations of Lady Dalhousie, declaring that it was "marvellously improved" by some 450 yards of rose chintz. Not content with redecorating indoors, Charlotte spent an equal amount of time laying out the Barrackpore gardens, including the one outside her bedroom window that replicated the garden at Highcliffe Castle, one of her family's homes on the Hampshire coast. She found Wellesley's original park "too English" and created an Italian garden as well as a walkway down to the river bordered by poinsettias and a host of exotic shrubs. Lady Ripon later created a shady tunnel of bamboo over this walkway, and also planted a rose garden. The Barrackpore gardens were Charlotte's primary legacy to India, and were enjoyed by all later vicereines and their families and guests as they strolled the wide, straight walk down to the river, or wandered through the exquisite gardens and terraces filled with bamboo, palms and poinsettias and floating lotus plants in ponds. Only the gardens between the house and the river were reserved for the viceroy's private use. The rest of the grounds were open to the public, and Lady Canning welcomed the sight: "…it looks cheerful to see people, and the regiments send their bands to play in the evenings, and it has quite a gay effect." [23] She also offered bungalows on the grounds to the wives of lower ranking Company officers and clergy as a place of rest and recovery. They even took their meals with the vicereine, and on rare occasions, her less hospitable husband.

When Lady Canning died of a fever aged 44, her faithless but grieving husband buried her in her beloved gardens at Barrackpore, since there was no burial place in India for governors general and their families. Her grave overlooks the river she was so fond of drawing, shaded from the sun by high trees and among shrubs and flowers she loved. A marble tomb and a cross designed by her sister, Lady Louisa Waterford, marked her grave, which became a pilgrimage site for all visitors to Barrackpore, a reminder of the ultimate sacrifice made by so many British women in India. The

The garden walk at Barrackpore close to the tomb of Charlotte Canning. The garden had been largely her creation.

Victorian vicereines were particularly sensitive to the Queen's devotion to Lady Canning. In 1894, Lady Elgin reported to Her Majesty that she had visited Charlotte's tomb, and laid a wreath of "beautiful Barrackpore roses" with a note saying that the flowers had been placed at the Queen's request.

Whenever possible, the vicereines extended Barrackpore weekends to 10 days or more. Here they could more easily arrange and enjoy morning tennis, hunting, picnics along the river, and quiet time with their husbands and children. Even the energetic Hariot Dufferin said that the restful times spent at Barrackpore were among her happiest in India, while Mary Curzon wrote to her family in America about the "delicious" air of Barrackpore after a rain. "We sat under trees and read and wrote – real *dolce far niente* existence, which as grateful to us over-tired people as water to a thirsty man."[24]

The relaxed atmosphere was enhanced by the quiet, a relief from the noise and bustle of the city that often penetrated even the family quarters in Calcutta. Barrackpore also offered more freedom of action to children and young people, as evidenced by the joy the three Minto girls took in driving a small carriage all over the grounds. Even here, however, viceregal protocol and order were evident. Mary Curzon described how the little

Curzon girls were driven out to take the air in a landau with three nurses, and two liveried footmen on the box and two standing behind. If they went out in their rickshaws, there was an "army of attendants" including the viceroy's policeman, who had the responsibility for carrying the girls' dolls.

Barrackpore was a favourite choice for family holiday celebrations. The Dufferins spent their last Christmas in India there in 1887, the holiday was made even happier by the prospect of an imminent return home and the presence of all of their children, an unusual circumstance for most vicereines. Hariot reported that they spent a quiet day, with church in the morning and then a visit to the elephants, with children's celebrations reserved until the next day. Similar simple pleasures were described by Lady Louisa Antrim, sister of Lady Minto, who spent part of her Christmas holiday in 1909 viewing the garden's architecture and monuments, which by this time included plaques to commemorate the battles of Maharajpur and Pannier[25] as well as several Imperial statues, including one of her brother-in-law the viceroy astride his favourite horse – most appropriate for a man who prided himself on his equestrian abilities. Eventually, many important figures of the Indian empire would end up in Charlotte's quiet garden, since statues of King George V, Robert Peel, Lord Roberts, Lord Napier, and viceroys Curzon, Minto, Mayo, and Lansdowne were moved to Barrackpore after independence.

Barrackpore remained a favourite of the viceregal families throughout the *Raj,* even though after 1864 they headed for the hills of Simla to escape the heat, and no longer spent several months at the former retreat. Steam launches replaced the houseboat, and the menagerie and elephants also disappeared. Lord Hardinge held onto Barrackpore for his visits to Calcutta after the seat of government was transferred to New Delhi in 1912, but his successor, Lord Chelmsford, preferred the proximity of Belvedere and gave up Barrackpore to the Governor of Bengal.

In the end, even Barrackpore's association with the tragic Charlotte Canning could not diminish the fondness all the vicereines had for this elegant country mansion. It was a haven, a family home where they could relax the stiff protocol that enveloped their daily activities, and enjoy the strange flora and fauna of the Indian countryside – albeit carefully manicured and constrained to fit English sensibilities. Gliding smoothly upriver, the vicereines could view India's verdant beauty, but from a distance, remaining isolated from the poverty and misery that many deemed the "real India." Lady Elizabeth Bruce, daughter of the 9th Earl of Elgin, described Barrackpore's magic most eloquently when she wrote of an evening drive to the retreat: "The stars were sparkling and the fireflies shone among the dark trees...I wished that Virgil had been in India to describe the beautiful nights."[26]

Once the British left India, the Barrackpore complex was no longer maintained, and a number of buildings were constructed in what had been the park. The main house was turned into a police hospital and training facility, although the Governor of West Bengal used one of the bungalows as a weekend retreat. As late as 1967, a visitor noted that despite the overgrown park and general disrepair of the site, a sentry still stood guard at the entrance to Lady Canning's grave, which remained in perfect order.

Mountain retreats: Simla, Mashobra and Naldera

Dealing with, and if possible, escaping, the sweltering heat of the plains was an all-consuming aspect of Anglo-Indian life, and viceregal families shared their subordinates' desire to escape the insufferable weather that began in April and lasted until late October. Despite the omnipresent *punkahs* and the open, high-ceilinged design of their residences, for seven or eight months of the year, life in Calcutta and elsewhere in India was almost unbearable for Europeans. But with the Himalayas so near, there had always been an alternative. Beginning in the early 19th century, the British cleared the virgin forest and built hill stations in the mountains, little half-timbered villages that looked as if they had been magically transported from Surrey, complete with mock-Tudor houses, Gothic churches, miniature theatres, teashops, and lines of English cottage gardens littered with croquet hoops and English roses – all clinging perilously to ledges thousands of feet above sea level. All those who could afford it – East India Company officials, businessmen, grass widows – sought refuge in rented houses in one of the hill stations, where provincial governments established themselves for the worst of the summer heat. Locations like Darjeeling, Naini Tal, or Ootacamund were the places where one could see the most energetic attempts to recreate England, in architectural style as well as social life.

The cool, damp weather allowed English-style gardens to flourish, and made the elaborate 19th century garb of upper class women a little easier to bear – there was a bit less chance of perspiring through one's layers of corsets, petticoats, and dresses here. Reaching these distant aeries meant a long, difficult journey, but the promise of cooler weather and "Scottish air" drew Anglo-Indians to the hills from the mid-1800s onward. Even the discomfort of the high altitudes, the monsoons which brought cold to unheated houses, and the mudslides which shifted houses, and shops and made riding on the steep slopes a special challenge did not dissuade them from their annual pilgrimages.

Like everything else connected to the British in India, the business of hill stations was shot through with concerns of precedence, status and the attendant snobbery. There were hill stations, and there were smart hill

stations, and then there was Simla. Simla was ultra chic – always in a different class from its rivals since from 1830 until 1947 it was the *de facto* and later, official, summer capital of the British Indian Empire. Nowhere in India was the pseudo-English country lifestyle more evident.

Adding sauce to the mix was remoteness. Situated at 7,000 feet, and more than 1,100 miles from Calcutta, Simla was extremely difficult to reach. By 1873, the railroad system reached only as far as Umballa, from where it was necessary to travel by post carriage to Kalka at the foot of the Himalyas, and from there – some 57 miles – to Simla. Until the rail line was extended in 1903, carriages could take as long as three days to cover the winding road to Simla. Individual horsemen could manage the trip in about 12 hours, so most men rode, while the women were carried in a *dhooly* or *dandy*. Not everyone saw the trip as burdensome: the adventurous Lady Dufferin wrote to Queen Victoria in 1885 that the road to Simla "…is a wonderful road, always on the edge of a precipice and twisting and turning."[27] Despite her optimistic report, the fact was, in the worst of the monsoon weather, when the trails were flooded, elephants were the only effective means of transportation.

A view of the Peterhof. The quaint and dilapidated house was home to the Viceroys in Simla, until Lord Dufferin commissioned the very much larger Viceregal Lodge.

Despite transportation advances in the 20th century, the trip to Simla never got all that much easier. On their first visit to Simla in the 1930s, the Irwins stopped at Dehra Dun in the Himalayan foothills to give the household staff and the government personnel time to get things organised before they arrived. They stayed at Circuit House, a lovely thatched bungalow which Lady Irwin found enchanting, particularly the gardens, which featured broad lawns shaded by mango, teak, cypress, Indian plum and Cypress trees. Palms, bamboos, and bougainvillea mingled with traditional English flowers such as lupins and marigolds, reminding her of the gardens at the Irwin estate of Garrowby in York. The pleasant atmosphere of Dehra Dun only added to Lady Irwin's apprehension about heading into the hills. She wrote in her diary: "We are packing up and leaving for Simla tonight, feeling very sad, for this place is perfect and such a holiday, and now we have to begin the job in real earnest, and the more I hear of Simla the less attractive it sounds. I am terribly afraid we shall all hate it, but I have never expected anything else as far as I am concerned, as I loathe living in mountains and this is the most concentrated mountain one could possibly imagine! It is like living on the edge of a knife."

Her negative feelings were no doubt increased by the fact that Irwin's private secretary, Sir Geoffrey de Montmorency, spent much of the trip giving "sardonic reflections on the horrors of Simla social life to come which he detested." [28] Dorothy described the misery of riding in a "rail-motor" after the broad-gauge viceregal train ended its run at Kalka, packed with their staff into an open railway carriage, which tended to make people riding it in quite nauseous as it twisted and turned during the five hour journey to Simla, a trip that Lady Wavell found quite literally sickening. By 1947, the Mountbattens were able to make the journey to Ambala by air, but still faced a three-hour drive in an open car up the twisting road to Simla.

Once in Simla, the trials of the journey were forgotten as the Himalayas worked their magic. Even the reluctant Lady Irwin was captivated, writing that after the monsoons set in, "Viceregal Lodge looked like a magic castle, as the stones turned pink in the sunset, then deep orange with a tinge of violet."[29] Her *volte face* about Simla was not unprecedented. More than one vicereine would find Simla's natural beauties an antidote for its inconveniences, stilted social order, and difficulties of travel. Even the critical Mary Curzon said that "…a look out the window makes up for it all, and I can live on views for five years." [30]

Although the distance from Calcutta and difficulty of access made Simla's selection as the home of the British Government in India for seven months each year a somewhat incredible decision, but the consensus of its British rulers was that the health benefits, and breathtaking views of the

Himalayas, more than made up for its inconvenient location. Whatever else it was, Simla was the place where the nostalgic Britons felt themselves almost at home, and to a great extent separated from the business of governing India. As one disapproving official put it, "sedition, unrest and even murderous riots may have been going on elsewhere in India, but in Simla the burning questions are polo finals, racing and the all-absorbing tennis tournaments." More than any other place they lived, Simla was where the vicereines could recreate the English country aristocratic lifestyle so familiar to them. All the ingredients were there: cool weather, a clear social hierarchy, and somewhat fewer demands on their time. It was, as Niall Ferguson wrote, "a strange little hybrid world – part Highlands, part Himalayas; part powerhouse, part playground."[31]

Simla owed much of its development to Major Charles Pratt Kennedy, Garrison Officer and later Political Agent and Commanding Officer who after the Gurkha wars in the early 1800's had a major position of power and influence, being responsible for the princely states' compliance with treaties. An aristocratic and dominating middle-aged bachelor, Kennedy had significant independence of action and power. He built the first permanent house at Simla in 1822, a gabled cottage he modestly named Kennedy House, and set out many of the guidelines for the town's development, choosing sites for houses, bazaars and roads among the heavily wooded hills. Nevertheless Simla was never a particularly attractive town. Even in its heyday, the architect Sir Edwin Lutyens remarked that if Simla had been built by monkeys one would have said, "What clever monkeys, they must be shot in case they do it again." Other observers likened the tinned-roofed government buildings to discarded tramcars, toast racks, salvaged junk, or armadillos.

Its buildings may not have been architecturally attractive or consistent, but once the hills were deemed to be relatively safe havens under Company control, British and Europeans suffering ill health and unable to afford a trip home began to build bungalows and cottages at Simla on land leased from local owners, or to rent houses from the Indian princes. The annual transfer of the Government to Simla began in 1827 with the visit of Governor General Lord Amherst, who came at Kennedy's invitation, travelling with his official entourage and some 1,700 coolies. Despite the difficulties of moving that many people from Calcutta to the mountains – a task that would increase dramatically over time – the visit convinced Amherst of the value of retreating from the heat and dust of the plains for several months of the year. After succeeding with Amherst, Kennedy continued to invite important Company officials to Simla, giving his guests superb dinners with the best wines, and by 1830 the East India Company had officially acquired the township, striking deals with various native rulers and exchanging villages within the Simla tract for villages elsewhere. With Governor General William Bentinck's visit in 1831, Simla received the establishment's stamp of approval when a new house, "Bentinck's Castle," was constructed especially for his use during the summer sojourn. Although Simla would not be officially designated as the summer capital for some 30 years, the presence of the Governor General encouraged more and more Europeans to come there, and the place took on the feel of an English country village, as cottages and bungalows were built and given names like Oakover, Ravenswood and Kelvin Grove.

All the Governors General after Amherst spent some time at Simla, although the first viceroy, Lord Canning, made only one visit, in 1860, at the end of his viceregal tour of the northern provinces. The Cannings stayed at Barnes Court, a large, half-timbered, ersatz Elizabethan manor house, but comfortable quarters did not improve their opinion of Simla. Neither Canning nor his wife warmed to the place. She found it much "too public" and was especially offended by the crowd which met daily on the mall to be seen and gossip. She even termed the Himalayas as "giants detestable to live among," although she said she was glad to have seen them.

In 1864, Canning's successor, Sir John Lawrence, officially designated Simla as a seat of government and ordered the annual move of the entire Government and his Council to the hills. In addition to the presumed health benefits, Lawrence also felt it important for the viceroy to be close to the governments of the Punjab and the Northwest Provinces for some part of the year. Over the years, critics would assail the inadvisability of this decision, citing the dangerous isolation of the rulers from the ruled for so much of the year. One of the most scathing critics was the ardent anti-imperialist Wilfred Scawen Blunt who in 1904 condemned the annual trek to Simla and the effect on the "impoverished millions" of Indians under British rule. The relocation of the Government he insisted represented "...the reckless extravagance of their effeminate rulers, living away from the people 9 months usually out of 12. You may put down much of Indian's woes to the farce of a government whose officials are perched away in the clouds, absorbed in their own amusements, etc. 'in the hills,' and unmindful of their duty to the people."[32] The viceroys however, were unanimous in their belief that the annual progress enabled them to do more work in a climate less draining on their health, and that the trek was essential to maintaining the health and well-being of their families. The fact that the viceroy's annual tours would have taken him out of Calcutta for some months in any case did not impress critics of the decision to move the government to Simla for half the year. In any event Lawrence's edict resulted in a building boom in Simla as Indians and British builders quickly put up structures to meet the demand for housing and government offices.

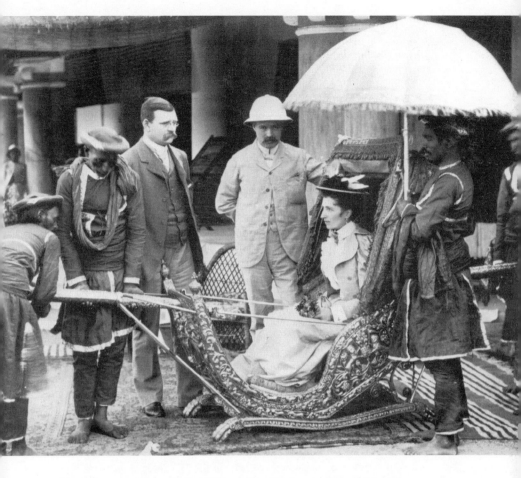

The Governors General who followed Bentinck – Auckland, Ellenbor-
ough, Hardinge, and Dalhousie – had lived in various rented quarters in
Simla, so it was Lord Elgin who lived in what would be the first official
viceregal residence, a large, chalet-like house called Peterhof. Also referred
to as the Governor's Lodge, Peterhof was rented to the government by the
Maharajah of Nahan, and although large by comparison to other houses in
Simla, it was a far cry from the grandeur of the viceregal palace in Calcutta.
Situated on a high ridge, Peterhof was a two-storey building with a gabled
roof of corrugated iron – a source of great noise during monsoons or when
the ubiquitous monkeys landed on it – and two levels of verandahs, one
atop the other. There was one large room for entertaining, but no suitable
indoor venue in which to hold *durbars* for native princes, or viceregal
receptions and investitures. When there was a ball, the entire house had
to be called into service – including the vicereine's private drawing room

Lady Elgin and attendants. She is about to be lifted and borne away in a silver Tanjan.

– as doors were taken off their hinges and verandahs closed in to provide the maximum amount of space for the guests. If the viceregal family was large, children had to live with their *ayahs* in bungalows situated in the estate's grounds. Some viceregal staffers and government officials were also housed in bungalows down the steep hills, and just getting up to Peterhof could be an adventure, especially during the monsoons.

The entire household – viceroy, family, staff, and servants – lived cheek by jowl. At night, native servants, following the custom of sleeping in the halls in case they were needed, took up most of the space, since the corridors of Peterhof were considerably narrower than those of the viceregal palace in Calcutta. Rain seeped into nearly every room, and mildew was not uncommon. The outdoors didn't offer much of an alternative. The house had very little front or back garden, making viceregal garden parties and other outdoor receptions difficult if not impossible. The rain also played havoc with the silk-lined and carpeted large tents or *shamianas* which were put up on the tiny lawn, seeping through the canvas tops and dripping on the viceroy's head as he sat on his silver chair of State, a disruption that significantly reduced the solemnity of the occasion. This same huge chair had to be lugged up and down the hills if the viceroy paid a return visit to one of the rajahs.

Despite its limitations, the Lawrences actually preferred Peterhof to the great palace in Calcutta, since they could escape the formality of the viceroyalty, and trudge happily up and down the zig-zag paths of the hills. The informality of the house and Simla itself reminded Harriette Lawrence of their earlier life in India, "…when we were very small people indeed."[33] She especially enjoyed the fact that her sitting room at Peterhof was close to Lawrence's office, so they saw much more of each other during the day. In the evenings, they often went for an outing, John walking, and Harriette being carried in a *jampan*. Lawrence did not address the issue of a viceregal residence during his term, but the topic remained of interest to Anglo-Indian society, always eager to gossip about the current vicereine's balls, state dinners and garden parties, and to judge her ability to maintain viceregal splendor in such a pokey residence. The speculation of a move from Peterhof even prompted one government secretary in the Mayo administration, Mr. A.O. Hume, to renovate and expand his home, Rothney Castle, in the hope that it would be purchased to replace Peterhof. He spent a fortune, adding enormous reception rooms suitable for large dinner parties and balls, as well as a magnificent conservatory and spacious hall where he displayed his superb collection of Indian horns. A European gardener transformed the castle grounds and conservatory into a magnificent garden and horticultural exhibit, which Hume opened to all visitors. Unfortunately, Rothney Castle's location atop a particularly steep hill made it as difficult to reach as Peterhof, rendering it impractical for an official residence, so Hume saw no return on his considerable investment.

The viceroys who followed Lawrence managed to survive rather comfortably at Peterhof, with the Mayos continuing in the smaller Simla residence the warm and generous hospitality for which they were known in Calcutta. Mayo's successor, Lord Northbrook, did what was necessary to keep up the viceregal tradition of entertainments in the hills, but preferred long walks and horseback rides for his own entertainment, and a quiet game of whist with his daughter in the evenings to a formal dinner party or ball. It took the imperious Lord Lytton to get the ball rolling toward a new and much grander residence. On his first visit to Simla, he was disgusted at being asked to live in a "pigsty," especially since he knew that the Governors of Madras and Bombay were building elaborate summer residences at the same time. Although declaring that Peterhof was the smallest house she had ever lived in, the aristocratic Lady Lytton was less harsh in her judgment than her husband, likening the residence to a large rectory – albeit staffed by some 300 servants and at least 100 cooks – and she was quite taken with the beauty of the rhododendrons surrounding the house. She described the furniture as "hideous stuff, but still old English shapes" which delighted her.

Entranced by the magnificent views, Lady Lytton found the house quite livable, even though her elder girls would have to go via *dhooly* to their lessons, since the main house had only five bedrooms and the govern-esses lived in a separate bungalow. As usual, his wife's willingness to make the best of things domestically had no effect on her husband's opinions, and Lytton directed his considerable energy and effort toward getting the Government to approve the construction of a new viceregal residence whose size and stature would demonstrate the imperial authority of the *Raj*, and its permanence. Lytton personally selected a site on the summit of Observatory Hill in western Simla for the new residence, but despite his best efforts, the project was stalled during his tenure. The initial design for a new Government House proved impractical, and its creator, Captain Cole, judged incapable of managing the complicated construction. Lytton's successor, the more modest and frugal Lord Ripon, felt that while pomp and circumstance might be justified in Calcutta, it was entirely unneces-sary at Simla, and made no effort to move the project forward. When told by engineers that Peterhof might slide down the hill, he remarked "I think it will last for my time."[34] He put Lytton's plans on hold, favouring instead a much less expensive expansion and overhaul of Peterhof with the addition of an additional storey, which would have included adding more comfort-able dressing rooms and bathrooms. All plans remained in abeyance as Ripon departed; he left the decision to his successor, Lord Dufferin.

As soon as she saw Peterhof, Lady Dufferin echoed Edith Lytton's opinion: "The house itself is a cottage, and would be very suitable for a family desiring to lead a domestic and not an official life...I have never lived in such a small house." She fully agreed with her husband that the house was entirely unsuitable even for a part-time viceregal establishment, their experiences in Canada and other European capitals having shown them what it took to create the right social and political environment. During Dufferin's time as Ambassador to Russia, they had spent considerable time and money (some of it their own) to redecorate and refurbish the Embassy House in St. Petersburg (including the stable), creating an establishment that became a social centre among the capital's diplomatic corps. A cultured and experienced diplomat who enjoyed the durbars, receptions, and fancy-dress balls that were an integral part of the viceroyalty, Dufferin urgently wanted a venue in Simla to maintain viceregal splendor, and pressed the government to act on the proposal for the new residence, which fortunately was received much more warmly by a new Secretary of State for India, Lord Randolph Churchill.

Initially, Dufferin had favoured the expansion of Peterhof, having a fondness for old buildings that had grown bit by bit. Eventually, the engineers again proclaimed that Peterhof was unsafe, and Dufferin was given the green light to proceed. His enthusiasm for the project grew out of his long-held desire to create a "romantic" house somewhere. He had wanted to do so at his Irish seat of Clandeboye, but family finances prevented that. He tried again as Governor General of Canada, adding a ballroom and the festive Tent Room for ceremonial events – as well as an indoor tennis court – to Rideau Hall, the official residence. Now, at last, he had the chance to fulfill his architectural dream – and at government expense. As the debate over the need for, and the cost, of a new viceregal mansion escalated, the ever-diplomatic Lady Dufferin wrote to the Queen in May 1885 about the issue, subtly sending the message that the Empire was not being well represented in Simla. The summer capital, she said, "... seems to us, I fear, a little common when looked upon as the capital of a Great Empire." Peterhof was just fine for a family home, she said, but not at all suitable for official entertainment, and that while they had hoped to build a new viceregal residence, Lord Dufferin had vetoed the project at the moment, as an "example of economy." [35] That wasn't entirely true, since Dufferin was determined to build the new residence, no matter what criticism arose, including the false rumour that the Indian income tax had been instituted specifically to pay for it.

Designed by Henry Irwin in English renaissance style, the new residence would have looked right at home as a country house in the Scottish Highlands. (In fact, a later Secretary of State for India, Lord

Montagu compared it to a "Scottish hydro;" even less favourable comparisons were made to St. Pancras Station and the Pentonville prison.) Work began in 1886, with Dufferin micromanaging the project every step of the way, even reviewing and modifying all the architectural drawings. For two Simla seasons, the construction was his primary concern, almost an obsession. He visited the building site morning and evening most days when in Simla, and like many eager homeowners, made changes that frustrated the builders of the Public Works Department. Whatever the state of the weather or construction, Dufferin insisted on taking visitors to view the progress of the house. Even such august royal guests as the Duke and Duchess of Connaught and the Duc d'Orleans were not spared: "We climbed up the most terrible places, and stood on single planks over yawning chasms," wrote Lady Dufferin, describing one such visit to the site.

The Dufferins depicted in print by the London Illustrated News. *They were the epitome of the High Victorian aristocracy and perfect candidates for the viceroyalty.*

She shared her husband's enthusiasm for the new house, and employed her well-known talent for organization in planning and overseeing every aspect of the interior decoration, ordering the furniture, wall and window coverings and discussing every detail with the builders. As she watched the building take shape, Hariot became fascinated with the appearance of the native labourers, especially the women, whom she characterised as "the most picturesque masons." She was impressed by their elegant and smooth carriage which she compared to that of empresses, and their ability to walk as easily on top of the roof as on the ground.

The 8,000-square-foot Viceregal Lodge slowly took shape, an ostentatious, extravagant residence which many judged suitable for the Lord of the Indian empire. From a distance, it did look something like a Scottish castle, with its grey limestone exterior, hundreds of mullioned windows, and towers and cupolas towering above the trees. It was the first truly modern viceregal residence, boasting electric light and European-style kitchens, an indoor tennis court, a tiled laundry, a Council chamber, and a half-timbered guardhouse at the gate. Visitors entered through a south-facing portico into the centrepiece of the house, the enormous great hall with its paneled walls of elaborately carved and moulded teak, walnut, or deodar, a Himalayan cedar. The central feature of the hall was a grand teak staircase that spiralled up three full floors, reaching the upper rooms as well as the surrounding gallery. The hall's enormous chimney-piece around the fireplace boasted carved heraldic beasts and royal arms; other public rooms were located around the main hall, enabling easy movement of large numbers of guests for receptions and state dinners. Lady Dufferin selected an unusual colour scheme for the main public rooms: brown and yellow silks were used in the large drawing room, while the ballroom walls were hung with a lighter yellow silk. When not in use, the ballroom's polished teak floor was covered in sumptuous oriental rugs, with French-style chairs and settees placed in conversational groups around the huge room. The walls of the grand state dining room were covered in rich, dark Spanish leather, enhanced by intricate pierced Elizabethan strapwork with the arms of former Governors General and viceroys – later corrected by George Curzon to ensure historical accuracy.

Below-stairs amenities included large modern kitchens, separate rooms for storing table linen, plates, china, and glass; a laundry; an enormous wine cellar; a room for storing luggage; boilers for central heating, and running hot and cold water in the bathrooms. Verandas and terraces surrounded the entire building at different levels, those at the lower level opening onto the lodge's grounds, while those on other floors provided superb views of mountains. The home's spacious interior was a welcome change from the cramped quarters of Peterhof, but the change was so dramatic that Lady

Dufferin initially wondered how they would fill it all up. Always ready to rise to a challenge, she ordered the necessary interior fabrics and furniture from Maples of London, and while she thought them quite sumptuous and the colour choices very stylish, later vicereines – Mary Curzon for one – would complain of their "middle class" appearance. Lady Curzon's criticism of Lady Dufferin's choices, while perhaps sharper than most, was not unusual. Almost every vicereine found something to fault regarding her predecessor's design choices and household administration, friendships notwithstanding. Hariot's successor (and friend) Maud Lansdowne earlier had expressed opinions similar to Lady Curzon's. She found much of the furniture in the house "...quite deplorable," as well as the combination and contrasts of furniture and fabrics, "...which would make you shudder." She was especially appalled at the fact that carpets had been purchased in England, and wondered why anyone would have chosen bland English patterns over the marvelous Indian carpets available locally.

The Dufferins were only able to enjoy the new mansion for part of their last Simla season, but they were delighted with the new house, both inside and out. Hariot's pride in what she believed to be her smart, elegant interior matched her husband's delight in the overall design, so any criticism of the house's architecture and décor was made privately, and none reached the Dufferins' ears. Although the Dufferin children were unenthusiastic about the move, preferring the more homelike atmosphere of Peterhof, their mother thought the new house was just right for all of them, and thoroughly enjoyed being mistress of the new mansion for the remainder of her time in India. She was particularly taken with the electric lights, finding it "...quite a pleasure to go round one's room touching a button here and there."[36] The new Secretary of State for India, Lord Cross, was less enthusiastic when presented with the bill: the house cost £100,000. To complete the new viceregal establishment, other houses on the estate were built for senior members of the viceroy's staff and the 15 acres of gardens were laid out in the traditional English style, overseen by some 40 gardeners, with an annual budget of £2,500. One viceregal expense unique to Simla was the cost of 10 watchmen employed to keep the omnipresent monkeys away from the house and the gardens.

In the short time she had left in Simla, Hariot quickly set the standard for viceregal entertainments befitting such a magnificent residence. Eager to show off the new mansion – and her decorating talents – she took full advantage of the new spacious public rooms, holding a number of lavish dinners, receptions, and balls to introduce the Lodge to official Simla. In the cool summer evenings, rickshaws lined up along the Lodge's drive, disgorging women in gorgeous ballgowns and jeweled tiaras, their escorts in evening dress or formal uniforms, and on occasion, princes and

Viceregal Lodge, Simla. Mary Curzon called it, "odiously vulgar." Edwina Mountbatten described it as, "Bogus English Baronial," and yet all of the vicereines grew to love the gardens, the views of the Himalayas and the sunsets that could be seen from the house.

maharajahs, whose outsized gems were so huge and numerous that they looked fake, outshining any jewels worn by the vicereine or any of her female guests. Describing similar costumes at a later date, Aldous Huxley wrote "...the diamonds were so large they looked like stage gems. It was impossible to believe that the pearls in the million-pound necklaces were the genuine excrement of oysters."[37] Hariot's formal evenings were the equal of anything seen in London or Calcutta, and could easily match the glamour of any party given by the viceroy's only real rival in Central Asia, the Tsar of Russia.

After all the time and effort she and her husband had put into creating the new residence, Hariot Dufferin would have been furious at the review Viceregal Lodge received from Mary Curzon in 1899. Arriving for her first visit in March (ahead of her husband) her first reaction was one of snide amusement, writing to George that Viceregal Lodge was "quaint" and exactly the kind of house "...every rich American builds..." "Everything suggests cheapness and lack of space and air...but you can't have palaces on mountaintops...and a Minneapolis millionaire would revel in this."[38] She was especially dismissive of Hariot's brown and yellow colour scheme, wondering why it had been chosen when such "noble colours" as crimson, blue, or green were available, and characterised the whole mansion as "odiously vulgar." Even the wallpaper did not escape comment: "Oh Lincrusta, you will turn us grey! It looks at you with pomegranate and pineapple eyes from every wall."[39]

Mary's feelings about the house only reinforced Curzon's already negative views of Simla. He hated the place; the altitude made sleeping difficult, and he loathed the endless round of social events they were required to host or attend. "I do not think there is a more pitiable position in the world than that of the Viceroy and his wife set down for 7 months amid that howling gang of jackals."[40] Still, with his customary obsession for detail, Curzon corrected several of the armorial devices in the dining room to ensure historical accuracy, and he, not Mary, altered the offending interior décor, replacing the Lincrusta wallpaper with damask, and bringing into the dining room a copy of the carved screen behind the Chinese emperor's throne in Peking. He also modified the structure of the house itself, raising the external tower which he thought to be out of proportion, and correcting structural defects. An earthquake in 1905 necessitated major repairs to Mary's bedroom and sitting room, and did nothing to improve the Curzons' opinion of the Lodge or the town itself. George always thought Simla to be decidedly middle class, where he was forced to mix and dine with a set of people well beneath his social status, who were interested only in athletic games and dancing.

He also despised sharing Simla's precipitous heights with two other worthies, the Commander-in-Chief and the Lieutenant Governor of the Punjab, both his informal social and formal political inferiors, and he was right. Simla was not large enough to contain this many lordly Sahibs, and certainly not with two having egos the magnitude of Curzon and Kitchener. The three competing social circles – Kitchener's at Snowdon – known for its fabulous balls; Barnes Court, the Lieutenant Governor's grand residence; and the Curzons' at Viceregal Lodge – each had their followers and critics, and the competition for social preeminence in such a limited space and society was fierce. By 1902, Mary's opinion of Simla had come to match her husband's, moving from amusement to loathing. She now hated everything about Simla, including its "cruel climate," and felt overburdened at having to represent George at a continual round of parties, races, concerts, and weddings given by people she judged to be her social inferiors.

Mary's only enjoyment in the mountains came when the family could escape to the Retreat at Mashobra just outside Simla, or to Naldera, a tented camp some 17 miles away, where George could work outdoors under a the stately deodar trees and the girls could play. The first Lord Elgin had spent several weekends at Mashobra in 1896, and shortly thereafter the government permanently leased a house there for the viceroy's use. A charming gabled cottage, the Retreat's smaller size and congenial setting enabled Mary to be closer to George – even though he worked at the same grinding pace – and to spend quiet time with her young daughters. The Dufferins had also enjoyed Mashobra, revelling in the country life atmosphere, where as Hariot said, it was possible to go on horseback or on foot (and "gloveless," she added) to quiet spots where tea would be served.

Originally called Oaklands, the Retreat was a romantic place, located among apple orchards and woods of oak and pine, which offered plenty of pretty spots for walks and picnics. The house was originally built as two separate flats, and in the Dufferins' time, Lord Roberts had the upper floor and Sir Edward Buck the lower, both of which were turned over to the viceroy at his request. All viceregal children especially enjoyed the freedom of the place and the opportunity to spend more time with their parents. It was as close to life at home as the families found while in India, and enabled the viceroy to relax and have a respite from the cares of office.

Despite Mashobra's charms, Naldera remained the Curzons' favourite mountain retreat; their third daughter was named Alexandra Naldera, after the place they loved most in India, and where she was most probably conceived.

By the Mintos' time, even Viceregal Lodge had become too small to meet the demands of a much expanded Simla society. The number of government officials, military personnel, as well as the "unofficial" population had doubled since the days of the Lyttons, creating additional headaches for the vicereines, who struggled with such problems as whom among this swelling crowd should be included in viceregal entertainments. Although the Warrant of Precedence maintained its hold over Anglo-Indian society, in the early 20th century, the line between the "elect" and the lesser elements of society had blurred just a bit. It was now common for 800 people to be invited to a ball, double the number ever invited to Peterhof. Adding to the crowd on the mountaintop was the increased number of servants; there were now almost as many domestic servants at Viceregal Lodge as there were in Calcutta.

While Viceregal Lodge remained the seat of government for the summer months up until World War II, its glory days were the years between 1912 when the viceroy left Calcutta and 1929 when the new residence in Delhi was ready for occupancy. During that time, the Lodge was the viceroy's primary residence, and many valuable artifacts, pictures, furniture, and other decorations removed from Calcutta in preparation for their eventual installation in the new residence added glamour and elegance to the mountaintop viceregal establishment. The silver state howdah sat at the foot of the main staircase, and portraits of Lady Bentinck, Louis XV and Queen Marie Leczinska (captured at the French settlement of Chandernagore in 1757) hung in the ballroom.

With only one residence to focus on, the vicereines of the period paid rather more attention to Viceregal Lodge. Even before she arrived in Simla in 1921, Alice Reading was preparing to make major changes. "I rather dread the house at Simla as I hear it needs so much doing to it. There is a special fund for it, but it seems a hard job to squeeze it out. I don't believe in 100's of servants, no hot water, 8 courses, not one good, magnificent car, shabby livery."[41] She moved quickly, redoing much of the interior decoration in shades of mauve and grey, sharing a predilection for that colour scheme with her successor, Lady Willingdon. She used the exotic and gorgeous artifacts brought from Calcutta as background for her dinner parties, balls, and receptions, and earned a reputation for orchestrating some of the most glittering entertainments ever held in Simla.

Fully aware of the scrutiny given to their domestic environments by Anglo-Indian society, all the vicereines who came to Simla felt the need to make some changes at Viceregal Lodge, either for purely esthetic reasons or to accommodate the needs of their families. They either redecorated the public rooms, or rearranged private quarters, no matter how short their stay. Some even took on the external environment. Mary Minto, for example, focused on completing the installation of the Lodge's extensive gardens, personally designing an elaborate rose garden that was a showpiece of the viceregal compound. She designed terraces and herbaceous borders, recreating as much as possible the garden environments of the places in England she knew intimately.

Doreen Linlithgow, the last vicereine to spend full seasons at Simla, suffered a great deal from the altitude, and was always glad to get back to New Delhi. However, once acclimated (she often had to take to her bed for a few days after arrival) both Doreen and her husband enjoyed the retreat from the plains, the somewhat reduced pomp of Viceregal Lodge, and above all, Mary's gardens. The house itself did not fare well in comparison with the mansion in Delhi: Doreen thought Viceregal Lodge to be "an ugly Victorian mansion" with none of the elegance so evident in Lutyens' creation.

Even the intrusion of menacing creatures into her environment didn't faze her. She wrote home to her children of finding a deadly snake in the garden, which, she reported, was killed "...by an ADC with a curved sword snatched from the hall." An excellent painter, Doreen's artistic vision was stimulated by the Himalayan vistas she could see from Mary's magnificent gardens. As with Mary Curzon and Dorothy Irwin before her, Simla's natural beauty and magnificent sunsets helped moderate her attitude toward the summer capital. She described the glorious sunsets: "The hills are every colour – those nearest a dirty green, the near distance sepia, the far distance indigo blue w/black shadows and beyond the last range of hills you can see the plain 120 miles away pale cobalt blue and pinky mauve seared w/silver bands, which are the rivers in flood. And the sky quite indescribable…[it] completes a picture which no artist could paint – Turner would have made the best job of it." [42]

Edwina Mountbatten also exulted over Simla's scenery and weather ("Snow peaked mountains, clear and bright and brilliant skies…")[43] but echoed the criticisms of Viceregal Lodge. "House hideous," she wrote in her diary. "Bogus English Baronial, Hollywood's idea of Viceregal Lodge."[44] Entertainment was hard to come by – the movie projector didn't work – and Edwina soon found that Mary Minto's gardens were a welcome relief from the huge dark rooms of the Lodge. Whenever possible, she worked with her assistants among the roses and rhododendrons, and then relaxed in the bright Himalayan sun. During one of her last visits to Simla in 1948, Edwina invited Nehru for his first visit to the Retreat at Mashobra, hoping that a few days in the mountains would help relieve his grief and self-doubt after Gandhi's assassination. During the visit, she made a point of introducing him to old Simla. Edwina, Nehru, and her daughter Pamela wandered among the old wooden houses and strolled along the well-worn paths of the Mall, followed by an admiring crowd.

Even at the end of the *Raj*, improvements in transportation technology had not eased the burdens of travel to and from Simla. A week after Nehru's departure, the last vicereine made her final exit from Simla in a sleek, open-topped red Talbot roadster – with Dickie at the wheel – down the twisting mountain roads toward the plains. Not much had changed in nearly 100 years: leaving Simla was as difficult and uncomfortable as arriving, with the heat increasing almost mile by mile "…hotter and hotter till Kalka where we stewed at 106 degrees," wrote Edwina. [45]

Certainly none of the 19th century vicereines and few of those who lived there in the first half of the 20th would recognize their mountaintop retreat in the 21st. Dufferin's castle remained an important site up to the end of the *Raj*; the 1945 Simla Conference was held here, and in 1947, the critical decision to partition India was made at Viceregal Lodge. After independence, the Lodge continued to be a seat of power, serving as the President of India's summer retreat until 1965 when the Indian Institute of Advanced Studies was installed. That brought significant changes to the building's interior: the state drawing room, ballroom, and dining room were combined to create a library; the Viceroy's office became the IIAS Director's office; and the conference hall, a seminar room for research scholars. Gone are the retinues of servants, the chintz-covered furniture, the gleaming silver, and crisp, snowy table linens so meticulously maintained. The ballrooms and reception rooms where vicereines once welcomed maharajahs are now the site of ponderous academic debates. Perhaps Mary Minto's garden is the saddest sight of all: the roses she so carefully chose and sited now run wild, the lawns are no longer cut close for croquet, and weeds can be seen between the carefully laid stone walkways, a metaphor for the transient impact of the British on India.

The last palace: Viceroy's House, New Delhi

At the 1911 Durbar, King George V announced to the gathered Indian princes that the new capital at Delhi would be "conceived with spaciousness and care so that the new creation would in every way be worthy of this ancient and beautiful city." It would also be the last gasp, architecturally speaking, of the imposition of British style on India. Once the decision was made, work began on the last viceregal palace, one that would literally be the centrepiece of the new imperial capital, and the grandest domestic establishment any vicereine ever enjoyed, as well as the last. The Indian superstition that the movement of any seat of government to Delhi signaled its downfall was ignored by the British, who preferred to see the shift as a continuation of the Moghul legacy. Lord Hardinge, the viceroy who announced and presided over the change of location, turned Government House in Calcutta over to the Governor of Bengal in March 1912, as the entire government made its move to temporary quarters in Delhi.

He and Winifred were happy to go; Winifred was almost as unpopular as her husband by that point, both having been the subject of cruel and angry articles in the Calcutta press over the proposed move. The Hardinges cheerfully put the turmoil of Calcutta behind them and began to focus on the new capital and the chance to create a brand new and, to their minds, permanent imperial city. It became their chief interest: Harcourt Butler wrote that Hardinge "...is mad on Delhi at present. I am afraid we shan't get much of a policy out of him, as he can think of little except Delhi."[46] After the Hardinges took up residence in Circuit House, it was quickly renamed Viceregal Lodge. A rather grand Indian bungalow of Palladian design built to accommodate George and Mary Curzon during the 1903 Durbar, it had a few large rooms suitable for entertaining and was a reasonably comfortable family home, but the viceroy's staff and guests had to make do with tents put up on the grounds, although like other tents used during the *Raj,* they had permanent floors and even fireplaces. In the 1920s, Alice Reading described the house as being like a "monster villa at Monte Carlo" marble balustrades, balconies of white marble, flowers and palms everywhere." Circuit House would remain the principal viceregal residence for the next 17 years, and five vicereines would spend much of their time "helping" Edwin Lutyens create the last great colonial palace.

As important as the new viceregal residence was, it was only part of

Circuit House later Government House, in Delhi, the temporary home to the viceroys. Alice Reading wrote that it was like a "monster villa at Monte Carlo."

the challenge faced by Lutyens, his colleague, Sir Herbert Baker, and their team of architects. Their most monumental task was to lay out the new city grid, design the principal government buildings as well as the viceroy's residence, and work with the senior ruling princes on the location and design of their palatial residences, which although only occupied a few weeks a year, were being built to demonstrate the princes' loyalty to the government and acceptance of the new capital. Baker was responsible for designing the twin Secretariat Buildings, as well as the circular Council Chamber (later known as Parliament House) and a number of smaller government offices while Lutyens focused on the viceroy's palace, and those of the Indian princes.

In the end, New Delhi took nearly 20 years to complete, and was only used by the British for a further 16 years. Lutyens and Baker created a city that was the polar opposite of Old Delhi, with its imposing Red Fort and narrow streets. New Delhi was to be a grand imperial citadel, with broad leafy boulevards lined with government buildings and private homes. From the time the change was announced – and certainly as the new city emerged, and the enormous costs became public, the erection of such magnificent and opulent government buildings, including a huge palace for the viceroy caused some Indians to view it as a further statement of the imposition of foreign rule, and lack of commitment by the British to some degree of Indian self-rule, despite periodic statements to the contrary.

The British deliberately chose a blend of neo-classical and traditional Indian architectural styles for their new capital, attempting on the one hand to demonstrate their power over the country, while at the same time showing deference to the country's cultural and traditions by including both Hindu and Muslim architectural elements in the capital's overall design. The result was a unique if somewhat strange "monumentality" throughout Delhi, with traditional European symbols such as obelisks, arches, columns, urns, and domes enhanced by Indian motifs such as the lotus-blossom, snake, elephant, and the Buddhist *stupa*. This attempt to intermarry cultures in architectural design was a source of friction between Lutyens and his first viceregal client. Hardinge wanted a capital that was British in look, as seen in the Gothic Indo-Saracenic buildings of Bombay, but with the addition of "vernacular" symbols such as a keel-arch or the occasional onion dome in order to pacify the native princes.

Although he had never been to India, and was known primarily as a country-house designer, Lutyens had several important viceregal connections that helped him in his dealings with not only the viceroy, but with the commission appointed to advise on the design and construction of the new city. He was married to Emily Lytton,[47] one of Lady Edith Lytton's two daughters, who had been present at the creation of the *Raj*, the Imperial Assemblage of 1877. Another commission member was the creative and enthusiastic Mary Minto, who maintained her interest in India long after her return to the United Kingdom. Most importantly, Lutyens enjoyed the full confidence of Winifred Hardinge, who fully supported his vision for the new capital, and who provided aid and comfort in his dealings with the viceroy. After his first meeting with the Hardinges, he declared Winifred to be "very cordial and pleasant" and Hardinge easy to work with.

Lutyens focused on developing an easy architect-client relationship with them in regard to the entire project, but especially the new viceregal residence, and he spent considerable time and effort maintaining that relationship. After some minor disagreement, Lutyens made a humble yet amusing apology to Winifred: "I will wash your feet with my tears and dry them with my hair. True, I have very little hair, but then you have very little feet." [48] In the end, the Viceroy's House – the name chosen by the King Emperor George V himself – did include elements of Buddhist culture in the form of *stupas*, in hopes of avoiding any Muslim versus Hindu debates, but Lutyens also merged Mughal architectural elements, balancing Indian motifs with the classical Palladian tradition.

Like the Dufferins at Simla, the Hardinges took a keen interest in the newest viceregal residence, and were not shy about expressing their opinions as to how the new city should look, particularly the new viceregal residence. Lord Hardinge was enamored of pointed arches for the windows and doors: "I should personally like to see buildings of a bold and plain character with oriental adaptation...call it bastard if you

Lord Hardinge with his wife Winifred, his daughter Diamond and his sons Alec and Edward. The template of the ideal Edwardian family. They suffered an assassination attempt and turbulent period of rule in India. Both Edward and Winifred were to die before the end of 1914.

like."[49] Lady Hardinge on the other hand thought that "high considerations of state" should dictate a capital and an imperial palace that was entirely Indian in design.

When the new capital was inaugurated in 1931, the magnificent Viceroy's House dominated the landscape from atop Raisina Hill, its dome rising high above the new city, sharing the high ground with the twin Secretariat buildings – a concession Lutyens later regretted as it seemed somehow to minimize the viceroy's supreme authority.

Covering more than 200,000 square feet, with 12 separate courtyards within its walls, Viceroy's House was larger than Versailles, and contained some 285 rooms of varying size and function located on four floors, which from the outside appeared to be only two. In the central core were the imposing state apartments, including the circular Durbar Hall, complete with thrones for the viceroy and vicereine; the 100-foot long state dining room (which could easily seat 104 guests); and three drawing rooms used exclusively for official events. The four wings of the house contained many State suites and guest bedrooms as well as viceregal offices, while one was designed almost as a self-contained English country house, with living, sleeping and guest rooms on three storeys and easy access to the gardens, ensuring that the viceroy's guests could visit in relative quiet and privacy without marching long distances through the house. Airy loggias and inner courtyards helped to keep the rooms comfortable and were designed to maximize cross-ventilation. On most of the shady verandahs, the temperature remained relatively pleasant even on the hottest day, thanks to the careful design that caught any breezes.

Lutyens had designed every feature of the house, from the paneled walls and coffered ceilings down to the chimney pieces, chairs, "soft squishy sofas" and even the nursery furniture. The door handles, for example, evoked regal grandeur as they were modeled in the shapes of lions in repose, wearing imperial crowns. The house contained all the "mod cons" of the time, plus the extra features required in an imperial palace: 37 lobbies, 35 loggias, 18 staircases, 37 fountains, and 10 elevators. There was a cinema on the lower floor, as well as a fully equipped printing press. Every aspect of domestic life had its own area: a bakery, a tailor's shop, linen rooms equal to those of a large hotel, baggage storage room, kitchens, sculleries and larders of all sorts, special baking rooms, and storage for the coal needed to heat the house in the winter. There was also a full dispensary with an operating theatre and a hospital ward for the use of the viceroy, his family and immediate staff. As an experienced country house architect and the designer of Hampstead Garden suburb, Lutyens appreciated the importance of the landscape that would surround the great palace. He knew that any garden that could survive in Delhi's dry climate would require irrigation, and he also wanted to include Indian design elements outside the house as well as inside. The result was a formal, carefully designed 13-acre garden incorporating both Mughal and Italian styles, with Mughal style canals, fountains and terraces at different levels with flowering shrubs and Western style lawns, hedges and flower beds, including 250 kinds of roses, marigolds, more than 60 cultivars of bougainvillea, and Sweet William, as well as groves of various trees. The pools, fountains, pergolas, gazebos, stone paths, squares of lawn and carefully tended flowerbeds created an oasis for the viceroy and his guests on the dry Delhi plains.

The hard work which maintained that oasis was overseen by a head gardener and a staff of more than 400, 50 of whom were assigned to keep birds away and another 20 whose job it was to arrange flowers for the house grown in a separate "utility garden," along with vegetables and fruits for the kitchens, and enough rose bushes to replace the 3,000 that

Edwin Lutyens' awe-inspiring front elevation of the Viceroy's house in New Delhi.

might be lost each year. The 300-acre estate also included a nine-hole golf course, a swimming pool, cricket pitch, squash court, eight tennis courts, and the requisite stables for horses and hounds of the Royal Delhi Hunt. The Government had authorised £400,000 for the building, but the long span of construction raised its cost to £877,136 (then Rs. 12.8 million).

This then was the last 20th century vicereines' seat of power: a magnificent palace, equal in size, pomp, and complexity to any royal residence in England – but with many more servants. As at previous viceregal sites, the vicereines oversaw this enormous enterprise via the Military Secretary and his subordinate, the Comptroller of the Household who was in charge of the house itself, and all the servants, both indoors and outside. He was in turn assisted by a deputy comptroller, a catering assistant and a housekeeper, each of whom had a coterie of servants to supervise: from table servants to the head silverman, butlers, cooks, scullery maids, bakers, even a chicken cleaner, who did only that, to storekeepers, tailors, carpenters, housemaids, lift boys, laundrymen, down to the sweepers and the *daftaries,* who were responsible for making sure that there was paper and ink on all the desks. By 1947, there were some 2,000 people serving the viceregal establishment in New Delhi: government functionaries, aides and clerks, police and soldiers, and a veritable army of servants working in the grounds, the garages, stables, post office, and dispensary. Some 6,000 persons had permanent housing at Raisina Hill, including staff, wives, children, and other dependents, with another 1,000 housed on viceregal estates in Simla and Calcutta.

Two of the vicereines who reigned in the interim before the new residence was completed – Frances Chelmsford and Alice Reading – were consulted by Lutyens as the project progressed, but with only varying levels of interest, well aware that they would never occupy Viceroy's House. Dorothy Irwin, on the other hand was actively involved with the project, as was her husband. Lutyens found the Irwins the most compatible of all the viceroys and vicereines with whom he worked, and he was grateful for their helpful advice, and sympathy for the problems he faced. Lord Irwin's interest extended beyond the house itself, and he raised funds to construct an Anglican church worthy of the imperial city. Lutyens found the Irwins' "patrician taste" entirely in sync with his own views; they had an "instinctive feel for classicism and the grand manner" he said, while in turn his grand visions sparked their imagination and creativity, and enabled them to make meaningful contributions to the house as it was being constructed.

Dorothy worked closely with Lutyens on the final details of the furnishings and decoration, and spent endless hours on the design and planting of the Moghul gardens, which she described as "strangely English" since they contain flowers usually seen in the high summer in England – hollyhocks, phlox, petunias, and verbena, in addition to the more traditional Indian plants. Like vicereines before her, Dorothy kept the Queen informed of the viceregal domestic arrangements and the progress on the new palace. Having visited twice, Queen Mary had a particular interest in India, and in 1930 she sent Dorothy a Chinese goldfish bowl for the new house that had belonged to the last King of Delhi, along with an inkstand. Dorothy thanked the Queen effusively for her generosity "on behalf of ourselves and future viceroys." She reported that she had been very busy getting the new house set up, and that the final version of the house and its furniture had "on the whole" been successful, neglecting to mention that plumbers were finishing their work the day before the Irwins arrived to take up residence in 1929.

Despite its grandeur, the Irwins found the House to be "essentially a liveable-in house." Irwin and his daughter Anne especially enjoyed the fact that its location enabled them to take early morning rides across the Delhi plains, sometimes taking their breakfast among the stone remains of the many tombs scattered across the landscape.[50] The great open spaces

The Mughal Garden of the Viceroy's House. The intricately planned formal gardens would employ a staff more than 400 gardeners, to maintain the oasis in a state of permanent perfection.

around the Viceroy's House offered more freedom to the viceregal families, who were formerly limited to riding on the Maidan in Calcutta. Here they could ride for miles with only one ADC in attendance. Shortly before his death, Lord Irwin (by then Lord Halifax) recalled that "every day that we lived there, we came to love it more."[51]

It was the next vicereine, Marie Willingdon, who had the greatest impact on not only the Viceroy's House, but the skyline of New Delhi itself with her extraordinary changes to Lutyens' elegant and carefully crafted interior décor and her involvement in the design of other major buildings. No stranger to positions of power, Marie was one about whom few had neutral feelings. Depending on to whom one listened, she was either a charming, yet strong-willed asset to her husband who had done a great deal of charitable work, or a pushy, indiscreet, self-absorbed social climber with ambition and lust for power far beyond that of her devoted spouse. She and Freeman loved the pomp and status the viceroyalty embodied, shared a genuine love for India itself, and were delighted when they had the opportunity to return to the subcontinent as its rulers. The years as the Governor's Lady in Madras and Bombay, and as the wife of the Governor General of Canada had given Marie a wealth of diplomatic and social experience which served her well in the "top job" in India. Having been denied the viceroyalty more than once due to the vagaries of politics, Marie was elated at finally reaching the very apex of Anglo-Indian society – a prospect made all the sweeter by the opportunity to redecorate the grandest palace in British India. No one ever approached the role of vicereine with more enthusiasm, or with a greater determination to leave her mark.

Once in residence, her first move was to reinstitute a more formal viceregal court, reversing what she saw as the "very sloppy" social conventions of the Irwin regime. The wearing of black tie at all except at the most formal occasions was quickly reversed, and to their great annoyance, the viceroy's staff officers now had to appear in white tie for all formal gatherings. As noted earlier, she then began her redecoration scheme for Lutyens' great mansion, with her favourite colour, mauve, as the central theme. Whether her fixation with this colour resulted from a desire to emulate the style and known colour preference of the late Queen Alexandra or not, Marie's love of mauve was a hallmark of her public persona, and often noted by the press. She used it in all her homes – public and private – even having her staterooms painted mauve for the voyages back and forth to England, and was always given at least one bouquet of mauve flowers at any official occasion. Her predilection was so well known, that one maharajah, eager to please the new vicereine, even ordered mauve toilet paper for a viceregal visit. It turned out not to be colourfast, with some embarrassing results.

Oblivious to the elegant ambiance and order Lutyens had created in the Viceroy's House, Marie moved quickly to put her own stamp on the barely completed mansion. She ordered many of the rooms to be repainted in mauve, and added insult to injury by further embellishing them with painted decorations described by one visitor as "wild duck falling into Dorothy Perkins roses."[52] Even the magnificent ballroom was not immune, its walls and ceiling being repainted with Moghul motifs and "gaudy arabesques." Not satisfied with making changes to the house's interior, Marie set about revamping the formal gardens, having stone elephants moved from the forecourt and placed throughout the garden. She also ordered many trees to be cut down, some to provide a football field for soldiers, and some to be replaced with cypresses, a variety she preferred but that was unsuitable for the climate. Her frenzied overhaul of the garden completely destroyed the order of plants and trees so carefully chosen ny Lutyens, who was distraught upon learning of the horrors inflicted upon his *magnum opus*, even more so because he understood the strong personality he was dealing with. He had originally met Marie in Bombay in 1912, and described her as "very brusque and rude" yet somewhat attractive with "an air of appealing pathos about her." At their next meeting in 1915, Lutyens was struck by how Marie's demeanor had changed after losing her son in the war. "Lady W is softer, but as energetic as ever. She still I am told believes her boy will turn up sometime, somehow."[53]

By the 1930s, however, whatever sympathy he might have felt for

Marie disappeared as she began to meddle with his life's work in New Delhi. Distressed at what he heard about her changes, he launched a major campaign to stop the revisions. At his request, Queen Mary wrote Marie a stern letter expressing her concern about the changes, but even a royal rebuke did not affect the supremely self-confident Marie. In 1934, when the Willingdons were home on leave, Lutyens asked to meet with Marie and presented his concerns in person, but to no avail. Describing the meeting, Lutyens wrote furiously "She combines bad manners with worse taste." At first, she and Lord Willingdon attempted to placate Lutyens by suggesting that a bust of him be installed in the new house near that of Lord Hardinge. Lutyens responded by recommending that the bust be placed in a niche he knew she had already eliminated. The meeting went downhill from there. He later recalled that during the somewhat heated discussion he had told her "...if she possessed the Parthenon, she would add bay windows to it. She said she did not like the Parthenon, but I hope and trust that the irony of my remark will eat into her soul. "[54] When Lutyens brought up the issue of cost, Marie claimed that her changes had not cost the government much money, since she had gotten a substantial contribution from the Nawab of Bhopal, and that the donation had been to the house, not to her personally. Lutyens saw this as her way of getting around the rule which required that any gift to an official of the government of India be reciprocated with one of equal value. As the discussion escalated, Marie even complained to Lutyens about the fact that the residence was called the Viceroy's House, not the Viceroy's Court, which she thought much more appropriate. "I did not call her a Pimlico Poo which she ranks with in taste," wrote a disgusted Lutyens.[55]

Having redone the palace to her satisfaction and re-established the splendor of the viceregal court, Marie extended her sphere of influence to New Delhi itself, thereby increasing Lutyens' fury at her interference. At her initiative, a new site for an Olympic stadium – dedicated to her and her husband – was selected at the Purana Quila end of Kingsway, obscuring the old fortress and significantly altering Lutyens' carefully crafted skyline which was to have only the war memorial – now known as India Gate – between the Viceroy's House and the Purana Quila. She further insisted that *chattris* be "dotted" along the outline of the stadium, despite the objections of the architect. At her order, the Anglican Church of the Redemption was given a tower in plastered brick instead of the sandstone used elsewhere in New Delhi, so that it would be higher than other buildings. Marie even took on the native princes, changing plans for several of their mansions as they were being constructed. The design of Jaipur House was changed and amplified, despite the Maharajah's objection. He later told Mountbatten: "No one could stand against her when she decided on something."

Once she had finished redoing the mansion and its environs, Marie turned her considerable energy to maintaining the glamour of the viceregal court, planning and organising elaborate fancy dress balls and overseeing with great delight the many requisite state balls, receptions, dinners, investitures, and garden parties. No vicereine loved the pomp and circumstance more, and none missed it more when it was over. In her defense, Marie truly loved India, and longed to stay for another 10 years, although whether she missed India itself or her tenure as its vice-queen remains an open question.

Marie may have won the battle, but she lost the war. When the Willingdons were replaced by the Linlithgows in 1936, one of Doreen Linlithgow's first acts was to set about restoring Viceroy's House to its former magnificence. Less concerned with the formal side of the viceroyalty than Marie, Doreen wanted the house to be more family-friendly, while at the same time, she recognised the need to reinstate Lutyens' original vision for the mansion and its gardens. In the autumn of 1938, she invited Lutyens to New Delhi to help her remove the "various vagaries" of Lady Willingdon both inside and out. He was so overjoyed at the prospect of returning the house and gardens to their original state, that he told Doreen "if she had not been a Queen I should like to kiss her. She at once put her arms around my neck and kissed me."[56] Confident that the Linlithgows were committed to putting the house back to the state in which he had left it, Lutyens happily oversaw the repainting and redecoration inside the house, including the painting over of the ducks and Dorothy Perkins roses, and moved furniture back to the location for which it had been designed, restoring the ambiance and style that had been destroyed, as one aide put it, through Lady Willingdon's "misplaced zeal."

Lutyens also supervised the restoration of the gardens to their manicured splendor, sending the stone elephants back to the forecourt, digging up the ill-chosen cypresses, replanting the original species of trees, and somewhat reluctantly designed a fountain to commemorate Marie's reign. Lutyens knew he could rely on Doreen to maintain his garden vision, because she was a keen gardener with a real sense of design. She, on the other hand, was delighted to find that her garden superintendent had formerly worked at Kew Gardens in London and had a wealth of experience to bring to this quasi-English, mostly Moghul landscape. Together, they devised colour schemes and plans for the garden, and he and his staff executed them. Doreen liked masses of single colours in varying shades, a design element she used in a little sunken garden where she and Lord Linlithgow often took tea, cherishing the few moments of peace in the evening. In addition to regular maintenance, the mansion's garden underwent a complete change twice a year: once when the Linlithgows came down from Simla

Doreen Linlithgow. The Viceroy Lord Linlithgow and the Maharaja of Bikaner at Bikaner Fort in 1937.

in the fall and again in February or March. Each change was completed overnight; a guest would go to bed having seen the garden in one set of plants and colours, and awaken to an entirely new landscape, a complete new set of plants having been put in place overnight by a silent troop of some 250 men.

Lutyens was so grateful for the changes Doreen made, and for her understanding and appreciation of his original vision and design, that he presented her a glass goblet, now at the family estate, Hopetoun House, outside Edinburgh, inscribed as follows:

To Her Excellency
The Marchioness Linlithgow
Whose Presence dignifies
Whose sovereign touch repairs the wounds
Inflicted by mistaken zeal upon
The Viceroy's House at Delhi
This goblet is humbly offered
As a token of gratitude
By him who has most reason
To be grateful.

E.L.

Viceroy's House was modernised over the years, even getting air conditioning in some of the rooms, but as the 20th century moved toward the halfway point, some elements of life in the great palace were reminiscent of those faced by the first vicereine, Charlotte Canning, such as the silent presence and hierarchical structure of the servant corps. One evening as she stood ready to receive dinner guests, Doreen Linlithgow's little dog made a mess on the carpet. She immediately rang for a servant to clean it up, but it took so long to find a servant of low enough rank to perform the task that she was cleaning it up herself as the first guests entered.

As Doreen presided over the house from 1938 to 1943, the onset and beginning of World War II dramatically changed the vicereine's role as the *Raj* began to crumble. By the time Doreen's successor arrived in New Delhi, Eugenie Wavell faced a world where interior design and garden maintenance were far down on the list of priorities for the vicereine. Despite a punishing schedule of visits to canteens, hospitals, welfare centres, and schools, both the wartime vicereines maintained a significant level of pomp and ceremony in Viceroy's House and carried the primary responsibility for an extensive domestic establishment. After 1941, the viceregal retreat at Simla was off limits, which reduced their administrative burden somewhat, but the Viceroy's House remained a focus of Anglo-Indian society throughout the war, with some of its former extravagances limited by the wartime realities.

It would be hard to find two women from more different backgrounds than the last two vicereines who reigned at Viceroy's House. Eugenie Wavell was raised in a middle-class family, a colonel's daughter with none of the aristocratic background or diplomatic know-how of earlier vicereines, but with a lifetime of experience as a soldier's daughter and wife that served her well in a world at war. "Queenie" as her family called her, focused on making the house a comfortable refuge for her hard-working husband, and on maintaining the Linlithgows' less intimidating and less

formal viceregal establishment. Friendly and charming, Queenie was a success as vicereine in a difficult time in the history of the *Raj*. When her husband was unceremoniously replaced by Mountbatten in 1947, Eugenie put aside her hurt feelings and tried to effect a smooth transition, writing friendly letters to Edwina Mountbatten on the running of the viceregal household, advising that there was sufficient glass, china, "electro-plate,– ample though not attractive" and some silver and gold plate for viceregal entertaining. Although a reluctant vicereine – she would have preferred to stay in Europe and continue her post-war relief work there – Edwina replied in kind, expressing her appreciation for Eugenie's advice, even though it was mostly unnecessary, given Edwina's background, fortune and ability to remake her domestic environment almost at will.

Edwina had spent her life in the literal lap of luxury and was skilled at overseeing large households, which she had done first for her grandfather, the financier and royal confidante, Sir Ernest Cassel, and later for her husband, whose ego and royal pretensions brought with them an expectation of a certain level of domestic luxury. No stranger to grandeur and able to spend money almost without thinking, even Edwina was impressed by magnificence of the viceregal establishment. She toured its vast state rooms and reception halls, wandered through the acres of elegant and exquisitely tended gardens, and saw for the first time, the literal regiments of servants. With her characteristic attention to detail, Edwina spent a fortnight thoroughly inspecting the palace and learning how it operated. The Comptroller of the Household was amazed at her detailed interest in schedules, menus, and costs of meals, the condition of linen and plate for entertaining, even the management of the gardens and the stables. Although no redecorating had been done during the war – a fact for which Lady Wavell apologised – Edwina quickly agreed that Eugenie had made a good decision, and since the war had changed so much and she would be in residence such a short time, she too made no plans for renovations or alterations. Instead, Edwina spent part of her initial tour checking on the living conditions of the multitude of servants whose homes were in the viceregal compound, and urged an immediate improvement of their wretched quarters. She also ordered a thorough house cleaning of cobwebs and dirty walls that now overshadowed its stately elegance.

As part of their efforts to smooth the transition, the Mountbattens made a point of opening Viceroy's House and gardens more often and to a more diverse group of guests, especially Indians, including those who had served time in prison for "nationalist" offenses. "I think Viceroy's House and grounds are now looked on more as a *part* of India than as a British stronghold," Edwina told her daughter. She had been amazed that fewer than six of all her Indian guests had ever been in the residence before, despite having been active in public life and politics for many years.[57]

These social innovations were extremely disquieting to the Anglo-Indian establishment – yet another reminder that the *Raj* they had known and served for so long was rapidly disappearing. The Mountbattens' seeming disregard for the established social norms and an openness to actual friendship with Indians gained them great popularity, but flew in the face of all that the Anglo-Indians had known and clung to. The social changes at Viceroy's House were among the most visible indications of the dramatic remarkable shift in British-Indian relationships, as Indians reached their long-promised independence.

After independence, Viceroy's House became known as the *Rashtrapati Bhavan*, or President's House, and has served as his primary residence. Lutyens' breathtaking architecture and interior décor remain intact for the most part; surely no other president of a democracy can boast of a residence so vast and so magnificent. Even the memory of the glamorous tiaraed vicereines is long gone, their decorating changes, elaborate entertainments, and family celebrations all but forgotten. In one small final irony, Lutyens' imposing mansion designed to showcase the majesty of a ruling elite now represents the power and authority of an independent people, and in another the bust of Lutyens proposed by the Willingdons remains in an alcove above one of the great staircases, while the portraits and sculptures of all the viceroys have long since been removed.

3
Mater Familias

One of the less visible dimensions of the vicereines' time in India is their family life. The powerful distorting influence of that grand imperial setting can be felt at a great distance in time as well as space. It was closest in essence among the outlying realms of empire in terms of structure, values and aura to the satraps and provinces of ancient empires, images and models of which were part of the "programming" of the young Britons who became the rulers of the greatest if not the grandest of all such hierarchies. But there was really no counterpart structurally to their roles in the *Imperium Romanum*. Wives of the Roman provincial governors were just that -- wives -- without the eminence and ceremony that surrounded the British vicereines, nor were the other principal overlords in the British Empire in Egypt and Canada labelled viceroys of anywhere near the eminence as the symbolic surrogates in India of British monarchs. But like Caesar's wife and the exemplary matrons of ancient Rome, models with which many of the *Raj*'s functionaries were familiar, the vicereines were to be above reproach, and stand as symbols of familial virtue. Although they were expected to strive toward the ideal of philosopher king and proconsul as many British colonial administrators did, vicereines in general did a better job of playing the role of *mater familias* than most viceroys did in their capacity as *pater familias*.

Whatever the vicereines' feelings about going off to play the most demanding and visible role in all the overseas Empire, most maintained a stoic mien when they became aware that their husbands were eagerly seeking the position, sometimes long in advance, sometimes when surprised by their husbands almost on the eve of departure. No matter how bitter and wearing the infighting involved in their husbands' struggling to gain the appointment, and how unhappy they might be about the prospect of at least five years in discomfiting exile, the vicereines all dutifully expressed enthusiasm in public. In most cases there was at least a tincture of sincerity, since most vicereines had spent their married lives in diplomatic or military postings in the hope that their husbands would rise to a very high position in the Imperial hierarchy. But even though becoming viceroy of India was the capstone in that careerist progression, vicereines often held strong reservations about that most exalted of assignments, just as all but the most grimly ambitious viceroys shared their wives' concerns about the impact of their elevation to the virtual summit of their ambition on their family's health and welfare. Most viceregal aspirants made at least some gesture toward weighing in their wife's opinion while considering whether or not they would accept the position. But once any agonising over the clash between personal and political ambition and their sense of duty versus family concerns was over and the decision was made, each viceroy expressed confidence in his wife's abilities to carry out her vice-reinal duties and praised her evident keenness for the facing the special challenges ahead.

Whatever contingencies the viceregal couple weighed as they prepared to go to for India, and whatever counsel was given them as to what they might anticipate, viceregal couples routinely encountered many aspects of service in India, both pleasant and discomfiting, that they did not, or, indeed, could not anticipate. After ascending the figurative throne in India, most viceroys found themselves depending on their wives for support and advice far more than they expected when it became apparent that there were very few people in India with whom they could speak freely or rely upon for unswerving support and political guidance. As noted earlier, the vicereines' role in gathering intelligence in social settings was especially important, as was their serving as links to key players in the game of power in India and at home. Not only did those viceregal couples blessed with sound marriages find that pressures of lofty power in India strengthened their bond, but those with shaky relationships often discovered, or re-discovered, aspects of their unions which brought them much closer together. And while some vicereines pursued charitable and political interests, warming to the special celebrity awarded to champions of the less fortunate, others came to see their vicereinal responsibilities as another bundle of burdens piled onto a life already over-taxed by child-bearing and child-rearing.

Aside from grave illness and death of loved ones, perhaps the sharpest and most nagging pain came from prolonged absence from children and/or aging parents, a burden they shared with all servants of the *Raj*, along with the substantial dangers and discomforts imposed by travel and climate. Here, too, they were compelled to suffer in silence. By the mid-19th century, the Victorian stereotype of the strong, stoic, self-sacrificing wife and mother had become firmly implanted among middle-class Britons throughout the Empire, and variants of it, both in substance and lip-service, endured almost to the end of the *Raj*. The vicereine was expected to embody that stoic ideal, whatever her personal wishes or worries about her children. As the stiff upper lip tradition evolved and flourished, the image of the happy, stable viceregal family in India mirrored the myth of a snugly happy and very proper bourgeois monarchy in Britain. Chilling as the prospect of playing a stolid Titania to the pseudo-court of the *Raj* was to any vicereine, and presiding over a kind of dim magic which was growing dimmer, doubts about going to India could be voiced only to family and close friends.

By the time the last vicereine, Lady Mountbatten, departed for India in 1947, concerns that bedevilled her predecessors had been eased by myriad technical advances. But even though vicereines in essence bore much the same load of personal concerns as "Judy O'Grady and the colonel's lady," their passage was along a much smoother road. A Victorian vicereine's wealth and aristocratic connections and access to medical care reduced the risk to their children, her husband and themselves. But as the threats posed by end-to-end pregnancies and tropical diseases diminished, latter-day vicereines faced an increasing likelihood of losing their sons in war, and indeed several did experience that tragedy. In an era when ruling elites shared the military risks of maintaining, expanding, and defending the empire, and as those hazards increased, viceregal families' anxieties and losses came closer to and sometimes exceeded those of their social peers in colonial wars, and of the masses in the conscript armies and navies of the World Wars. Lesser in degree, but a more prolonged pang was leave-taking for extended separation. It was one thing, as most British middle and upper class parents did, to send a young boy off to public school 200 miles away, knowing he would be home for vacations and could be visited, and quite another, as British parents headed for India did, to say goodbye, knowing that reunion lay several years in the future. Sad little letters from lonely children caused the same pain and heartache whether their mother was a vicereine or the wife of a district commissioner. But most imperial elites of all ranks saw no valid alternative.

The risks of such separations were measured to a great extent in medical terms. Although medical and preventive health improved by leaps and bounds throughout the mid- and late 19th century, and odds of surviving Indian service far exceeded those in the days of the Honourable East India

Company, Britons faced much greater chances of serious illness in India than at home until the last days of the *Raj*. Vicereines who brought their families to India, like Europeans whose children were born there, watched them carefully for signs of the many illnesses that could kill within hours. Viceregal children were closely guarded, and grew accustomed to the tall silent bodyguards who watched them play on the broad lawns, or led them on ponies around the compound or parade ground.

Closely linked to that concern was the spectrum of gynaecological problems that afflicted British and European women in India during their childbearing years. As the rise of awareness of microbial contagion from the 1870s onward led to the rapid evolution of "modern medicine," many vicereines, most notably Constance Elgin, Mary Curzon, Winifred Hardinge, Frances Chelmsford, Alice Reading, and Edwina Mountbatten, suffered from various "female complaints" during their reigns, and were generally recognised as being in somewhat precarious health. Their difficulties were aggravated by intense heat and humidity, and the stresses of being "on stage" when they would have much preferred to put their feet up or go to bed. Each of them in letters, diaries or memoirs recalled occasions when a *samurai*-like spirit of doing their duty prevailed over personal desire, or common sense, as they ground their way through a long dinner party or state reception, struggling to smile through their pain. On the other hand, such robust vicereines as Ladies Dufferin, Lansdowne, Minto, Willingdon, and Wavell were rarely ill, and proudly proclaimed their good health, as if it were a matter of choice rather than fate. Newspaper accounts of their prowess at games – horseback riding, tennis, and golf – and references to their stamina reinforced the paradoxical and incongruent images of their being stalwart and softly feminine at the same time.

Servants of the crown in their exile found themselves paying the price of imperial glory in many different kinds of coinage. Good health and a steady world-view provided British functionaries overseas no defense against the chronic concerns for their children at home, whether in infancy or fully grown, and with whom communications were uneven and uncertain. Until the late 19th century, those on extended service abroad might not hear of a family member or friend's death or illness until weeks or months after the event. That nagging pain, however, was eased in stages by the expansion of the vast network of transoceanic cables, and improvement of postal traffic by rail, steamship, and finally aircraft. But even during the final phase of empire, parents among the servants of the *Raj* had no quick or easy way to deal with letters from lonely children begging Mummy to come home, a plight dramatised by Kipling in his tear-jerking short story "Baa-baa Black Sheep." The best they could do was to write an immediate response explaining why they couldn't come, and suggest when Mama and Papa might next be home, hoping that the child's unhappiness would have abated by the time the letter reached them.

The threat of personal danger threw an even darker shadow over the vicereines, especially after the untimely deaths of Lady Dalhousie and Lady Canning less than a decade apart. The hazards of living in India were manifold, and risks oscillated due to medical advances and political conditions, making the overall hazard incalculable, as was striking a balance between the well-being of their children and wanting to be with their husbands. The childless Charlotte Canning's concerns about her own health were trumped by the importance of her husband's being viceroy, since she always acceded to his wishes and the demands of his career. Although Mary Louisa Elgin and Harriette Lawrence had devoted husbands and very happy marriages, neither was keen to make the difficult voyage to India with their children. Harriette had a clearer picture of what she would face, since she had already experienced the harshness of garrison life on the plains, the Mutiny, the death of a son, and an eight-year separation from her daughters who were sent home for their safety. Although Mary Louisa had not been to India, she had raised children alone, most recently while her husband spent two years in China. When Elgin was named viceroy, the family had been together for only 11 months after a long separation, and the thought of uprooting them again, even for the honour of being elevated to viceroy, was depressing to the Elgins.

Being dutiful Victorian wives, Lady Lawrence and Lady Elgin conformed to their husbands' interests, as they went off to India with less than full enthusiasm. So did many of their successors, and in some cases, their husbands. Virtually all of the viceroys appreciated the inconveniences and dangers that faced them and their families, and some suffered as much or more than their wives from separations, brief or extended. Elgin's and Lawrence's letters written while travelling to India reflect a deep devotion to their wives and children, and the agony of being parted from the. Elgin wrote daily of his longing for home, family and most of all, his wife, recalling family dinners and happy Sundays spent together at Broomhall, the Elgin estate in Scotland, reminding himself of happier times but heightening his misery at being parted from his family. Lawrence also suffered from family separations, but in keeping with the Victorian adage "distance lends enchantment," he was overjoyed to see his wife after nearly a year's separation. "You cannot think," John wrote to a friend in England," what a difference the arrival of my wife has made to me." Their wives made decisions of the kind that many British families were also forced to make as they selected some of their children to accompany them to India while leaving others at home. Sometimes things became very complicated indeed. Lady Lawrence, for example, brought her two eldest

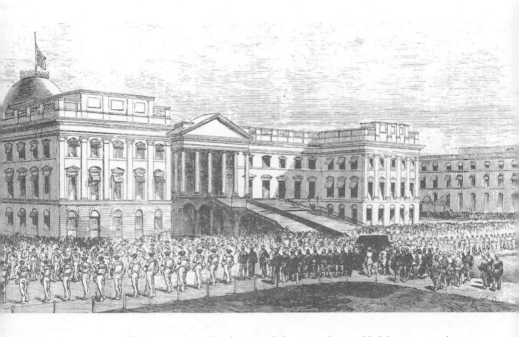

The
assassination
of the popular
and effective
Viceroy, Lord
Mayo, deeply
shocked Britain
and India. A
contemporary
engraving of
his funeral
cortege passing
Government
House in
Calcutta in
1872.

and two youngest daughters with her to India, and left her sons in the care of her sister-in-law, Letitia Hayes. When Mrs. Hayes died, Harriette was forced to make other arrangements, and eventually returned to England to look after them before Lawrence's tenure ended. And after all the years apart, Lady Elgin spent less than a year in India, heading home unexpectedly after the sudden death of her husband in 1863 to bring up her stepdaughter and three sons.

Julia Mayo was the other vicereine whose husband died during his stint in India. After agonising over whether or not to stay at home, Lady Mayo decided to leave her three elder sons (all in their teens) at home, and brought her four-year-old son and young daughter with her to India, believing that her husband needed her more than her elder children. He certainly seemed to think so. During Julia's trip home in 1870 to see the boys, Mayo wrote to her: "We have never been separated before for any length of time. I hope you dislike it!"[1] She did indeed, and after making sure that all was well with the children in England, she accompanied the viceroy on his annual processional throughout India.

Tragedy struck on February 8, 1872, when she was aboard *Glasgow*, one of two steamers carrying the viceregal party on a tour of Burma and the Andaman Island penal colony. Lord Mayo, an advocate of improved prison conditions, first in Ireland and now in India, was returning from a climb to the top of Mount Harriett above Hope Town where he inspected a hilltop site under consideration for a prison sanitarium. In the dim evening light, Lady Mayo saw the torches of the party approach the jetty to board the launch for the short run back to the ship. As she ordered the band to strike up "Rule Britannia," she saw a convict stab her husband in the back as he stepped onto the jetty.[2] The viceroy fell into the shallow water, and was dragged out, still conscious. Bleeding heavily, Mayo died before they reached the doctor aboard the *Glasgow*. Although numbed by grief, Lady Mayo managed to recover by the time the ship reached Calcutta, and her quiet dignity during the lying-in-state and official mourning earned her high praise in India and at home. A few months later, when Mayo's assassin was convicted, the viceroy's children sent him a telegram, "May God forgive you," a comment in keeping with their liberal father's senti-ments, and which was probably encouraged or at least approved by their mother. The message infuriated Sir Donald Stewart, Superintendent of the Andaman Island penal colony, who saw the statement as giving way in the face of insurgency rather than a Christian expression of charity.

Mayo's fate gave his successor, Lord Northbrook, considerable pause when he was offered the viceregal throne.[3] While his experience in the India Office during the post-Mutiny organization of an Indian government was cited by Lord Halifax[4] and other supporters, those favouring the affable Lord Dufferin's candidacy suggested that Northbrook lacked the "right" personality and social skills for the post. The fact that he was a widower also was held against him on the grounds that even though the role of vicereine was not formal but honorific, and appeared on no organizational chart, an unmarried viceroy would face a significant handicap in meeting his extensive social obligations without a helpmate. Having lost his wife in 1867 and three years later his son Arthur, Northbrook hesitated when first approached about the viceregal position out of concern for the potential effects of Indian service on his surviving children, Emma and Frank. He would not entertain the option of leaving the children home, since raising the children alone had increased his paternal devotion. After Halifax and others in the government persuaded him that becoming viceroy was his duty, Northbrook and his children embarked for India in late 1872.

The fears of danger were borne out during the Calcutta famine of 1874, when the viceroy sent both youngsters back to England to stay with an uncle. After they returned in late 1875, Frank blotted the proverbial copybook by establishing an "attachment" to a married woman he had met in Simla. That led Northbrook to request an early release, citing "duty to his children" as the primary reason. After agreeing to stay in India to host the Prince of Wales's tour in December and January, the viceroy managed to keep Frank out of trouble and away from his paramour during the visit. In contrast to her brother's hi-jinks, Emma served as her father as *ipso facto* vicereine, ably overseeing and presiding at many official ceremonies and social events, including a state banquet at Government House, several investitures, and a host of smaller dinners and receptions, winning widespread praise for meeting the exacting demands of Anglo-Indian protocol in spite of her youth.

Throughout the late 19th century and into the twentieth, western technology was brought to bear against the various climatic extremes that European and American merchants, soldiers, sailors and explorers encountered in their traffics and discoveries around the world. While much of that effort was medical, including microbiology, immunology, and preventive and educational campaigns, a substantial amount of energy was expended on attempts to temporize temperature extremes. Beyond the creation of summer refuges for British administrators in the foothills of India's mountain ranges and *punkahs* was the adoption of desert and jungle dwellers' architecture and clothing, and the flow of ice in insulated ships and railcars, the product of the "ice-farming" on frozen lakes in northern latitudes. Electric fans came into widespread use from the 1920s on but mechanical refrigeration would have relatively little effect on the overlords' comfort level by the time the *Raj* came to an end.

By the time Lady Edith Lytton was preparing to depart for India in 1876 with her daughters in tow, Northbrook was able to advise the new viceroy that his daughter had suffered no ill effects from the climate, and that excellent medical care was available to the viceroy and his family. That did not really matter to Lady Lytton, who never considered staying at home or leaving her daughters behind. Having already lost two sons, and pregnant with a third, she packed up her girls, the youngest barely two years old, and embarked on what she expected to be a great adventure. Concern for her children's well-being and caring for an infant, aside from providing some distraction from Robert's compulsive flirtations, provided the façade of a an ideal Victorian family – handsome well-placed husband, dedicated to serving the Empire, aided in doing his duty by a devoted wife and mother, and charming, happy, and healthy children. Lady Lytton fully understood that it was her job to maintain that picture-perfect image and conceal the hard realities that lay beneath.

When the defeat of the Conservatives in 1880 put William Gladstone, one of Robert's harshest critics, into office as prime minister, Lytton felt compelled to resign and prepared to go home even though his term was not up. That political defeat and being assailed by the press in India and at home as "the black *Raj*" for his liberal policies toward the "natives" fuelled a depression arising from spending in excess of his income, which had been reduced by a declining rent roll at the family estate Knebworth, and sizable investment losses. But he tended to see the dark side of things, and the Queen's public approval of Lytton's service – and her ill-disguised

Few viceroys enjoyed the fanfare and flummery of the role as much as Lord Lytton, he is seen here in his Star of India robes.

dislike of Gladstone, expressed in very concrete terms by her awarding him an earldom, did not soothe Lytton's easily-bruised ego. As Lady Lytton did her best to comfort her husband and express sympathy for what he saw as ill treatment by the government, she was secretly delighted by the prospect of going home, even to what she called "a pauper earldom." Ever subservient and self-denying, Edith tried to offset her husband's financial excesses by living frugally. "I shall live with the children in great retirement," she wrote to a friend, declaring that she "would rather have only a tallow candle than run risks" of overspending.[5]

Faced with imminent departure from India, for once, Lytton seemed to be willing to put his wife and children first when his successor Lord Ripon was appointed in June. Lytton advised Gladstone that his family could not possibly leave India during the height of the summer, for it wouldn't be safe for his wife and the children to go to Bombay until the cooling rains arrived. Queen Victoria weighed in on the side of the viceroy, writing to

Lytton that "his dear Lordship" should not move "a day sooner than is safe for himself and his family."[6] It did not matter. The prime minister ignored Lytton's pleas and the monarch's recommendation, and sent Ripon to India immediately, so quickly that his wife was left behind to deal with arrangements for bringing her family out. Caught in the crossfire between viceroy and prime minister, Ripon reluctantly took over Peterhof when he arrived as the Lyttons moved into General Roberts' house in Simla, which the commander-in-chief was renting from a maharajah. After a few weeks of the former and current viceroy's awkward co-location, the Lyttons left, with Edith looking forward eagerly to a life with "no flies, no glare, and no biting things."[7]

Lady Lytton's successor, the Marchioness of Ripon, was one of the few vicereines who came out to India with a relatively easy mind in terms of her children, since her only son was 28 years old and firmly on his own. Having lost an infant daughter years before, Henrietta[8] and Ripon were devoted to each other and to their surviving son. She unquestioningly accepted his political and social opinions as her own – even his politically difficult conversion to Catholicism. With no young children to tend, Lady Ripon was able to serve as her husband's principal political advisor and supporter as she had throughout their marriage, and encourage his attempts to impose liberal policies in India. Distantly related to her husband's great uncle, Earl de Grey, Lady Ripon's abilities as a political hostess were praised by Gladstone and Disraeli, and may well have influenced the former's decision to offer Ripon the viceroyalty.

Lady Ripon's good offices and political acumen were urgently needed in India, and her skill at entertaining and wooing those who opposed her husband was a major asset of his administration. A radical even among the liberal Gladstonians, Ripon began to make major changes in India as soon as he arrived, based on the knowledge he had gained from his years in the India Office. His first act was to end the protracted Anglo-Afghan hostilities. He entered into a peace treaty with the new Afghan Amir Abdur Rahman. Later, in 1882, Ripon proposed a dramatic change in local government, splitting Local Boards into smaller, more efficient units, with elections replacing the old nomination process. His recommendations met with strong objections from British officials and civilians who believed that the "natives" were not yet ready for an electoral system, and Ripon was unable to fully implement it. But his most controversial proposal was yet to come – the idea that Indian magistrates should have jurisdiction over British subjects. When the Law member of the Viceroy's Council, Sir Courtenay Ilbert – at the viceroy's urging – introduced a bill that would make British subjects subject to courts over which Indian magistrates presided, the Anglo-Indian community erupted in fury, especially the

European business community in Calcutta and the Bengal indigo planters. Much was made of the possibility of British women enduring the indignity of having to appear before a native judge, although in practice that was a highly unlikely occurrence. Eventually a compromise was reached in which a British subject could request a jury if he or she were brought before an Indian judge, half of which had to be Europeans. The new Westernised Indian middle class felt slighted by this arrangement, and the incident did much to give Indian national feeling a political forum. Ripon further displeased the British community when he repealed the controversial Vernacular Press Act of 1878 that required the editors of Indian newspapers to agree not to publish any material objectionable to the government and in questionable cases, to submit proofs before publication. While the Indian press hailed this action, the British-run papers and the Anglo-Indian community once again voiced their objections to what they saw as Ripon's ultra-liberal proposal. In this case, Ripon was able to prevail, sealing his reputation as the most liberal of the viceroys. By the time he left India, he and Lady Ripon were beloved by many in the Indian ruling and emerging middle classes, feelings not shared by the bulk of Britons in India.

Lady Ripon was succeeded by one of the brightest gems in the figurative tiara of Indian vicereinity, Lady Hariot Dufferin, who was especially well prepared for the role in terms of personal traits and experience. By the time she arrived in India in 1884, Hariot had endured many separations from her seven children, spending most of her married life apart from her school-age sons while her husband served in various diplomatic posts around the Empire. It was never easy for them, since the Dufferins were devoted to their children, and Lord Dufferin was especially close to their three daughters, grieving when each one married. Like several other viceregal couples, the Dufferins' closeness was in good part due to their shared ancestry and upbringing in Ireland, and the 17-year difference in their ages was not unusual in that era. While Lady Dufferin presented a public image of independence and an overpowering personality, things were quite different when the proverbial doors were closed. She was passionately devoted to Dufferin, and saw him as the centre of her universe, "the glittering orb"[9] around which she and her children circled. Hariot never addressed her husband by his Christian name, even in family settings, and stopped talking when he entered the room. Dufferin returned that devotion in equal measure, telling his mother-in-law that after 35 years of marriage, he owed his happiness "and the greater part of his success" to his wife.

Lady Dufferin's excitement at the prospect of going to India was marred only by worry about her eldest son Archie, who decided to head for South Africa and join the military just as the Dufferins were departing. She

No vicereine took the words of Queen Victoria quite as literally as Hariot Dufferin. The legacy of her devotion to health services in India would outlast even her own long lifetime.

expressed her concern in her letters to Queen Victoria, and was comforted by the Queen's diplomatic advice regarding the difficulties of "managing" grown children. Her other three sons stayed at home in school, but came out to India several times during Dufferin's viceroyalty. Archie's various misadventures aside, the Dufferin family enjoyed their time in the sub-continent, and brought new energy to the viceregal residences. The staff soon grew accustomed to the Dufferin girls, already veterans of official life, skipping down the marble halls of Government House in cool white linen dresses, giggling at some secret or other, heedless of the silent sentries standing along the walls. When the Dufferins arrived, Nelly, at 21 was already "out" in society and thus could be included in viceregal events, but Hermione, 15, and Victoria, 11, were only allowed to participate in family social occasions, and had to watch from afar as their mother and father presided at innumerable balls, banquets, and receptions. In Simla, the family had more opportunities to be together, and the girls frequently joined their parents on picnics, horseback and carriage rides, and games on the lawn of Peterhof.

As noted earlier, Hariot's negative opinions aside, the girls found the smaller house in Simla much more congenial than the new mansion under construction, and were not at all eager to move into Viceregal Lodge, a fact they tried in vain to conceal from their father. When the time finally came to move, each girl chose her own room and Hariot allowed them some say – but not much – in choosing decorations in an attempt to smooth the transition. Their aversion to the new house may have accounted for the special delight with which the Dufferin children reacted to the news that their father had opted for an early exit from India to become the British ambassador in Rome. Lady Dufferin's unhappiness at leaving her Dufferin Fund efforts unfinished was offset by her daughters' approaching the age of searching for suitable husbands. Rome would offer many more "appropriate" prospects of making a "good" marriage.[10]

The Lansdownes' diplomatic family life had mirrored the Dufferins with more separations from their children than they would have preferred. That led Lady Lansdowne to insist on taking their youngest girl, eleven-year-old Beatrix, with them to India, although the boys – Henry, 16 and Charles, 14 – had to remain in public school in Britain through most of the year and come out to India during their long summer vacations. Uneasy about the difficulties of life in India, Lansdowne was comforted by the viceroy's assurance that the climate had no ill effects on Dufferin's family, and that any dangers involved in bringing Beatrix out were small compared to those of leaving a girl of her age at home. As a result, Government House became considerably quieter than it had been in days of the Dufferins with only one small girl in the viceregal household. Beatrix enjoyed being the centre of attention, as various staff members took special care to keep her from being lonely when her parents were travelling or otherwise occupied. In 1892, at the age of 15, Beatrix accompanied Lady Lansdowne home for her sister Evelyn's marriage to Victor Cavendish, heir to the Devonshire dukedom,[11] an especially grand event, although Beatrix was not deemed old enough to enjoy the attendant social events. After serving as a bridesmaid, her first formal introduction to aristocratic society,[12] she returned with her mother for the remainder of her father's term as viceroy. The Lansdownes were now able to enjoy several years together as a family, although both of their sons served in the Boer War, Charles as an ADC to Lord Roberts, and in World War I. Charles' death in combat on October 30, 1914 was a terrible blow to both Lansdownes, and it spurred Maud to begin a long volunteer career with the British Red Cross, both during and after the war. The Lansdownes also opened their family home, Bowood, as a military hospital throughout the war.

Another dramatic shift in the composition of the viceregal household occurred when Lord Elgin succeeded Lansdowne, bringing his steadily increasing family, the largest ever to occupy the viceregal mansions. The staffs at the various residences were wrenched out of the placid routine of looking after one young girl to meeting the demands and requirements of 10 children ranging in age from 2 to 17. By the time Lady Constance Elgin arrived in India in 1894, she had already produced ten children, and she would give birth to her last son during her reign as vicereine. [13] Although Lady Elgin struggled to strike a balance between official duties and her husband and children, she was for the most part occupied in taking care of the latter.

Even at a time when large families were normative, the scale of the Elgin contingent stirred comment among *memsahibs* who saw something unseemly in a vicereine's trying to oversee sons, six and two years old, and five daughters, four, nine, 14, 15 and 17 and then producing yet another child while in India. Since she left no diary and little correspondence, there is no clear evidence of her feelings in dealing with that sizable brood. Although it may be assumed that she missed the boys, it also seems likely that she was at least somewhat relieved when they went off to Eton. While British nannies and governesses were primary tenders of aristocratic and bourgeois children throughout the Empire, and in India they were assisted by *ayahs*, even with that support, Lady Elgin spent much of her time and effort sorting out the children's problems, and tending to their needs, ailments, small accidents, and desires.

The Elgin's last child, born in Calcutta on April 14, 1897, was, like Edith Lytton's son born in 1876, named Victor Alexander for his father, and in honour of the Queen who volunteered to be his godmother, as she often did for children of those she favoured. With the Indian summer approaching, as soon as Constance was able to travel, she took the baby and the other Elgin children to Simla to escape the heat of Calcutta. Victor was christened a few weeks later, after Constance recovered from the arduous trip to the hills, and regained her slim figure. The Archdeacon of Simla presided over a small private ceremony in a small chapel near Viceregal Lodge. Lady White, wife of the Commander-in-Chief General Sir George Stuart White, stood in for the Queen, while other godparents in England were represented by various members of the Viceroy's Council. In one of her letters to the Queen, Lady Elgin described the christening in detail, and thanked her at length for honouring the family by being godmother, and for the traditional gift of an initialed silver cup. She also explained why she intended to leave the baby in Simla when the family returned to the plains in the fall: "Calcutta does not suit young children," and assured the monarch that the baby and his nurse would join the family once the weather moderated.[14]

After recovering from the birth of her son, Constance undertook the planning of the wedding of her eldest daughter, Bessie, to Henry Babington-Smith, Elgin's private secretary, on September 22, 1898. The wedding, judged hugely successful by the media and the *Raj*'s socialites,

Lady Elizabeth 'Bessie' Bruce, The weddings of viceregal daughters were rare events in India, her ceremony in 1898 was considered a great success.

was Lady Elgin's last performance as First Hostess. Shortly afterward, and the Elgins and all their children sailed safely home, but tragedy soon followed when their 16-year-old daughter, Marjorie, died in 1901. Grief-stricken, and thereafter chronically ill, Constance never recovered from the blow and died in 1909.

The viceregal family ambience shifted from near-chaos to calm formality when the Curzons and their two daughters arrived. Arguably, aside from Edwina Mountbatten, no vicereine arrived in India with as much fanfare as Mary Curzon, whose beauty, fortune, and prominence as a celebrity in British high society had been widely reported in the popular press throughout the world. When she landed with Irene, aged two, and the five-month-old Cynthia ("Cimmie"), she and Curzon were recovering from their most recent disappointment in their attempt to have a son. At that point, they assumed there was still plenty of time for that, and the girls provided a diversion from the strains of the viceroyalty. At Curzon's insistence, Mary had remained in Britain until she was fully recovered from Cimmie's birth and the brutal heat of India's summer had eased. By the time she landed in Bombay, Lady Curzon was able to show off her extensive new Worth wardrobe to full advantage. Media images of the trim and beautiful vicereine and her stylishly dressed little girls reinforced the latest iteration of the "perfect" viceregal family.

In fact, Lady Curzon suffered considerably more than her two aristo-cratic predecessors from the vagaries of the Indian climate, often coming down with fevers and being bedridden for weeks at a time. It is not clear how much these afflictions aggravated the heart condition that later ended her life prematurely, or if that weakness made her more vulnerable to illness. She also suffered from migraine headaches which sometimes made her social duties an agony. "I nearly fainted twice dressing, and nothing but my will carried me through," she wrote to her mother, describing a dinner party to which she and George had been invited. "The only thing I ate was a water-biscuit and a teaspoonful of brandy. I collapsed in a heap in the carriage on our way home."[15] Her poor health also contributed to Mary's growing unhappiness with her life in India.

While she never failed in her devotion to her girls or her husband, or in fulfilling her role as vicereine, her nearly constant health complaints may suggest some sort of cry for the attention of her work-obsessed husband. Nor did ill-health put to rest the on-going issue of a male heir. Curzon loved his girls deeply, often writing little notes to be carried by a turbaned servant across the vast marbled expanse of Government House to their nursery, where the nanny read them to the girls. But such affection did not diminish his increasingly urgent desire for a son to carry on the family name. When Mary became pregnant in 1901, Curzon insisted that she and the girls return to England to ensure the best possible care for what they both expected would be a son. Grief stricken by a miscarriage, Mary struggled to remain positive: "Never mind, my husband, next time, next time," she wrote to George,[16] then made the long voyage back to India to join George for his greatest triumph, the Coronation Durbar of 1903.

After exhausting herself during the durbar festivities, Lady Curzon went to Simla to recover her health. By the end of the year, pregnant again, she went back to Britain again to await the birth. The stress, both physical and psychic, was now evocative of Catherine of Aragon's. Surely she could not fail her husband again; this time the baby would surely be a healthy boy. The pressure was augmented by George's joining her for a four-month home leave, since he had just been appointed to an unprecedented second term as viceroy. But there was no relief. The Curzons' disappointment mounted further when their third daughter, Alexandra – "Baba" – was born in 1904. As soon as medical conditions allowed, Mary became pregnant again. This last pregnancy was her most difficult. Not only was she ill almost the entire time, but the resulting miscarriage nearly ended her life. For 10 days, she hovered between life and death at Walmer Castle in Kent,[17] so certain of death that she dictated pages and pages of her last wishes to a panicked and grieving Curzon, including a request that her children not return to India. She knew that Curzon would go back whether she recovered or not, and she begged George to "ask Mama…to come and take them to some warm place and look after them."[18] But in the end, she recovered.

For a woman with a long history of ill health, Mary Curzon proved remarkably tough, surviving peritonitis, phlebitis, and pneumonia after her miscarriage. She spent months recovering, part of the time at Highcliffe Castle where Charlotte Canning had spent so many happy days. George returned to India once it was clear that Mary had pulled through, and as she improved, she felt that she had no choice but to join him, despite her earlier grim predictions that India's climate would be her undoing. Curzon was so delighted by her returning that he uncharacteristically set aside his official duties to meet his wife and daughters as they disembarked at Bombay. Lady Curzon's appearance at the Gate of India as heroine, the pale, fragile, yet beautiful vicereine returning to her husband and her duties with her children at her side was the ultimate personification of wifely devotion, and duly appreciated by the men and women of the *Raj*.

George and Mary Curzon sit beside the Maharaja of Bikaner in 1902. The cultivated and industrious Maharaja became one of the Viceroy's favourites.

Mary's days of glory were few and fleeting. By August of 1905, Curzon had resigned after losing a classic full-scale push-and-shove bureaucratic dominance game with the C-in-C Lord Kitchener over a minor organizational point that determined who would control the army of India. Lady Curzon had done her best to try to mediate that clash between the two giant egos, supporting George's position, even when she realised he was making a major error in judgment. The stress of being caught up in the dispute, and, as the Curzons saw it, George being humiliated by the home government, further undermined Lady Curzon's delicate health, although he was so focused on his own misery that he failed to sense the effects of the Kitchener-Curzon conflict and the solitude she endured because of his constant work. The girls offered some comfort, but they were now a secondary consideration as Mary focused all her rapidly declining energies on supporting and soothing her suffering spouse. As the Curzons left India in disgrace, they did not know how little time they would be together. Mary's death within a year of their return plunged Curzon into near-suicidal grief. While Curzon eventually remarried, his second wife was nowhere as devoted as his first, although she too brought a sizable dowry. Sadly, when his daughters reached maturity, their father opened fierce legal battles with them over the control of their mother's fortune, and Irene was estranged from her father at the time of his death.

The next Mary to ascend the viceregal throne, Lady Minto, was the polar opposite of Lady Curzon in terms of health and family. The Mintos, stereotypically healthy, robust, and rosy-cheeked Scots, gave illness little thought as they prepared to leave for India. Once again, the viceroy's family fit the Victorian ideal: three beautiful, pleasant and unassuming daughters – Eileen, 21; Ruby, 19; and Violet, 16; their strong and energetic brothers, Larry and Esmond; and attractive aristocratic devoted parents. The children recalled their father reading to them nearly every night when they were young, taking special pleasure in regaling the children with tales of his Scottish ancestry and the Borders region. He also set an example for all the family with his almost manic athleticism, introducing them to bicycling long before it became a major fad. He and his wife thought nothing of riding miles in the pouring rain along the Caledonian Canal, and continued their athletic pursuits wherever they were. In Canada, Lady Minto gained some recognition for her skill as an excellent figure skater. There, she also took up photography, and rode a short distance on the "cow catcher" of the viceregal train to get a better picture of some buffalos, alarming her husband and his aides. When not on extended overseas diplomatic service, the family spent a month each summer on the continent, introducing the children to the glories of Florence, Venice, and Spain, and enjoying the time together.

In contrast to the tense and oft-ailing Curzons, the Mintos quickly gained widespread affection in the social circles of the *Raj*, and were an immediate hit with British India. Their family's viceregal tour in Canada had been very positive and enjoyable, leading the girls to expect a similar experience in India. Nor were they disappointed; to their delight, their photographs soon appeared in the newspapers alongside articles describing their social life, including what they wore, in great detail. The

society press began suggesting possible matches for the eligible Minto girls; if any of them danced with one young man more than another at a ball, reporters' imaginations were inflamed. Being aristocrats, the Mintos disapproved of their girls becoming celebrities as such, but were pleased by the warm reception given them by British Indian society, even as they kept a sharp eye out for inappropriate behaviour. The staff loved all three girls; they were polite, clever, and fun-loving, and brightened viceregal gatherings, leading the viceroy's Private Secretary, James Dunlop-Smith, to gush in his journal:

The sporting Mintos with their daughter, Lady Eileen Elliot, and the Maharaja of Bikaner together with their trophies, two black buck. After a day's hunting in Bikaner State 1908.

> *They are such dear natural girls. Lady Eileen is a bright happy creature with an enormous capacity for enjoying life. Ly V [Violet]*

has by far the strongest character and has all her father's downright honesty as well as his passion for sport. But I think I have finally made up my mind that it is Lady Ruby I am in love with![19]

Lord Minto especially enjoyed early morning rides with Violet, often farther afield than his wife preferred, and with only one ADC accompanying them – a secret Dunlop-Smith kept from the vicereine.

The only visible flaw in that tapestry of family happiness was the boys' absence, both being enrolled at Eton. The family had been together in Canada, so it was especially painful for Lady Minto to leave her sons behind, even though her sister, Louisa, Countess of Antrim, stayed in close touch with them at school and entertained them during vacations. When Louisa brought the boys for a visit to India during the Mintos' reign, it added further lustre to the family's image as a "perfect" family.

By the time she left, Lady Minto had become widely admired by the media, *memsahibs,* the viceroy's staff, and many with whom she came in contact. In some respects she left India with a stronger personal reputation than her husband. Although Minto played a major role in devising and overseeing implementation of the India Act of 1909 which introduced a separate electorate for Muslims, and the inclusions of Indians on the central, provincial and government councils, with the goal of making a start toward representative government, many in India and the home government considered him an amiable "lightweight."[20] Once again, the vicereine outshone her husband, although the devoted Lady Minto would never have admitted it. Her energy, her obvious enjoyment of the social side of the viceroyalty, her warm, yet dignified style of entertaining, and "perfect" family all gained her points on the playing field of social approval. On the eve of her departure, a deputation of women presented Lady Minto with a diamond brooch in the shape of the lotus flower, not a unique practice, but the first time that Indian and English women jointly made such a presentation.

Lady Minto's interest in India did not end with her leave-taking. She kept up a regular, gossipy correspondence with Dunlop-Smith, who advanced to political ADC to the SOSI in London, and others on the viceroy's staff who sent her accounts of social life in India. She reported to Dunlop-Smith on what she had heard from India about Winifred Hardinge's arrival and the first impression she made – "rather distressing accounts," she wrote.[21] Lady Hardinge apparently had been ill and unable to attend the first Drawing Rooms of her reign, a nearly unforgivable slight to British India's socialites eagerly awaiting a chance to "review" the new vicereine. Even more shocking, Lord Hardinge nearly fainted during his first levee, and sat on a chair during the last half of the ceremony. Such signs of proconsular weakness were widely viewed as inexcusable, and got Hardinge's viceroy-alty off to a bad start. Lady Minto also heard from other staff members who were unhappy with the new viceregal couple's approach to their duties. "It doesn't sound like a happy party does it?" she wrote, with just a hint of *schadenfreude*, and a tinge of pleasure at her successor falling well short of her own vicereinal success.[22]

While Winifred Hardinge's connections to the royal family were not as longstanding as Mary Minto's, she was completely at ease with royalty, having spent most of her life in the inner circle of King Edward VII when he was Prince of Wales. Like the grandfather of another vicereine, Lady Edwina Mountbatten, Winifred's father, Gerald Sturt, 1st Baron Alington of Crichel, was a close confidant and financial advisor of the monarch. He had also served in Parliament, and more importantly, made a fortune in investments.[23] As soon as she was "out" in society, Winifred joined the Marlborough House social set, and became especially close to Princess Alexandra, who found Winifred bright and charming and became one of her strongest allies in the battle to convince Alington that Charles Hardinge was a suitable match for his beloved daughter. It was an uphill fight never-theless. When the match was first proposed to him, Gerald exclaimed: "What, Charlie Hardinge marry my little Bena?[24] *Never!*" His main objec-tions were the fact that Winifred and Hardinge were first cousins, and the Hardinges not nearly as grand as his wealthy and influential family. Since the Sturts had lived at the palatial Crichel House in Dorset from the mid-1800s, Alington felt his pedigree was at least equal to, if not superior, to the Hardinges', even though the Hardinge viscountancy technically outranked Alington's relatively new baronetcy.

Family lineage notwithstanding, by the time Hardinge formally proposed in 1889, his diplomatic career was well under way as he followed in the footsteps of his grandfather who served as Governor General of India from 1844 to 1848. After a protracted siege, Alington succumbed to his much-loved daughter's pleas and the advice of friends who convinced him that Hardinge's diplomatic career was steeply ascendent. Once the match was made, Alington supported Hardinge's upward mobility, visiting the couple whenever he could, and bringing a touch of "new money" flam-boyance to their more modest diplomatic household, lavishing jewels on Winifred and expensive gifts on all the children. Charlie's elevation to the peerage as the 1st Baron Hardinge when he was named viceroy greatly improved his standing with his father-in-law, who was elated at his daugh-ter's becoming a vice-queen.

The Hardinges brought their 10-year-old daughter Diamond (named in honour of Queen Victoria's Diamond Jubilee) with them to India, after the Mintos and Lansdownes assured them that her health and well being would not be compromised by the Indian experience. Diamond was a cheerful child, the apple of her father's eye, and he spoiled her terribly. Even though her irrepressible high spirits often brightened his darker days, Diamond could be a proverbial handful. Hardinge's dignified demeanor, that expected of a serious diplomat, and Diamond's sprightliness, and especially her compulsion to play practical jokes frequently generated tensions in the viceregal entourage.

During a visit by the Maharajah of Gwalior, Diamond conspired with several household servants (who refused the little *memsahib* nothing) to remake the potentate's bed in an "apple pie" fashion, that is, putting flour on both top and bottom sheets. When the prince emerged from his bed covered with white dust, he saw no humor in the prank, although many others in the family and staff found it hilarious. Her father, however, did not share their amusement, fearing that the dimension of different skin colours that made the prank seem humorous to some Europeans would add a layer of unforgivable insult to the incident. But, as usual, the much-indulged Diamond was forgiven. Her father sometimes even conspired with her to add some levity to viceregal events. For example, Hardinge would enter the room in his usual dignified manner, followed by Diamond zooming about on roller skates across the polished marble floors and grasping the columns to avoid falling. In a somber counterpoint, fate made Hardinge his daughter's primary caregiver. Lady Hardinge, afflicted by a weak heart, was often exhausted by her charitable and social responsibilities, and after a long day of official engagements would retire to her room for a rest and a light dinner in bed. Attempting to fill the gap, Hardinge allotted as much of his time as possible to Diamond, and the two became very close.

The Hardinges came together for the last time when the boys came out for the Coronation Durbar of 1911. From that point on, the family suffered a series of tragedies, the first of which was the assassination attempt on Hardinge in 1912. Although the boys were back in England by then, Diamond was caught up the chaos and fear that permeated the viceregal household. She watched in horror as the viceroy was carried into Government House bleeding profusely from his wounds, and although Winifred rushed to reassure her that he would survive, she was traumatised at the thought of losing her father. In the following days, Lady Hardinge strove to comfort Diamond and help her cope with the aftermath of terror, and brought her to her father's bedside frequently to see her father improving.

In June 1914, worn out by the Indian climate and still suffering from the trauma of the assassination attempt, Winifred went home for a rest and to consult with British doctors, leaving Diamond behind with her father. On July 11, Hardinge received a cable telling of her death from heart failure. The loss of his wife of 24 years brought Hardinge close to collapse, but

Lord Hardinge stands in the garden of Government House, Calcutta with Winifred and Diamond.

despite the tragic circumstances, there was, as noted earlier, no provision for his taking leave. Making funeral arrangements and dealing with the after effects of her sudden death fell to his young sons, while Diamond and Hardinge shared their grief in India. Condolences and sympathies poured in from England and throughout the Empire, including cables from the King and Queen and Queen Alexandra, lamenting the loss of "...your beloved Bena, so precious to us all." Indian rulers were similarly effusive and occasionally hyperbolic, like the Maharajah of Alwar: "...our whole country will mourn one of the noblest Vicereines and one of the finest samples of womanhood that ever trod our soil." [25]

Diamond's comforting presence and the surge in work resulting from the onset of World War I provided Hardinge some distraction, but the flow of sadness did not ease. His elder son Edward, a lieutenant in the 15th Kings Hussars, went to the front in France almost immediately when the war began, and was wounded in the fall of 1914. The Hardinges' younger son Alec, who had come out to India to be with his father and sister after his mother's death, returned to England to help care for his wounded brother, who appeared to be on the mend. But in December, Edward died from complications of his wounds, plunging Hardinge even deeper into grief. That left Alec alone to handle matters while dealing with his own sorrow. As soon as his brother was buried, Hardinge insisted that Alec come to India and serve as one of his ADCs, a position he held until his father's viceroyalty ended in 1916.[26]

By the time Hardinge's extended tenure was over, the new viceroy, Lord Chelmsford, encountered increasing political turmoil in India, and a widespread global conflict whose outcome was by no means certain. The revolutionary forces set loose by the Great War were threatening long-established regimes from America to the Far East. In mid-1916, the gigantic and unprecedented grinding battle at Verdun was underway; the less than salutary deployment of an Indian corps on the Western Front had dashed British hopes of mobilising larger forces as the French had; and British and Indian forces had been humiliated by the Turks' capture of Kut al Amara in Mesopotamia. German manipulation of Muslim anti-British sentiments throughout the empire was paralleled by rising nationalist agitation in India.

The India Act of 1919, based on the Montagu-Chelmsford report (Montagu being the SOSI) was the result of discussions between the viceroy, the SOSI and leaders of the Indian community on the concept of limited self-government for the nation and the protection of minority communities such as Muslims and Sikhs. What became known as the Montagu-Chelmsford reforms extended the franchise to more Indians, gave increased authority to central and provincial legislative councils, and introduced the concept of "dyarchy," whereby some government departments – agriculture, education, public works, etc. – were placed under ministers responsible to the elected and now more Indian Legislative Council. The key departments of finance, revenue and home affairs continued to be subject to the viceroy's Executive Council, and were generally, but not always, British in membership, and responsible directly to the viceroy.

The 1919 reforms did not satisfy Indian political demands, and Chelmsford's reign continued to be a turbulent one as the British repressed opposition, and restrictions on the press and on movement were reenacted in the Rowlatt Acts introduced in 1919. These measures were rammed through the Legislative Council with the unanimous opposition of the Indian members, several of whom resigned in protest. The Amritsar massacre in 1919 and the upwelling of British support for General Dyer, who commanded the British troops and gave the order to fire into the crowd, further alienated a growing class of political activists who increasingly began to support Gandhi's idea of *swaraj*, or self-rule for India, and a policy of non-cooperation with the British on any issue. Chelmsford was consumed by these thorny issues, and by almost constant strife with the home government.

The price of empire was exacted on a personal level in the immediate domain of the viceroy when the Chelmsfords' son, Frederick Ivor, was killed in Mesopotamia in May 1917, which may have accounted for Frances's reputation for moodiness and erratic behaviour when she was vicereine. The Maharajah of Bikaner later told Lady Reading that when invited to Viceregal Lodge, he prayed that someone of higher rank would be in attendance so he would be spared the misery of sitting next to Lady Chelmsford.

The Chelmsford girls – Joan, 21; Anne, 18; Bridget, 16; and Margaret, five – apparently followed their mother's lead in terms of demeanour. Their bad behaviour from the time they arrived in India presented the staff with ongoing difficulties, and their arrogance and rudeness led their governess, Miss Hogge, an elderly unmarried lady, to take to her bed in despair. When she finally summoned up enough courage to advise Frances of the staff's opinions regarding her ill-behaved daughters, the vicereine was furious at the governess's boldness. She rejected Miss Hogge's comments until the MilSec, Colonel Ralph Verney, confirmed the charges in a tense meeting at Viceregal Lodge during which he provided further details of the girls' beastliness, and the girls, properly chastised at last, returned from a banishment at Simla promising to do better.

The apparent calm was momentary, and soon Verney found himself entangled in another family upheaval. Bridget ("Biddy") rebelled against being confined to the schoolroom by beginning a flirtation with Aubrey Metcalfe, an Assistant Private Secretary to the viceroy.[27] When the redoubtable Miss Hogge reported the situation to the vicereine, Lady Chelmsford was unwilling to accept that Biddy might have been an active participant, and insisted that her husband discipline Metcalfe. Chelmsford became "white with rage" when he heard of Metcalfe's purported boldness, and sent Verney to investigate. While the MilSec's investigation quickly revealed that Miss Hogge had exaggerated the intensity of the relationship, Biddy sought release from the schoolroom, a request the vicereine, for once, denied, threatening boarding school at home as the alternative.[28]

Determined to escape parental control, Biddy attracted a proposal of marriage from Major Richard Sheepshanks of the Indian Army in 1919, and insisted on being married in England in an elaborate wedding organised by her mother, after which the couple returned to India. Now a guest in

Frances Chelmsford in an official portrait. Her years as vicereine were marked by personal loss and the rise of political activism in India.

her parents' home, Biddy remained a source of discord. In October 1920, she accepted an invitation from the Maharajah of Bikaner for herself and her husband to accompany the viceroy on his forthcoming visit. A few days later, she decided not to go to Bikaner but to join the viceroy's train there, and continue on to Jodhpur, the next stop on the viceregal tour. Now MilSec Verney was caught between Biddy's inappropriate demands, supported by her mother, to be included in an official visit, and viceregal protocol, under which Biddy, not having been invited to Jodhpur, could not simply attach herself and her husband, the unpopular "Sheepers," to the viceregal party, familial links notwithstanding. Eventually, the viceroy himself had to tell Biddy that she and Sheepers could not go, souring familial relations further.[29]

Lady Chelmsford's departure from India was as painful as most of her tenure had been. Both of the Chelmsfords were stunned when he was named merely a viscount for his viceregal service, rather than receiving the more customary earldom. Their being succeeded by someone whom they viewed as a mere *parvenu* earl compounded their umbrage. The never-too-diplomatic Frances was barely civil to Rufus and Alice Isaacs, now the Earl and Countess of Reading, when they arrived. Even without the Chelmsfords' dismay at this seeming back-of-the-hand treatment from the government and monarch, the Chelmsford-Reading transition would have been uneasy. The Readings being Jewish and non-aristocratic put them at odds with race and class-conscious British India, despite Isaacs' distinguished career as a jurist and diplomat and Lady Reading's reputation as a charming, if infrequent hostess. Early in her reign, she wrote to her son of a conversation reported to her which reflected veering attitudes in the British Indian community toward the Readings: "We trembled when we heard the Readings were coming, *Jews too!* We knew they had brains but it was the social part we felt so alarmed about, now we have never had such hosts…"[30]

Fortunately for the Readings, they were able to laugh at these kind of parochial views. They were a devoted couple, and had weathered many storms together, beginning with their courtship and marriage. Both had grown up in Hampstead's Jewish community; Alice's father, Albert Cohen, a German immigrant, became wealthy in the import-export business, while Reading's father was a prominent merchant and shipbroker in the City of London. While it was a reasonable match from the standpoint of social equivalency, Cohen opposed to their marrying since Rufus had not completed his legal studies. Beyond that, Albert deemed the Isaacs as much more "liberal" than his himself, and saw the handsome Rufus as a rake and playboy. Rufus's intellectual prowess, already demonstrated in his studies, weighed little with Albert.

Even if he had been willing to acknowledge Rufus's potential, Albert could never have envisioned that this marriage would ultimately elevate his daughter to the highest role in imperial governance to which a woman not born to eminence could aspire. Alice, devastated by her father's refusal, resorted to a stratagem that she would use all her life – she took to her bed, where her fragile health rapidly worsened. The family doctor was unable to cure her ailments, but was reluctant to cite thwarted love as a cause of

her decline. He called in a more prominent physician, Sir William Gull, who bluntly told Mr. Cohen: "Give her the young man, and I promise she will recover; otherwise she will die."[31] That broke down Cohen's defences, and he now agreed that the couple could marry when Rufus completed his studies. At the wedding some months later, in December 1887, Alice, now recovered, was a tall, slim and elegant bride, and the couple's good looks enhanced by obvious mutual devotion to each other which endured throughout the 42 years of their marriage.

Viceroyalty marked a significant shift in the Reading viceregal family dynamics. Children of vicereines who came to India after 1920 were usually grown and married, or in their late teens or early twenties and able to accompany their parents, or at least visit regularly. Although the possibility of sudden tragedy remained, especially for viceregal families with sons in military service, the constant worry about children's health and education that beclouded the lives of the 19th century vicereines was much diminished. But these later vicereines, somewhat older than their predecessors and beyond childbearing, were still haunted by possible ill effects of India on their own health.

Alice Reading's semi-invalid status almost kept her husband from becoming viceroy, and she had surgery for uterine cancer while in India. Still, she soldiered on. With no children to watch over, Lady Reading was free to focus her limited energy on vicereinal charities and social responsibilities and on supporting her husband, even though her ill health was the family's prime concern throughout their years in India as it would be for the rest of her life. She wrote to her son that her rheumatism had become much more painful due to humidity, and that the decline in her hearing presented a special difficulty when chatting with soft-spoken Indians.

Like her predecessors, Lady Reading did the best she could, and the Readings' considerate behaviour earned the staff's respect. The vicereine's personal secretaries, however, had a different view of her, both of them describing in their diaries a pricklier personality than what most people saw. Whatever transpired offstage, it appeared to outsiders that the couple's deep affection for each other and Reading's constant concern for his wife's well-being and her easy grace as a hostess helped to blunt the initial reluctance of the elites of British India and even some Indian rulers to accept the Readings as social and political leaders. They attended Church of England services on the prescribed occasions, apparently having suspended their religious beliefs *pro tempore ex officio*. The ever-sensitive Alice, however, never lost her awareness of the special scrutiny aimed at the viceregal couple because of their faith, however restrained their display of it, and concerted efforts to seem as aristocratic as her predecessors were sometimes taken as snobbery or arrogance.

Overall, Lady Reading received high marks as vicereine, and scored some substantial coups in charming Indian potentates, confirming the British folklore noted earlier that held that a Jewish viceroy and vicereine might have an advantage in establishing rapport with "Orientals" due to a sensitivity arising from their "Eastern" origins. The vicereine especially enjoyed in the official visits to the various rulers' palaces, and included lengthy detailed accounts in her letters home of those establishments, including descriptions of furniture, architectures, costumes, and finery. The

Maharajah of Bikaner, she wrote, wore jewels so huge that "…those of the Maharajah of Benares are splinters in comparison. Strings of pearls and emeralds (6 chains of emeralds held together by knobs of uncut emeralds and diamonds)." [32] Despite her fascination with that exoticism, Alice found it difficult to distinguish Hindus from Muslims. Not only was travelling to various principalities one of her greatest joys, but she encouraged Reading to invite their rulers to Viceregal Lodge as overnight guests more frequently than other viceroys did.

Sadly, Lady Reading's cancer returned shortly after she returned from India, and further treatments failed to stay the progress of the disease, but she continued to support her husband's career. Often confined to her bed, she insisted that he attend social events alone, and when he showed reluctance to leave her for an evening, she reminded him of how important such gatherings were for informal networking and politicking. Although she had shown little interest in London high society prior to going to India, when her waning strength permitted, Alice entertained Reading's colleagues and friends at home, having learned in India what might be gained by her interacting with his friends and supporters. But in time, those agonising efforts became impossible, and in her last year, her devoted husband rarely left her side, and grieved deeply when she died in 1930.

Even though India had worn Lady Reading down physically, she was still reluctant to leave when the time came. When Dorothy Irwin met her in 1926, she noted the vicereine's face was pale and drawn, and sensed a great depression in addition to physical weakness. "Her great adventure is over," Dorothy wrote, implying that Alice regretted leaving India more than her husband. She loved all the aspects of being a vicereine that Dorothy would come to loathe, and openly admitted her delight at having been a "queen."

Soon after the Readings left, the new vicereine grasped the full extent of the prejudice that the Readings – especially Alice – had been forced to endure. The suave, thoroughly Westernised and snobbish Maharajah of Bikaner aimed some snideries at Lady Irwin's predecessor while welcoming her warmly. "It is very nice that Lady Reading enjoyed India so much," he said. "She positively radiated happiness but it was a pity that she had eaten cheese on her knife." While listening politely, Lady Irwin could not help but wonder what he and others would say about her after she left. In reporting that bit of cattiness to her husband, Dorothy expressed surprise at someone disliking Alice and her husband "…not only an outstanding viceroy, but a man of unusual charm."[33]

Lady Irwin had sensed Lady Reading's weakened condition when they met in India, although she was not aware of the extent of her illness. Initially a reluctant vicereine, Lady Irwin had the appropriate aristocratic pedigree as the daughter of the Earl of Onslow, and was by all reports happily married and closely involved with her husband's work. She had been immediately drawn to Irwin when they met in 1908 at the Berwick-on-Tweed railway station where both were changing trains on their way to a ball at Kelso. He was similarly smitten, and after a rapid courtship, the couple married in 1909.

Unlike the Readings, both families approved, and Dorothy became a favourite of her father-in-law, who, shortly after the wedding wrote to his son: "We have all done nothing but sing her praises. We began to love her for your sake, now we are going, indeed we are a long way on the road to love her a great deal more for her own. This is not flummery but the truth."[34] Her charm and vivacity were matched by a quick mind and superb

organizational sense, all major assets to Irwin's political career. Lady Irwin, following the custom of her class at that time in molding herself to her husband's needs, made his well being and comfort her first priority, and softened his natural brittleness by creating a happy and informal family atmosphere wherever they lived.[35] As a hostess, Dorothy eschewed excessive formality, and being a quick study and clever was able to deal with sudden changes of course, abilities that were at a premium in India.

The Irwin's family grew rapidly. Although Mary, one of twin girls born in 1910, died four days after being born; births of three sons followed – Charles (1912), Peter (1916) and Richard (1920). Only their surviving daughter Anne accompanied her parents to India in 1926 since Charles was already at public school and the two younger boys were looked after by friends who supervised their early education as they prepared to join their brother at Eton. Although Irwin was a strict, no-nonsense father, he missed his sons as much as their mother, and looked forward to their visits during school vacations. The young ADCs on his staff filled the gap as a kind of surrogate family, often joining the Irwins after dinner to listen to the radio or to play charades, the viceroy's favourite game. Lady Irwin and her husband, in turn, served as parents *in absentia* to these young men, offering advice on romance when asked, and comforting those with broken hearts. Reportedly, the junior officers thoroughly enjoyed living in the viceregal mansion thanks to the vicereine's ability to keeps things relaxed amid the obtrusive splendor of the viceroy's mansions. Visitors reported the viceregal mansions in Delhi and Simla echoing with laughter as Anne and the young men created their own entertainments, amusing the Irwins and their guests.

Lady Irwin spent considerable effort at trying to re-create within the viceregal residences the country house atmosphere of the family home at Garrowby in York by bringing along many personal possessions, including plate, pictures, and books, disregarding the advice of more seasoned India hands that leather-bound books would do badly in the Indian climate, with unfortunate results as the warnings were borne out. Irwin, being a country gentleman, had his pack of hounds sent out, and took his children on hunts across the Delhi plains whenever possible. As time passed, the vicereine came to love India, while Irwin warmed to being viceroy and to the people he worked with. After Lady Irwin took Anne home in 1928 to help her prepare for her debut in the coming London season, her husband joined her the following summer, the first viceroy to go on home leave during his reign, Curzon's absence in 1905 having been between viceregal terms. When the couple returned in the autumn, they took up residence in Lutyens' massive new Viceroy's House in New Delhi. Very pleased by the new residence, Lady Irwin sensed the historical significance of living in such a palace as well as its luxury. Although Gandhi's star was already on the rise, there was no way for her to know that it would serve as the viceregal residence for barely a half-generation

On the eve of returning home in 1931, Lady Irwin found that rather than being relieved by the prospect of departing as she expected, she felt heavy-hearted at leaving what she had come to see as the magic of India. During his reign, Irwin had grappled with major issues as politicians at home argued how far and fast India should move toward dominion status, let alone toward the grail of independence which seemed very far off in Westminster and Whitehall. Within three years of their returning from India, Irwin had succeeded his father as Earl of Halifax, and in World War II, served as Foreign Secretary and Ambassador to the United States.[36] In Washington, Dorothy, now Lady Halifax, was credited with much of Halifax's success during his first few months in America when isolationism was running strong, as well as substantial Anglophobia. She became a popular speaker at women's clubs, and active in leadership of British war relief efforts in America as well as other local charity work. When the Halifaxes traveled across the country, Lady Halifax exuded enough charm

Dorothy Irwin dreaded the role of Vicereine, but when the time came for her to leave India it was with a heavy heart. Further duties lay ahead of her. Lord Irwin would be made British Ambassador to the United States on the eve of the Second World War.

to compensate for her less socially adept husband's gaffes. She was especially pleased to be made a deputy sheriff in Prescott, Arizona, an honour far, far from being formally invested with the Crown of India medal a decade earlier.

Dorothy's popularity in America was all the more remarkable in view of the deep tragedy and pain which the war brought her family. Two of her three sons served in the military: Peter was killed in 1942 in North Africa, and Richard was severely wounded in early 1943, losing both legs. After receiving the telegram which told him of Peter's death, Halifax sought comfort in church before sharing the tragic news with his wife as they walked around the Naval Observatory. Although shattered, Dorothy somehow found the strength to carry on, concealing her grief as she fulfilled her public duties. Halifax, marveling at her steadfastness in the face of tragedy, wrote to a friend in England: "As you would guess, [she has been] wonderful, brave, carrying on, never a word of self-pity or anything of that sort. And that just wrings one's heart, for I know how she feels and it hurts me to see how much it hurts her."[37]

A few months later, when the Halifaxes learned of Richard's grievous wounds, President Roosevelt offered to send the Halifaxes to Cairo aboard his private plane to visit their son, who was not expected to live. Halifax thanked FDR for his generous offer, but rejected it. He felt that since their son was in a hospital with many wounded soldiers whose fathers were not ambassadors, he could not in good conscience take advantage of his position. While Halifax did not publicize the offer or his rejection of it, the story soon found its way into the diplomatic community rumour circuit, gaining the Irwins widespread admiration for holding onto their ethics in such distress, as well as their dignity in grief. The Halifax's American friends were amazed by the couple's self-control and keeping on with their work, giving substance to the proverbial British stiff upper lip.

All that sadness lay in the future as the Halifaxes (still the Irwins) made the transition from viceroyalty to private life and passed the reins of power to the Willingdons in 1931. Dorothy's successor, Lady Marie Willingdon, came directly to India from a popular reign as wife of the Governor General of Canada. She was ecstatic at returning to India, especially to the viceregal throne which she long felt was her husband's – and her – due. During those early years, Lady Willingdon established a reputation as an energetic, committed volunteer in a host of charitable activities. Although respected and even admired for her many good deeds, her domineering, often eccentric behaviour caused gossip among the *memsahibs* of British India.

While not an hereditary aristocrat (her father, a Liberal politician, was created Baron Brassey in 1886 and Earl Brassey in 1911), Marie felt fully confident about her qualifications to be vicereine. As a baron's daughter, she had brought a certain cachet to her marriage in 1892 to Freeman Freeman-Thomas, a rising Liberal politician, to whom she devoted her full energies from the day they married. That was literally true, since Freeman-Thomas's first major administrative post was as an ADC to his father-in-law, who was Governor General of Victoria in Australia 1897–1900, where his performance marked him as very able, and bound for great things in politics and diplomacy. After bearing two sons, Gerard (1893) and Inigo (1899), Marie focused her energies on helping her husband move ahead. Freeman's intelligence, energy and political and social astuteness, backed by Marie's use of whatever tactics were necessary to bend people to her will, made the Willingdons a formidable couple. Throughout his career, Freeman never failed to recognize her role in his success, and she was more than willing to take the credit.

A large, "zestful" woman, Lady Willingdon had seemingly unlimited energy. During World War I, when she worked tirelessly in Bombay running hospitals for troops returning from Mesopotamia. Although many with whom she came in contact found her overbearing personality hard to take, paradoxically, she was an early albeit low-key advocate for women's rights in India. Marie relished each advance in her husband's rank from baron to viscount and finally to marquess, but was especially pleased by Willingdon's service as Lord-in-Waiting to and tennis partner of King George V, which brought her into close contact with the royal family. Within the inner keep, she developed many habits and eccentricities more appropriate to the upper tier of the royal milieu than a mere "Excellency."

As noted earlier, few vicereines were as controversial or had such a mixed reputation as Lady Willingdon. In her early years in Bombay and Madras, she became known as a gracious hostess who personally inspected every visitor's room to make sure that they had everything they needed, even the maids' rooms. While in Canada, she was praised for blending her personal collection of rare carpets and furniture from Asia with the traditional European décor of Rideau Hall, the Governor General's residence. That portrait of a considerate hostess with an elegant sense of taste contrasted sharply with her insistence on "re-arranging" Lutyens' new Viceroy's House, heedless of or rejecting the master architects' designs.

By the time she ascended to the viceroyalty, Lady Willingdon's strengths – and foibles – had become legendary throughout the British diplomatic corps, and many in India awaited her return with some trepidation. One Bombay newspaper wrote on her arrival:

> The extent to which the Viceroy-designate has been inspired and assisted by Lady Willingdon is well known. Of her it may be said without disrespect that she is like the leader of a dog team in Canada: the more she leads, the better she pulls. If a word of caution could be allowed, it would be to remind her that, though her husband's courage is as high as her own, his strength is of a lesser standard.[38]

It was a not-terribly subtle reference to the fact that Willingdon, at 65, as Lord Minto was when he became viceroy, was one of the oldest men ever appointed to that post. Whether she intended to highlight the contrast or not, Lady Willingdon announced to the press that she was in excellent

Marie Willingdon (seated on the right) was an inexhaustible woman. She was fearless enough to ignore even Queen Mary's direction, that she cease vandalising Sir Edwin Lutyens' finished designs for New Delhi.

health, and that she was confident that the Indian climate would have no ill effects on her. Public appearances of the viceregal couple reinforced the view of the new vicereine as being the "real" power. A vigorous, almost frenetically active woman, she wore a fixed smile, and a broad sash with all her decorations on every possible occasion. The viceroy, more relaxed and affable even in his full viceregal regalia, radiated far less an aura of strength and authority than his spouse.

Lady Willingdon's ardent pursuit of notoriety and publicity led her to encourage newspaper coverage of her activities. In 1934, a book entitled *Lord Willingdon in India* appeared in India, authored by a pseudonymous "Victor French." Its adulation of the Willingdons raised suspicions among servants of the *Raj* at all levels of hierarchy that either the vicereine had commissioned it, or had some hand in its publication, perhaps to offset the furor arising over her controversial and extensive decorative changes of the Viceroy's House. The publisher's note fed such suspicions in averring that "no work on Lord Willingdon's career can be adequate without reference to the dynamic personality of Lady Willingdon, who, it may be stated without exaggeration is chiefly responsible for the brilliance of his colonial career." The author (or authoress) chose to remain anonymous, the note indicated, "to avoid publicity," but claimed, "he has had exceptional opportunities to witness events at close quarters…" While the recounting of Willingdon's achievements in India was straightforward, the book included many references to Lady Willingdon's "charm of manner and incomparable strength of character" and other positive attributes. "If ever there was a power behind the throne," wrote "Victor French" effusively and awkwardly, "Lady Willingdon has been, specially in the field of social movements [sic]. The stamp of her personal endeavor will for ever remain on the non-official up-life activities in Bombay, Madras and Delhi."[39] The book became the talk of British India for weeks, reinforcing the belief that the vicereine was a self-serving publicity seeker, her good works notwithstanding.

Despite her flamboyance and verve, Marie concealed continuing sadness over the death of her son Gerard in World War I. In the 1930s, a visitor observed that when she spoke of him it was as if she expected to see him walk into the room at any moment. That tragedy was compounded when Freeman died five years after they left India. While the stress of the viceroyalty had exhausted her husband, Lady Willingdon would have been happy to stay on indefinitely. She left as she had arrived, feisty, full of strong opinions, and dismissive of Lord Linlithgow, Freeman's successor: "He's terribly pompous," she told one of Linlithgow's ADCs, indifferent to the fact that he was duty-bound to repeat the barb to his boss.

If the departing vicereine's disparaging remark had reached Linlithgow's ears, neither he nor his wife would have paid any attention. Their aristocratic pedigree far exceeded the Willingdons', and Linlithgow's having chaired several royal commissions in India and his extensive political connections left no question of his fitness to be viceroy.[40] The Hope family earldom – later the Marquessate of Linlithgow – was one of the oldest seats in Scotland, having been established in the 18th century. The family residence, Hopetoun House, was a vast Georgian mansion situated in 150 acres of parkland near Edinburgh with broad views of the Firth of Forth. Linlithgow's father, a distinguished politician and diplomat, was a close friend of Queen Victoria, having served her as Lord Chamberlain and a Lord-in-Waiting, and been raised to a marquessate in 1902, six years before he died. While Lady Doreen Linlithgow's family lacked royal linkages, her lineage was more than adequate for marriage to a marquess.

The Milners had been Yorkshire baronets since the 1700s, and her father was the 7th baronet. She was raised in the family home, Nun Appleton Hall, built on the site of a nunnery destroyed in the reign of Henry VIII. The Milners distantly related to the Duke of Portland, and it was at his estate at Welbeck that Lord and Lady Linlithgow first met. He was enchanted by her beauty, artistic temperament, high spirits, and the fact that she was close to his height of six foot five.

The Linlithgow family grew quickly with the birth of twin sons, Charlie and John in 1912; twin girls in 1914, of which only Anne survived; and two more daughters, Joan, born in 1915, and Doreen in 1920. During

World War I Linlithgow served with the local Lothian yeomanry in France, and commanded a battalion of the Royal Scots in Ireland in 1918. Back from the war, he entered politics as a Conservative, but when financial reverses forced him to close Hopetoun House for several months he went into business, where his successes allowed him to re-open the family home. Despite the size of their family, the Linlithgows found time to enjoy their shared literary tastes (biography and essays rather than novels), and managed to allot time for each child, especially the twins. A man of many interests, including medical research (a result of his bout with polio), and science and technology, Linlithgow also enjoyed singing, and the family often gathered around the piano.

Charlie and John, who both graduated from Oxford in 1936, had no interest in accompanying their parents to India. John went directly into the military after college, while Charlie held a series of jobs. Lady Linlithgow opposed leaving her three daughters at home, so they were reluctantly brought along to India, none of them knowing that war would prolong their father's reign from five to seven years. While the girls shared their mother's initial lack of enthusiasm for going overseas, they warmed to the experience when they realised how many social opportunities were available to a viceroy's daughter, and their exalted status in the realm of the *Raj*. Like the Minto girls before them, the Linlithgows' daughters became popular with their father's staff officers and officials as well as with other "eligible" young men amid the social whirl of Delhi and Simla. The boys visited India only once, in 1938, and when war broke out, both became officers in the Scots Guards. The girls also did their bit in the war effort, working along with their mother in military hospitals, and helping Lady Linlithgow introduce TB treatment centres throughout the country.

Striving to maintain a "family" atmosphere in the viceregal residences, Lady Linlithgow followed Marie Willingdon's practice of establishing the family quarters on the east side of Lutyens' gigantic mansion to avoid the worst of the heat and be close to the viceroy's office. In the prewar years, she and the viceroy were able to have breakfast together in the colourful gardens she took such pleasure in, but as his work load increased, that small pleasure had to be forgone as breakfast meetings with his private secretary became part of his daily routine. Despite the mounting demands of a wartime viceroyalty, Lady Linlithgow struggled to try to find time for the family to be alone, scheduling private lunches or dinners during openings in the schedule of official activities. As the war extended from months to years, and intensified in the Far East after Pearl Harbor, bringing large Japanese forces to the frontiers of India, British officials, including the viceregal family, found keeping up appearances more and more difficult.

With the enemy at the proverbial gates and dissidence erupting in India,

The Linlithgows on the viceregal thrones, their pages comprised four young maharajas.

Linlithgow's strength was taxed to the limit and he became increasingly embroiled in the struggles over India's future. During the opening months of the war, the Linlithgows, far from the ravages of the Blitz and privations that affected Britons of all classes, lived in relative luxury, although Lady Linlithgow instituted rationing throughout the viceregal establishments, and kept official entertaining to an absolute minimum. With two sons in the military, they faced the same worries as millions back home. The news that Charlie had been captured in Africa in 1939 stunned the Linlithgows, and the viceroy desperately sought any information he could get about his son's well being. Charlie, serving as a lieutenant in the Scots Guards, was liberated from a POW camp in 1940, and spent the rest of the war as a captain in the Lothian and Border Horse Royal Armoured Corps of the Territorial Army. John served with distinction in the Scots Guards, and was mentioned in despatches several times, which made his parents very proud, even if it did not relieve their concern for his safety.

By 1943, when Linlithgow went home after seeing Wavell installed as his successor, he had spent nearly seven years as viceroy in arguably the most turbulent era of the *Raj*. Wavell had been Linlithgow's C-in-C, so even though he and his wife were freshly elevated to the peerage, they were familiar with the routines and vicissitudes of viceregal life, and had some sense of its abrasion of family. The Wavells, like the Readings, were a viceregal family without an aristocratic heritage, both having come from upper-middle class military families. Wavell's viscountancy gave him and his wife the obligatory viceregal peerage, but both felt it was slightly anachronistic in an era of global conflict. Their family life had already been heavily battered by the war, both by Wavell's series of high-level commands and their son, Archibald John, being a serving officer.

After Wavell underwent a briefing in London, his three unmarried daughters – Pamela, 25, Felicity, 23, and Joan, 20 – accompanied him and his wife to India where all began working in military hospitals and assisting their mother with her many charitable activities. The new Lady Wavell had seen enough of the diminished viceregal splendor during the Linlithgow's reign to know what was expected of her, and she more than met the social expectations of British India, attempting to keep up appearances in what many now sensed was a failing concern. During the twilight of the *Raj,* she, like her predecessor, struggled to maintain some semblance of a family life and thereby ease the tremendous strain under which her husband laboured. She held informal gatherings in the mansion to divert the family's and the viceroy's retinue from the gloom of war, if only briefly. If only for a moment now and then, young, attractive women brightened the gloom of the viceroy's residence, flirting with their father's aides, and enjoying the last flickers of up-scale social life in Delhi.

As British-Indian relations rapidly evolved, Lady Wavell was often drawn into the delicate web of negotiations and contacts with various Indian political factions. In April 1946 for example, Gandhi sent Rajkumari Amrit Kaur, one of his leading female lieutenants in the "Quit India!" movement, and a British educated social worker, to meet with the vicereine regarding social welfare programs in an independent India. Kaur's secondary mission was to convey the Mahatma's hopes for India becoming a united nation when independence came. Gandhi hoped that persuading Lady Wavell might in turn bring the viceroy to support his position. The vicereine had met Kaur through her work with various women's organizations and while she had no intention of interfering with her husband's administration, being approached gratified her. A member of the Kapurthala royal family, and advocate of female education and abolishing regressive Indian traditions like child marriage and female infanticide, Kaur was a member of the Indian delegation to the 1946 UNESCO conference in Paris, and went on to serve as Minister of Health, the first female in the new Indian government's cabinet.

Both her being approached on a political matter, and the vicereine's discussing vital political and social issues with a woman once jailed by the *Raj* for sedition reflected the transition in British-Indian relations, and a maturing of the vicereine's role in the matrix of power that would continue

until Partition, and afterward. But this was not Lady Wavell's first involvement in sub-continental politics. Before coming out to India in 1943,
she had been approached by Cornelia Sorabji, noted lawyer and author
who represented the interests of women property holders who lived in
purdah, and who supported continued British rule. Although Lady Wavell
gently parried Cornelia's pleas for assistance with women's legal matters,
and referred her to provincial authorities, their meeting led to a spirited
correspondence about improvements in public health, both agreeing that
special attention should be paid to the problems of infant mortality, better
prenatal care, and the building of additional well-baby clinics. The vicereine's experience with Indian hospitals during the war had opened her
eyes to the urgent need for more Indian nurses, and she used her contacts
with Sorabji to encourage Indian women to pursue advanced education
and nurses' training.

When the war ended, Lady Wavell, looking forward to completing her
husband's reign and returning to England to enjoy retirement with him, was
shocked when Wavell was summarily dismissed as viceroy in early 1947.
Masking her resentment at this humiliation of her husband, one of a series
at the hands of Churchill as well as Attlee, she did her best to ease the transition, including sending her successor, Edwina Mountbatten, the names
of servants who would look after her personal needs – her *dhodie* (bearer),
the *dorsa* (tailor), *characid* (messenger), and *khitmagar* (waiter). Like many
soldier's wives, Lady Wavell packed up her family's belongings one last
time and accompanied her weary husband home and into retirement. The
awarding of the traditional earldom given to departing viceroys soothed
the Wavells' feelings somewhat, but did nothing to restore Wavell's failing
health worn down by a series of onerous high command assignments and
the stress of viceroyalty. The Wavell earldom was brief. The Field Marshal
died in 1950, and his son, Archie was killed in a Mau Mau raid in Kenya
in 1953, leaving Queenie another sad viceregal widow.

Any resentments among Britons in India regarding the Wavells' uncere-
monious departure were quickly eclipsed with the highly publicised arrival
of glamorous successors who brought a tinge of the mystique of "real"
royalty to Viceroy's House. In many ways, this last viceregal family exemplified the qualities of leadership that Britons in India had most valued
in their viceroys – if they ignored the Mountbattens' liberal politics and
his German origins. Louis Mountbatten's connections to the royal family
were solid enough: he was a great-grandson of Queen Victoria, who stood
sponsor at his christening, a cousin of the current King, George VI, and
personally known to nearly every other member of the royal family. Edwina
– known throughout the Empire as "Lady Louis" because of her heartfelt
work in wartime charities – could not match "Dickie's" pedigree,[41] but

held her own with her striking beauty, sophistication, and a wardrobe and jewels that outshone anything seen in India since the reign of Mary Curzon.

Whenever the Mountbattens appeared in full viceregal regalia, those who strained to catch a glimpse of their new rulers and were impatient to review their costumes and deportment were routinely impressed. The viceroy, a fanatic uniform collector, was always immaculately outfitted, and fully bemedalled. The vicereine's showed her slim figure to its best advantage in flowing gowns, the left side of which was almost hidden with her own decorations including her newly obtained CI, the Grand Cross of St. John, and the Australian Conspicuous Service Medal. Along with her huge diamond chokers and earrings, she wore several inches of diamond bracelets atop elbow-length kid gloves, and a large tiara with five stars in diamonds and pearls atop her carefully coiffed hair. The radiant glory of the Mountbattens enthroned in Delhi obscured the essential subtext: they had come to power to end power, charged to end the very system that they so effectively symbolised.

The Mountbattens' attributes and assets for viceroyalty went well beyond mere lineage and charm. Beyond his mixed reputation within the government, "Dickie" was renowned in Britain and the United States as a celebrity war hero who had survived the sinking of his ship to become head of Combined Operations, and then became theater commander in Southeast Asia, nicknamed "El Supremo." During the war, his fame was substantially amplified by being portrayed by Noel Coward in his well-received film *In Which We Serve*, and by a brief appearance in Milton Caniff's popular comic strip *Terry and the Pirates*. In the late 1940s, he gained further visibility from being featured in Lowell Thomas' popular account of Orde Wingate's Long Range Penetration force in Burma, the Chindits. Lady Mountbatten also became a media celebrity of substantial magnitude for involvement in the direction of war-related relief activities. The glow of their fame eclipsed the fact that they had sent their teen-aged daughters, Patricia and Pamela, to the United States early in the war as many prominent people had – but not the royal family[42]

Nor was that the only discontinuity between image and substance. Despite myriad media depictions of their marriage as glamorous and "ideal," mutual infidelity and emotional distance marked their union over the years. Both Mountbattens were remarkably candid with their daughters about their stormy marriage, including their extramarital relationships, and occasionally dragooned Patricia and/or Pamela as go-betweens to explain or excuse misbehaviour or seek a truce. As the girls became young adults, their relations with their parents became increasingly tense, especially when Edwina, in the throes of menopause, became markedly jealous of her husband's close relationship with Patricia.

When the young Edwina and Mountbatten first met at a ball in 1920 all that sadness and misery lay far off in the future. Both were untitled (although Edwina was an "Honourable" because of her grandfather's rank) and thus somewhat on the fringes of "true" aristocratic high life, and the couple often attended the same parties during that social season. When Dickie's father and Edwina's grandfather died a few weeks apart, they had spent enough time together to share their grief. Both were upset at the prospect of being separated when Mountbatten was invited to accompany the Prince of Wales on his tour of India and Japan, and letters flew back and forth across the miles. The future viceroy's missives included descriptions of athletic events, hunting, and pig-sticking interwoven with details

The ultimate Viceroy and Vicereine, Louis and Edwina Mountbatten, they posed for this photograph at the Viceroy's House to celebrate their silver wedding anniversary in July 1947.

of balls and receptions and his encounters with attractive women which prompted Edwina to write equally effusive letters about her social activities. The resultant jealousy threw the intensity of their feelings for each other into bold relief. They were therefore delighted when Lady Reading invited Edwina to come to Delhi in January as a member of the house party entertaining the Prince.

In what a Victorian novelist might have deemed the first flush of young love, the couple toured historic sites, rode together in the early mornings, and spent every evening in each other's company. By February, they had become covertly engaged – although nearly everyone in the viceregal entourage had guessed their secret. As the couple discussed the mechanics of making a public announcement, Lord Reading, as Edwina's host and a friend of her grandfather's, and concerned that proper arrangements be made to assure that Edwina would retain control of her fortune, weighed in. "In plain English, Edwina, in my opinion, brings far more than she gets by the marriage," he wrote to Mrs. Cassel, Edwina's great aunt. "If all went well with the marriage, then no harm would be done, but if "Heaven forbid" things did not work out, "…she will be in a far better position if she has control of the money." [43]In the way of a further complication, Mountbatten's being a member of the royal family meant that nothing could be said publicly until the King gave his consent.

Once the couple were back in England, although Edwina's father, Wilfred Ashley, was annoyed when he learned that the King was informed before he had received Mountbatten's formal request for Edwina's hand, Wilfred finally gave his consent when the financial details were arranged and the wedding date, July 18,1922, set to mesh with King and Queen's schedule, proved to be the highlight of the social season. A host of pre-wedding events were given by notables of London society, as well as the Cornelius Vanderbilts[44] who were in Britain for the summer. Brook House, Edwina's grandfather's London residence, quickly was glutted with wedding presents, including diamond jewelry from Edwina's family and Mountbatten's royal relations, bejewelled boxes and clocks from maharajahs, as well as the traditional flat silver and plate. After the ceremony at St. Margaret's Westminster, the wedding party proceeded to Brook House, which had been transformed for the reception by the planting of ten-foot-high orange trees, enormous footed vases of lilies and delphiniums, and hundreds of carnations, Edwina's tribute to her grandfather who always wore one in his buttonhole.

After the merger of a beautiful heiress with a cousin of the King filled the society pages for weeks on end, the couple settled into relative anonymity. When their daughters were born – Patricia in 1924 and Pamela in 1929 – Edwina followed the traditional upper class model of parenting by giving babies to the care of nannies and governesses as soon as possible. Nevertheless, she was an affectionate and caring mother, writing faithfully to the girls during their school years and their absence in America. Mountbatten was closer to them; like many fathers, he was captivated by his daughters from the day they were born, never expressing a desire for a male heir to carry on his family name and titles.[45] He, too, was a tireless correspondent, and with his passion to control and organize, ordained that the girls should write alternate weekly letters from their American exile during World War II: one week, Patricia would write to Edwina and the next to him, with Pamela doing the reverse.

When the Mountbattens went back out to India in 1947, Pamela went with her parents, but not Patricia, who had married John Knatchbull, (later 7th Baron Brabourne of Brabourne), and one of Mountbatten's wartime ADCs. "Operation Wedding" as Edwina called it, was a major and complex undertaking, and provided a magnificent spectacle in a Britain still dulled by the wartime damage and privation.

When it was decided that Pamela would accompany her parents on what the new vicereine called the "Indian saga,"[46] she was enthusiastic after her long separation from her parents throughout most of the war and having been on her own after her sister's marriage. Nearing 18, and attractive, charming, and an heiress of some substance, she gained immediate popularity with the young men on her father's staff and among functionaries of the nearly moribund *Raj*. For the most part, Pammy was on her own, but she also helped her mother with her various charitable activities and in entertaining groups of women at the residence, British, Indian, and foreign visitors. Content with that arrangement, she took full advantage of being the viceroy's daughter at the epicentre of the post-war social whirl in the last days of the *Raj*. Despite their punishing schedules, both parents were able to divert some time and attention to Pamela. Mountbatten scheduled an early morning ride with Pamela, and Lady Mountbatten ordered that unless there was an official engagement, lunch would be served informally each day by the pool, with no ADCs or staff in attendance. On Pamela's 18th birthday, in lieu of a formal debut, the Mountbattens gave a small poolside dance in her honour that allowed guests to enjoy the relative cool of the evening and the ambience of the extensive and closely tended gardens.

Despite Edwina's best efforts, however, the family's time together was limited as the August deadline for Indo-Pakistani independence approached. The surge in crucial issues consumed Mountbatten's full attention and energy, and Lady Mountbatten was immersed, as she had been during the war, in overseeing massive relief efforts, travelling throughout the country amid the ultimately bloody turmoil of Partition, visiting hospitals, relief stations, and public health facilities, while assisting her husband in his delicate political negotiations. Family concerns had to take a back seat to other, more immediate problems. Ever the compulsive correspondent, Lady Mountbatten described of all their activities in her letters to Patricia, including fears and worries. While her husband, she reported, was "enjoying it all *madly*, thank God," the last vicereine struggled to pretend that she enjoyed the "great adventure," all the while longing for the green of southern England and her spacious estate.

Like most of their predecessors, and despite the various stresses within their own family, the Mountbattens managed to maintain the public image of the perfect viceregal family. Once again, in keeping with the three and-a-half centuries of the British presence in India, and the widely accepted stereotype of *Albion perfid*, public images masked the inner reality. Not all looking on in Britain or India approved of the Mountbattens' actions or style. But as the *Raj* was dismantled, their public demeanor provided a compensating version of how British functionaries in India saw themselves: dedicated servants of the crown, comporting themselves admirably, remaining steady while risking their own safety and their family's as the stewards of their subjects' welfare. Whatever their initial reaction to assuming that burden had been – enthusiasm, reluctance, or fear of the known and the unknown – virtually all vicereines gave their proverbial all, with varying degrees of success, to playing one of the most visible and demanding roles in the grand masque of imperial symbolism, and provided much of substance as well.

4
Grand Hotel

Very soon after arriving in India, vicereines lacking experience in diplomatic settings found that to be a very great deficit indeed as they were immersed in the vast and steady flow of diverse guests. While visits from friends and family from England were usually welcomed, and even longed for, many other visitors, frequently unknown to either the viceroy or vicereine, showed up with little or no warning. Those who "dropped in" expected reception and entertainment in a manner befitting lofty personages, whether or not they actually were of such status in terms of protocol and rank. Lady Curzon, for example, shortly after her arrival in India, began to get requests for hospitality from Americans whom she had met only once but barely recalled, or did not remember at all, certain that an American vicereine would be eager to see someone from "home." In addition to the parade of politicians, foreign dignitaries, and film stars seeking reflected publicity and name-dropping fare were Britons without such axes to grind. Some among those, although wealthy, saw Government House as a free grand hostelry wherein they might help themselves to cigars and viceregal stationery as mementos of their subcontinental sojourn. Lord Minto summed up the dilemma in a letter to the SOSI, Lord Morley, in January 1908:

> This house is simply becoming an Hotel. Everyone who passes through, and their name is legion, hopes to be put up here ... M.P.s abound and ask one terrible conundrums on Indian affairs. A ponderous politician, a Staffordshire member I think, fired off every conceivable riddle at my head. As far as I can make out, he

*is bent on earning an Indian reputation in the House of Commons.
Possibly he may afford you some amusement.[1]*

Carried along by that powerful and expanding social torrent, the
vicereines found themselves functioning as the manager of several major
facilities. Fortunately, they were able to draw on the support and experience of the Military Secretary and his staff, which made their relationship
with those functionaries even more crucial in the social and administrative dimensions of viceregality. Hosting and arranging amusements for
guests, especially uninvited ones, or politicians, foreign dignitaries, or
journalists critical of their husbands' administration, added another level
of complexity to being vicereine. Some visitors stayed on for weeks, or
even months, in contrast to the short and hectic pace of the country house
weekend party. Often, they used the viceregal residence as a base for
touring the countryside, absenting themselves for a week or more, then
returning and expecting their rooms to be in the same order as they left
them.

Like any good hostess, regardless of personal feelings, the vicereine
had to handle such matters with full diplomatic sensitivity, and fit the
needs and desires of all guests into the routine of a household, which
was virtually never routine. And beyond the dimensions of protocol
and sensibilities, the entertaining was damnably expensive, since most
viceroys spent substantial portions of their own funds on maintaining the
viceregal establishment. Sometimes guests – particularly uninvited ones –
seriously complicated schedules, especially when major dignitaries were
passing through. Despite the enormous capacity of viceregal residences,
finding sufficient bedrooms for visitors and their servants became a major
problem, and often led to tents being erected on the lawn to accommodate
guests, staff members and servants. Although the vicereine relied on the
staff to make these temporary quarters as comfortable as possible, she was
ultimately responsible for orchestrating such matters, and poured considerable energy into ensuring their suitability.

When guests arrived from abroad during the viceroy's annual stay
at Simla, logistical problems were even greater as even Viceregal Lodge
filled up, and tents were set up on the lawns of the Lodge as the hordes
of guests eager to see the Himalayas at the viceroy's expense increased
over the years. That trend was complicated by fewer official entertainments and ceremonials compared with the court in Calcutta and then
New Delhi, although the English weather of the mountains and the opportunity for more informal interaction with the viceroy and the Simla social
community were some degree of compensation. Even the difficult trip up
from the plains did not discourage them, although most European visitors

deliberately chose to visit India in the "cold" weather, and thus did not come to the viceroy's mountain aerie. But those adventurous souls who did make that trip were rewarded with some of the planet's incredible mountain vistas, diverse open air activities, and the creative entertainments that blossomed in British-Indian up-country retreats.

While high-ranking and royal visitors and celebrities significantly multiplied logistical and protocol complications for the vicereine, they also attracted widespread publicity as each detail was reported in minute detail in the Indian, British, and international press, as well as in dispatches, letters home, and personal conversations upon return. Although the viceroy and vicereine and the staff were responsible for ensuring that protocol was strictly observed and that the visitor received the honours due to his or her station during any official ceremonies, the vicereine oversaw the "private" social side of such visits, assuring that luminaries enjoyed themselves and were comfortably situated.

Beyond arranging sumptuous lodgings, properly elegant feasts, and extravagant entertainments, the list of activities included providing advice on the obligatory tour of the country, ostensibly aimed at expanding the dignitaries' knowledge of the India and its peoples, but in fact a series of meetings with British officials and Indian rulers in pleasant and often splendid settings far from the hard realities of day-to-day life. Visitors usually wanted to see some of the glories of India, the stereotypical mountain, jungle and lakeside vistas, caves, ancient sites, and vivid pornographic sculptures, as well as the local rulers' vast and ornate palaces, huge jewels, and presumably beautiful veiled women gazing from the shrouds of purdah or from behind the screens of the *zenanah*. To fulfill their guests' fantasies, the viceroys and vicereines depended on the good will, grace, and extravagant hospitality of those major potentates inclined to demonstrate their loyalty to the *Raj* by providing the viceroy's European visitors an intimate view of their palaces, finery, rituals, and customs, and for a more select few, lush accommodations and picturesque entertainments.

Some Indian rulers, striving to outshine their princely peers, mounted elaborate hunting expeditions that allowed visitors to shoot big game in safe and comfortable conditions provided by small armies of servants and *shikaris*. Hence the massive denuding of Hindic wildlife traced out in the shooting lists of many greater and myriad lesser hunts, and in hundreds of cliché photos of great beasts in stacks or rows flanked or surmounted by *topi*-wearing, gun-brandishing Europeans. Beyond that was the taxidermic residue, ranging from stuffed beasts, heads, and horns to tiger skin rugs and elephant foot umbrella stands that cluttered the homes of the British aristocracy and *haut bourgeois*, as well as those of other nations' luminaries who were wealthy enough to visit India and eager to join in what a

few contemporaries and many post-imperial critics would deem an eco-
(seated on the atrocity. Some Indian rulers, eager to appear British and display their skill
left) was a rare at sports learned during their days at public school, put polo and cricket
instance. The on the schedule of activities. Since the vicereines had usually visited
daughter of the palaces chosen for royal tours, they were able to comment on details, and
only widowed offer insights on what visitors might expect in the way of accommodation
Viceroy, Lord and entertainment, along with special opportunities for interested female
Northbrook, she travelers to visit schools, hospitals, or other social welfare centres.
was required
to step into the The vicereines themselves accompanied most British royals on at least
role of vicereine part of their tour, adding to the complexity of logistics and protocol by an
for the Prince of order of magnitude. Those visits presented a special dilemma since the
Wales' tour of viceroy, as the monarch's representative, outranked any member of the
India in 1875. king or queen's immediate family. Inasmuch as royal guests were used
to pre-eminence in most situations at home, and in other domains of the
British Empire, India presented an imbalance, the management of which
required special diplomacy and adroitness on the part of the vicereine.
Even when no female royal person was on a tour, protocol required the
viceroy to have a lady present to assist him in his social duties.

During Edward Prince of Wales's tour in 1875–76, the first visit of a
future monarch to the "jewel" in his mother's crown, Lord Northbrook,
the widowed viceroy, had his daughter Emma return from London (where

she had gone to restore her health) to serve as his hostess and domestic overseer. Although only in her mid-twenties, Emma demonstrated a notable grace in aiding her father through that ordeal. Despite Emma's efforts, the lack of an "official" vicereine offered other protocol challenges as senior Government of India officials and staffers' wives competed for the Edward's attention, some pushing themselves forward at every opportunity. A man notorious for pursuing attractive women, the Prince of Wales was cordial to all, but especially so to the most attractive, regardless of their rank. On the one hand, Princess Alexandra's remaining in England made Emma's work easier, but on the other, it increased the Prince's opportunity for twinkling and flirting. But despite that, the future king managed to maintain balance as he personally invested new members with of the Star of India order, and completed a full program of official events before visiting the Maharajahs of Kashmir, Patiala, Gwalior, and Jaipur while touring the subcontinent to slaughter droves of tigers, elephants, and other large animals.

Sir Bartle Frere, former Governor of Bombay and the leader of the Prince's expedition, wrote to the Queen that the trip was an unqualified success. Edward had won the affection of the "common people" of India, Frere said, as well as the respect and admiration of the Indian ruling class. With this extensive tour Frere suggested, the Prince had firmly established a personal relationship for the royal family with the people of India like the one they had with the people of England. The extensive program of social and military events organised for the Prince also highlighted the importance of carefully aligning royal protocol with that of the viceroy's court.

The arrival in India of European royals could also pose problems for the viceroy and vicereine. The visit of Tsarevitch Nicholas of Russia in 1891 presented Lord and Lady Lansdowne with especially sticky protocol difficulties, mainly due to Queen Victoria's unwelcome intervention. Nicholas, the monarch's grand-nephew by marriage, was also heir-apparent to the second largest empire in the world, which rivaled Britain for dominance of South-Central and Southwest Asia. India was only one stop on the tsarevitch's tour, which included Egypt and Japan, and Nicholas's travelling companions included his cousin, Prince George of Greece and three young Russian noblemen, thereby adding another layer of protocol intricacy to the planning.

From the moment the intended tour was announced, Victoria took intense interest in all aspects of the visit. She asked Lansdowne for details of arrangements, especially public ceremonies and occasions where issues of rank and precedence were salient, and such matters as the number of guns to be fired in salute. Lord Cross, the SOSI, advised Lansdowne that the tsarevitch would receive 21 on his arrival in India under the logic that since "… the Prince of Wales would receive a like salute in Russia, reciprocity governs the question." Ever-loyal and sensitive to the Queen's feelings concerns regarding protocol, especially in respect to her own family, Lansdowne reported to Cross that he had given the tsarevitch every courtesy, including seating Nicholas on the viceroy's right in the carriage during the drive from the railroad station to Government House, something not done even for the Queen's grandson, the Duke of Clarence, during his visit. Although Lansdowne was not inclined to pay that honour to a visiting prince, he saw that the Queen felt strongly about the issue, and having "no personal feeling in the matter," conceded the point, despite his view that the Queen's representative "should on all occasions take rank before anyone else."[2]

The Queen's concerns about Nicholas's Indian experience may have been heightened by her awareness that her grand-nephew lacked enthusiasm for the trip, which had been arranged mainly to separate him from his inamorata.[3] Unaware of the lovesickness of her royal guest, Lady Lansdowne was duly diligent in preparing for the visit, and spent days organising housing and domestic arrangements for Nicholas and his entourage. She presided over all major social events held in the tsarevitch's honour, sending particulars of each occasion to the Queen, and always careful to award her husband credit for its diplomatic success. But Victoria sought further information, pressing Lady Lansdowne about her grand-nephew's effect on the Indian people, which led the vicereine to write long detailed letters describing the tsarevitch's demeanour, and the public's reaction to every event.

After Nicholas' party had left India, the Lansdownes were relieved to hear from Lord Cross that the Queen was very pleased with their reports, and considered the visit highly successful, diplomatically and personally. And Nicholas was able to conceal his feelings about the trip from his hosts. When he met his brother-in-law in Colombo, he expressed his boredom with the exercise: "Palaces and generals are the same the world over, and that is all I am permitted to see. I could have just as well stayed at home."[4]

While the tsarevitch's visit was accounted a success for the Lansdownes in the highest circles of the British Empire, they were not eager to repeat anything like that experience. When advised that Prince George, another grandson of the Queen, was proposing that he tour India during the winter of 1892, Lansdowne told Cross that since he planned to go to Burma in January, the Prince's arrival would "inconvenience" him. "No one, "he observed, "has any idea of the trouble which such visits give to all our officials, as well as to the native states included in the program."[5] Although Lansdowne did not include his wife in his list of those adversely affected by royal visits, it was generally recognised that much of the burden for coordination and administration of such events fell on her and the viceregal functionaries with whom she worked closely.

At the same time, Lady Lansdowne, like all vicereines, saw visits by royalty as a mixed blessing. As First Hostess of the *Raj,* her domestic and social skills were on show as she orchestrated the viceregal system to provide luxurious accommodations, met each worthy's personal need and comfort, and designed and oversaw lavish entertainments exceeding those of the most eminent London hostess. On the other hand, she had to cope with the royals' whims and demands without murmur or complaint. Not only could they be especially demanding, but most were insensitive to the peculiarities of India and its social fabric, and eager to get to the real "business" of the visit – bagging big game and seeing the sights. And all the while, even though the vicereine had substantial control over the design and execution of the royal visit, she shared her husband's concern about the impression that their efforts made on royal visitors, and their effect on princes and maharajahs he would visit, and to a lesser extent, on the "natives."

Entertaining royals was especially burdensome when the visit coincided with a major ceremony, such as the monarch's brother and sister-in-law, the Duke and Duchess of Connaught's representing of King Edward VII at the 1903 Durbar. On that occasion, as Lady Curzon struggled to balance her position of superiority in the Indian hierarchy to that of visiting royals, she was aided by the King and her husband's expertise in royal and viceregal protocol, and their complete agreement regarding precedence at ceremonies and social occasions. At that durbar, the zenith of Curzon's viceroyalty, the royal duke's presence was only one of many irons in the proverbial fire in terms of planning and organization.

With characteristic arrogance, Curzon envisioned the duke and duchess as mere supporting players in the grand pageant which he created and played out on a stage designed to highlight him and his wife. In the metaphorical battle for female supremacy that raged during the durbar, Mary Curzon had many advantages, including youth, great beauty, and significant wealth. As a result, no woman present of any rank outshone her, as Mary became the centre of attention throughout the durbar, her own impressive jewel collection enhanced by the "bags" of diamonds brought to India by her mother specifically for the occasion. Well aware that her presence was equal to that of any royal, she more than fulfilled her husband's expectations, especially in the role of hostess to the Connaughts, who, when they returned home, joined other notable British durbar guests in spreading the story of Mary's triumph among their aristocratic friends.

All the grandeur and sense of triumph suffusing the 1903 Durbar proved brief and fragile as the kudos earned by the Curzons were negated by their rudeness toward the next wave of visiting British royals. While Curzon had hoped to host the future King-Emperor and Queen-Empress, by the time the Prince and Princess of Wales arrived in 1905, the viceroy had resigned. Despite his pleading to the home government that he allowed to remain in India throughout the royal visit, he and his wife were allowed to stay only long enough to welcome the royal couple in Bombay. It fell to Lord and Lady Minto to execute Curzon's carefully planned visit for the Wales, including their triumphal tour of the subcontinent. On the eve of the arrival, Curzon's pointed insults to the recently arrived viceroy and his lady were already a widespread subject of gossip in India, and his rough treatment of the Wales furthered his reputation for arrogance and rudeness. Although he and Lady Curzon were on hand to welcome the royal couple ashore in Bombay, he had failed to ensure that their temporary quarters in Government House were ready. In a repeat of Mary Minto's experience in Calcutta, Princess Mary found servants changing the beds as she arrived since their rooms were occupied by others almost up until that moment. Curzon also kept the viceregal train for his own use until the last possible moment, and when the Wales came aboard, they found it in a grubby condition.

Common displeasure at the departing viceroy's boorishness added further cement to the Mintos' and Wales's association, already solidified by the new vicereine's having grown up at Windsor. Beyond that bonding, the inauspicious beginning provided an implicit irony – things were bound to improve. Lady Minto, supremely confident that the remainder of the visit would be a success, personally took charge of overseeing the Wales's accommodations, and with her customary energy and attention to detail gave meticulous instructions on how their quarters were to be arranged. Some 700 men worked feverishly painting, cleaning and preparing Government House in Calcutta for the royal visit, and erecting 50 large tents to accommodate the staff and servants, shelters similar to those used at the Delhi Durbar – huge rooms with brick floors covered with carpets, each tent containing a bedroom, a sitting room, and bathroom. In her journal, Lady Minto noted that "Even the valets have two arm chairs apiece." And beyond that, on the backside of the façade of imperial grandeur, some five hundred coolies were engaged to handle the royal party's luggage alone.

Naturally enough, both the Mintos and the Wales both grasped and scrupulously adhered to the convoluted rules of protocol. Well-schooled in such matters by his father, the Prince made sure that the viceroy and vicereine took precedence at every public occasion. At the first dinner party of the visit, the Prince mentioned to Lady Minto that he hoped the Viceroy understood that he would come to Minto's place at the table after dessert, not the other way around. When Lady Minto indicated that her husband felt very awkward about the situation, the Prince replied, "Surely I [should be] the first person to show consideration to my father's representative." He then wrote a note to Minto on the back of the printed dinner menu: "You must remain in your place. I will come and sit beside you when the ladies leave the dining-room."[6] When such instances of potential uncertainty or friction arose, the Prince and Princess adapted easily to the social rules of British India with balletic grace and ease, earning admiration and fulsome praise beyond the usual hyperbolic gushing for their easeful adaptability. Lady Minto reported how a rumour that the Prince would be leaving at a certain time triggered a free-for all in which proverbial Britannic sang-froid was literally trampled underfoot as men crowded toward the head of the receiving line. "Men fainted and were nearly trampled on," she reported. "Their coats were torn, plaster broken off pillars, the barriers were thrown down. The maimed and bleeding of course had to return home, but the remaining 2,123 were disposed of in an hour and three quarters."[7]

The Prince, following the relatively liberal path set by his grandmother and father, expressed displeasure about the rude treatment of Indians, especially the local rulers and aristocrats. Late in her reign, Victoria had urged keener awareness of the feelings of her Indian subjects, and expressed the hope that "The future Vice Roy…[should] do what he thinks right and not be guided by the *snobbish* and vulgar, over-bearing and offensive behaviour of our Civil and Political Agents…"[8] In a similar vein, the Prince was displeased by British-Indian functionaries denigrating their subjects, and was especially offended when he heard military officers calling them "niggers." He was further taken aback when he learned that no Indian of any level of education or birth could be considered as a member of any British club, and was concerned about relationships between potentates and the government, urging that they should be treated "more as equals than inferiors."[9] His views may well have been shaped during his tour by seeing the "Europeanization" of Indian rulers, many of whose sons went to public school in Britain, whose palaces were furnished with Louis XIV-style furnishings, and who had become obsessed with cricket and polo.

Despite any lingering concern about the long-term prospects of the British in India, the Prince and Princess proclaimed their visit a complete success, and praised the Mintos, as did the press, for their brilliant hospitality and efficient organization of the royal tour. During their 18 weeks in India, the Wales travelled 9,000 miles by train, and hundreds more by carriage and motor car, not to mention occasional triumphal processions and hunts atop elephants. Princess Mary became enchanted by it all, and as they departed aboard HMS *Renown* she wrote in her diary that: "We went on the bridge and watched dear beautiful India vanish from our sight."[10] She would happily return in 1911 for the Coronation Durbar, and remain fascinated with Indian affairs the rest of her life, asking one of her attendant ladies the night before she died to read aloud to her from a book about India.

The global publicity churned up by the royal visits encouraged other minor British and European royalty to come out to India both before and after World War I. However, it was not until 1921–22 that another vicereine hosted a future British monarch – the "playboy prince," Edward, Prince of Wales, later Edward VIII and Duke of Windsor, who arrived in Bombay in December 1921 for an extended tour of India and Japan.

Various misfortunes and discomforts converged to complicate matters. Political tensions were heightened when a *hartal* or general strike was called by Gandhi to protest the Prince's visit, all the more ominous in the immediate aftermath of the Amritsar massacre, while Alice Reading's attack of sciatica made preparing for his visit that much more difficult. House-bound during the month preceding his arrival, she was able to inspect the Prince's quarters only shortly before he was due to appear in New Delhi. Although the government had been transferred there in 1911, Lutyens' grandiose viceregal residence was still in progress, requiring the Readings to "camp out" in Viceregal Lodge. While spacious and elegant, it could not accommodate them and the future monarch and his entourage.

Alice oversaw construction of the Prince's Pavilion on the grounds of Viceregal Lodge, a bungalow featuring a huge gilded wood reproduction of the Prince of Wales' feathers above the entrance, above which the Royal Standard was displayed when the Prince was in residence. Alice personally selected decorations for the Prince's rooms, and designed the garden surrounding the bungalow, which included a large sitting room and bedroom, and adjoining bathroom with running water and electricity. The rooms were furnished with the very best in the way of comfortable beds, huge wardrobes, large writing tables, comfortable chairs, and luxurious carpets. When Alice ordered pictures brought from Viceregal Lodge at Simla to cover the bare walls, she rejected the "fly-blown hunting scenes" that were sent at first, and demanded that paintings matching her chosen colour scheme of green and gold be dispatched forthwith. Her efforts were rewarded (and she was enormously relieved) when the Prince pronounced the bungalow not just comfortable, but his first "home" ashore since leaving England. His retinue was housed nearby in splendid tents, also carpeted and furnished with comfy sofas, lamps, and paintings. After a final inspection, Alice declared that "…anything so unlike a tent cannot be imagined," although she had to acknowledge that it was impossible to prevent the buildup of heat during the day even though batteries of electric fans blew steady streams of air through the damp grass *tattis* at several points around the tent.[11]

There were some 115 tents in the Camp in addition to the Royal Pavilion built for the Prince, whose roommate was his cousin and best friend, Lord Louis Mountbatten. As for other royal visits, a small, leather-bound booklet had been prepared for all those living in the Camp. It contained an hour-by-hour schedule for each day of the visit; a list of house party members and the staffs of the Prince and viceroy, as well as the orders of all processions (including the composition of escorts) and details for each major event: the unveiling ceremony for the All India King Edward VII Memorial, the Durbar, the laying of the foundation stone for Kitchener College, and the State banquet. One of the most scrutinised lists was that which named the select few granted admission to the reserved enclosure where the viceroy and honoured guests would watch the Prince play polo.

No detail was overlooked, including instructions for guests at the State Ball. Here again, precedence ruled: those guests whose automobiles carry the label "special" were granted "private entrée" and sent to the porch outside the ADC's office to be admitted early into the royal presence. Those without such labels were instructed to go to the platform north of the ADC's waiting room to be admitted later. Public entrée guests waited in tents pitched on the grounds. All private entrée guests were escorted by ADCs, while the lesser lights were merely directed toward the ballroom by other staff members. The booklet advised that the Prince and the Readings would arrive at 9:45, and supper would be served after the fifth dance, with the usual musical accompaniment, the "Roast Beef of Old England."

More mundane but essential details in the booklet included a "Distri-bution of Accommodations" which revealed who was staying in what tents – proximity to the Royal Pavilion indicating one's rank and importance – and who had been assigned motor cars, another status symbol. For security reasons, all motor cars were issued a number; those assigned to Viceregal Lodge bore a red crown and a special pass issued by the Foreign and Political Department. Those assigned cars were advised that they could obtain petrol from the head chauffeur of the viceregal garage by sending a written request with their drivers. Camp dwellers were also warned to keep their money and jewelry "carefully locked up" and to report any losses to Inspector Powis in Tent No. 14 as soon as property or cash was missed. Any delay, the warning continued, would make it that much more difficult to trace any missing possessions "owing to the presence of so many strange servants in the Camp." [12]

Ill-health aside, Lady Reading was actively engaged in planning the Prince's social schedule in Delhi. "We are letting him off very lightly here in the way of ceremonies," she wrote to her son. "Only one state dinner, one large ball, then one gay fancy dress dance, and a dinner and dance here of young people with a jazz band." She took part in nearly all the events associated with the Prince's visit in Delhi, including a durbar for native rulers held at the Red Fort during which she sat on a gold throne chair's scarlet velvet cushions while wearing a petunia pink satin dress. "I hope I looked like a fuchsia," she wrote her son, and described the Prince as too preoccupied with his constricting tunic and his speech to notice her sartorial discomfort.

The durbar was followed by a garden party and an enormous fireworks display of the Fort and its gardens, then polo and a dinner given by the native princes in Edward's honour. The vicereine Alice may have thought the schedule was light, but Edwina Ashley (soon to be Mountbatten) had insights into the "Little Prince's" views about the tour. The Prince was "quite fed up" with…the terrific pomp and ceremony" and felt quite undone by the scorching heat. "What they called a tiny dinner party was one for only eighty people," Edwina reported.[13] Edwina herself was appalled by the excessive ceremony: "Quite overpowering," she wrote to her great aunt; "the curtseying and etiquette are awful."[14]

Any trepidation Lady Reading had about her social skills ebbed as she spent time with the Prince, whom she found easy to talk to, and very grateful for her efforts to ensure his comfort and pleasure. Her arthritic knees did not keep her from enjoying the State Ball, and she was "breathless with laughter" after performing the exhausting "State Lancers" – a version of a Scottish Highland reel very popular at the time in viceregal social circles, but new to the Prince. The last day of the Delhi visit, the vicereine accompanied Prince Edward to a "People's Fair" on the Maidan, where a crowd of some 15,000 to 20,000 had gathered to see the Prince arrive on horseback. Although the Readings were alarmed at the prospect of the Prince displaying himself so openly to such a huge crowd, he insisted on doing so, since the main purpose of his visit was improvement of the political climate in India, in a downward spiral since the Amritsar massacre three years earlier. In the end, no serious security problems emerged, and the Prince was warmly welcomed – especially by the Indian princes and British-Indian society, although the growing unrest flickered into view from time to time, in the empty streets at Allahabad University and in Benares, in large public demonstrations in Madras, and when shots were fired without effect at the Prince's ADC's car in Patiala.

The tour inadvertently had introduced a future viceroy and vicereine to their future domain since, as noted earlier, Edward had invited his cousin and close friend, Louis "Dickie" Mountbatten, then a junior naval officer, to accompany him on the tour. Ever eager to increase his royal cachet, Mountbatten was eager to go, even though it meant leaving behind Edwina Ashley, with whom he had fallen deeply in love. When Lady Reading invited Edwina to India (through her old friend and Edwina's great aunt,

Mrs. Cassel) she seized the chance to join her intended and wired Dickie of her impending arrival. Even as a young man, Mountbatten was compulsive about details and a stickler for royal protocol. Eager that his intended should make the very best impression, Dickie sent Edwina long letters on just how she should prepare for the trip: get a lady's *topi* from Henry Heath or Ranken; bring "lightish" eyeglasses to reduce or eliminate harmful solar rays; and bring riding and tennis clothes. She must be careful about the food she ate and what she drank during the voyage to avoid illness, and always protect her head against sunstroke, "especially between nine in the morning and four in the afternoon." Mountbatten also provided lists of the viceroy's staff, grouped by category and order of precedence, as well as group photos with individuals identified so Edwina would recognize them when she was introduced, and with brief biographies of the members of the Prince's retinue.

Despite a childhood and adolescence in her grandfather's splendid homes filled with priceless art treasures and antiques, Edwina's first exposure to viceregal grandeur literally took her breath away. From the time she was welcomed in Bombay and brought to Calcutta on the viceregal train, she was overwhelmed by the magnificence of the viceregal establishment and the complex rituals of British-Indian protocol. She was one of two guests (the other was Mrs. Ronnie Greville, the famous political hostess) staying in Viceregal Lodge itself, whose thick walls and large, dark rooms kept the oppressive heat somewhat at bay. Although it would soon be surpassed by Lutyen's new 340-room Viceroy's House which she would occupy some 25 years later, Edwina was impressed by the marble and inlaid wood hallways leading from one cavernous reception room to another, and by the hordes of servants. "I can't tell you how smart and rich one feels here," she wrote to her great aunt. "A car whenever you want one. About ten servants for everything; special flowers for each dress, etc."[15] In the mornings, she luxuriated in cool sheets, listening to the sounds of the Lodge awakening – birds singing, fountains babbling, and the soft swish of brooms as sweepers cleared verandahs. The intricacies of viceregal protocol were equally astounding to Edwina: a daily printed program describing every event, from times of arrival and departure to seating plans, required dress, and, of course, in the number of guns to be fired in salutes. The exotic setting and the glamour surrounding them fuelled the aura of romance, and Dickie and Edwina became engaged on February 10.

The Readings welcomed many other notable houseguests during their reign, including the Duke and Duchess of Connaught and the Scottish entertainer Sir Harry Lauder at Christmastime 1924. Alice's "Scotch Dinner" on Christmas Day was marred by the Duchess's absence with stomach trouble, but Alice's unique decorations – three illuminated Christmas trees and helium-filled balloons tied to the backs of chairs – were much admired, and the skirl of bagpipes after dinner introduced a round of Highland dancing.

Up until WWII, even though the imperial twilight deepened, and tremors of political turmoil intensified, India was a favourite destination for British aristocrats as well as European royals and foreign luminaries. In that interval, vicereines continued to be responsible for accommodating all sorts of guests, some of whom came for political reasons, others simply to enjoy viceregal hospitality, and still others to attend weddings or other family celebrations. As the years passed, little changed in the way of protocol and ritual, until economies were put in place during World War II as the viceregal family set an example in British India which would play well in a Britain under siege and wartime privations. Most of the wartime houseguests were military or political leaders, and as the war intensified and Britain's military fortunes declined, Doreen Linlithgow and Eugenie Wavell struggled with balancing the vestiges of viceregal grandeur against the privations of war, including massive political turbulence and the threat of air attack and invasion from 1942 to 1944. Even as independence loomed ever larger on the horizon, the vicereines continued to welcome visitors to an imperial guesthouse that would soon become the property of those who had been denied entry for so many years.

Edwina's memories of her initial romantic stay in India would colour the rest of her life, and gave her something of an advantage when she became the premier hostess of the *Raj*. Ironically, a generation later, the vicereine who enjoyed viceregal hospitality at its zenith presided over the most revolutionary changes in that milieu during the last days of Britain's suzerainty over India.

Pride and Precedence

John Lehman's definition of "A great hostess and creator of a salon" applied to the essence of being a vicereine of India. "She needs an unflagging curiosity about other people," he suggested," a flair for making them feel at home, or at least stimulated in her circle, almost unlimited time to organize her entertainments and to devote herself to the pursuit and domestication of those rising celebrities her shrewdly selective eye has marked down; and plenty of money."[1]

Few would have considered the viceregal court anything like a salon, with its intellectual conversation about literature or politics, nor would they have seen the creation of such an appropriate role for the vicereine. Most Britons in India saw the vicereine's most salient duty attendant to her lofty position – seen by some as exalted, and by others as empty and ceremonial – was that of grand hostess of the Indian Empire. Trollope's Lady Glencora Palliser might well have filled the bill: being aristocratic, and therefore at ease in all settings, and wealthy as well, allowing her to display a fabulous wardrobe and jewels that outshone most within her circle. Less tangible, but major assets all the same were Lady Glencora's charm, intuition, and political acumen that permitted her to use social occasions to further her husband's and her family's interests, including soothing ruffled feelings, and gathering intelligence. Glencora's political "crushes" – semi-formal assemblages – which she staged at their palatial country seats to promote her husband Plantagenet's agendas corresponded with fetes at Simla's Viceregal Lodge and New Delhi's Viceroy's House. The texture and scale of the latter were, of course, much grander due to the exotic settings, elaborate uniforms, and the glitter provided by bejeweled potentates, all part of the façade of Britain appearing to share power with overlords of many dozens of semi-autonomous states and principalities.

In India, home of the caste system, the cultures of the dominant and subservient mirrored each other in the sense that social levels among Britons and Indians alike were as sharply demarcated as anywhere in the world at that time. And the vicereine, at the very apex of that needle-like pinnacle, was responsible for overseeing an intricate social milieu. Most vicereines' reputation as a hostess preceded them, setting expectations of Britons serving the Raj as to how solid a standard she herself might set for British-Indian society. Grace, charm, and above all, stamina were at a premium in that little world which was, as Vita Sackville-West said, "a collection of people thrown together through a purely fortuitous circumstance, with nothing in common except the place we happen to find ourselves in."[2] Although the vicereine's social circle was not a salon in the spirit of Madame de Stael's, it set the social rules and standards of British India, and viceroys and vicereines were fully aware of the pitfalls of modifying its strict etiquette. Any social innovation or deviation from form might be perceived as "radical" and tarnish a viceroy's reputation as a leader, for if he was not master of his own entourage, how could he oversee the greatest of Britain's imperial domains? As a result, vicereines laboured under the constraints of British-Indian society's expectation that she create a glittering social ambience tinctured with glitter and novelty despite her minimal latitude to vary the forms or people taking part in occasions from a Great Durbar to a lawn party.

While even the vicereines who lacked aristocratic status and connections arrived in India well aware of the rigid stratification of the British-Indian hierarchy, those who were raised in the highest tiers of English society more easily identified the manifold differences between the two systems. Although inherited rank and wealth set fundamental baselines in Britain and Ireland, including manners and deportment, and served to block and thwart the rise of those from the lower tiers of society, some did manage to move up to the highest levels. This trend to mobility gained momentum late in the 19th century as wealthy scions "bought" knighthoods or even peerages along with the requisite country estates and London town houses, thus gaining social access to aristocrats of long lineage, and something akin to their status, even though "climbers" were often looked down upon within the inner keep. Such social ascendance was far more rare in India due the much more rigid and complex system ruled by the "demon of precedence" and a very strict if not clinically obsessive conformance to the rules of etiquette.[3]

Formal order of rank was the keel of British Indian Imperial protocol.

A preoccupation with pecking order shaped every facet of ceremony and behaviour, from the sequence in which Britons went in to and sat at dinner, and departed at the end. Exceptions or irregularities were duly noted, and cautions and penalties firmly imposed. For example, the highest ranking European woman present always received some sort of formal recognition of the primacy of her precedence, whether that might be a "reserved" seat on a certain sofa at the Club, or sitting at the host's right hand at dinner. From the mid-1800s onward, British India's social system was defined by the *Warrant of Precedence*, which listed all positions – civil and military – and a related rank assigned to wives or female relatives." "The "book," as the *Warrant* was widely known, was published by the Government of India to serve as a guide to the placement of Government servants at official occasions. By the middle of the 19th century, the *Warrant* had become the social "bible" of every hostess, from vicereine to governor's wives to wives of district or provincial officers.

The listing of sequence in "the book," starting with the viceroy and vicereine and ending with Sub Deputy Opium Agents, included members of the Viceroy's Council, presidents, governors or lieutenant governors, military commanders, and district judges. The *Warrant* also spelled out the detailed rankings of status and function. Officers of the covenanted Indian Civil Service, for example, outranked members of the Indian Political Service, the Indian Medical Service, and senior officials of the Public Works Department, while heads of such departments as the Department of Education ranked lower, with consequent subordination in social circles. However, although businessmen and planters were at the bottom of the ladder, they were still part of the ruling caste, and therefore superior to all "natives."

Within the tight social circle of viceregal establishments, precedence set the templates in organising any social or official event. Rank determined who was worthy of a private entrée to a viceregal investiture, levée, or other official function as well as their order of reception. Needless to say, any departure from the prescribed routine became a matter of deep concern, from buzzing and conversation at the moment of or immediately after the breach, or after the event. Yet despite the *Warrant*'s tortuous detail, "the book" was sometimes found wanting, as in the instance when it failed to specify whether a recent arrival should be ranked as a major general or as a peer.[4]

Such hairsplitting reflected the Veblenian progression from the nabob scandals through the Macaulay Memorandum and the Mutiny as vanity replaced greed as the driving force of careerism in the sub-Continent. By 1881, the *Warrant of Precedence* identified 77 separate ranks to guide Britons in India in avoiding deference, and to the extent that it was feasible, advancement. As in England, socially ambitious Britons in India worked energetically to gain royal – or viceregal – honours. The senior order, the Order of the Star of India, was conferred upon princes and chiefs of Indian states and senior British civil servants working in India. The junior order, the Order of the Indian Empire, like the Star of India, excluded women. Founded in 1877 as a less exclusive version of the Star of India, the OIE rewarded British and native officials, and was far more widely bestowed.[5] Especially sought-after was the Most Distinguished Order of St. Michael and St. George, founded in 1818 by George, Prince of Wales (later George IV), to honour individuals who rendered important services to the Empire or foreign nations. Sixth among Imperial decorations, the St. Michael and St. George award's device appeared on the viceroy's flag, and receipt of this honour was seen as capstone to a career in Indian service. In the popular culture of British India, the levels of the St. Michael and St. George awards were deemed Companion (CMG – Call Me God), Knight or Dame Commander (KCMG – Kindly Call Me God) and the very top tier, usually reserved for governors, Knight or Dame Grand Cross (GCMG – God Calls Me God).

The vicereines were not without their own honours. Topmost among the "gongs" worn by vicereines on formal occasions was the Order of the Crown of India, created in 1878 in recognition of the Queen's accession as Empress of India, and awarded to every vicereine (and one viceroy's daughter, Emma Baring) thereafter. Ranked 12th among British honours, it carried no title or precedence beyond honourees being permitted to add the letters "CI" after their name. Women eligible for the CI in addition to the vicereine included British princesses, wives and female relatives of Indian princes, and of the governors of Bombay, Madras, and Bengal, the SOSI, and the Commander-in-Chief in India. Vicereines with more personal connections to the monarch (Dufferin, Lansdowne, Irwin and Mountbatten) also received the Order of Victoria and Albert, or the Royal Victorian Order.[6] Ladies Dufferin, Lansdowne, Chelmsford, Reading, Willingdon, and Mountbatten were awarded various classes of the Order of the British Empire, while Ladies Lansdowne, Minto, Irwin, Willingdon, Linlithgow, and Mountbatten were presented with the Most Venerable Order of the Hospital of St. John of Jerusalem for their work with the order's hospitals and ambulance brigades.

Queen Victoria had made St. John's a Royal Order of Chivalry in 1888, in appreciation for its spreading western medical practices throughout the Empire. That royal recognition, along with Hariot Dufferin's scheme to provide female medical aid to Indian women, encouraged wives of senior officials of the *Raj* to become more engaged in health care and medical issues, especially during the world wars. Lady Mountbatten, the vicereine most closely connected to St. John's, was highly visible in her work for that agency in Britain, Europe, and Southeast Asia during World War II, becoming Superintendent-in-Chief of the Nursing Division, the highest post a woman could hold in the Ambulance Brigade.

The most sought-after and prestigious award for women of the *Raj* beyond the traditional British honours was the *Kaisar-i-Hind* medal, created in 1900, officially to recognize outstanding public service in India, but most often given to vicereines or wives of high officials. Only the sovereign could award the first class of the order (gold) while the viceroy could award the second class (silver). Mary Curzon, Winfred Hardinge, Alice Reading, Marie Willingdon, and Doreen Linlithgow received the gold Kaisar-i-Hind, while many Anglo-Indian women received the silver. And while all vicereines modestly declared that such honours were of little importance to them, they never missed an opportunity to display them at official events, despite the damage that the heavy pins and medals often did to expensive gowns.

Those with multiple honours wore each in the proper place on their bosoms or a sash, well aware that any breach of medal etiquette would cause comments and criticism. Most visible was the Crown of India medal, with diamond, pearl, and turquoise jewels of the Queen's cipher ensigned with an enamelled Imperial Crown suspended from a light blue and white watered silk ribbon and worn on the left shoulder, or on the left side of an evening gown.

While rank and title were prime factors in determining precedence in British India, rituals also determined eligibility for access to the viceregal inner keep. When a new viceroy arrived in Calcutta, Delhi or Simla, officials and their wives above a certain level in government or the military would pay a welcoming call on the new viceregal couple and sign a book to confirm that the visit had been made in person. Each day, the Military Secretary carefully checked the signatures to see if anyone had called whose title or position warranted an invitation to an upcoming entertainment or some other response from the viceroy or vicereine. He also had the frustrating job of sorting out constant "scrambles" for tickets to various events, as people attempted to finagle entry into the inner circle. Often the vicereine reviewed the signature book, usually with the MilSec, and decided whether someone outside the normal social order warranted being invited to a function. Invitations might also be extended if a vicereine found someone particularly interesting or charming, but rarely without first verifying that that individual was indeed "worthy" of inclusion in the charmed viceregal circle.

Although the custom of paying a call and signing the book endured into the twilight of the *Raj*, the vicereines gradually extended invitations

to persons other those who had paid formal calls. Lady Mountbatten, who most freely invited new faces to the Viceroy's House, made it clear at the outset that she did not intend to rely on names in "the book" for her invitation lists, but preferred to meet those "…who are really making some contributions to the problems of India, high and low alike."[7] From the beginning of her vicereinal tenure, Lady Mountbatten sought aid from British-Indian women who shared her interests and views on race, to draw up a list of "useful Indian contacts" whom she set about getting to know by organising teas and luncheons.[8]

The displays of ritual and grandeur in viceregal courts, ostensibly in emulation of Mughal pomp and pageantry, increased throughout the last half of the 1800s, and peaked in the early 20th Century, although many of the ceremonies remained almost unchanged until the end of the *Raj*. There were alterations however, as some social customs at the viceregal court waxed and waned from the time Queen Victoria was named Empress of India until the final wave of revolutionary changes instituted by the Mountbattens in 1947.

The progression toward courtly formality had begun with Lord Lytton, who, next to Curzon, was the most concerned of viceroys about rules and behaviour. Somehow, in the midst of overseeing the wars in Afghanistan and dealing with the myriad issues of an expanding Empire, Lytton found time to involve himself in the question of what level of formality was appropriate for a now-Imperial viceregal court. The viceroy was especially frustrated by the variety of costumes worn at court, and most especially by the fact that ladies often appeared without trains on their gowns. In a thinly veiled threat, Lytton told the Queen that unless an official decision enabled him to set some guidelines, he would recommend that they abandon all pretense of court ceremonial "...which ceases to be impressive when it is careless."[9] Lytton was confident that the Queen would come down on his side of the debate, because he knew how strongly she felt about maintaining the proper status of her personal representative in India. The members of the Viceroy's Council, on the other hand, being bureaucrats themselves, were reluctant to impose the cost of special dress require-ments on civil servants.

As rumours of Lytton's request spread, the ladies of the *Raj* were in an uproar at the prospect of having to acquire new gowns to comply with any such order – and not only because of the expense, but also the incon-venience and delay involved in procuring the appropriate garb, making them unable to appear at Government House until the new gowns were ready. In the end, the Queen supported Lytton, and the Lord Chamber-lain's office in London decreed that ladies would wear trains at viceregal evening parties. An editorial in the Calcutta *Statesman* blamed both of the Lyttons for the new dress code, which required an outlay of about Rs 1000 for a man with a wife and two daughters – no small sum, even for a senior government official. As in many other of his actions, Lytton's preference for form over substance increased the negative opinion of many British in India of him and the vicereine. A later decree that made the wearing of trains voluntary failed to repair the damage to the Lyttons' reputation.

Lytton's successor, Lord Ripon strove to minimize his predecessor's grandeur whenever he could and worked with his wife to impart a less imperial feeling at the viceregal court. A true British grandee with vast estates in Yorkshire and Lincolnshire yet a confirmed radical liberal in his politics, Ripon was appalled at the "autocratic rule and regal splendour" of the viceroy's court, which, he wrote to his wife, made him "more radical every day."[10] He was determined to "cut down the swagger" as much as possible by wearing a shooting jacket and dispensing with bodyguards – a fact that caused his wife great anxiety. Despite his committed liberalism, even Ripon saw the importance of his wife's position in British-Indian society. He seriously considered buying Lady Ripon a £2,000 necklace in preparation for her new viceregal role, insisting that he was not becoming "kingly" but was merely ensuring that his beloved wife would not be

The Ripons were less formal and more liberal than any of their viceregal predecessors.

embarrassed by her lack of appropriate jewellry as she reigned over the viceregal court.

Lady Ripon was probably the most openly political of the vicereines, although most of her influence was applied behind the scenes. She unwaveringly supporting her husband's controversial decisions designed to move India toward self-government, and used her intellect and charm to persuade political opponents of the importance of these liberal policies. She felt particularly strongly about the controversial Ilbert Bill, and constantly urged her husband not to waver from his decision. He wrote to a colleague in London: "The Anglo-Indian row has done her a world of good; she is as strong and bold as a lioness and would soon recall me to a proper frame of mind if I were in the least inclined to waver."[11] The Ripons were only marginally successful at reducing the pomp of the viceregal court, but even those who opposed her husband's politics agreed that Lady Ripon had earned good marks as a hostess. She dutifully entertained the "right" people, and her aristocratic demeanour added lustre to the formal rituals of the *Raj*.

The obsession with rank, precedence and court protocol was not limited to men; many vicereines were not shy about insisting on respect for their own exalted position. At all official events and in correspondence, vicereines were referred to as "Her Excellency," even as the viceroy was "His Excellency." Most quickly grew accustomed to the new title, and some relished it, but a few were less than enthused about elevation to that exalted status. Naturally, proponents of formality in the viceregal court were more insistent on its use, like Lady Chelmsford, who insisted that everyone, personal staff included, address her as Her Excellency, as did Lady Reading, although both of the latter's private secretaries, Yvonne Fitzroy and Stella Charnaud (later the second Lady Reading) found her insistence on use of the title in all settings burdensome. Lady Reading's successor, Dorothy Irwin, viewed viceregal protocol as ridiculous: "It also gets on my nerves to be called 'Your Excellency'[12] which I am sure is overdone by the ex-Reading staff. One hardly ever calls the Q and K 'Your Majesty'; it seems to me rather vulgar."[13] Lady Irwin was generally annoyed by the formality imposed on the household by her predecessor and deemed such customs as waiting to be called by an ADC to lunch as unnecessary and yet another cause of the separation she and her husband felt from the staff.

The vicereines were not the only rank-conscious women in British India, but being at the top of the ladder, they had substantial influence on the social order. Over the years, several of them were offended by provincial governors' wives calling themselves "Her Excellency," and sought to end that practice through their husbands. In July, 1922, following the unsuccessful lead of his predecessors Minto, Hardinge, and Chelmsford, Lord Reading advised the SOSI, Lord Peel, that he also objected to the provincial governors' spouses using a title reserved for vicereines and wives of other governors general throughout the Empire. He asked Lord Peel to end this "unauthorised and incorrect practice" and so advise the governors immediately. After months of correspondence on the issue which eventually led to the King's involvement, Peel effected a compromise. The flood of memos and telegrams generated by that seemingly trivial change in protocol reflected the fixation on precedence and title and bureaucratic procedure in the *Raj* even as defeat, humiliation, and extinction loomed on the horizon.

This rigid social system hampered anyone who tried to effect change in the ambiance of the marble palaces in which the viceregal families lived. The early vicereines kept to the traditional role of devoted wife and gracious hostess, entertaining senior government officials and their wives, most of whom they found dull, pretentious, and utterly without charm. Lady Charlotte Canning exemplified appropriate conduct for Victorian women: doing her very best within her tightly circumscribed position in society, dutifully playing that frustrating game while bearing the extra burdens of her husband's marital infidelity and her own infertility. As the experienced wife of a diplomat, she strove to strengthen her position as consort to the viceroy, which had been established by her friend and predecessor, the "exemplary" (and recently deceased) Lady Dalhousie. Relying on her experience as a Lady-in-Waiting to the Queen and her familiarity with the intricacies of royal protocol, Lady Canning tried to introduce some European tone and elegance to brighten up the stilted viceregal ceremonies and social events. Recognising its symbolic and political importance, Charlotte insisted that she and Canning enter ballrooms and the marble halls together, rather than her slipping in through a side door as had been the custom previously. However small that victory, it meant a great deal to Charlotte, for entering on the viceroy's arm not only bolstered her position as vicereine, but also signaled flirtatious women present that despite Charles's wandering eye, *she* was his wife and would remain so.

Although most vicereines lacked the benefit of having served in the royal court, the social skills required at the peak of Indian society were well known to aristocratic women. From childhood onward, members of the British upper class were made familiar with myriad social rules and niceties, and those who ascended to the higher tiers of public and diplomatic service encountered much that they had long been familiar with, albeit now under much greater public and private scrutiny. Vicereines arriving in India with substantial experience in formal entertaining were more able to easily design events and oversee the court's social affair in a way that solidified their positions atop the social heap. However, those lacking such experience quickly made up for their shortcomings.

Neither Alice Reading nor Mary Curzon were raised in the British landed aristocracy, and both felt initially insecure about their ability to hold their own in India's social milieu, yet each managed to overcome their perceived deficiencies. Alice and Rufus Reading, aware that their family background "in trade" and as Jews exposed them to social pressure and invidious comparisons, took ballroom dancing and riding lessons under the logic that these were two of the most visible skills expected of aristocrats. Rufus also sharpened his marksmanship to prepare for going on the hunting expeditions that had become a major part of the annual viceregal tours of princely states. Mary Curzon, in advanced pregnancy during the months before her scheduled departure, read widely about India in books provided by her husband, from Indian history to descriptions of the social demands she could look forward to. While such efforts at expanding their knowledge yielded some benefits, including the approval of British and Indian elites, almost every vicereine was judged by the templates of social skill applied to women of the upper classes throughout the Western world during the last phase of imperialism – personal appearance, charm, social grace, and the capacity to handle both intricate rituals and unexpected situations with aplomb.

The mechanism that supported the vicereine and her husband in their official duties and closely linked social functions was the viceroy's personal staff, which over time would grow to well over a hundred. The viceroy's Military Secretary and his staff were the vicereine's principal guides as she navigated the complex shoals of titles, invitation lists and seating arrangements, and potential missteps. In practical terms, the position of the MilSec, also designated by the acronym MSV, and always a serving officer, was much like that of a feudal seneschal. In essence, his functions encompassed the modern military roles of Headquarters Commandant and aide-de-camp, but with several layers of formal and informal intricacy added on. As the major-domo of the viceregal establishment, the MilSec was responsible for arranging the personal and social life of the viceregal family, as well as official ceremonies. Beyond the substantial burden of dealing with the great tangle of personal and official matters, the MSV's tasks included overseeing some 4,000-plus servants who staffed the various households, the Comptroller of the Household, at least four ADCs, and the viceroy's bodyguard and its officers.[14] Each ADC had specific clusters of responsibilities – invitations and the printing operations, stables, garages, etc. – in addition to planning and assisting at ceremonies and social events. Even after the outbreak of World War II, the MilSec and his staff continued to oversee the administration and staging of viceregal events – investitures, receptions, state visits, banquets, (including one honouring the viceroy that was held at a maharajah's palace), as well as a garden party for 2,000 held in a stadium. The voluminous guidelines included details of how the viceroy and vicereine were to be received at a wedding, and the procedure for their signing the guest book. (One assumes the viceroy and vicereine did not stand in the signing or receiving lines.)

These capable individuals were particularly valuable assistants to the vicereine in essentially private family affairs like weddings. Given the choice, the vicereines preferred to hold their daughters' weddings in London with the attendant glamour and excitement only available in the Imperial capital – pre-wedding parties given by noble friends, and the ceremony itself in either the obligatory St. Margaret's Westminster in London or the church at the family's traditional country seat. A significant downside to that plan was the fact that until the 1920s when home leave was enacted, the viceroy could not attend. This – and the fact that an Indian venue would ensure a significant increase in pageantry – led several viceregal daughters to choose to marry in India. The burden of planning, organization, invitations, transportation, security, as well as the selection of flowers, food, and accommodations for guests all fell to the viceregal staff, under the close and sometimes oppressive supervision of the vicereine. No expense was spared and the similarities to a "real" royal wedding were unmistakable: the magnificent procession to and from the church, with brightly uniformed troops who held back huge crowds eager to catch a glimpse of their rulers in full majesty, the reception at the viceregal residence, with the music of the viceroy's band drifting down from the gallery, and huge urns of flowers decorating the marble halls; and finally, the requisite six-foot-high wedding cake exquisitely designed and prepared by the viceregal bakers towering over the lavish spread of refreshments.

Fortunately for the viceregal staffs, there were only a few such events: Lady Elgin's daughter Bessie was married at Simla in 1898, and the Minto and Lansdowne families were joined by the wedding of Violet Minto to Charles Petty-Fitzmaurice in Calcutta in 1909 – the only marriage between two viceregal families.[15] The cream of British aristocratic society used the Minto wedding as an excuse to escape London's winter gloom and see the subcontinent. Dukes and duchesses, earls and countesses were lavishly entertained by the Mintos before departing to the marble palaces of friendly rajahs and some serious big-game hunting. The last viceregal wedding was that of the Linlithgow's daughter, Lady Anne Hope, who married Lt. P.H.J. Southby, RN in 1939 in New Delhi. A somewhat less lavish but no less carefully orchestrated event than the Mintos', the Linlithgow wedding was rendered all the more poignant by the impending departure of the groom to his wartime duty station.

Each of these family spectacles offered the vicereine the opportunity to shine. All protocol requirements were met thanks to the meticulous planning and support of the viceregal staff, yet with food, decorations and music to remind guests of home, and the inclusion of the "right" Indians for a dash of local colour and culture. The brides however, had to return the lavish gifts proffered by the Indian princes, because government rules forbade the viceroy or his family from accepting anything more than modest tokens of appreciation.

A family wedding may have been rare within the viceregal social calendar, but in these cases, as in all aspects of her life, the vicereine's every decision was likely to be dissected and discussed by Anglo-Indian society, especially those to whom gossip was the staff of life. Like their counterparts at home, most British women in India, aside from nurses, teachers, and a handful of professionals, were primarily involved with their families and social life. In a special irony, the empty time that fuelled their loneliness was widened by the abundance of low-paid Indian servants who tended children and housekeeping, setting the stage for the long, sad days and even emptier hearts that followed their children going off to England for schooling. Although often punctuated by illness, accidents, tragedies, and occasional adventures and misadventures, the daily schedule of *memshabibs* for the most part tended to be grindingly boring. After a brief meeting in the morning to arrange menus, and perhaps a visit with sellers of various goods, they performed such routine tasks as writing invitations and thank-you notes, correspondence, flower arranging, usually in hour or two, leaving the rest of the day open for such pastimes as riding in the cooler hours, sketching, reading, paying calls, a visit to the club, gossip, meetings related to a charity, organising, discussing or planning events, and resting. By the late 19th century, the addition of some athletic activities to their schedule – archery, badminton, croquet, tennis, and golf – provided additional opportunities for social interaction. But even then, the tight constraints of precedence persisted, including such absurd traditions as serving the first shuttlecock in a game of badminton to the senior lady present on the court.

Finding new ways to break the tedium of their daily routine in India challenged the imaginations of men and women alike, especially at Simla and other hill stations where cool weather made activity more comfortable, and stimulated their creative – and often, romantic – impulses. Even before Simla became the summertime seat of the Indian government, it had developed a reputation for being a "fast" society in which grass widows – women whose husbands sent them to the hills while they remained at their posts in the sweltering plains and jungles – engaged in flirtations, or more intense romantic relationships, as Kipling hinted obliquely in his early short stories. Opportunities to spend time with the opposite sex in public without any social onus included treasure hunts, amateur theatricals, a seemingly endless procession of balls – State balls, regimental, fancy dress or costume balls – as well as dinners, garden parties, and receptions. Beyond those were omnipresent horse racing and other equestrian sporting events, most especially gymkhanas – tournaments that included a range of contests like spearing tent-pegs with lances, and steeplechasing.

Naturally enough, the early Victorian vicereines were appalled by Simla's freewheeling atmosphere. Charlotte Canning was revolted by the gossip and rumours arising from the daily promenade along the crowded Mall, and John and Harriette Lawrence, the first viceregal couple to spend a good deal of time at Simla, avoided its many "diversions," although Lady Lawrence's attempts to vary activities by holding Shakespeare readings and arranging *tableaux vivant* met with little success.

Simla's racy reputation seems to have peaked during the Lytton viceroyalty of the late 1870s, when flirtations and gambling became more rule rather than exception. At that time, the artist Val Prinsep[16] described "Simla itself" as "an English watering-place gone mad" where "except for the fact that the people one meets are those who rule and make our history, one could as easily be at Margate."[17] Perhaps Prinsep's perceptions were shaped by his disdain for Lytton's questionable behaviour, and the generally lax social climate which the viceroy tolerated and sometimes seemed to encourage, but Simla's lurid reputation endured long after

Lytton's reign. That led authoress Maud Diver to warn a few years later that the two greatest dangers facing a woman in India were military men away from their wives, and participation in amateur theatricals – both of which were mainstays of Simla's social routine. Some have argued that Simla's reported looseness was exaggerated in historical accounts and gossip alike because the press at the time chose to emphasize trivial aspects of Britons' lives in India. Others have suggested that play tended to trump work during the government's annual deployment to the grandest of all hill stations, and elsewhere as well.

Whatever else was going on, the official functions scheduled by the viceregal court were the first considerations for the Simla social calendar, although other "traditional" events were more greatly anticipated. Among the unique highlights of the Simla season were balls given by The Most Hospitable Order of Knights of the Black Heart, an exclusive society founded in 1891, suspended during the First World War, and re-activated in 1920 to entertain its members and friends. Limited to 24 Knights, Black Heart membership rules provided that candidates "should not be living in open matrimony," which allowed bachelors and "grass widowers" to enter the Order. The Black Hearts became known for their ingenious and enjoyable entertainments, and for the costumes worn at their annual revels which burlesqued the Order of the Bath: full evening dress with knee breeches and black silk stockings, a knee-length scarlet cloak, with Black Heart over the left breast and a red band around the left knee. Grass widower Knights selected when their wives were away were allowed to attend functions when their spouses returned, but in a revised uniform whose red knee-band was replaced by a white one, and without the Order's collar badge, "… for he had lost his Heart."

All three of the Black Hearts' masked balls held during the annual season – one of them a widely renowned fancy dress ball – took place on the tennis court at the United Services Club, which was turned into a gaudily decorated ballroom festooned with Black Hearts decorations and coloured lights. Since romance and entertaining was the Order's *raison d'etre*, secretive sitting areas known as *kala juggas* were sited around the ballroom, wherein young men and women might briefly disappear. The ground-rule provided that once a couple went into one of these niches, they were to be left alone, but not long enough for any serious dalliance, since they were to reappear when the next dance began.

Although vicereines initially made little headway in their head-on attempts to brake the trends toward a certain social looseness – indeed, most eagerly looked forward to the Black Hearts revels, whatever their reputation – the Indian Government's and the viceregal court's summer migration to Simla became increasingly routinised, and regularity allowed morality to gain hold. As vicereines became interested in social welfare efforts, Simla society followed suit, with wives and daughters of senior officials of the *Raj* engaging in such respectable activities as the formation and support of charitable societies, mission work, and fine art exhibitions, as well as more athletic pursuits. Although the "daily doings" of the viceregal court remained a prime focus of interest among women who met along the Mall, as time passed, Simla society became as decorous and proper as other British communities in India, with a full schedule of proper activities filling up the bright cool days and brisk evenings.

Whether in Simla, Calcutta, Delhi, or Barrackpore, vicereines not actively engaged in childbearing or child rearing were as eager as anyone in British India to create or take part in diversionary entertainments. Most were accustomed to the lively, less rigid social atmosphere of the upper classes in Britain – compared to India, at least – where witty conversation in elegant surroundings was an ideal if not universal practice. As noted earlier, several vicereines had aided their husbands' diplomatic careers by artfully applying their social skills in highly formal settings, and expected to do so in India. But most were dismayed when they found themselves enmeshed in a parody of high society whose rituals were basically familiar, but very different in tone from their prior experience. Most quickly came to terms with the demands of viceregal entertaining, and some were stimulated by the constant social whirl and throngs invited to major events. What never really changed was how boring and isolated British Indian society was.

Even the usually upbeat and lively Mary Minto was initially overwhelmed by loneliness and tedium:

Letters are brought in from the ADC's saying they await my commands – at present I have none to give them. Apparently in future I shall have to send for anyone I may wish to see, as no one intrudes upon the sacred presence uninvited. I am bound to say a deep depression has taken possession of my soul!"[18]

Lady Minto's dismay at the parochial formality of the viceregal court was especially surprising in view of her earlier performance as wife of the Governor General of Canada which was marked by her imposition of what she saw as proper levels of order and decorum after the somewhat less rigid social regime of her predecessor, the Countess of Aberdeen. She purged the Aberdeens' guest lists, demanded strict observance of precedence and court etiquette, curtailed what she saw as excessive entertainments, and insisted on strict punctuality, thus terrorising many guests who feared that they might violate one of her rules. By the time she got to India,

Lady Minto had developed a more relaxed view of viceregal protocol, and proved one of the most popular and best-loved of all vicereines.

But however charming and polite most aristocratic vicereines were in public, and gracious as hostesses, in private they felt superior to most of the women – and men – with whom they came in contact, very few of whom were "people like us." The British elite strata in India – officials, military and civilian, and their spouses – was overwhelmingly recruited from the middle and upper middle class, with a sprinkling of peers drawn to careers in the sub-continent by the romance of the region, a thirst for adventure, the lure of financial opportunity, or because they had no meaningful prospects at home. For the most part, wives mirrored their husbands' values and personalities, balancing dangers and discomforts against living in an exotic domain in which their roles were clearly defined and might be enhanced by their husband's rising to higher administrative rank. A poem published in the 1920s encapsulated the *memsahibs'* social aspirations:

> *If I was Mrs.What's-her-name*
> *I would, I would, I would –*
> *I'd get my husband made a K*
> *And see the Viceroy every day*
> *I would I would I would.*[19]

Despite the drawbacks of being surrounded by an abundance of low-paid servants as noted earlier, that and relatively good pay gave most memsahibs a lifestyle closer to the aristocracy at home than to the social strata from which most of them came. Even hostesses married to officials of lower rank were able to station turbaned servants behind each chair at an eight-course dinner party, or arrange elaborate picnics with rugs, chairs, cushions, hampers of food, and stoves – whatever the *sahibs* and *memsahibs* desired – brought to the site and returned with minimum fuss.

There were, of course, limits to those benefits and advantages. Emulating what one perceived as the manners and graces of the aristocracy did not an aristocrat make, nor make possible scintillating conversation in a society in which the topics discussed among the upper crust were limited in range and depth. After years in British embassies abroad and within the British royal household as a lady-in-waiting, Charlotte Canning found Calcutta society excruciatingly dull, far more than she had expected. It was a world in which she noted "dinner parties are to be endured rather than enjoyed." Widely known to be a lively and charming conversationalist, Lady Canning tried in vain to draw her guests out of themselves, and was stunned to find that no one seemed to want to talk to her. Eventually, she realised that everyone, especially the women, became shy and even tongue-tied in the vicereine's presence, and were intimidated by her well-informed and intelligent conversation. In the end, she recognised that there was really no cure for that malaise.

Lady Edith Lytton also tried to liven things up by receiving callers in the afternoon, thus attracting gentlemen as well as ladies, "who seem to be a better type..." perhaps not recognising that only men of the upper hierarchy could manage to break free from work for such gatherings. She wrote to her sister that she couldn't imagine ever being popular in British-Indian society: "The ladies are not at all my type, either dowdy or fast."[20] Nevertheless, she sought opportunities to see English women of the lower social echelons, like nurses, soldiers' wives, and missionaries, trying to leaven her ritualised social activities with something more meaningful. "One loves to see all one's countrywomen so far away in India... nice English nurses so full of courage and cheerful patience," she wrote. Breaking with protocol, Lady Lytton invited soldiers' wives and children to a grand fête at Government House, serving the women tea in the imposing marble hall and offering games, presents, and balloons to the children in the garden. At the same time, she found it difficult to make friends or even enjoy balls; no one asked her to dance except for the "official" quadrilles, so she spent most evenings alone seated in a recessed corner of the ballroom.

Although Edith understood that it was her position and not her personality that kept people at a distance, she found the situation unpleasant, since she had always found it easy to mix and make friends at functions in her husband's earlier diplomatic posts. Lady Lytton's efforts at implementing changes were hampered significantly by her husband's instituting bold and controversial exceptions to established social practices. Soon after arriving in India, as he began altering points of protocol and ritual, Lytton was quickly labelled an eccentric by Anglo-Indian society. That wave of hostility put the vicereine in the uncomfortable position of trying to play the role of social buffer when Lytton steered outside the bounds, like his upsetting Calcutta worthies by writing private notes to his Council members, smoking cigars between courses at dinner, or sprawling on the viceregal throne during levées (few knew that his recumbancy was dictated by painful hemmorhoids.) Lytton's private calls on the wives of government officials, also much resented, were consistent with a reputation for flirting that preceded him to India.

Anglo-Indians were further disconcerted by the Viceroy's introducing evening rather than daytime levées. All of these audacious moves exacerbated Lady Lytton's relationship with Anglo-Indian society. Their pity for a slighted wife combined with their reluctance to interact with the vicereine on the more casual basis she sought further isolated Edith, and made her reign even more difficult.

Even the outgoing and vivacious Hariot Dufferin described Anglo-Indian society as "...the most difficult of all the societies I have ever had to do with."[21] She, too, found it nearly impossible to get to know people when social convention demanded only that they come to the viceregal residence, write their names in "the book," and leave. To rectify the situation, Hariot established "at homes" from 12 until 2 o'clock two days a week, at which callers were expected to enter and visit, not just sign in. But that attempt to open things up could not remedy the dearth of conversational topics and lucidity. Any discussion of religion was out of bounds, and vicereines avoided politics, literature, or the arts except when talking with social equals or close friends. Nearly every male whom the vicereine met worked for her husband, and every woman was the wife, daughter, or sister of a member of the viceroy's government or staff at some level. That left children, servants, and the weather as acceptable topics for casual chats. As a result, conversations were generally terse, vapid, and uneasy in spite of the vicereine's attempts to put her guests at their ease.

Large public events were often the most boring. Since no conversation was required at formal drawing rooms or levees, they required little effort from the vicereines beyond the raw stamina needed to stand and smile for hours as hundreds of ladies being presented filed past and curtseyed before the viceroy and vicereine. Other public events like state dinners were even more trying, particularly the practice of ADCs bringing guests up to the viceregal throne to be introduced – a custom which lasted until the Linlithgow viceroyalty. Every three minutes, a "suitable" person or couple was brought forward and introduced, followed by stilted and awkward conversation, then a curtsey or bow, after which the victim was led away, to be replaced by yet another equally nervous guest.[22] In an attempt to make guests feel that they received special viceregal attention at these large events, Edith Lytton began the practice of circumnavigating the room in one direction, the viceroy in another, speaking to each person in turn, a time-consuming and less than satisfactory activity, especially in view of the viceroy's proclivities for flirting with pretty women and being rude to older and less attractive female guests. Even a "small" dinner could mean that the vicereine would be introduced to several dozen people, and after making constant conversation during dinner, then be required to privately visit for a few minutes with each lady present afterwards.

However demanding the social calendar, few if any excuses for the vicereine's absence from a formal function were acceptable. They understood that they were to be present – and charming – at all official gatherings, however they might be feeling, or whatever was happening in their personal lives. As royal representatives, they were not allowed to display human fallibility or weakness; they were the living symbols of British imperial sovereignty, and symbolism was the currency of their realm. Late pregnancy, recovery from childbirth, or major surgery were the only excuses deemed acceptable for their absence; "minor" health ailments or overpowering heat and humidity were not.

In addition to the rote learning of and adhering to accepted social norms, and dealing with great numbers of people whom she found uninteresting, a vicereine also had to consider the complex political, religious and cultural implications of her decisions and actions. She alone got credit or blame for the social atmospherics of the viceregal court, with every element – guest list, wardrobe and jewelry, table arrangements and menus – critically reviewed by those attending a particular occasion – and even more so by those who were not included. Major viceregal entertainments such as state dinners, garden parties, levées, and drawing rooms were covered extensively by the press, and their reports, albeit formalistic, superficial and self-censored, were closely read by the British Indian community.

Many formal rituals remained basically unchanged from the 1870s to the 1930s. Lady Linlithgow's description of a mid-1930s investiture for the Order of the Star of India was almost exactly the same as that recorded in the diaries of Ladies Dufferin and Minto. Some 400 people were invited to the ceremony , which was preceded by a "small" dinner in the elegant columned dining room of the Viceroy's House in New Delhi of a hundred or so guests to fete the evening's honorees and other special invitees. After dinner, the guests joined those less-privileged folk who had been invited only to the ceremony in the Durbar Hall to await the arrival of Their Excellencies. At precisely 9:45, a trumpet fanfare signaled the beginning of the ceremony, and Lord and Lady Linlithgow were led into the hall by the viceroy's senior staff wearing full dress scarlet and gold uniforms. The viceroy wore a Privy Councillor's uniform and the pale blue velvet mantle of the Order. Lady Linlithgow's simple gown of white satin was enhanced by her Crown of India medal, a diamond tiara and necklace; an ermine trimmed velvet mantle like her husband's fell from her shoulders. The viceregal trains were carried by young Indian princes in bejeweled turbans, with large gems sparkling on their fingers and ears, and whose satin coats and trousers in pale blue satin matched the Order's colour. The Linlithgows' height – both were over six feet tall – added further to their impressive and regal appearance. As protocol prescribed, they moved slowly down the centre of the room without acknowledging the curtsies and bows of the crowd, to sit up their huge gold and scarlet-cushioned thrones while the young princes carefully arranged their trains. When the investiture of some sixty-six Britons and Indians was completed close to 11 p.m., the procession reformed and the Linlithgows left the hall, hand-in-hand, to the accompaniment of the National Anthem. Such splendid ceremonies, deemed by many observers the equal of those held at Buckingham Palace, reinforced, as it was supposed to, it the "royal" aura of the viceregal court.

A good part of the fascination of media accounts and accompanying illustrations – and later photographs – of viceregal ceremonies was the exotic texture, especially the images of Indian rulers and their entourages. Since most Indians were prohibited by religious custom from dining with Westerners, they either ate separately, or more often, joined dinner parties, balls, and other official events later in the evening after banquets ended. The viceregal court provided a safe setting for British Indian society to mingle with aristocratic Indians, and offered the British glimpses of their hidden life. In this comfortable, safe little world in which the rules of contact were clearly laid out, British women could smile graciously at the princes and make polite conversation, while studying the details of elaborate silk or satin costumes, counting ropes of pearls, and estimating the carats of huge emeralds, sapphires, rubies, and diamonds on the Indian notables' fingers or headdresses, or around their waists, knees, ankles, and wrists. These spectacles provided grist for the next day's gossip to regale friends and acquaintances not fortunate enough to have been invited to that particular event. On these occasions, the vicereine's manner of greeting and conversing with local rulers and dignitaries set the benchmark for the European ladies watching how she approached each one, and following her lead. It was readily clear that more senior and "Westernised" rulers received a warmer and effusive greeting than those of lesser ilk and status, and those whose policies and behaviour had displeased the *Raj*.

Early in her reign, Hariot Dufferin established the custom of going to meet with any rulers invited to a viceregal function, but who for reasons of religion or caste declined to dine with the rest of the party. The rajahs and princes were charmed at this special attention from the vicereine, which she used as an opportunity to discuss her female medical "scheme." At one such event at Barrackpore in January 1886, the Maharajah of Durbungha told Hariot he would build and fund a female dispensary if Lady Dufferin would come and lay the foundation stone. She quickly agreed ("...it is only 20 hours away, a mere nothing") and did as she promised. Hariot's success set a precedent; from her reign forward the vicereines often used gala occasions to raise funds for their particular charity, exploiting the eagerness of some potentates to gain the viceroy's favour by urging them to subscribe to one or another of the vicereine's pet charities. The pledge of a few thousand rupees guaranteed at least a modicum of her attention, and a warmer reception from other ladies involved with the vicereine's cause.

Given all such complicated rituals and the established routine of the court, even the most energetic vicereine found the social whirl punishing. In the few months that viceroy and vicereine spent in Calcutta each year – December to February or March – they held a long series of grand occasions and entertainments which might include a state dinner and evening party, a garden party, a dance every fortnight, a drawing room, a levee, an investiture or two, a weekly dinner for up to 120 people, and several smaller dinners or lunches each week, in addition to dining out with important dignitaries. As suggested previously these were also the months when guests usually arrived from Europe, putting an ongoing stress on the viceregal household and staff.

Official functions that brought large numbers of guests to the viceregal residence were not, strictly speaking, the vicereine's responsibility. Each was organised according to well-established rules of protocol by the MilSec and his staff, which allowed her to focus on her principal concerns: her appearance and maintaining the stamina she required to endure hours of standing in a receiving line and making polite conversation. Despite the support and guidance provided by the MilSec, the vicereine was still the hostess, and had to be alert for any missteps or breaches of protocol. Those vicereines who developed a trusting relationship with the MilSec were the most successful. The combination of an experienced political hostess with the protocol expertise and ability to execute complex rituals was invaluable, and the vicereines who had the best reputations enjoyed that kind of close working partnership.

The most elaborate and ornamented costumes were *de rigeur* for investitures and other evening events – a tiara was an absolute must, except during the last half of World War II – while garden parties and daytime occasions required less formal, but still eye-catching dresses and hats. Details of the vicereine's costumery were usually adumbrated in the press, even if no reporters were present. Guests commonly described her gowns and jewels to friends at length (and sometimes to the press) to demonstrate their inclusion in the charmed viceregal circle, and build credits with the fourth estate. Throughout the century of viceregality, as styles changed, extravagance remained the central motif, and continued to fascinate newspaper reporters and readers alike. Alice Reading's appearance at a state ball in a magnificent dress of soft gold tissue fabric, shot through with mauve, and embroidered with real gold thread was the topic of conversation for days, mainly because it was reported that both the gold and the embroidery had been a gift of the Nawab of Rampur.

As the viceroy and vicereine stood together in the limelight while being honoured or hosted by Indian rulers, they frequently found themselves overwhelmingly upstaged in respect to their dress, decorations and jewelry. Throughout the days of the *Raj*, Indian potentates maintained grand residences at Simla (and later in Delhi) in which they often entertained the social upper crust of British India. These major establishments demonstrated their loyalty to the *Raj* and desire to be included in Indian high society, and more and more provided them with their own stage on which they could display their "British" traits.

One such event was a ball given for the Mayos by the Maharajah of Jaipur at the Assembly Rooms, a British government building complex at Simla on September 6, 1869. The occasion was described extensively in the *Illustrated London News*, its correspondent listing the splendid decorations worn by luminaries, the gowns and jewels worn by the vicereine and other ladies, and praising the Maharajah's dancing ability. The Assembly Rooms were transformed for the occasion, the *ILN* reported, with the main stage turned into a dais with a throne for the viceroy, large mirrors, lounges, and rich carpeting, while a nearby supper room for some 200 guests was draped in pink and white. The band of the 41st Regiment of Foot provided dance music, while the viceroy's band rendered martial salutes during the viceregal arrival and departure.[23] A heavy mountain rainstorm broke out, but did not deter guests from attending, nor did it douse the thousands of iron braziers placed along the two miles between Peterhof and the Assembly Rooms.

The Maharajah had the honour of partnering Lady Mayo in the opening quadrille, having been under "terpsichorean instruction" for the past week that enabled him to "acquit himself remarkably well, though somewhat stiffly." His ability to put on his white kid gloves "without the slightest hurry" was noted, as was his moving through the five figures of the quadrille without error. To the strains of "The Roast Beef of Old England," the company moved into an extravagant supper at half-past twelve, served up "in excellent style," after which Lord and Lady Mayo were accompanied by the Maharajah to the outer doors of the Assembly Rooms, departing with the customary viceregal honours.[24]

While reporting such details of viceregal activities was common, even for private functions, society writers paid especially close attention to entertainments planned for the viceroys' aristocratic and royal visitors, recounting who was invited to dine with a duke and duchess, who played polo with a prince, and which ladies accompanied the vicereine on a late afternoon carriage ride. And yet whatever pain the transient royalty atop what was essentially an *haute bourgeois* pyramid in India might suffer, it was more symbolic than actual. Their real and alleged missteps might be grist for the rumour and journalistic mills, and serve to puncture the bubble of their reputations, but none was sent home for social *faux pas*, however humiliated they might be by a particular gaffe.

Entertaining – and being entertained by – Indians was a particular challenge for the vicereines. In the aftermath of the Indian Mutiny, most British women in the subcontinent spent most of their time within their gated and guarded compounds, limiting their contacts with Indian men or women. In fact, there was always limited contact between the vicereines and the regional rulers during the annual viceregal fall tours, but again, like so much that surrounded the vicereines, such interaction was carefully regulated (for the comfort of both sides) and minimal. So little had changed by 1877 that the appearance of Lady Edith Lytton and her daughters at the great Imperial Assemblage in front of the native princes generated considerable interest – and some disapproval – among the British in India. Even 19 years on, the threat of a recurrence of the Great Mutiny haunted the *Raj* – and would do so to the end of British rule. That anxiety was compounded by the fear of the influence of the sensuality of Indian culture, and, as in all European and American overseas possessions, by growing awareness of how diseases were spread. As most British women isolated themselves, they came to view Indian women – even those of the highest caste and aristocratic rank – as one with those of the "lower orders," with whom they had little in common, and could never be real friends.

Nevertheless, some tentative and cautious contacts between Indian and British women began during the Cannings' post-Mutiny tour of 1859 that was intended to reinforce British suzerainty. Lady Canning established the custom of going to see the women of the *zenanah* in the palaces that she and the viceroy visited, although the language barrier along with the restrictions of *purdah* generally made such visits uncomfortable for guests and hostesses. While such visits and tours of girls' schools or the few existing women's hospitals soon became an integral part of viceregal tours, broader social contact with Indian women remained limited until the 1880s when Hariot Dufferin made a concerted effort to improve medical care for women. Her natural curiosity and energy combined with her determination to fathom the complex problems of providing health care led her to seek out opportunities to meet with and learn from Indian women.

Despite her bold and thrustful approach, Lady Dufferin was careful to stay within the boundaries of Indian mores as she began to contact both Muslim and Hindu women. She evoked the "common bond of womanhood" to justify her Association's work and her increased involvement with Indian women that led to increased social interaction in the field of health care years that followed. While viceregal protocol and British security concerns usually trumped social concern, Lady Dufferin was able to capitalize on the trends in medicine and sanitation that highlighted the link between maintaining the health of Indians and Britons in urging more substantive contact between European and Indian women. Most importantly, she got the ball rolling which many of her successors gave a further kick downfield, as they sought to improve the welfare of Indian women, and used their position to gain insights into women's lives and to encourage progress in education, medical care, and eventually, politics. While no vicereine would have been categorised as a feminist, several did speak out on the need for Indian women to be treated more equitably and play a more active role in public affairs. Their increasing contacts with Indian women led them to understand, if not fully appreciate, the grim conditions in which these women had to operate. Although such efforts highlighted the double bind of the *Raj* striking a pose of steward and beneficent overlord while exploiting India, improving education and health care for women and children were relatively non-controversial vicereinal platforms.

By the 1920s and '30s, the vicereines met prominent Indian women regularly, as the latter assumed leadership positions in charitable organizations formerly held by Indian men. They became increasingly comfortable with these relationships, and some, like Lady Mountbatten, formed close friendships with women who would later become important political and social leaders.

Despite the gradual thaw in the relationship between British and Indian women over the years, most of the social barriers between rulers and ruled remained in place until the final years of the *Raj*. Since both Hindu and Muslim tenets forbade women from publicly participating in official ceremonies or entertainments, the most common social gathering for women was the "*purdah* party." One such event in March 1909, at which Mary Minto was the honoured guest, was described in great detail by the Calcutta *Statesman*. That party, given by Mrs. Zahid Suhrawardy at her Calcutta home, was the first time that a vicereine met with such a diverse gathering of women – Muslim, Hindu and European – outside a viceregal residence. Mary was accompanied by her daughter Lady Eileen Elliot, and Lady Baker, wife of the Lieutenant Governor of Bengal, all attired in cool linen afternoon dresses and wide-brimmed flower-bedecked hats, topped by matching parasols to ward off the heat of the Calcutta spring. The guests included the Maharanis of Cooch Behar, Mourbhanj, and Nattore, young princesses from Oudh and Mysore, wives of senior British officials, and Cornelia Sorabji, a well-known lawyer and advocate for the interests of women property holders who lived in *purdah*.

As with all viceregal social events, the agenda was formal and carefully timed. The vicereine's carriage arrived promptly at 5: 30 p.m, when the hostess escorted her honoured guest behind the *purdah* walls to a gold embroidered *shamiana* supported by silver pillars. Lady Minto was led to the omnipresent viceregal throne where she received bouquets from the young princesses, and listened intently as Mrs. Suhrawardy gave an address. The hostess expressed her thanks that the "august consort and daughter of the Representative of the Emperor of India, had seen fit to come to this unique gathering of "…princesses of houses once Imperial and royal, descendants of the Emperors of Delhi, the Kings of Oudh…" and other sultans and nawabs, and to honour the distinguished heritage they represented.

Mrs. Sahrawardy went on to extol the work of the Ladies Branch of the National Indian Association (which would later meld with the Congress Party) and express her regret that many Indian women could not participate in many of its activities due to religious constraints, which made this gathering even more important. She concluded by thanking Lady Minto once again for coming and for her "deep and active sympathy…connected with the welfare and advancement of the womankind of India." Lady Minto, in her formal reply reprinted in the *Statesman*, thanked her "sisters and friends" for their warm welcome and generous hospitality, and expressed her appreciation of their proud heritage. Acknowledging the "powerful influence" that the women of India had on private and public affairs, the vicereine also stated that cultural differences between the British and the Indians "are not so great as to keep us altogether apart." In conclusion, she expressed her gratitude for the latter's willingness to bring their nfluence to bear on behalf of "the highest and purest interests of your own country," and promised to carry their message to the viceroy, and through him, to the King and Queen.

Following the custom at such gatherings, Mrs. Suhrawardy's address had been illuminated and printed on white silk, and after being signed by many of the women who attended, it was placed in an ivory casket by the Begum of Murshidabad and presented to Lady Minto, who then spent time walking among the guests, silently marveling at their gorgeous costumes and splendid jewels. When it was over, the vicereine and her party went off in their carriage, leaving the media to lay forth impressions of the event. The *Indian Mirror*, for example, described the gathering as "one of the most unique and interesting social functions ever held in the metropolis," and praised the National Indian Association for its leadership in encouraging "excellent opportunities of social intercourse between European and Indian ladies." It was, the correspondent for the *Indian Mirror* averred, another example of "the modern spirit" among women of all nationalities. The vicereine – "the highest and most honoured lady of the land – received effusive thanks for her "unsparing efforts to ameliorate the condition of Indian womanhood."[25]

A similar but less formal event hosted by Lady Reading in 1921 revealed how slight a change had taken place in social relations between European and Indian women in the intervening 12 years. Her gathering, held at the Viceregal Lodge in Simla, was also an afternoon tea. In a letter to her daughter-in-law, Alice described how the "Hindoo" [sic] ladies remained behind a screen eating the fruit and sweets that had been brought by their servants, along with plates and cups to be used by the ladies only. When the Begum of Bhopal[26] arrived swathed in a "partly *purdah*" costume topped with a small crown of magnificent diamonds, the vicereine realised why the Indian ladies had strongly suggested that she too wear a tiara, even though the event was taking place at four o'clock in the afternoon.

After the refreshments, the ladies walked to another secluded location to view a film – specially selected by the vicereine – that stressed the importance of regular health care for children. Many had never seen a film before, and in an effort to be sociable, sat with their backs to the screen, worried that their hostess would think them rude otherwise. She asked several of her Indian guests to explain that the movie was intended for their entertainment, but they found it difficult to explain the concept behind a movie, so the film's message was lost on many of the guests.

Purdah parties were one of the few occasions where the vicereine was really on her own as a hostess, although in most cases, wives of senior administrators who had more experience in this complex and delicate arena usually provided assistance. These events, offering the rare chance for vicereines to meaningfully connect with Indian women, were always well attended. Few Indians resisted the lure of a viceregal invitation, but the contacts made were generally superficial, and rarely forged substantive links, as Lady Reading learned in 1925 when she opened a Social and Health Centre for Purdah Ladies in Delhi City to instruct women in sewing and knitting, and expand their capacity and inclination to do something for themselves beyond tending their children. By this time, the vicereine had spent considerable time with Indian women, working with them on health and welfare projects, and entertaining them regularly at the viceregal residence, so she anticipated that many would attend the opening of this important centre. But she was stunned and disappointed when none of the women whom she had met or whom the Centre was intended to serve showed up. Instead, they were represented by their husbands, fathers and/ or brothers. The only Indian woman present was the wife of one of the speakers, Mr. Sultan Singh, who celebrated the example his wife had set by freeing herself from the burdens of *purdah,* especially he said, "in this most conservative of cities."[27]

New rules: entertaining excess in the High Raj

Although the vicereines were able to some extent to fine-tune their entertainments when hosting groups of Indian women or other non-official gatherings, they were less successful in recalibrating protocol details which had remained in place long after they had any real significance. One such long-standing tradition, established in 1905 by Lord Minto (at his wife's urging), was that of ladies curtseying individually as they left the dining room after dinner. At the close of the meal, the viceroy would rise from his seat, followed by all the men. First the vicereine and then the ranking female guest rose and walked to the doorway, then turned and curtseyed to the viceroy, who returned the courtesy with the proscribed court bow, from the neck only. (The ability to execute this maneuver gracefully was much admired, and Hariot Dufferin's manner of holding her torso rigid while making a low and sweeping curtsey was recollected for years throughout British India.) As every other woman then followed suit, regardless of age or infirmity, the ADCs of the Reading era staved off boredom by placing bets on which elderly women's knees would crack noisily while curtseying. Despite the discomfiture of many female guests, this archaic custom was still in place in 1925 despite efforts by the acting viceroy, Lord Lytton, son of the earlier viceroy, who had urged Lord Irwin to do away with the post-dinner curtsey, deeming it a "a dreadful formality…which ruins all viceregal parties." Ultimately, Lord Irwin was able to introduce the practice of the British royal court, with curtseys required only of ladies seated on either side of the ruler at dinner, but only after personally presenting that change to George V, since the monarch's approval was required to modify any detail in protocol or ceremony pertaining to his chief Indian representative.

Beyond all the rituals and rules that applied at a particular time in the evolution of the *Raj* over nearly a century, each vicereine's personality and social skills also shaped viceregal life. Edith Lytton, the first who attempted to put her own stamp on entertaining, introduced the use of several small round tables at dinner parties in Simla to encourage conversation, a practice she had found highly successful in earlier diplomatic posts. A talented musician as well as an artist, Lady Lytton regularly attended public concerts, and liked to play duets and sing with or accompany those who performed at her dinner parties. She also encouraged theatricals both at Peterhof and at the Gaiety Theatre through the Simla Amateur Dramatic Society, with casts made up of officers and their wives or sweethearts, or anyone who wanted to act.

From the late 1800s onward, as elsewhere in the Empire, amateur theatricals became a craze in Simla, and a mainstay of the social season. Acting at Simla became so respectable that in 1910, when Lady Eileen Elliot, one of three beauteous viceregal daughters, took part in a melodrama, she received rave reviews in the newspapers and her performance was said to have brought tears to the eyes of Lord Kitchener and the Maharajah of Scindia. Complications ensued as it became apparent that Eileen had caught the acting bug, and when the family returned home, she announced her intent to go on the stage, a career her father successfully discouraged.[28]

Nor did Lady Lytton's other attempts to raise the tone of society in the summer capital fare so well. During her first season in the mountains, she was especially miffed when only 250 of 300 people invited showed up for a ball, and the others sent no regrets, and by the time supper was served in a *shamiana* on the lawn, only 200 remained. She wrote to her sister, the Marchioness of Waterford, of the contrast between Anglo-Indian society and that at home: "...so vulgar, [the people] so cold, so flat, and dancing so badly....it will be *so* difficult to congregate with them often."[29]

Although she felt herself unsuccessful, Lady Lytton's attempts to instill more decorum did in fact begin the gradual trend toward a more formal viceregal court at Simla. Lord Curzon, who shared her low opinion of the "quality" of most members of Simla society, strove to raise the level of pomp and ceremony at Viceregal Lodge, aiming at a summer capital with the same level of protocol (and work schedule) as in Calcutta. He increased the servant staff to 400, roughly the same number at the much larger viceregal establishment in Bengal, considering that level of support as the minimum need for him to maintain headway against a torrent of work while maintaining an exhausting social schedule.

Curzon, not his wife, also revised the etiquette for Simla's garden parties, which, not surprisingly, made more demands on Lady Curzon's time and stamina than on his. Under the new ground-rules, the vicereine would arrive and receive guests as they were announced by an ADC, to the accompaniment of the Viceroy's Band. Much later in the schedule than under the previous arrangements, Curzon would enter to the strains of the National Anthem, always wearing a frock coat and top hat. Walking through the crowd, stiffly acknowledging greetings, he proceeded to the *shamiana*, where he and his wife took their seats on large, throne-like chairs. Once the Curzons were enthroned, the crowd was then free to resume visiting, eating and drinking while the band played softer, less martial music. At some point, Lady Curzon would leave the tent and walk among the guests, chatting graciously, quietly enjoying their evident admiration for her ever-exquisite costumery,[30] and trying in vain to turn their attention from the fact that the viceroy had left as soon as he possibly could. Although many saw his quick exits as him simply avoiding his social obligations, some more familiar with the practical side of viceroyalty excused him, aware of his grinding workload, and a few were aware of his severe back ailment, and the corset he wore to alleviate the pain which made standing for long periods pure agony.

Not all of the viceroys and vicereines saw these entertainment obligations as burdensome. The gregarious Lord Dufferin thoroughly enjoyed the social interaction that Curzon hated. Well-grounded in the court manners and life (he wrote the most flowery and complimentary letters to the Queen of any Viceroy), Dufferin was also widely viewed as an intellectual lightweight, and lazy. Although he and Lady Dufferin saw viceroyalty as tremendously hard work, many in India and England faulted his lack of interest in policy and administration, which he tended to pass off or to leave to others.

Beyond his administrative failings, Dufferin thoroughly enjoyed the social aspects of his role that brought him in contact with attractive women. While he was devoted to Hariot, he also missed the elegant charm and clever conversation of women he had met in his earlier diplomatic posts, and shared most viceregal couples' views about the shortcomings of those "in society" in India. Determined to find some way to enjoy viceregal events, he briefed his staff on how he wished ceremonial functions to be conducted and how his guests should be attended to. "I want you to quite understand," he said, "that I expect you to devote your energies to the elderly ladies. You need not trouble about the young and pretty ones. I will look after them myself!"[31]

The Dufferins' reign sparkled in the realm of social affairs, in good part due to the fact that Lady Dufferin enjoyed her husband's full confidence and support. Dufferin appreciated her skill in organising parties and never failed to praise the care she took with her appearance. "Oh, Lal, how well that gown becomes you! How beautiful you look tonight!" was his typical welcome when his wife entered the room, whether dressed for a family dinner or a viceregal investiture. Over the years of her marriage, Hariot's intelligence, quick wit, and unceasing curiosity about the world she inhabited had enabled her to develop a personal style which overcame her quiet upbringing in the Irish countryside, and an innate shyness. Dufferin fostered and encouraged her evolution into a polished and gracious diplomatic wife, and one day proudly told his eldest son, "The King of Greece told his sister that there was no lady in Europe who could enter a room like Lady Dufferin."[32]

Lady Dufferin set standards that future vicereines followed to varying degrees of success. Often called the "perfect vicereine," her personality and charm served her well in social settings, and especially in her groundbreaking charity work. Her reputation for grace and dignity remained unrivaled through all the days of the *Raj* in good part because she shared her husband's enjoyment of ceremonial as well as social aspects of viceregal life, especially those occasions which called for enthronement, since both delighted in being escorted to gold and velvet thrones and presiding over official ceremonies and on tour, being surrounded by scarlet-clad attendants bearing peacock fans and the other emblems of their exalted position. In keeping with the spirit of conspicuous consumption, Lady Dufferin routinely ordered new gowns from Paris to avoid being seen as repeating her fashion statements. While the Dufferins' entertainments in Calcutta and Simla exceeded those of their predecessors in scale and cost, they also charmed almost everyone they met, and Lady Dufferin's ability to break through the shyness and apprehension of women in receiving lines was especially appreciated by the *memsahibs*. In the way of another asset, the Dufferins' children added further glamour to the viceregal court: three attractive daughters, the Ladies Helen, Hermione, and Victoria Blackwood were with the Dufferins for most of their tenure and their handsome son Archie, a serving officer, and his other brothers visited when they could.

As vicereine, Lady Dufferin enjoyed the support of an especially efficient Military Secretary, Lord William Beresford, and his staff of capable ADCs. Beresford, a charming Irishman, was an aristocrat – the son of the Marquess of Waterford – and had won the Victoria Cross in the Zulu wars. He became Dufferin's MilSec after serving as ADC to viceroys Lytton and Ripon, and remained in that role through the Lansdowne administration. Hariot had great respect and personal affection for Beresford, and his attention to detail: "From the highest military affairs in the land to a mosquito inside my Excellency's curtain or a bolt on my door…he does all equally well," wrote Hariot. [33]

She took special pride in devising party themes to amuse her fun-loving husband who enjoyed parties so much that Hariot often found it difficult to pull him away at the proper moment, reinforcing the belief in British India that he really wasn't all that interested in his viceregal duties. Whatever gossip-mongers may have surmised, protocol was changed so that guests could leave social events before the viceregal couple retired, although few took advantage of it because they were having such a good time. The viceroy was equally at home at outdoor social events, played excellent tennis, and enjoyed pig-sticking and tiger shooting, while Lady Dufferin satisfied her longing for outdoor experiences in camping "expeditions" with her daughter outside Simla. She quickly discovered that camping had a different meaning for a vicereine: "We have tried hard to see wherein lies the roughing it," she wrote, and "can only discover that we have had to do without champagne and without cheese and that for three days out of five we have had no coffee after dinner."[34]

Lady Dufferin and the able Beresford were literally immersed in viceregal entertaining. As Hariot noted in her diary for 1887, during one Simla season, the Dufferins had held 54 separate functions: 12 "big dinners" for up to 50 guests; 29 "small dinners" for six to 15 people; a state ball, a fancy dress ball, a children's fancy dress ball, six other dances for 250 guests each, two garden parties, and two evening parties. Not only did more than 644 people dine at Viceregal Lodge that season, but the Dufferins also attended numerous parties and balls at other houses, as well as race meets and other sporting activities. Since balls were the highlight of every season, Hariot took special care with her turnout for Lady Roberts' Jubilee Ball at Snowdon in 1887, choosing a fancy dress ensemble in which she had celebrated the Dufferin's recent silver wedding anniversary, an elegant gray satin dress trimmed with silvery fringe whose long transparent silver sleeves almost touched the floor. Her hair was powdered in the style of the eighteenth century, and a long silver veil fell from her diamond crown, while diamond ornaments enhanced the glitter of her dress and she carried a tall silver stick with "XXV" in large silver figures on the top, tied with a silver bow embroidered with the Arabic numeral twenty-five, lest anyone mistake the meaning of the Roman numerals. Her costume was the most elaborate at the party, and was the talk of Simla for days afterward.

Eventually, the thrill of viceregal pomp and circumstance and the fun of entertaining and being entertained paled for Dufferin, and he saw the viceroyalty more and more as merely a burden. After three years, he wrote to a friend that:

>...dulness [sic] is the central characteristic of an Indian viceroy's life. All the people around him are younger than himself; he has no companions or playfellows; even the pretty women who might condescend to cheer him, it is better for him to keep at a distance; and, except occasionally, the business he has to deal with is of a very uninteresting and terre a terre description.[35]

Once Dufferin was able to secure an appointment as Ambassador to Rome, he submitted his resignation and left India before his term was up, ostensibly to allow him to be closer to his two growing sons. Lady Dufferin left India with a strong sense of unfulfilled mission, wishing she had at least one more year to devote to her efforts to improve medical care for women.

Mark Bence-Jones labelled the Lansdowne and Elgin administrations that followed Dufferin's as the "Imperial siesta," a time when India was ruled by two men who were unremarkable in their contributions to Indian history, and who could have been more appropriately called "Great Ornamentals" – an appellation that had been suggested in the press in the 1880s for the viceroy and his court. As in Canada, the Dufferins' successors were

Picnics with the Viceroy were seldom informal affairs. Here the Lansdownes and their party settle under the trees at Simla for an open air lunch.

the Marquess and Marchioness of Lansdowne, a couple with an even loftier aristocratic family background than the Dufferins. Maud Lansdowne was a daughter of the first Duke of Abercorn, her sister was married to the heir to the Marlborough dukedom, and Lansdowne himself was already the fifth marquess in the Petty-Fitzmaurice family when appointed viceroy. He and Dufferin shared an impressive political and diplomatic background, and Lady Lansdowne arrived in India well aware of the high standards of viceregal entertaining set by her predecessor. Lansdowne himself hated the pomp and circumstance of the viceroyalty, but played his part to perfection, with a grace and ease that made an excellent impression on British India and on prominent Indians.

Lady Lansdowne's reputation as a superb hostess and helpmate to her husband's political career preceded her to India, so Britons there had reason to expect a continuation of the Dufferin years. During the years as Lansdowne rose through the diplomatic and political ranks, Maud had become renowned for the glittering soirees she held at the family's

London mansion. Guests at Lansdowne House floated between the gallery containing one of the best private sculpture collections in the world, and elegant drawing rooms hung with rich silks and velvets, containing priceless paintings and superb French furniture. Beyond the elegant ambience, Maud became known as a hostess who required more from her guests than just rank, wealth, or position. In addition to members of the government, she liked to mix guests from different social strata – within certain limits, of course – especially witty and attractive men and women who could add sparkle to conversation. Those kinds of free-ranging guest lists would not be possible in the constricted Indian setting, but Maud did her best to bridge the gap, and tried to bring together small groups of interesting people whenever possible.

As vicereine, she also drew on her London experience when deciding where and how to set up a particular dinner or ball. While she could not replicate the historic surroundings of Lansdowne House in London, Lady Lansdowne took full advantage of the architecture and treasures in the viceroy's mansions to create a similarly elegant and welcoming environment. She even brought along the famous Lansdowne plate, and at formal dinners, the splendid Fitzmaurice silver candelabra gleamed along the huge dining table, interspersed with massive silver bowls, each filled with fragrant flowers. Few in the Anglo-Indian establishment had ever seen such a display of aristocratic wealth, which served to impress, and mask the Lansdownes' true financial status. The fact that Lady Lansdowne never appeared without the famous Lansdowne pearls or other "historic" family jewels further enhanced her reputation as a hostess of taste and elegance.

The glory days of viceregal entertaining came to an abrupt halt with the arrival of Lady Constance Elgin in 1894. A reluctant vicereine, she had neither the family heirlooms nor her predecessors' energy or interest in entertaining, nor their diplomatic experience. Although her husband's father, the eighth earl, had a long and distinguished political career before he died while viceroy, his son's career was undistinguished, and he accepted viceroyalty only after extended persuasion had been brought to bear by his friend the Earl of Rosebery. Preoccupied by economic stringency and growing political unrest, Elgin showed little enthusiasm for the pomp and ceremony associated with viceroyalty. Although he presided over the expected number of viceregal entertainments and ceremonials, Elgin was somewhat shy and quiet, and often ill at ease in crowds. His blatant apathy and his wife's involvement with her brood of 11 children created something of a social vacuum in British India's elite circles. Although Constance's beauty overshadowed that of all in her retinue, she was in chronic ill-health, and complained of the Indian climate. However, with the help of her older daughter, Bessie, Constance did her best to meet her social obligations, and presided over the requisite balls, dinners, and receptions, but overall, the Elgins' much simpler life than their immediate predecessors was widely noted by British-Indian society and the media, and undermined Constance's prestige as vicereine. While poor health was often cited as a reason for restricting the number of official and private social events, the *memsahibs* gave no quarter, and interpreted the excuses as evidence of the Elgins' disinterest in the social side of their role.

Although Constance's successor, the newly enobled Mary Curzon, knew she was following a relatively unpopular vicereine, it provided her little comfort as she nervously prepared to depart for India. She had seen enough in the press and heard enough on the aristocratic rumour circuit to sense that she could outdo Constance Elgin in the social arena, even though she too was in her childbearing years, and pregnant. Her husband insisted she recover fully from the birth before setting out for India, and thus arrive in the proverbial pink, with her tiny figure restored and clothed to perfection in a superb (and expensive) wardrobe. Bent on total conquest of British-Indian society, Lady Curzon faced the special problem of convincing the elites in Britain and the sub-continent that she was a worthy consort to her adored husband, and able to deal with all the niceties and demands of her office, even though she was of the American *haute bourgeoisie*.

Few who knew Curzon were surprised that when he and his wife arrived in India in December 1898, they brought the level of imperial ceremony and social activities to new levels of intensity. Curzon, in sharp contrast to his predecessor, insisted on strict standards of behaviour, viewing state rituals not only as consistent with Britain's succession to the Mughal rule, but a necessity in meeting the expectations of most British officials and subjects in India regarding the dominant posture and image of their governance. Curzon insisted that the head of government and of Anglo-Indian society deal with native rulers and upper echelons of the Raj "....on a footing not merely of equality, but of vantage."[36]

Lady Curzon shared her husband's views of the importance of ritual and protocol, and set about proving herself worthy of her august position, as well as doing what she could to compensate for her husband's aloof and arrogant personality, which marred many social events. Even she had not been raised in the aristocratic milieu, Mary outdid herself in the role of viceregal hostess. Months before she arrived, reports of her youth, beauty, American heritage, and the estimated size of her fortune stirred widespread speculation. Would she be able to grasp the nuances of viceregal protocol? Could any American, however glamorous, well brought up, and wealthy manage to play the role of first hostess of India? Was not an aristocratic background a *sine qua non*? As one titled lady sniffed, she was not "one of us." It soon became clear that Mary's extensive encounters with the legendary snideness and hauteur of British aristocratic society at the centre of Empire had prepared her for the close and hostile scrutiny that awaited her in India. Determined to win over British-Indian society for George's sake at least as much as for her own, Mary rode to battle with energy and enthusiasm, much as she had days before her marriage when she had been a widely admired society beauty, except that now she was not one of many, but alone atop the swaying tip of the social ladder. Funds provided by her generous father allowed her to amass an impressive wardrobe and glittering jewelry, and well tutored by her husband in detailed knowledge of royal protocol, Lady Curzon proceeded to dazzle British-Indian society.

During her first two months in Calcutta, the new vicereine presided over a Drawing Room, a garden party, a state ball for 1,600, a state evening party for 1,500, several smaller balls for 600 or so, and many official dinners with a minimum of 100 guests, as well as many smaller "private" dinners and informal evening dances. She shone brightly at each one, usually wearing one of her many Worth gowns, which were rarely seen more than once, and various sets of jewelry, each outfit highlighting her youthful beauty. Her turn-out for her first Drawing Room, a gown of white satin, embroidered with an Indian motif, the lotus leaf, subtly acknowledged her new connection with India, one of the few times – her famous Durbar peacock dress being the other – that her carefully designed wardrobe demonstrated a connection with India. At each event, she missed no steps as she met every expectation in terms of protocol, appearance, and personal charm. When the vicereine entered a room, every eye was on her, and she loved it – initially at least.

Lady Curzon was, like several other vicereines, the more popular half of the viceregal team. Almost from the day she landed, she found herself called upon by circumstance to offset her husband's ill-disguised arrogance, with more and more detriment to her health. Although her husband fully comprehended the function of viceregal ceremony and formal entertaining as elements of power, he was compulsively engaged in his administrative work, viewing viceroyalty as his personal preserve, and expressing little confidence in subordinates. Curzon saw social events as pointless intrusions on his labours, and could barely conceal his detestation for having to deal with people he did not know or respect. On one occasion at least, during a large dinner party, he reviewed proofs of a report ignoring the stares of his insulted guests.

Curzon's penchant for doing everything himself frequently led him to interfere with what should have been his wife's responsibilities, such as drawing up guest lists and planning menus, even unto writing place cards for dinner parties, all to the great annoyance of the MilSec and his ADCs upon whose bureaucratic domains he intruded compusively. Mary quietly ignored such intrusions and boorishness, and remained the proverbial good soldier, often attending functions alone, and making apologies for the absent viceroy. She aired her frustrations and criticisms (and George's failings) only to her family, who unintentionally damaged her carefully crafted image by reinforcing Anglo-Indian prejudices about uncouth Americans. During her sisters' visit to Simla, Mary was faulted for giving them "royal rank" by placing them on either side of the viceroy at a dinner party, a clear violation of protocol. Anglo-Indian socialites were further offended when Mary's siblings made exaggerated obeisances to George in public, and flirted outrageously with young officers and ADCs. Although she was furious with her sisters, and tried without result to alter their behaviour, the press showed no empathy or mercy. "The world," she wrote to her father, "is a miserable carping place,"[37] after having read several articles in the press critical of her sisters' behaviour. Nor did Nancy and Daisy respond to tugs on the bridle over time. They failed to dress properly, wore "huge sham pearls" instead of real ones, and secretly visited a rajah until recalled by a telegram from the viceroy, which advised them that this particular potentate was *persona non grata* to the *Raj*. Sir Walter Roper Lawrence, the viceroy's private secretary summed up the visit: "Socially, the advent of the Leiters has done great harm."[38]

Since Lady Curzon recovered from the negative publicity and gossip, by the time she and the viceroy left India in 1905, it was clear that she had more than held up her end of the bargain, even trying to rectify the huge social gaffes her husband created with his outrageous behaviour when his successor arrived in India. The disrespect and deliberate rudeness Curzon displayed during the transition was his way of demonstrating his profound indignation at the choice of the new viceroy, and his fury at what he saw as treachery by the home government.

Lady Curzon did her best to smooth the way for her successor, another Mary, Lady Minto, who was initially bemused by the "marvelous ritual" of the viceregal household. Shortly after her arrival she wrote in her diary: "Francis Grenfell told me he expected a picnic luncheon [after a ride] but I informed him that the VR must have his silver plate, his Star of India china and every variety of wine, even if he happens to be on the highest pinnacle of the Himalaya mountains, and somehow they always appear as if by magic!" The new vicereine also witnessed first-hand other lingering effects of Curzon's increased formality at Simla. On an evening when she and her husband were "absolutely alone" for dinner, 19 servants stood in attendance in the passage outside the living room while 32 bandsmen played below.[39] Even for someone raised in Windsor Castle, it all seemed a bit too much. Shortly after their arrival, the Mintos agreed that they would try to reduce the rigid formalism and bring a "lighter touch" to viceroyalty, while not diminishing its authority or majesty. The change was necessary, Mary wrote in her diary, because Curzon had "strained the patience of his subjects almost beyond endurance...treat[ing] the 300,000,000 people as puppets."[40]

Mary Minto's lively personality and demeanor sharply contrasted with her American predecessor, more closely resembling Lady Dufferin, thriving on challenges posed by her position, and approaching myriad duties and projects with eagerness. She was not in the least intimidated by the fame of Lady Curzon, and had enough experience in aristocratic society – not to mention personal friendships with the sovereign and his wife– to understand how the game was played. Lady Minto also had the advantage that many among the British-Indian elite saw her as "one of us" – a British aristocrat, well suited to oversee the viceregal court. In their view, the new vicereine's breadth of experience as a diplomatic hostess easily trumped Lady Curzon's wealth and fragile beauty.[41]

As she had in Canada, Lady Minto took full charge of viceregal entertaining, aided by the very able James Dunlop-Smith, the viceroy's Personal Secretary, a dutiful and trusted courtier at the outset who ultimately became her devoted friend. And while not so glamorous as her predecessor, Lady Minto was petite and slim-waisted, with "bronze" wavy hair, bright blue eyes, and a warm smile. She had a great sense of style, and although she lacked the massive trove of jewelry of many earlier vicereines, she had enough tiaras, coronets, necklaces, and chokers to maintain her social standing symbolically. Very much in the spirit of Edwardian decorative excess, she appeared in a blazing array of her jewelry in a photograph taken for her daughter Violet's wedding in 1909. The front page of a special edition of the *Indian Mirror* showed the vicereine in an elaborate satin gown trimmed with elegant Brussels lace on the neckline and sleeves, wearing her Crown of India medal, a diamond choker (a la Queen Alexandra), a diamond and ruby necklace, and a rope of large pearls reaching to her waist, topped off by the requisite tiara. A sheer lace shawl draped over her left arm and roses in her right hand completed the image of a woman self-assured in her appearance and rank in the final days of *La Belle Epoque*.

Unlike some vicereines, Lady Minto genuinely enjoyed mingling with people. Guests at the viceregal court always felt welcome, whatever their rank or race. Her charisma was much like that ascribed to successful politicians – the ability to make everyone she encountered in social settings believe that they were the only person in the room with whom she wished to talk. As she moved easily and confidently through crowds, it was rarely necessary for her to ask an ADC to coach her regarding names. Like several vicereines before her, Lady Minto used her position and strength

'A proper sort of woman in charge'. Lady Mary Minto, a confident and adroit vicereine with the air of the Belle Epoque, *she made the role appear to be easy.*

of personality and quick-wittedness to further her favourite charitable causes, wheedling donations from Indian rulers at every opportunity, but her constant efforts on behalf of worthy projects did not keep her from attending to her family or the social demands of the viceroyalty.

While the Mintos were known for their athleticism, Mary outdid them all, even the viceroy, who some saw as diverting too much of his energy from his viceregal duties to sport. Lady Minto shared her husband's equestrian passion, and rode as many mornings as possible. Late in the Minto's last Calcutta season, Mary took a "fearful smash" on a steeplechase course one morning, breaking her hand and suffering many bruises, but after being bandaged, entertained some 2,300 people at a garden party that afternoon. Such displays of spunk and charm gained Mary a substantial following among Britons and Indians alike. The Mintos were equally enthusiastic about dancing. At one Black Hearts Ball, Lady Minto danced a reel so wildly that she fell and slid across the floor, with no ill effects, but horrifying many onlookers. She also reported that at a viceregal ball, her elegant gown had been ripped by the spurs of her partner during a particularly vigorous dance. Privately, Lady Minto shared her predecessors' low opinion of the "quality" of some of those whom she was required to entertain, but she, too, managed to keep such feelings from her guests, and within a short time of her arrival, Lady Minto won the hearts of the British Indian elites. *Memsahibs* expressed pleasure at the changes she had instituted in the viceregal court, and were delighted by the entire Minto family. For British Indian society, it seemed that all was now right in their domain; the proper sort of woman was in charge.

The new era: 1911–1936 the age of uncertainty

Few post-Edwardian vicereines who followed the indomitable Lady Minto approached the viceregal social whirl with her energy and enthusiasm. Some enjoyed it, others pretended to, and some were unable to mask their disinterest, or didn't care. Even in the second decade of the new century, their attitude could have significant repercussions because in addition to her own reputation as a figurehead and hostess, a vicereine's standing in British India and at home was often influenced by visitors' views of their husbands. Sometimes, it was not a pretty picture. For example, even though Winifred Hardinge was widely praised in Britain and India for her display of courage at the time of her husband's attempted assassination in 1912, she was savaged a few months later by Sybil Sassoon Rocksavage, who, with her husband, the Earl of Rocksavage, the Marquess of Cholmondeley's eldest son, were honoured guests of the Hardinges during their tour of South Asia. Sybil and her brother, Sir Philip Sassoon, were among the most glamorous members of the British aristocracy, their Jewish heritage notwithstanding. In marrying Rocksavage, Sybil had moved into the highest levels of British society, and clearly felt herself the Hardinge's social superior, despite Winifred having been a lady-in-waiting to Queen Alexandra and Hardinge's close friendship with Edward VII.

Sybil and her husband, close allies of both Edwin Lutyens and Herbert Baker, the architects designing the capitol in New Delhi, saw both of the Hardinges as obstacles to the realising of their friends' great vision. Lutyens and Baker, she wrote are "full of brilliant ideas, but Ld H pours sarcasm & cold water on their most charming schemes – he has the obstinacy which goes with extreme stupidity & is ignorant as a coot." Sybil was equally offended by Winifred's flirting with her husband, deemed the Hardinge court "inexpressibly boring" and gleefully described how she and her husband scandalised the entire viceregal court by dancing only with each other, then leaving the party without taking leave of the viceroy or vicereine. In sum, Sybil found the Hardinges "very tiresome."

Despite Sybil's disdain, Lady Hardinge had earned generally high marks as a hostess during the Coronation Durbar of 1911, and she tried hard to maintain that level of excellence, despite the onset of the heart disease which ultimately felled her in 1914. Often weak and sickly, she gamely met as many viceregal social obligations as she could, even regularly entertaining Indian children so that her young daughter Diamond could meet young girls of her own age. Still, Winifred and her husband were never wildly popular with Anglo-Indian society, perhaps because senior administrators of the *Raj* saw the vicereine as wielding too much power and intruding into matters far outside her purview and too deeply within theirs. Hardinge's sharp sensitivity to criticism led him to hold the reins too closely and rely on only a very few trusted advisors, of whom Winifred was the foremost. Extensive service on the Viceroy's Council led Sir Harcourt Butler to observe acidly that "Hardinge has Crewe [the SOSI] in his pocket, and Lady Hardinge has Hardinge."[42] In a sad bit of irony, her reputation gained fresh lustre after her sudden death, followed closely by her son's, heaped tragedy upon Hardinge and his surviving children. Perhaps due to undercurrents of guilt within the *Raj*, by the 1920s, Winifred was revered as a stoic survivor of a terrorist attack, and a crusader for improved nursing and medical education for women, and any social failings were forgotten.

Several viceregal families lost sons in the Great War. Despite the dual tragedies, and under pressure from the home government, Hardinge extended his tenure to 1916 so that by the time the Chelmsfords arrived, the grim effects of World War I were beginning to be felt by nearly every family in the British aristocracy. Soon after their arrival in India, the Chelmsfords learned that their son, Frederick Ivor, had died from wounds received in Mesopotamia, a blow which affected Lady Chelmsford's public and private behaviour throughout most of her reign. Her attempts to "rule" Anglo-Indian society from her viceregal perch were not helped by the fact that Lord Chelmsford himself did not inspire confidence among some in British India, with Sir Stanley Reed, long-time editor of the *Times of India*, describing him as a man with "a good brain…not overburdened with imagination."[43] His administration was marked by the cautious advance toward Indian self-government through what came to be known as the Montagu-Chelmsford reforms, formally known as The Government of India Act of 1919. These controversial provisions introduced the concept of dyarchy, a two-tiered structure of Indian government, which while expanding Indian participation and greater control over some provincial matters, kept central control firmly in British hands.

Lady Chelmsford did not have the ability or the desire to try to counter her husband's growing unpopularity, even though she often tried to push herself forward at some official functions. She and her girls were bored with life in India; from the day they arrived they made life difficult if not downright unpleasant for most of the staff. Their condescending and demanding attitudes only added to the generally tense atmosphere in Government House staff, some of whom made the unfavourable comparison with other, more congenial, viceregal children. Lady Chelmsford's unhappiness played itself out most often in her demand for strict viceregal formality at all times, and her constant interference with affairs of state. Her daughters reflected their mother's views, and unlike the charming and well-liked Minto girls, the Chelmsford daughters were a constant source of irritation and concern.

Within the social circles of British India, Lady Chelmsford was judged to be an adequate if not exceptional viceregal hostess, and the *memsahibs* softened their criticism somewhat after the death of the Chelmsfords' son. That loss only deepened Frances's dissatisfaction with India, and she became unable to mask her disdain for most of the people she entertained. Despite her work with the Dufferin Fund which brought her in close contact with such women as the Begam of Bhopal, Sultan Jahan, Lady Chelmsford never warmed to the Indian people as had some of her predecessors. She met them when she had to, and did her charity work as required (her rude daughters mocked her work for what they called "Mother's brown babies"), but her consistently superior attitude was off-putting to many who were used to more warm hospitality at the viceregal residences. Lady Chelmsford continued to cause difficulties and embarrassment for the viceroy wherever she went. As on one occasion in 1919, when she insisted upon going into a Hindu temple that was forbidden to Europeans. Even the angry throng screaming and making rude and threatening gestures did not dissuade Frances from her purpose – to sketch the inside of the building. She alighted from her car and surveyed the scene, and then, ignoring the obvious danger and warnings of her military escorts, ordered the party to proceed into the temple.

This kind of callous disregard for local traditions by vicereines was not often seen publicly, but when it did occur, it was fodder for gossip among Anglo-Indian society, and also spread quickly among those Indian princes in close contact with the viceregal court. An even more public gaffe than that of Lady Chelmsford occurred at the grand banquet which Lord and Lady Willingdon gave for the Maharajah of Alwar in the 1930s, an error in judgment all the more remarkable because of the Willingdons' long diplomatic experience in both India and Canada. However, Lady Willingdon's years on the high rungs of the social ladder bolstered her tendency to disregard official protocol, and occasionally, to disregard Indian customs and practices.

On this occasion, struck by a magnificent diamond ring which the ruler wore on his right hand, Lady Willingdon exclaimed "How fabulous!" and asked to examine it more closely. With a great flourish, the Maharajah removed the ring and handed it to her. After she scrutinised it from all angles for a few minutes, turning it over and over in her ungloved palm, Marie held it out to the Maharajah, who refused to accept it, but asked a retainer to bring a fingerbowl and wash the ring. As the astonished viceroy and his wife watched, he then put the now-cleansed ring back on his finger. The Willingdons and the assembled diners watched in embarrassed silence as the Maharajah demonstrated devotion to his religious beliefs, and a sense of superiority to his hosts, as he stuck a proverbial thumb in their eye. Tides were turning, and not only among the masses being stirred to nationalist action by Gandhi and the Congress Party.

Perhaps the most controversial of vicereines, Lady Willingdon, ever high-strung and bustling about, tended to create uncomfortable social situations, however unwittingly, which reverberated into the domain of her husband's political activities. Perhaps most critically in the long run was her role in aggravating the tense relationship between Willingdon and Muhammed Ali Jinnah, the Muslim leader. Some observers traced that antipathy to 1918, when Willingdon was Governor of Bombay and the Jinnahs attended a reception at Government House. When Mme. Jinnah entered wearing a fashionable, low-cut, Paris gown, Marie ordered a servant to bring Mrs. Jinnah a wrap "in case she felt cold." Jinnah, furious at this slight, replied "When Mrs. Jinnah feels cold, she will say so and ask for a wrap herself," and the Jinnahs departed. Whatever Marie's intentions, many onlookers felt she had made the gesture more out of envy rather than concern for maintaining viceregal decorum.

Paradoxically, such heedlessness to Indian mores stood apposite to Marie and her husband's vigorous attempts to expand British-Indian social interactions. During his 1905 tour of India as Prince of Wales, King George V had been stunned to learn that no Indian, whatever his education or birth, was allowed to join any European club. But the royal writ ran thin in some crannies of the Empire, and his indignation provoked no lowering of the colour bar. Despite his expressions of displeasure, no clubs opened their membership rolls to "the locals", even to the wealthiest British-educated potentates who could easily afford the dues, and held high honours from the Crown and the *Raj*. A few years later, Willingdon, as Governor of Bombay, led in the creation of the Willingdon Sports Club open to all races, which he hoped might be a proper site for young Indian princes to keep a hand in on sports and games they learned during their school years

in England. However, partly due to an architecturally "undistinguished" clubhouse and extremely high subscription fees, few Anglo-Indians joined, eschewing the chance to mingle with the wealthiest Indian aristocrats.[44] Lady Willingdon strongly supported her husband's controversial effort, and followed his lead by starting a ladies club in Madras with membership open to all regardless of race or caste.

By the time the Willingdons were enthroned in 1931, Anglo-Indian society had survived (as they viewed it) the reign of the Readings, the first Jewish viceroy and vicereine. Social order had been restored by Lady Irwin, whose impeccable aristocratic credentials as the daughter of the Earl of Onslow combined with her husband's family's connections to India had created a viceregal court deemed acceptable to Anglo-Indian society.

Dorothy Irwin's keen sense of style brought an aura of Twenties chic to official duties. She is seen here on the right with Lord Irwin and the Maharaja of Gwalior.

The fact that Lord and Lady Irwin were known to be close friends of the Duke and Duchess of York (later King George VI and Queen Elizabeth) only added to Lady Irwin's social cachet.

The excess that was Delhi Week was reaching its peak as Lady Willingdon assumed the throne. When the capital was transferred from Calcutta, each Indian potentate of the highest status had built a palace, many of them designed, or at least overseen in construction, by Lutyens. Although spacious and luxurious, these grand buildings were rarely occupied for more than two or three weeks a year, normally in February, when the rulers came to Delhi for the meeting of the Chamber of Princes. Over the years, as these meetings generated an ever-expanding social calendar, the princes sought to outdo each other in entertaining the officials of the *Raj*, a round of activities which became known as Delhi Week. Ultimately, until the middle of World War II, the week was expanded to a fortnight packed with such annual athletic and social events as the Imperial Horse Show, the All-India Polo Tournament, the Delhi Hunt Ball, the Freemasons' Ball, a viceregal ball and garden party, and a State investiture. Officers and wives accompanied their regimental polo teams as nearly all of "official" India descended upon Delhi: governors, residents, ministers of state, and their retinues – eager to mingle with the very uppermost of the British and Indian elites.

Delhi Week also had some of the elements of the great durbars of the past. The viceroy and his consort opened the Week in a ceremony at the new stadium, entering in their carriage under the traditional huge golden umbrella after the other guests were assembled, and surrounded by the scarlet-uniformed lancers of the Viceroy's Bodyguard. Circling the stadium to acknowledge the cheers of the throng with nods and waves, they proceeded to the viceregal box where, once seated, they were joined by the viceregal party, the men exchanging *topis* – sun helmets – for more traditional felt top hats presented on trays by scarlet-clad orderlies.[45]

Having longed for the post of vicereine for years, Lady Willingdon was in her element during Delhi Week, relishing every minute as she and the viceroy presided at official events and were honoured guests at a series of balls, receptions, dinners and garden parties. It was a demanding schedule, both in terms of stamina and wardrobe, but Lady Willingdon never tired of the spotlight and receiving the adulation of her subjects, however obligatory and less than spontaneous they might have been. She brooked no breach of viceregal protocol, insisting that firm dress guidelines for each event be issued well in advance. This prompted all the ladies who expected, or hoped, to be invited to order or purchase a complete Delhi Week wardrobe – new daywear, with broad-brimmed and elaborately flowered or feathered hats to ward off the sun, and elegant brocade or silken evening gowns.

The wartime vicereines – 1936–1947

After the indefatigable Lady Willingdon reigned over British Indian society for five years, she reluctantly ceded her position in 1936 as First Hostess to Lady Linlithgow, a woman whose style and sense of taste far exceeded that of her predecessor. In addition to overseeing a full expunging of Marie's "improvements" to Viceroy's House, Lady Linlithgow dismantled much of her predecessor's rigid protocol in favour of informality and comfort, aiming to make her family's quarters and lifestyle her first priority. Amid the growing turbulence in India and the world at large, the Linlithgow family was well received by Anglo-Indian society. Lady Linlithgow, a congenial hostess, artistic, and easy in her manner helped overcome her husband, "Hopie's," apparent shyness and discomfiture at social gatherings. The viceregal couple's impressive height and dignified bearing belied his shyness, and reinforced the impression of a ruler and his consort perfectly at ease, whether in viceregal robes or more ordinary costumes. By 1937, the two older girls – Anne and Joan – had overcome their initial homesickness, and were enjoying the perquisites of viceregal life as they became belles of the ball. A gaggle of presentable ADCs and military officers surrounded them at every party; they never lacked for a tennis or bridge partner; and their father's position brought them invitations to every significant social event in New Delhi.

In counterpoint to those diversions and pleasantries, clouds were gathering on the international scene, at a distance, nearby, and within India. But as major wars raged in Spain and China, threatened in Europe, and campaigns mounted in intensity on the Northwest Frontier, viceregal entertaining continued with the usual cycles of garden parties, state dinners, receptions, drawing rooms, and balls. After war broke out in Europe in September 1939, there appeared to be little change in the Indian social scene beyond the normal transition in the style of dress, and the easing of some traditional constraints. The Linlithgows did revise their social schedule somewhat, cutting back on dinners and receptions, but not official ceremonies or standard state functions.

As relaxed as the Linlithgows seemed about social standards in some respects, they did not steer all that far from the predecessors in relying on ritual to maintaining the façade of the *Raj*, even as it was becoming more and more just that – a façade. Linlithgow, perhaps more than any viceroy, had become aware of the steep angle of decline in the late 1930s as he grappled with mobilising the resources of a populous domain that lacked much of the infrastructure of a modern power. A classic double-bind of imperialism became more and more apparent as the priorities of the *Raj* versus those of Britain as Mother Country clashed. The debits of keeping Indians from full economic and military partnership in the structuring of

The Linlithgows, in perfect morning dress, preside over a garden party at the Viceroy's House.

the industry and armed forces of the sub-continent while trying to raise large armies far from home able to stand up against modern military power was thrown into increasingly sharp relief. In his viceregal role of proconsul and premier battle captain, Linlithgow dealt with an almost two-year long, nerve-wracking interval when the Soviets were virtual allies of Nazi Germany while India was tasked with providing men and materiel for the campaigns in North and East Africa, and the Middle East 1940–42. The vice grew tightest in early in 1942 as British-Indian martial fortunes reached their nadir at Singapore and in Burma, disasters which Gandhi and the Congress Party and other nationalist factions exploited in the "Quit India!" movement as did the Japanese in forming the Indian National Army from 70,000 Indian prisoners of war.

As the viceroy and his wife stood fast amid the quickening torrent, Doreen continued to order custom-made gowns from London, and stuck to a busy schedule of charitable and social activities more and more related to the war effort. As the "general situation" in the Middle and Far East worsened from mid-1940 onward, the girls' social life was curtailed as they began to work as nurse's aides in military hospitals, while Lady Linlithgow directed her efforts toward broader public health issues, focusing her attention on establishing a tuberculosis centre in every province. Whatever British-Indians thought of her social skills became less and less important as she earned widespread respect for directing the fight against TB, and for her deft balancing of viceregality and wartime priorities. By the time the Linlithgows went home in 1943, they were eager to leave the pomp and circumstance of viceroyalty, even though after seven years the routines and demands had become second nature for the once-reluctant viceroy. At a luncheon party given in Cairo honour of the new viceroy, Field Marshal and now Viscount Wavell, when Linlithgow stepped forward to enter the dining room in keeping viceregal protocol, Lady Linlithgow gently but firmly held him back, whispering "No, you've done that for the last time."[46]

With a major Japanese invasion of India looming, Bengal ravaged by famine, and political unrest simmering throughout the sub-continent as the Wavells took the viceregal thrones. Called Queenie by her family, Eugenie Wavell's lack of aristocratic pedigree, which would have once been seen as intolerable in some circles in British-India and Britain, made barely a ripple, socially or politically. Lady Wavell was able to "look the part" of a vicereine when necessary: a portrait taken by Cecil Beaton shows her seated in one of the marble halls of the Viceroy's House in Delhi wearing a silk jersey evening gown and matching coat, her white hair softly framing her face, topped by a delicate tiara. No decorations are in view, and the image is of an elegant yet distinctly "un-royal" vicereine. A colonel's daughter, the new Lady Wavell had spent her life in the military, including several years as the wife of a senior general and field marshal on foreign postings, including the USSR, the Middle East, India, and Southeast Asia. Since Wavell had held two theater commands, and was most recently Commander-in-Chief India, she was well grounded in helping the fighting men and their families, and supporting her husband in matters of protocol. Especially alert for innovative ways to improve morale, soon after Wavell's viceroyalty began, she and her husband hosted a garden party for winners of Victoria and George Crosses, and the Guards of Honour and their families, some 500 people in all. The event was greatly appreciated by the honorees, and the function was well reviewed in the press.

Despite her non-aristocratic background, overall, Lady Wavell received high ratings as a wartime vicereine from the media in India and in Britain, and from her husband, who regularly acknowledged her contributions to the viceroyalty and positive impressions she made. As he noted in his diary: "One way or another – parades, parties, green boxes, red carpet – Her Ex and I earned our keep today." At the end of 1944, Wavell summed up his first year as viceroy: "It is hard to say how we have done on the social side, all right I hope. Her Ex is of course an outstanding success as Vicereine. I think the atmosphere in the VR's house is friendly w/o loss of dignity and the Staff have done their work well….it is hard work and very easy to make a bad mistake and we may have made some already."

Whether or not the Wavells bungled badly in the domain of viceregal protocol or not, they were unceremoniously ushered out of Viceroy's House in 1947 to be succeeded by a viceroy as close in bearing and family links to an actual royal personage as possible. Admiral Lord Louis Mountbatten, "Dickie," war hero, chief of Combined Operations and the Commandos early in the war, Supreme Allied Commander in Southeast Asia in the last two years of World War II – a "glamorpuss" in the slang of the 1940s – was a martial super-celebrity widely featured in the media and popular culture in Britain and the U.S. With his impressive presence and egomaniacal personality, his wife had her hands full trying to keep from being eclipsed. Edwina Mountbatten, however, managed to more than hold her own. From the moment that Mountbatten's viceregal appointment was announced, the couple were viewed with suspicion by many within the Anglo-Indian community, primarily because of their reputation for liberalism in Britain. Edwina's wealth and well-publicised charm, along with Louis' celebrity status and close royal connections as a grandson of Queen Victoria and a cousin of the reigning monarch were obvious pluses, but some of their controversial acts amid the turmoil as India approached independence were very unpopular with many in the Anglo-Indian community, and die-hard imperialists at home.

Although he was charged with orchestrating India's transition from imperial domain to independent state, Lord Mountbatten maintained the magnificence of his retinue close to the level of late 19th century viceroys. While he faced a myriad of daunting tasks, the prospect of living in a real palace was especially alluring to someone renowned for his vanity, and who had spent his life on the fringes of British royalty, with no formal household of his own. With this appointment he would reside in one of the most magnificent residences in the Empire and the world at large. His love of dressing up in uniforms or other ceremonial garb was another attraction of viceroyalty. With Edwina's slim beauty and sense of style enhancing his regal appearance, the Mountbattens were as royal and impressive appearing a viceregal couple as India had ever seen, even though Lady Louis did not share her husband's "mad" enjoyment of the ceremonial side of the viceroyalty. It was, she wrote to her daughter, "a great adventure... and I love the work and my Indians...but how I long for Broadlands ... even ringing a bell and no one answering!"[47]

Although often exhausted by long journeys in punishing heat, Lady Louis kept up with the ceremonial and social side of her job. In the space of a day, she could transmute from the hardworking volunteer in a Red Cross uniform with a turban around her hair to the most glamorous of vicereines – hair and make-up perfect, wearing a satin gown bedecked with her CI and several other medals, elbow length gloves topped with glittering diamond bracelets, and a magnificent tiara. No one who saw her walk proudly and easily down the marble stairs of Viceroy's House to open a state dinner, head held high, gazing straight ahead, acknowledging no one as she glided across the gleaming marble floor, would have suspected that she had just returned from spending the day with wounded veterans and liberated POWs, and longed only for a quiet evening with dinner on a tray. Nor did would they have realised that, in that pre-contact lens era, without her glasses, she could barely make out shapes, let alone faces.

Despite the viceroy's obsession with feudal finery, when the Mountbattens entertained Indian leaders and their families at formal and informal occasions, the social ambience at Viceroy's House reflected their liberal policies. Both strove to balance the formality with more personal hospitality at Viceroy's House. The viceroy might host Gandhi alone for breakfast, but he and his wife also knew how to entertain grandly when necessary. Edwina wrote her daughter that on "big pompous occasions all the *right* people come with the gold plate out and God Savers and all the Panoply but we have tried to unbend and become more approachable and more human."[48] Recognising the importance of viceregal symbolism, she suggested rewording the Court Circular demonstrating the couple's wish to no longer "honour" people with their "august presence" but to simply "invite" them to Viceroy's House. The last vicereine recognised that at this point in the history of the *Raj*, "...words and pompous notices" alone would not keep up the "prestige of the Crown and one's country," but rather one's "behaviour and example."[49]

Lady Mountbatten's time as vicereine and later as the wife of India's first Governor General was remarkable not only because of the glamour she brought to the position of vicereine, but also because of her efforts to effect a social transition that would parallel the dramatic political changes. As the last vicereine, she was determined to end her reign in a way that both dignified the years of British sovereignty in India and at the same time reflected the new era that was emerging and her own liberal politics. Her sincere interest in improving the lives of Indians was balanced with her understanding of how anxious the long-time servants of the *Raj* were about the future of a country many had served loyally and with dedication and their need to see the pomp of the viceroyalty maintained until the last possible moment. By the time she left India, Edwina had initiated dramatic changes in protocol and had successfully overcome the "demon of precedence" that had held British India captive for nearly 100 years, while at the same time maintaining a level of glamour and elegance equal to that of Lady Mary Curzon.

The new vicereine's bringing growing numbers of Indian men and women into the viceregal inner circle fuelled criticism, public and private, as many found it difficult to accept the *Raj* was crumbling, or that many of Indians formerly shunned or excluded from elite functions and who were now being entertained would soon rule the subcontinent. The Mountbattens, fully aware that many Britons in India and Britain distrusted them as agents of Attlee's Labour government bent on quickly toppling the world as they knew it, played their roles, even in the eyes of admirers, with dizzying enthusiasm and self-confidence. Over the years, British women in influential positions had made friends with Indian women and even invited them into their homes, but Lady Louis, as she was generally known, was the first vicereine to make such contacts on a large scale and a hallmark of her entertaining. As the mid-August 1947 deadline rapidly approached for the partition of British India into the independent Dominions of India and Pakistan, Lady Mountbatten helped her husband by developing close links with Indian leaders, something that their predecessors trapped in the role of proconsuls, and the pervasive racism of British imperialism had been unable to do, even the liberally disposed Wavell and his wife. While Lady Mountbatten's deep involvement in social welfare efforts important to Indian women was not wildly different than some of her predecessors, more unique, however, was her aggressive dismantling of social barriers, including caste, class and race, including very personal contacts with Indian politicians, and most shockingly to many, as details emerged later in the 20th century, her relationship with Jawaharlal Nehru.

Edwina's brief reign as vicereine was followed by a slightly longer stint as the Governor General's lady. The transfer of power took place barely five months after the Mountbattens arrived in India. On a hot August day, Mountbatten in full regalia and Edwina in an evening gown, made their way to the golden thrones of the Durbar Hall for his swearing-in as Governor General of an independent India. Following the ceremony – and a momentary panic as a flashbulb exploded – the Mountbattens drove in the blinding sun to the Council Chamber for another ceremony. The high point of the long-awaited day occurred in late afternoon with the dramatic unfurling of the Indian flag near the War Memorial at Princes Park. The

crowd was so huge that Mountbattens' carriage was unable to reach the
grandstand and the formal program had to be abandoned. As Lord Mountbatten gave orders to hoist the saffron, green, and white banner and to
fire the salute, a tumultuous crowd of 500,000 boisterously cheered. That
evening Mountbatten, in full regal dress replete with medals and ribbons,
and Edwina, wearing a gold brocade gown with a red, white, and blue
shoulder sash and a diamond tiara and necklaces, received 3,000 guests
in the State drawing rooms and reception rooms of Viceroy's House, now
to be known as Government House. Guests wandered in the illuminated
Moghul gardens, as the Viceroy's Band played its final airs.

The Mountbattens sit enthroned in the Durbar Hall of Viceroy's House in New Delhi 1947.

Amid the tragedy and turmoil of India's transition to independence,
Lady Mountbatten's schedule was a maelstrom of travelling, charity work,
disaster relief, diplomacy, entertaining, and keeping as closely in touch
with her family as possible. Once so loathe to go to India, she now found
herself dreading departure. Even the Delhi heat didn't change her opinion:
"...the hot wind has commenced and scorching dust storms are upon us.
But I love Delhi like this and India and the Indians and my heart aches at

the thought of leaving them so soon."[50] She was especially grateful for a final trip to Mashobra with a few close friends before the final onslaught of official entertaining: the visit of the Governor of the Punjab and his wife; a farewell party for the Indian and foreign press; the last-ever dinner celebrating the King's birthday; and a series of receptions for various echelons of staff, including the indoor and outdoor native servants. At each event, Edwina appeared the perfect Governor General's Lady, whether elegantly gowned and bejeweled at grand gatherings, or warm and congenial in more private settings. She managed to mask her deep grief at leaving until the very end. When Mountbatten wrote "Tears all round. Left at 8:20" in his diary, his terse report spoke volumes, some of which would not be opened for many years.

In those final months, the last vicereine had brought Viceroy's House – now Government House – back from wartime grubbiness to its full glory, and restored viceregal entertaining to a most royal stature. The Mountbattens' connections with the monarchy helped return some of the old aura, and Edwina, her frenzied schedule notwithstanding, managed to exceed the expectations of the last cohort of the *Raj*. Despite her political stance, she had everything they expected or wanted in a vicereine –wealth, aristocratic heritage, glamour, and a confidence in diplomatic and social settings that every *memsahib* in that final phase envied. Her entertainments were brilliant yet enjoyable as she balanced the dignity of her office with her genuine love of people. And the last vicereine left more than a bright memory of her social skills. Always meticulous in her note-taking and organising, Edwina tried to make sure that those following her, in whatever capacity, would benefit of her experience, preparing detailed notebooks on the variety of entertainments, including suggestions for how they might be modified to align with in the new era of independence. Whether the successors of the *Raj* used them or not, it was a last gesture to render service in the spirit of all the Grand Hostesses who tried to leave their mark on India's high society over a century of viceroyalty in India.

As the transfer of power became a reality, some Indians began to vent their real feelings about how the British had demonstrated their power through symbols and ceremonies. Jawaharlal Nehru commented scornfully on the arrogant self-portrayal of colonial power: "Their court ceremonies, their *durbars* and investitures, their parades, their dinners and evening dress, their pompous utterances." An interesting observation from one who was "socialised in Britain" so close to the last viceroy, and perhaps even closer to the last vicereine.[51]

Whatever their feelings about the British, the Indians adopted much from the *Raj* in the way of ceremony and symbolism in government. Each year, on January 26, Indians celebrate Republic Day with a huge parade which includes representatives of India's many cultures and regions. The lines of turbaned scarlet-clad lancers, and bands on foot or horseback or camelback would not have seemed out of place in a ceremony organised by the ultimate ceremonial viceroy, Lord Curzon. The fact that the parade takes place on *Rajpath*, formerly King's Way, offers another irony.

6

Stagecraft of Empire

If, as Jan Morris wrote, "Spectacle was always an instrument of British imperialism,"[1] nowhere in the empire was that more true than in India, which would blend British ritual manifestations of spectacle with their own rich tradition of ostentatious ceremony and vast princely wealth. In the late 18th Century, the British in India began to see that the theory and practice of caste in India created a society that resembled their own in many ways. They saw Indian society as "ordered, traditional and layered hierarchically,"[2] and thus worth supporting, and insofar as possible, kept intact to ensure orderly governance. This meant that those on the top of the heap, the Indian princes, should be considered 'natural aristocrats' and treated as social equals by British aristocrats in India – within limits.

The Marquess of Wellesley was the first Governor General to appreciate and articulate the need for a governmental residence and lifestyle worthy of a ruling class. His famous statement, that "India must be ruled from a palace, not a counting house; with the ideals of a prince, not those of a retail dealer in muslin and indigo" would echo through the years of the viceroyalty, justifying not only military expansion and control, but the imposition of a system of honours, extravagant lifestyles, the construction and maintenance of huge palaces, and ceremonies designed to surpass anything the earlier Mughal rulers could have imagined. Wellesley's dictum was repeatedly trotted out as justification for the ever-increasing hierarchy and the imperial ceremonies of the Raj that began when the Honourable East India Company turned over direct control of India to the British government in 1858, and which reached its apogee in the late 19th and early 20th century.[3]

In 1799, without consulting his superiors in London on either design or cost, Wellesley decided to build a residence in Calcutta worthy of his position – a residence at least equal to those of the princes he hoped – and expected – to rule. Government House would be the centre point of British sovereignty and Anglo-Indian society until 1912 when the central government was transferred by King George V to the new capital to be constructed in its entirety at Delhi, the former seat of the Mughal emperors.

The importance of India within the British government also was becoming more evident by the mid-1800s. In 1868 India's unique position within the emerging empire was showcased in splendid new premises of the India Office in Whitehall. The building contained a three-storey glass-roofed Durbar Court, with a Wedgewood frieze running along the four walls, and niches for busts of senior Indian administrators. The Secretary of State for India was ensconced in an oak-paneled office decorated with Indian miniatures that had been "liberated" from the famous Mughal Red Fort at Delhi. There were even two identical doors to the office, set side by side, so that if the Secretary had to receive two Indian princes of equal rank, they could step across the threshold simultaneously, neither giving precedence to the other. Even in London, Indian insistence on deference to rank and protocol was respected, and influenced British behaviour.

There were never more than 300,000 Britons in India, while the indigenous population was some 250 million. Maintaining that lopsided power depended upon convincing the population of Britain's ability to rule effectively and fairly, and – equally importantly – the cooptation of those already in power – the princes of India who ruled some forty percent of the country. Believing that it takes one to rule one, the British believed that only aristocrats could effectively impose and maintain a social and political structure much like that in England.

The British monarchy was supported by an aristocratic hierarchy which had survived the late 18th mid-century European tumult and revolution unscathed, and which, despite a rising tide of democracy, felt secure in its environment. The aphorism, "Everybody loves a duke," was an indication of the deference, if not affection, given to the nobility, which in turn, gave them supreme confidence in their ability to govern – and undoubtedly improve – "lesser" peoples throughout the world. That category included the hereditary Indian princes, albeit under close British supervision after 1858. They were seen as the Indian equivalent to the British landed gentry, whose cooperation was essential to maintaining British suzerainty. The Queen's post-Mutiny proclamation had promised "respect [for] the rights, dignity and honour of native princes as our own" because they were the 'natural leaders' of South Asian society,[4] but that respect and honour required strict adherence to British control.

If the ruling princes were the natural aristocrats of India, then only British aristocrats, supremely confident of the inherent superiority of their education, character, and morality would be able to understand and replicate in the Empire the complicated ceremonies, hierarchy, honours, and social systems that had kept them in power in the British Isles for hundreds of years. Who else but an aristocrat, with his (and her) firm belief in their own social and racial supremacy, could deal successfully with a culture in which many rulers of principalities had greater wealth, more ostentatious palaces and jewelry than the British monarchy itself? To rule effectively, the British believed that they had to equal, if not surpass, the traditional splendor of India, both by appointing only aristocrats as proconsuls, and by overwhelming their native subjects with displays and ceremonies that strengthened their hold on the country. Despite statements to the contrary, the British were determined that the Indians should perceive the *Raj*'s presence to be a permanent one, and representative of a ruling tradition that was at least the equal, if not the superior, of any Indian prince, however long his history.

As important as the investiture and other ceremonies, dinners, balls, and receptions over which the viceroy and vicereine presided were to Anglo-Indian society and the Indian aristocracy, the public face of the *Raj* was most often shown in the large public spectacles designed to demonstrate martial power and governmental authority, in which the vicereines had little direct involvement other than attending and looking their best or ensuring the comfort of noble visitors. The British had a rich tradition of military and royal pageantry upon which to draw in designing these events, which had an important if unspoken governmental function. Given the relatively small number of British in India, it was essential to regularly "remind" the natives of the superiority of the British army, even though much of that army was made up of Indian volunteers. The glint of the sun on swords and lances, the flags whipping in the breeze, the blare of trumpets and the thump and rattle of drums – all reinforced British imperial strength and permanence.

Almost from the time they arrived in India in the 1700s, the East India Company's Governors-General and other officials took part in elaborate military reviews, and held or attended *durbars* with local rulers as part of imposing and maintaining military and commercial control. Mughal emperors had regularly staged *durbars* at which sultans, nawabs, nizams and maharajahs would come to pay tribute, bearing expensive gifts and accompanied by retinues carefully selected to demonstrate their status within the empire. Recognising the power of such spectacles, the British seized the concept, added their own flair – including demonstrations of military might – and used them to reinforce the assumed linkage between the old Mughal empire and the new British rulers, and to publicly demon-strate their connection to, and understanding of, regional social hierarchy. Except in the case of the few female rulers, Indian women generally did not take part in these events except perhaps as veiled spectators. This meant that British women, even the wives and female members of the Governor-General's family and those of other senior officials, did not have a role in most *durbars*,[5] particularly when native princes were to be in close proximity to the British. It was believed that for European women to "show themselves" to natives would lower their standing in the eyes of Indians. And as fascinated as many British women were with the exotic costumes and elaborate jewels worn by the natives, few were interested in having any real social interaction with them or learning about their lives.

In the years following the Indian Mutiny, imperial images were dissem-inated throughout the world on an increasing scale by a vast expanding network of telegraph and suboceanic cable systems. Descriptions and scenes of British, German, and Russian royal and imperial pageantry were regularly featured in the mass media, and especially images of the grandest and most exotic imperial bastion of the greatest empire of all, that of Britain, in the proverbially mysterious East – the Indian empire. At the same time, whether due to such imagery or despite it, anti-imperial sentiment was rising throughout Europe and much of the world. In an especially bizarre instance of politics producing strange bedfellows, both Marx and Bismarck deemed empires immoral and unprofitable. Others, including Rudyard Kipling, nurtured in the mystique of the *Raj*, and his pen-pal Teddy Roosevelt waxed lyrical over "dominion over palm and pine," since both saw major industrial powers in the role of imperial mother countries, conquering and ruling by force, as part of the natural order of things.

Amid those contradictions, the grand ceremonies and rituals of empire served as kind of political Rorschach test. While millions were disinter-ested in such matters, many were fascinated by the gaudy spectacles, or horrified at feudal power and privilege being flaunted amid grim poverty. For all the expense and effort involved in *durbars* and other major ceremo-nials, it was not all that clear, even to those who were staging them, just what they were meant to do – impress imperial rivals, subject peoples, or the folks back home. One apparent function was to hearten the rela-tively tiny bands of functionaries in the overseas empires who kept the "Great Powers" flags flying at great risk of health, comfort, and sanity. But such garish cheerleading led both observers and participants in the "Great Game" of Empire to wonder, in private for the most part, whether the pinnacle of the *Raj* had already been reached. Such a premonition led Kipling to sound a pessimistic note of doubt in his somber poem "Reces-sional" during Victoria's Diamond Jubilee in 1897.

Few among the crowds of Britons or Indians cheering the Prince of Wales' stately progress across India in 1875–76, or the millions around the world who saw pictures of those splendors could foresee that almost the entire superstructure of imperialism would be swept away within the next two generations. On the contrary, *Pax Brittanica*, now a century old, seemed very sturdy to critics and enthusiasts alike, despite some surging social and political counter-currents. And yet, somehow, the institution of viceroyalty in India seemed immune to those trends, and appeared to be more fully bathed in an aura of feudal grandeur and actual power than the monarchy in Britain as the Anglo-Indian community of functionaries and soldiers in India seemed to be evolving in the opposite direction as a kind of pseudo-aristocracy emerged from bourgeois forms. Perhaps that stemmed from British officials in India seeking a counterbalance to their discomfort, isolation, and the rising threat of Indian nationalism, and the fact that few at home, or in the world at large showed much interest or sympathy for their privations and efforts.

Whatever the causes and roots of their plight, British elites in India from the Great Mutiny to independence became heavily enmeshed in self-deception and denial. As previously noted, for example, Sir Bartle Frere, former Governor of Bombay and orchestrator of the Prince of Wales's visit, described the trip in a letter to Queen Victoria as an unqualified success. Edward had won the affection of India's common people he reported, along with the respect and admiration of the Indian potentates. Like many officials, he saw the Prince as providing a personal link between British royalty and Indian rulers that was much like his relationship with British aristocrats at home. The emerging literate, intelligent, proto-middle class in Indian was left well out of focus. Beyond weaving fantasies about masses of loyal subjects, the British derived more practical lessons in overseeing all the social and military events that accompanied the Prince's visit, made all the more complicated by the fact that it coincided with political initiatives under way in Britain to give Victoria the title of Empress of India, a change that would have a dramatic affect on the current and all future vicereines.

Prince Albert had first raised the prospect of awarding her that imperious title in 1858, and proposed that, in India, the Queen's formal designation should be "the Great Mughal," making the Queen the symbolic heiress of the Mughal dynasty. Whether due to common sense in high places, since that suggestion ran counter to the promise of eventual Indian self-government included in the 1858 proclamation, it was not adopted at the time. Bringing up the question, however, did warm the queen's interest in the idea of that she should assume some sort of imperial title. Victoria felt she was entitled to that, if for no other reason than to clarify her somewhat ambiguous position in the array of European royalty, some of whom bore higher titles. She became especially concerned with precedence and status in that milieu after William I of Prussia was proclaimed Emperor of Germany in 1871. Since that placed her daughter Vicky in line to become an empress when her husband Frederick succeeded his father, the Queen complained of being "handicapped by not being an Empress." Three years later, when the Conservative government proposed the Imperial Titles Act which would name Victoria Empress of India, political opponents assailed it as a grotesque capstone to Benjamin Disraeli's imperialist foreign policy. The bill passed through Parliament comfortably, but only after triggering substantial and unexpected controversy in Parliament and the press, as well as some organised agitation, alarming the Queen, who saw them as dangerous indicators of growing republicanism.

The reaction of the viceroy at the time, Lord Lytton, was more to Victoria's liking, however blatantly opportunistic as it seemed in many quarters. Immediately after the bill was passed, Lytton began planning the first of a projected series of ceremonies on a scale far greater than the Mughal *durbars* which were intended to symbolize India reunified under a new ruler. The son of Edward Bulwer Lytton, a well-known Victorian novelist and poet, Robert Lytton was the most controversial and unconventional of viceroys up to that time. An experienced, but unorthodox, diplomat, Lytton was at heart a Bohemian, a romantic poet drawn to symbols of medieval ceremony and ritual, a lover of ease, luxury, and exotic costumes, and, as noted earlier, something of a lecher. As viceroy, he united most of those predispositions with British imperial statecraft in a ceremony that was the first of its kind in India or anywhere in the Empire, and which churned up condemnation from many points on the political compass. Lytton consciously labelled this first grand gathering, scheduled for January 1, 1877, an Imperial Assemblage rather than a *durbar*. Lytton meant his Assemblage, structured around the proclaiming of Queen Victoria Empress of India, to differ "materially and essentially" from any previous *durbar*, in essence and in scale.[6] Beyond the question of European royal hierarchy, elevation to Queen-Empress had a more practical effect in the context of Indian politics by making Victoria paramount among Indian princes and nobles. Their formal professions of fealty during the ceremony would highlight the role of the Crown as the basic source of symbolic legitimation in much the same way that aristocrats' pledges to the monarch did in the British coronation ceremony.

Lytton hoped that the Assemblage ceremony would, all at once, solidify the system of Indian governance around the Queen Empress, properly honour his sovereign, and recognize the veterans of the campaigns of 1857–58. He was enthusiastically supported in his grand plans by his wife,

The Lyttons and
family gather for
a photograph
outside
Government
Lodge in
Calcutta.

the quintessential Victorian spouse who deeply loved her husband, and strove mightily to advance his career. As wife and vicereine, Lady Lytton ardently supported Lytton's plans for the Imperial Assemblage, sharing his vision of the event as the hallmark of his viceroyalty, and was eager to contribute ideas, if allowed.

Lytton's "Orientalist" view of India, and especially his fascination with Eastern art and costume, led him to take special pains to make sure that the "great feudal aristocracy" of India was honoured appropriately at the Assemblage, and that they in return formally deferred to the *Raj*. Like many other Europeans, and viceroys, he saw Indian peasants as an "inert mass," led and manipulated by their princes, simple folk easily impressed by grandiose symbols. "The further East you go," he wrote, "the greater becomes the importance of a bit of bunting."[7] Since the Assemblage was so closely followed by the formation of the Indian National Congress, one can only speculate as to how much the occasion stirred anti-British sentiment among the Indian middle class intellectuals and professional. Lytton was only following the pattern of British official disdain for *babus* who wrote their seditious "tripe" in the indigenous press.

Beyond Lytton's bullying style and the arrogance of British overlords in India, Victoria's becoming Queen Empress raised constitutional sticky points in Britain, which was itself in the cleft stick of being an imperial mother country evolving in fits and starts toward a full-blown democracy.

Whatever British elites did at home or in the subcontinent affected India constitutionally and procedurally as well. The 1875 visit of the Prince of Wales had heightened that paradox as the Government of India operated under royal protocol in the Indian milieu. The exceptional level (judged by some to be inordinate) of protocol and pageantry attending the royal representative's processional through India raised the question of how much more in the way of ritual would be required for someone standing in for an Empress or Emperor and his consort. Despite the rising tide of democracy in Britain, India, and much of the world, the Anglo-Indian social and political life became increasingly ornate and formalistic over the next generation, reaching its apex in the coronation durbar of the King-Emperor and Queen Empress in 1911.

One early index of that trend was Lytton's formal proposal to the Queen regarding the Assemblage that she publicly show her high regard for India's hereditary aristocracy by sanctioning such "acts of grace" as an increase of one in the number of guns fired to salute princes, except for those already entitled to the maximum of 21, and presenting them with gold or silver guns as mementos of the change. Rising further into the domain of cloudy fantasy, he also suggested establishing a Herald's College at Calcutta, and passing legislation in India to organize a Native Peerage of the Indian Empire, with permission granted to regional potentates to attend the Legislative Council when they visited the viceregal court after a number of years. Lytton's final suggestion was to distribute "moderate" amounts of largesse and sweetmeats to the poor,[8] since he believed that such lavish and elaborate rituals during the Assemblage would reinforce the Indian aristocracy's attraction and deference to strength and authority, most especially the displays of martial power included in the ceremonies. His hope was that the potentates, in turn, would exercise greater authority over their peoples, thereby strengthening the power and "increas[ing] the *éclat* of Your Majesty's Indian Empire"[9] Not surprisingly, his elaborate "proclamation schemes" were not well received by press or government in Britain. Even the archetypal imperialist Disraeli observed that they "read like the Thousand and One Nights."[10]

The site that Lytton chose for the assemblage was just outside the old Mughal capital at Delhi, on the Ridge where British-led forces recaptured the city at the end of the 1857 rebellion. For over a year, Lytton worked obsessively to create an imperial spectacle that would put to rest British and Anglo-Indian fears about bestowing the title of Empress on Britain's monarch, and solidify British rule over India's diverse elements by invoking ancient forms and ceremonies. The viceroy invited governors, lieutenant-governors, and heads of administration from all regions of India, as well as some 400 princes, chiefs, and nobles "in whose persons the antiquity of the past is associated with the prosperity of the present, and who so worthily contribute to the splendor and stability of this great empire."

Beyond that, Lytton spared no expense and brooked no obstacle as he designed a ceremony meant to be a great historical event in itself. Nor did he hesitate in reaching for funds outside ordinary channels, or in setting new ground rules. In addition to decreeing that the Princes and their entourages should travel to the assemblage in full-court dress at private expense, the viceroy announced that Lady Lytton would attend the formal Proclamation ceremony and other parties associated with the Assemblage – the first time that a female member of the viceroy's family would take part in a public function which Indians attended. With memories of the 1857 uprising still clear and painful, and racism flowering throughout much of the Western world, many in the Anglo-Indian establishment saw that European ladies' appearance at such functions as highly inappropriate. Whatever prominent Anglo-Indians thought or said, Lady Lytton was thrilled to be included in state occasions. In a letter to her family, she described the major banquet of the Assemblage, attended by many Indian notables and "all the swellest Europeans." Many of the former asked to be presented to her "… which is a great change, but I have been more brought forward than any lady yet in India."[11] Despite her experience with extravagant displays of riches and splendors in Europe and while touring the princely states, Edith was truly bedazzled by the glittering spectacle of the Assemblage. Determined to wear the very latest styles, and to appear welcoming and self-possessed at every appearance, before leaving for India, she had arranged for the House of Worth in Paris to regularly supply her with new gowns worthy of her high station. That outlay paid great social dividends during and after the Assemblage, as details of her fashionable dresses were widely and favourably reported in the Indian and British press.

The two weeks of official festivities attendant to the Assemblage began on December 23, when the Lyttons arrived in Delhi aboard the viceregal train. There, Lytton welcomed chiefs and princes in an elaborate dominance game that worked both ways, since only half the invitees deigned to appear. Following the official welcome, the viceroy and vicereine mounted a gaudily decorated state elephant complete with a silver *howdah* – plush seats within heavy boxes, shaded by gaudy silk canopies – to lead a spectacular three-hour procession through Delhi to the viceregal camp. Despite searing heat and glaring sunlight, every prince in the parade attempted to outshine the others in magnificence. Attendants and elephants alike glittered, the latter swathed in ropes and cloths of gold, or scarlet-and-blue embroidered in gold and silver.

A damp and dust-caked vicereine and her children arrived several hours later at the site of the *durbar* camp. Beyond large pavilions built for the official ceremonies, the plains outside Delhi were densely dotted with a vast temporary city of luxurious tents erected for European and Indian guests. All their needs and wants were provided for: roads for carriages and elephants, sanitation facilities, and servants' quarters, with myriad tents arrayed in strict order of precedence.

In that Anglo-Indian version of a pleasure-dome, the Lyttons and their guests slept, dined, entertained, and periodically sallied forth in the appropriate ornate regalia to take part in various ceremonies and military reviews. Naturally, the viceroy and his family had the most elaborate and extensive appointments, with a separate sleeping tent each for Lord and Lady Lytton, and another for the children and their nannies. Close by were fully furnished and carpeted quarters for viceregal entertaining, fronted by a huge *shamiana,* to which fabric walls could be attached in cooler weather.

Despite twinges of social conscience as she saw the miserable lean-tos where the lesser servants slept, offering no protection from dust or cold, the vicereine enjoyed the series of state dinners, receptions, and other entertainments, and relished her central position in a great moment of state. Sadly, Lytton took her presence and aid for granted, spending most of his time checking and rechecking arrangements for the Assemblage, attending official events, or meeting with government officials to discuss ways to deal with a major outbreak of famine in Madras. As a result, on New Year's Eve, Lady Lytton sat alone in her luxurious tent, hoping for a visit from her husband as a far-off band played "Auld Lang Syne." Despite the presence of her "dear girls," the woman at the top of the Anglo-Indian social pyramid felt very much alone, and all the vicereinal trappings and appointments provided little comfort to a forlorn, neglected, and oft-slighted wife.

Putting personal misery aside, Lady Lytton sallied forth the next morning in a brocaded dark blue velvet and silk gown by Worth to attend the Assemblage. To a flourish of trumpets, the viceroy and vicereine and their two small daughters walked slowly to the large hexagonal throne-pavilion draped with brilliant red, blue, and white satin streamers ornately embroidered in gold with appropriate emblems. The vicereine sensed the disapproval of senior British officials at her presence, but maintained her best royal demeanor and watched adoringly as the viceroy led the ceremonies. After guards of honour crashed to present arms and massed bands blared a thundering rendition of the National Anthem, the entire crowd stood as the viceroy commanded the chief herald to read the proclamation announcing Her Majesty's elevation to Empress of India.

The glory of the day was marred when the salute of 101 guns panicked the elephants, several of whom pulled tether and ran amok, trampling and killing some Indian spectators among the general crowd. Terrified, Lady Lytton tried frantically to divert her girls from viewing the gruesome scene, and calm was ultimately restored. The Assemblage concluded as Lytton joined the troops in several ringing cheers in honour of the Queen-Empress. At the state banquet and evening party that followed, the vicereine appeared in yet another Worth gown, this one all white and embroidered with gold and faux pearls. She was amused by the stares of the princes at the ball, who thought the pearls on her gown were real, like those on their own elaborate costumes. At bedtime, ever-dutiful Edith wrote in her diary: "And so ended the greatest day in our lives, and what a position for my dear husband!"[12]

For three days after the Assemblage, Lord Lytton received the princes individually, presenting each with a silken banner embroidered with a distinctive heraldic device which he himself had designed. As the viceroy was receiving the potentates, the vicereine entertained ladies of high station every afternoon from three till five in her tent, her easy manner, grace, and charm evident to all who attended. When the Assemblage ended, Lady Lytton left the site with a sense of relief. "We are alive, that is all I can say," she wrote. "But we are dead tired...The continual banging of guns, the dust and the duties made the time very trying, still it was splendid... and we are most thankful."[13] As empty and vainglorious as it came to be seen later, the great event marked the pinnacle of her stint as vicereine and many among the British elites at home and India as well as journalists felt that the widespread praise for her conduct was well-deserved.

While imperialists praised the gathering as an impressive show of British imperial power and majesty, the pseudo-coronation in absentia failed to squelch the controversy at home surrounding the Queen's assumption of the title of Empress. Beyond that, it stirred things up in other respects. Many Britons in India were incensed at official attention being paid to Indians, while some Indian journalists questioned the appropriateness of staging of such splendor while famine was ravaging much of southern India. The handful of middle class educated Indians attending were also appalled by the wasteful spectacle, and by the *Raj*'s usurpation of traditional Indian ceremonies and bending of history. As vicereine, Lady Lytton was caught up in that socio-political vortex, and its more serious consequences. While most Europeans in India derided Lord Lytton's including his wife and daughters in the Assemblage ceremonies, their presence was well-received by most Indian rulers. Lytton hoped that this bold new social interaction would help bridge what he called the "inconvenient and deplorable gulf existing between English and native society." But, as with so many of his visions, proposals, decisions and actions, the viceroy found himself alone, and in this case in a heavy crossfire of condemnations. Lytton's view of "Indian society," was limited to the very thin outer rind, and his unashamed romanticism prevented his appreciating the racism of the Anglo-Indians, and the fact many foreigners and Indians, and some Britons as well were appalled by the raw gaucherie of the Assemblage. Also dismaying to the viceroy was observers' condemnation of the flaunting of imperial power, and ostentatious displays of Indian princely wealth. Even the British ladies arriving in Delhi with trunks of new dresses who learned that that "dark gentlemen" would be present at all the balls and parties as part of viceroy's honouring of Indian potentates turned on Lytton. Their ire was matched by that of most Anglo-Indians, who excluded "locals" from their social life.

Such routinely blatant lack of respect for his role, the Crown, and British majesty in a broader sense led Anglo-Indians to label Lytton's vice-royalty the "Black *Raj*" as they viewed each of his revisions of customs and procedures as an attempt to unduly accommodate Indian potentates. Lady Lytton suffered as well, encountering mounting disrespect and coldness from Anglo-Indians as she strove to use her considerable charm and reputation for warm hospitality to repair relationships damaged by Lytton's often bizarre behaviour. The widespread view of the Lytton court as a moral slough was strongly reinforced when the vicereine's cousin, Colonel George Villiers of the Grenadier Guards, created a scandal with an "inappropriate" liaison with a married woman. The upwelling of outrage, layered onto recurrent rumours of Lytton's infidelity, and his open flirting with staff members' wives, crested with a lurid rumour that Lytton had sired the son of Lady Jane, wife of Sir John Strachey, Financial Member of the Viceroy's Council. Although it was untrue, Edith found her attempts to quell the resultant gossip all in vain.

The glories of the Assemblage – if not the odd behaviour of Lord Lytton – were long forgotten by the time the next imperial ceremony was announced in 1903. No British luminary was better suited or more eager to design and conduct a grand imperial ceremony than George Nathaniel Curzon. Academically gifted, a lucid writer, and patently ambition-driven in politics, he clung to the manners and customs of the fading aristocratic order that had left his family and himself somewhat land-poor. Not only did he seem unaware of the political costs of his adhering to those forms, and the increasing extent to which they were seen as absurd or wasteful, but he dedicated his life to ascending that rickety ladder. Indeed, Curzon spent much of his young adulthood preparing for the viceroyalty, travelling extensively in the East, and studying the region intensively against the day when the call might come.

That was slightly less true of Curzon's wife, the American heiress, Mary Leiter, whose father, Levi Leiter, had made his fortune in as a founding

George Nathaniel Curzon a dynamic and driven viceroy he would transform the Durbar ceremony into a glittering imperial event.

member of Field, Leiter & Co. which evolved into the department store empire, Marshall Field. Well-read, witty, and attractive, Mary was also able to hold her own as a super-rich American luminary in Britain alongside Consuelo Vanderbilt Marlborough and Jennie Jerome Churchill. Once Curzon's viceregal appointment was announced, she regained her momentary loss of a sense of social balance, promising her parents that she would do her best to fill "...the greatest place ever held by an American abroad."[14] The titles Baron and Lady Curzon of Kedleston fuelled Mary's eagerness to go to India, and she exclaimed in a letter to her parents: "Oh the ladyships! I feel like a ship in full sail on the high seas of dignity."[15]

While at Windsor for the traditional pre-departure "dine and sleep" in 1899, the viceregal couple visited with the widowed Lady Lytton, then a Lady-in-Waiting to the Queen, to learn something of what was in store for them in the East. At that point, Edith was unaware that the new viceroy intended to organize a grand fete intending to surpass the ceremonial magnificence of her beloved husband's Imperial Assemblage. Had she known, she might have been a bit less courteous and forthcoming with advice to her American successor. But after the death of Queen Victoria in 1901 and the accession of Edward VII, Curzon proposed a special ceremony on the plain at Delhi at which the new King would actually be crowned as Emperor-in-India – *Kaiser-i-Hind*. As the seat of the last true Indian empire, Delhi was the obvious choice for the 1903 (and later, the 1911) Coronation *Durbar*. Like Lytton, Curzon saw such a re-enactment of the age-old *durbar* ritual as a significant milestone in the history of British India, and of his own career, as well as the perfect expression of his somewhat feudal views. All obviously hinged on the monarch's presence, and the new King initially was quite keen on the idea, since he was eager to return to India. However, his ministers pointed out that if he were crowned in India, all the other dominions would demand an equivalent honour, so he agreed that the viceroy should stand in his place at the ceremony, and sent his brother, the Duke of Connaught, as his representative. This meant that the Curzons would be the salient personages at the *durbar*, despite the presence of the royal Duke and Duchess, since only a British monarch outranked the viceroy on the Indian chessboard.

The Curzons, realising the need to deftly balance formalities of viceregal ritual and routine against princely sensitivities, strove most carefully to avoid giving any slight or offense. But despite all its constraints and delicate points of protocol, the *durbar* offered the ultimate opportunity for an imperial zealot to design, organize, and officiate at the most imposing ceremonial ever seen in India. Curzon would now be able to frame an event that would recreate the pageantry of the ancient kings of India in a way that honoured its new rulers while manifesting an Indian subcontinent unified under British rule.

The daunting agenda of ceremonial details was, of course, right up George's alley, for throughout his life, Curzon had demonstrated a compulsion to control his environment. To his already overwhelming workload ("Do everything yourself" was his maxim in all matters) the viceroy now nearly exhausted himself overseeing the *durbar's* arrangements, including attending hundreds of hours of meetings, and constantly reviewing plans and designs. He even organised an exhibition of Indian arts and crafts to highlight the skill and artisanship of native jewelers and craftsmen, excluding insofar as possible any items that even hinted at Western influences. His critics, with no reference to the obvious Freudian paradigms, saw his obsession as some kind of pathology, and the *durbar* arrangements as more of a personal glorification of the viceroy than homage to the King. Some snidely deemed the durbar the "Curzonation," while others saw his compulsive immersion in *durbar* details as merely one of many expressions of his confidence that no one could do anything as well as himself, let alone to an adequate level of perfection.

In the months preceding the *durbar*, as Curzon's involvement with the great event left his wife more and more on her own, her health began to decline. Never of strong constitution, she suffered some sort of collapse – probably related to her weak heart – as the great event approached. Off in Dehra Dun for a rest, she wrote in a somewhat dramatic tone to George about her weak condition, expressing the fear that the day was coming when she would not be able to fulfill her duties, for "India...slowly but surely murders women."[16] Like earlier vicereines – and most especially Charlotte Canning and Edith Lytton – Mary had completely bent her wishes and desires to her husband's, and in the deepest of funks at Dehra Dun, she resigned herself to an early death as the final dismal reward for her sacrifice. But that pessimism proved both transient and misplaced, as Mary recovered her health before the great event began, allowing her to assume her key role and duties in the *durbar* festivities.

Curzon's exhaustion and concern for his wife's ill health were not the only shadows falling over the durbar preparations. British soldiers' ill-treatment of "natives," a chronic problem in India since the Mutiny, surfaced again just before the great event. In the months leading up to the *durbar*, members of several British regiments – most notably the 9th Lancers and the West Kent regiment – were accused of raping and murdering Indians. But when two military inquiries found no evidence to bring against specific individuals, a furious Curzon ordered those regiments publicly censured and punished. Despite support from Army leaders in India and the Balfour government, Curzon was assailed by the British press. The Lancers' substantial aristocratic connections at home offset the Indian press's praise for the viceroy's actions. Condemnations from various quarters in England blended with club society in British India labelling Curzon a "nigger lover." Curzon's elaborate *durbar* plans were also crimped by the home government who rejected his plan to announce a tax reduction at the event, bringing him to the point of resignation – a ploy he would use later with disastrous results.

Aware that Lytton's garish medieval trappings had been widely criticised and ridiculed, Curzon designed the *durbar* setting to present his vision of the epitome of British dignity and taste. The main horseshoe-shaped amphitheater encompassed a huge arena in which the troops were to pass in review. Dominating that scene, at the apex of the horseshoe arch, was the main dais, a relatively simple structure, at least when compared with Lytton's elaborate design, its white and gold onion-shaped dome offering an abstraction of a Mughal motif. The covered stand with benches or chairs surrounding the amphitheater was divided into blocs reserved for lesser dignitaries, the military, and 6,000 places for the general public. The entire structure was constructed of bamboo and grass fiber, or pith, a traditional medium for sculpture in India.

Principal dignitaries on the dais included the viceroy and vicereine, the Duke and Duchess of Connaught, other British government and military officials, and the principal maharajahs and princes. Closest to the viceregal thrones was the literally glittering firmament of the Curzons' personal guests who came from afar, including such worthies as the Dukes and Duchesses of Marlborough and Portland, Lord and Lady Crewe, Lord and Lady Derby and other members of Curzon's "set", as well as European royals like the Grand Duke of Hesse. In contrast to the Lyttons, who had only four such notables at their Assemblage, Curzon had invited 160 distinguished personages from Britain who traveled aboard *SS Arabia*. (Of course, the comfort, reliability, and speed of ocean transport had improved at least an order of magnitude between the two events.) The tons of baggage stacked in *Arabia*'s hold included dresses and uniforms appropriate to the many dinners, parties, receptions, reviews and other events associated with the *durbar*. In the book which Dorothy, daughter of artist Mortimer Menpes, wrote and which he illustrated on their travel to the *durbar*, described the distinguished travelers aboard *Arabia* in great and no wholly loving detail, as "Grosvenor Square... judges, peers, duchesses, and celebrities of all kinds ..." Beyond describing their vast wardrobes, and shipboard entertainments, she included vignettes of their bouts of seasickness, with a subtle humor that only partly masked a lack of respect for such august personages.[17] Not everyone was oblivious to the self-parodying aspect of the occasion, and while *Punch* correspondents and cartoonists pulled their punches, there were jabs all the same.

Lady Curzon's mother and sister Daisy were also on hand for the celebrations, as was one of George's closest friends, and former paramour, the author Pearl Craigie. Hired by London's *Daily Graphic* and New York's *Collier's Weekly* to report on the *durbar*, Pearl was no longer a romantic threat, but her easy manner with Curzon irked Mary, who knew she could not compete with either as an intellectual equal. Pearl's effusive compliments in her articles about the *durbar*, and glowing tributes to the Curzons were later compiled in a book entitled *Imperial India*, published under her usual pseudonym, John Oliver Hobbes. These public comments sharply contrasted with her remarks to others that Curzon was trapped in a "loveless" and "tragic" marriage, and was bored by his American wife.[18] Whether or not Pearl's comments were a former lover's wishful thinking, she proudly reported in letters to friends in London that she was seated next to the viceroy three times at dinner, and twice at lunch in a single week. Beyond all the intricate social dynamics of the European attendees,

The Curzons
atop the largest
domesticated
elephant
in India,
borrowed from
the Maharaja
of Benares,
process towards
the Delhi
Durbar of 1902.

the presence of all those noteworthy visitors heightened the glamour of the event, and blunted the negative effect of the King Emperor's absence.

The two-week long celebration began on December 29, 1902, as the viceroy and vicereine led the four-mile long State Entry into Delhi, riding atop the largest elephant in India, once again loaned by the Maharajah of Benares, who had provided the same creature to Lord Lytton in 1877. It was a society journalist's dream. Enshrouded in gaudy Eastern luxury, the Curzons were aloft in the same boat-shaped silver *howdah* used by the Prince of Wales in 1875 and the Lyttons in 1877. Mary, aware that all eyes were on them, but her especially, wore a fashion editor's vision – a brilliant white dress, caught up on either side with bunches of violets replicated in paintings on her pale violet parasol. Seated beside her beloved husband, enveloped in luxury, and accepting the cheers of thousands, she was exultant. Now, neither heat, nor dust, nor concerns over her health could mar her happiness. It proved to be most memorable moment of her life. One can only speculate as to what her little girls thought as they waved from the steps of India's largest mosque, the Jama Masjid, as their parents rode by.

There seemed to be no end to the splendor of it as the impressive procession of rulers and ruled lumbered majestically down the *Chandni*

Chowk, the "Silver Road," the grandest of Indian streets. Each of the 150 elephants in the procession bore a gold or silver *howdah*, some encrusted with gems, and all swathed in cloth of gold or silver, and accompanied by escorts of mounted and marching troops, spearmen, and macebearers. Everything seemed designed to boggle the mind of even the most sophisticated viewer, from servants with spears holding elephants to prevent their bolting into the crowds; ordered hordes of soldiers; retainers and functionaries by the tens of thousands; and throngs all along the route, paying homage to their British monarch, and celebrating his accession.

Faded photographs and newspaper drawings of the time present only a faint limning of the scale and magnificence of the event, and the vast and complex *durbar* camp. Roads and railways were laid, and arrangements made for electric lights, sanitation, water supplies, medical, and police presence. As in 1877, accommodations in the *durbar* camps for European and Indian guests were luxurious. The lists in account books showing prices paid for such items as satin toilet covers, damask teapot covers, pastry doilies, damask tray cloths, and satin counterpanes reflect something close to a pinnacle of Veblenian excess. Walkways were bordered by flowers and swept clean several times a day so that guests could walk in relative cleanliness between the various tents. Myriad servants ensured that gowns and uniforms were pressed and ready for all occasions. Transport was always at hand, as stylishly dressed ladies, uniformed European guests, and bejeweled maharajahs stepped into elegant carriages to be conveyed from event to event. There were few idle or empty moments for servers or the served, since official ceremonies extended well beyond the *durbar* itself. Two investitures, a state ball, a review of the troops, and a viceregal reception of ruling chiefs were orchestrated to reinforce the image the British as legitimate heirs of the Mughal empire which ruled much of India from Delhi for so long.

The great *durbar* began on January 1, 1903, and as any event organised by Curzon, precisely at the scheduled time, 11 a.m. The throng of some 26,000 in the arena was entertained by massed bands and choirs until the ceremony began.

Most European guests were captivated by Indian rulers and their entourages' finery. As befit the foci of the spectacle, Lord and Lady Curzon arrived last into the arena in a four-horse carriage accompanied by outriders clad in scarlet and gold. The vicereine, in a gown of pale blue chiffon heavily embroidered in gold, alighted from her carriage, glided up the gold-embroidered carpet, curtsied low, and gracefully took her place beside the Duchess of Connaught, while the viceroy made a low, courtly bow to the Duchess and the Duke before ascending the silver viceregal throne. After a musical interlude and an imperial salute by the assembled troops, the herald read the official Proclamation declaring Edward VII King-Emperor. Curzon then read out the King's message to his subjects and with a final flourish of trumpets and troops, the *durbar* ended.

As much it may have seemed to be the apex of the celebrations, much more was in store. Later in the week, a great march-past of British and Indian troops took place, with Mutiny veterans given pride of place in the procession of loyal Indian forces. The viceroy and his guests were also offered more well-sanitised vignettes of the "real India" during the Parade of States, with various tribes of India saluting the viceroy in a long and exotic procession, overwhelmingly picturesque, if less than authentically representative of village India. An especially gaudy spectacle was a gold and silver cannon in the entourage of the Gaekwar of Baroda, drawn by white oxen covered with nearly transparent gold cloth, with gold-encased horns. That panoply of excess was only the first phase of two full weeks of official events interwoven with polo and cricket matches, gymkhanas, receptions, garden parties, dinners, balls, and fireworks, until, as Mortimer Menpes observed, everyone was "simply gorged with gaiety." The full array of events was, the *Daily Telegraph* reported, "at least five or six times as great as Lord Lytton's Durbar," just the kind of praise Curzon hungered for.[19]

And at the centre of the grand whirl was the vicereine, the symbolic queen of it all, appearing throughout in a series of new and ever more stunning costumes as she moved through the many sub-fetes and the great forest of guests' tents to be sure all was in order. Her presiding over all with Titania-like grace and slightly shimmering presence surprised many visitors who knew her in her chrysalis days in England as a shy, reserved young woman. Now her confidence and charm enhanced every occasion she attended, and she handled the steady flow of minor crises with an easy sureness and grace, all the more notable to the onlookers for her American origins, the grinding wheel of her schedule, and the underlying ever so faint, but ever present tremor of danger in settings in which terrorism might erupt at any moment despite all the efforts of the invisible but formidable security services.

Concerns about her lineage and heritage were put wholly to rest by her performance, as she received kudos from Curzon's aristocratic friends when they returned home. Even her mother and sister Daisy were awed by her regal performance, and Mortimer Menpes, despite the reflexive skepticism of the artist, found himself enchanted by her:

"Lady Curzon swept into the room, a vision of beauty in the palest of lilac gowns ...What an ideal wife for a Viceroy, I thought...and when I asked her if she did not feel the effects of the Durbar she said that work was meat and drink to her."[20]

Mary Curzon stands in her renowned peacock dress. For a while it was the most famous gown in the world.

But she also had her detractors, especially the waspish Pearl Craigie who publicly praised Mary and her diverse finery, but wrote to her friend Rev. W.F. Brown about the vicereine's flirtation with a handsome young Army doctor, Captain Armstrong, whom Pearl had met on the voyage out on the *SS Arabia*. Armstrong, she related, had told her that Lady Curzon "had the coarsest mind and *ways* of any woman he had ever known of *any* class." Even the prejudiced Pearl found this a bit hard to believe: "Curious. She looks so flower-like."[21] While determining where truth lay in all this must be left to speculation, Mary's triumph of the *Durbar*, and arguably of her reign as vicereine, came at the final event, the State Ball, held on

January 6. The setting for that final burgeoning of excessive display was the Emperor Shah Jehan's Diwan-i-Khas – the Private Hall of Audience – in Delhi's Mughal Palace, a huge pillared marble room, its walls inlaid with intricate patterns of pale amethyst, black onyx, bright cherry cornelian, shiny multi-coloured agate, and yellowish-green jasper. Curzon, seeking to highlight the gaudy ostentation, designed a system of hidden electric bulbs that lit the arches and the multi-coloured walls with a soft glow, but not too much, as some 4,000 guests, including 50 bejeweled and extravagantly costumed rulers, flowed from the main hall into adjoining supper rooms. As the Curzons prepared to make their grand entrance, guests formed an aisle down the centre of the main hall, those farther back straining or standing on chairs to see the *Raj*'s glamorous first couple. Media throughout the world soon presented images of Mary's dramatic entrance in her "peacock" dress, which became the most enduring after-image of vicereinity.

Taking her lead from her husband's attention to detail, Lady Curzon had carefully orchestrated her appearance. She spent weeks overseeing the design and creation of her gown, enduring endless fittings, and once it was completed, posed for a series of photographs and commissioned a large oil portrait of herself in the gown, in hopes that her triumph – and Curzon's – would be long remembered. So it was that when she entered the great hall, quiet gasps rippled throughout the assemblage as spectators reacted to her gown. A not-so-subtle homage to the lost Peacock Throne of the Mughal emperors, her cloth-of-gold dress was covered with tiny peacock feathers delicately stitched with gold thread, an emerald in each feather's eye, the skirt trimmed with white roses, and the bodice with lace. Highlighting the ensemble were the glittering diamond and platinum tiara of collet-set brilliants in a fleur-de-lys pattern, designed by Boucheron in Paris and paid for by her father, her Crown of India medal, and sparkling diamonds at her throat and wrists.[22] In a special irony, it was here that an American woman became one of the most enduring symbols of British rule in India, for no vicereine who followed would match her radiant feminine presence on that occasion.

All the efforts proved to be worth it as Lady Curzon received rave reviews. "You cannot conceive what a dream she looked," wrote one eyewitness, while another swooned: "Such beauty is not given to one woman in a million."[23] Even Pearl Craigie had to concede success in her written account of the ball: "Among the many charming beings to be seen in the vast crowd, the woman who presented the most romantic appearance and embodied the romantic ideal was Lady Curzon herself," wrote Pearl. She praised Mary's "fragile beauty" and her decision not to "smear her face with red-and-white washes" nor pile on her head "the [usual] pyramids of curls, pads, fringes, tulle and ribbons...pinned on without regard for proportion, balance, or line..."[24]

When, at last, the guests departed, and the *durbar* camp was struck, the exhausted viceroy and vicereine savoured their shared triumphs. From Dehra Dun, where she had gone to recover once again, she wrote George: "The Connaughts were no more than an extra gargoyle to a most intricate and wondrous building, every stone of which had been carved and placed by you. ...she is only a German *hausfrau*... But now that it is all over, every civilian in India knows to whom the credit is due..."[25] Despite his micro-management of every element of the two-week long celebration, Curzon awarded his wife her due: "For the splendid triumph of the social side, yours is the credit. Your beauty, your charm, your absolute unselfishness in looking after others...these it was that carried through the whole camp life...on the crest of an unbroken wave of success, while to all the public ceremonial you lent a grace and distinction the more marked from the utter inability of even the smartest and the most beautiful of our English ladies to contest it."[26] In India, Mary Curzon seemed to have at last conquered British high society and become one of them, an American as *grande* a *dame* as any aristocratic predecessor.

The ebbing of the glow of glory was, of course, inevitable, but the intrusion of fiscal concerns sped the descent. Many dissented from Curzon's assertion that the £180,000 cost of the *durbar* (roughly $40 million in 21st century dollars) was well-spent in terms of increasing British and royal prestige and re-confirming Britain's commitment to its Indian empire. At a time when liberalism was on the ascendancy in many quarters, both British and American newspapers saw that expenditure as excessive, especially in light of conditions in India. Some papers cited the starving Indians "who asked for bread and had been given a *durbar* instead... Such extravagance is a shameful manifestation of the cruelty of Lord Curzon's craze for impe-rialistic display."[27] To the charge that he had staged the event for his own glorification rather than to honour his King and Empire Curzon responded that "...the effect produced by this overwhelming display of unity and patriotism is still alive and will not perish."[28]. Although he claimed that the *durbar* was in celebration of British power in India, the one element of Indian society that kept the system running, the "Bengali *babus*" – members of the "uncovenanted" Indian Civil Service – went unrecognised. Curzon's disdain for "ordinary" and lower-caste Indians and his belief that they would never be able to rule themselves shone through in his design of the *durbar*. Only the rulers really mattered, and then only in terms of their "cooperation" in maintaining the Empire

Beyond all the acclaim in British and Indian social circles, and jour-nalistic kudos, the *durbar* was an enormous personal triumph for the vicereine, as much as any bourgeois American woman could aspire to. Steering well away from the stirrings of militant feminism that were arising in the early 20th century, Lady Curzon emulated Edith Lytton's behaviour, playing the role of a dutiful wife, subordinating her needs and bending her behaviour to serve those of her husband's career and personal ambitions. His successes and failures became hers, and his enemies, her enemies, as she played the role of submissive helpmate. During the *durbar*, however, she was allowed to soar, and earned very high marks for her performance in support of George's imperial vision. That grandest of all occasions marked more than one zenith for the Curzons. Sadly, from that point onward, Curzon found himself descending a very steep political slope that led him to depart from Bombay in humiliation after losing a power struggle with the charismatic Commander-in-Chief, Lord Kitchener. While he managed to conceal rhis embitterment in most events and rituals surrounding his departure, it shone through brightly in his later writings about his Indian experience. His wife shared that sense of betrayal by what should have been a supportive government, and by his old friend and her admirer, Arthur Balfour. All the couple's hard work seemed to have gone for naught, and the grand imperial triumph a mere curiosity. In the few years that were left to her, Lady Curzon did not realize that she would be remembered as the most iconic of vicereines, not only because she was an American, but because her poise and beauty, and public demeanor set the highest standard for those women who followed her, and surpassed all her predecessors.

The last *Durbar*

In the end, Lady Curzon's graces overshadowed her husband's lack of them. As the Curzons prepared to leave India in November 1905, the departing viceroy behaved in a manner which his enemies deemed characteristic, by deliberately insulting his immediate successor, Lord Minto, preferring to expend his energies on the more politically expedient move of ensuring an appropriate welcome for the Prince and Princess of Wales, who were embarking on a tour of India.

While the Mintos did indeed have the honour of hosting the Wales in 1905, it fell to their successors, Lord and Lady Hardinge, to oversee the final *durbar* of the *Raj*, the Coronation *Durbar* of 1911 – the only time a reigning British monarch came to India. The tall, statuesque Lady Hardinge was fully at ease in associating with royalty, having been a lady-in-waiting to Queen Alexandra, and a close friend of the Queen's sister, the Dowager Empress of Russia. Her husband, Sir Charles Hardinge, first Baron Hardinge of Penshurst, a prominent diplomat as well as a close friend and trusted advisor of Edward VII, had eagerly sought the viceroy-alty – but the appointment was opposed by the King who preferred that Hardinge remain at the Foreign Office. After waiting out the Minto vice-royalty and the old King's death, Hardinge was finally offered the post and eagerly accepted – after getting positive counsel from Lord Lansdowne about the financial and family health concerns.

After the Hardinges arrived in Bombay on November 18, 1910, the new viceroy's first act was to announce a *durbar* celebrating the corona-tion of George V and Queen Mary as King-Emperor and Queen-Empress the following December – the first and only time a British monarch would be crowned outside the confines of the British Isles. The King proudly announced that this was "entirely my own idea"[29] and dismissed the concerns of the cabinet: namely, lack of precedence for such a long absence of the monarch from Britain, and the cost, at a time when the political climate at home was less and less likely to support "imperial" excesses.

While the main reason for holding the ceremony was to reinforce the monarch's personal connection to India, a secondary but important political purpose was to pacify Bengali agitators who were increasingly militant, demanding the reunion of Bengal, the release of political prisoners, and various local government, education and army reforms. Concerned that Bengali nationalists might be joined by militants in other regions of India, Hardinge and his Council resolved secretly to meet many nation-alist demands, despite their concerns that such concessions might trigger further unrest and create new opposition fronts among affected Muslims on the other side of the conflict. Faced with this dilemma, the Secretary of State for India persuaded members of the British cabinet to agree to use the *durbar* to have the King-Emperor announce as royal favours the reversal of the controversial partition of Bengal, and the transfer of the capital of British India from Calcutta to Delhi. To avoid controversy before the King's formal pronouncement, fewer than 30 people (the so-called "Masonic Circle") in London and India knew about the proposed changes. Even the Queen was kept out of the loop until she reached Bombay.

As the *durbar* approached, viceregal mail and telegraph lines were glutted with message traffic between the Government of India and the India Office in London regarding protocol issues. Within the web of the bureaucracy, it seemed as though the future success of the *Raj* depended more on the manipulation of public images and symbols and following the minute niceties of arcane and bizarre rituals than it did on competent administration. As with the previous *durbars*, and British ceremonials in India in general, the grand occasion set loose waves of obsessive concern about precedence, honours, and dress. The blizzard of cables and letters

The Hardinges riding an elephant in procession in 1913.

between Calcutta and London addressed such questions as who was of appropriate rank to attend the King and Queen, and to whom and in what sequence honours should be given during the royal visit. The Queen picked up on the spirit of things by demanding that only ladies from the higher ranks of the peerage serve as her attendants. Eventually the Duchesses of Devonshire and Shaftesbury were selected, although the Queen insisted on calling the latter "my woman Shaftesbury," much to the Duchess's annoyance.

Foremost and most difficult to resolve among all the discussions of precedence and protocol was the coronation ceremony. George, sharing his grandmother's special concern for India, recognised the importance of ceremony and ritual among its people. With that in view, he proposed crowning himself in full view of the populace, a Napoleonic gesture vigorously opposed by the Archbishop of Canterbury, among others. A coronation ceremony with its Christian consecration, the prelate pointed out, would offend Hindu and Muslim religious sensibilities alike. Others brought up the concern first raised in 1903 in the case of Edward VII, that if the monarch were "officially" crowned in one dominion, all the others would demand an equivalent ceremony. Ultimately, it was settled by having the King arrive at the *durbar* wearing his crown. But that led to another quandary: just which crown would he wear? Since an Act of Parliament forbade the Imperial Crown of State or St. Edward's Crown from leaving England, Garrard, the crown jeweler, was ordered to make a new crown, at an expected cost of some £60,000 – roughly 12 million 21st century dollars. That estimate assumed that most of the precious jewels required would be "donated" by Indian princes. Hardinge vetoed that proposal as politically unsupportable. It was, he felt, most undesirable that the viceroy and the government should virtually beg the princes for jewels to inset in their ruler's crown, especially since the flagrant brigandage that marked earlier British incursions in India had been substantially dampened by the passage of time, and the evolution of imperialist forms and customs.

Hardinge and his Council also opposed the proposal, worthy of a Galsworthy *haute bourgeois* scion, that Garrard create the special crown, "hire" it out for the *durbar* for £4,400, then break it up upon its return to London. Those in India realised how much damage that would do to the image of an all-powerful *Raj*, especially among the ruling princes if they saw the ultimate symbol of British power and majesty was a temporary, contrived trinket "on loan" from a jeweler. In the end, a new crown was designed and fabricated for the *durbar* by Garrard's for £60,000 – The Imperial Crown of India – featuring a jeweled headband and alternating arches and fleurs-de-lis, eight half-arches embellished with over 6,000 small diamonds, as well as dozens of larger sapphires, emeralds, rubies, and a velvet and miniver cap. Weighing in at over two pounds, it was the heaviest crown ever made, and George V would complain of its heft before and after the *durbar* ceremony. Even though the crown had been created for this singular event, and was paid for by taxes raised in India, it would not remain there, mainly because of Hardinge's fear that it would be a tempting symbol for a would-be usurper, or dissident. After being briefly displayed to the Indian public following the *durbar*, the crown was sent back to London and placed among other British crown jewels at the Tower of London,[30] including a special crown created for Queen Mary to wear at the *durbar*. Neither crown has ever been worn again.

Although it was not apparent when the Grand *Durbar* was held on December 12, 1911, it was the last such Indian imperial ceremony. It was inadvertently appropriate that in preparing for it, Hardinge showed an obsessional fervor about the details almost equal to Curzon's. Like his predecessor, he laboured in the shadow of what his legacy in India would be, and what Curzon's fête had set as a standard. He was determined that this would be a political and social triumph worthy of the second Hardinge to govern India, and that he and his wife would receive all the recognition and honour that was due the first family of the overseas Empire. But things went awry, in good part due to the King-Emperor's presence, which in effect "demoted" Hardinge to Governor-General, since there was no "vice-king" in India when the monarch was there. That alteration of precedence generated considerable confusion, since some in the King's suite, under the impression that Hardinge held no authority at all after the King arrived, failed to offer the honours usually accorded the viceroy when he boarded the King's ship, the *Medina,* in Bombay harbour. Hardinge, greatly offended, expressed his displeasure bluntly to the King's aides, and his irritation was evident to the King, who resolved to reverse the slight sometime during the visit.

The King-Emperor and Queen-Empress came ashore through a hastily erected white plaster ceremonial arch that later became a permanent monument to their visit and Bombay's signature landmark, the Gateway of India. Completed in 1924 and enhanced with decorative carvings and delicate *jharoka* work (window carvings), the 85-foot high stone archway of honey-coloured basalt was inspired by 16th century Gujerat architectural style. After 1911, that site became place of welcomes and farewells for all vicereines, and many British, European, and Indian dignitaries, as well the final farewell as the Last Post was sounded there when, in 1947, the last vicereine, Lady Edwina Mountbatten and the last British troops departed, after nearly three-and-a-half centuries of an official British presence in India, and nearly a century of direct rule.

The arrival of the British monarchs was welcomed by a 101 gun salute, and a series of public events in Bombay designed to demonstrate India's enthusiasm and loyalty for the ruler. They proceeded to Delhi by rail where another elaborate welcome was staged by the viceroy and vicereine in which the King created a huge protocol flap by refusing to ride an elephant for his State Entry. Instead of appearing in the traditional silver *howdah* and thus clearly visible to the assembled throngs, the monarch, with no royal standard preceding him, appeared astride a small horse and dressed as a Field Marshal, his face half-hidden by a white *topee.* The result was a considerably less enthusiastic welcome than the King expected. Once the viceroy explained – as diplomatically as he could – the cause for the lacklustre response, the King's disappointment soon ebbed

As with the two previous imperial ceremonials, exhaustive – and very expensive – arrangements were made to ensure the comfort of guests. Once again, the *durbar* camp, as elaborate and well-organised as that of 1903, was a virtual small city outside Delhi – a complex of 40,000 tents covering 45 square miles, including habitations for 300,000 people, and provisions for food, and sanitation, and quarters for their animals. Within the "mushroom city" covering 28 square miles there was a tent camp for each major Indian ruler, complete with roads, arched gateways, lampposts, instant gardens of potted plants, and flags. At night the camp took on what to observers seemed a magical glow as the tents and roads were outlined by hundreds of electric lights. Hardinge, concerned about Delhi's reputation as being located on a "malarial plain" and bent on preventing any major health problems from erupting among the visitors, ordered the eradication of the rat population to help prevent the spread of disease. Whether or not, as the viceroy claimed, 90,000 rats were actually killed to assure the monarchs' safety and well-being, the King and Queen enjoyed the most luxurious accommodations. Lady Hardinge had personally overseen the decoration of several lavish tents which were connected to form the royal apartments and was relieved when Queen Mary pronounced the quarters "delightful," since she had initially expressed a preference for more solidly built accommodations.

Despite lingering weakness and lack of stamina due to poor health, Lady Hardinge became as fully caught up in the *durbar* as Lady Curzon had been. Cheered by the arrival of her two sons from England, she was able to play her central role with apparent ease at the many receptions, garden parties, dinners, and official ceremonies. Working with the Military Secretary, she oversaw the comfort and well-being of her invited guests in the *durbar* camps, personally inspecting the carpeted and luxuriously appointed tents prepared for European guests, and making sure that the Indian princes and notables were well-cared for in separate and (nearly) equal quarters.

Despite the meticulous planning and administration and extensive safety provisions things went awry from time to time. Since the hundreds of closely arrayed tents presented a special danger from fire, guests were advised that matches were not needed inasmuch as tents were lighted by electricity. But despite such cautions, a blaze broke out that destroyed the fireworks prepared for the King's garden party, and another drove the Duchess of Devonshire from her tent clad only in a dressing gown. A huge stockpile of fireworks intended for the "People's Fete" exploded just before an equally spectacular fire consumed a multi-coloured tent purportedly covering 200,000 square yards lent by the Nawab of Bhawalpur for the princes' reception for the King.

Not surprisingly, some superstitious Indians saw those conflagrations as ominous portents. But despite such obstacles and difficulties, the third, last, and most elaborate *durbar* of the *Raj* was held on December 12, 1911. It had brought together a quarter of a million people from every part of the Indian Empire, and cost £660,000, more than three times the expense of Curzon's extravaganza. The durbar site consisted of two concentric amphitheaters, the larger one for the European guests, and the smaller for ruling

princes and other notables. More than 100,000 people filled the huge arena as 20,000 troops massed in the centre of the amphitheater. As the highest ranking 12,000 guests sat beneath the crimson and gold canopy of a *shamiana,* the bejeweled turbans of princes blended with the huge feathered hats of women guests, and white *topees* and helmets of British civil and military officials. The princes' multi-hued robes presented a grand moiré effect, running from purple and scarlet to rose, pink, light blue, and orange, and once again, as in 1903, everywhere embroidered with gold. Each potentate wore their best and most spectacular jewels: emeralds, diamonds, rubies, and sapphires glittered from turbans, necklaces, bracelets, rings, headdresses and nose jewels.

In the spectator stands, covered to protect the great and good from the punishing heat of the Indian sun, they walked on soft red carpets to their selected seats, where golden chains marked the bounds between the highest social tiers and the less and less privileged. At noon, all eyes turned toward the Royal Pavilion with its two high thrones beneath a golden dome as a flourish of trumpets and roll of drums marked the beginning of the grandest of events. Preceded by 14 mace bearers who wore white satin with robes of purple velvet edged in gold, their Majesties processed to the Pavilion. Very grandly dressed in their Imperial robes and wearing the crowns of India, they walked slowly to the golden-domed dais, under which they sat on thrones of solid silver, atop cloth-of-gold carpets to receive the formal allegiances of the viceroy and his Council, followed by the Princes of India and their families. The glitter of the latter's jewels and raiment rivaled the King and Queen, whose thrones were flanked by gold statues of trumpeting elephants, gleaming emblems of authority.

And as in 1903, the crowd included leaders of the Anglo-Indian community, women in fine silk gowns, and, for the most part, military officers and officials in full-dress uniforms. Once again the official *durbar* proclamation was read in English and Urdu by heralds in tabards emblazoned with the royal arms, followed by the viceroy's speech announcing the proposed administrative changes. The city which for 50 years had been nothing more than a major provincial town suddenly became an imperial capital, the primary seat of power in the subcontinent. The crowd gave three cheers for the King and his consort who then slowly and gracefully processed back to the *shamiana*, having fulfilled their obligations as the living embodiment of imperial power. The announcement was followed later by a ceremony held on December 15 for the laying of foundation stones to mark the restoration of Delhi as the capital city of India, wherein the King proclaimed that no capital "…ever held promise of greater permanence or of a more prosperous and glorious future."

To further solidify the image of the British crown as the legitimate and rightful heirs of the former Indian rulers, the King-Emperor and Queen-Empress attended ceremonies in full raiment at several places along the route of their tour of India after the *durbar*. In their appearance atop the walls of the famous Red Fort, ancient symbol of the Mughal empire, and site of a decisive battle during the "Great Mutiny," their Majesties were attended by young maharajahs and other sons of Indian potentates dressed as pages

(Opposite) The great imperial spectacle of the Delhi Durbar of 1911. The Nizam of Hyderabad, then reputed to be the richest man in the world, pays homage to the King Emperor George V and Queen Empress Mary.

in white or gold silk with turbans of embroidered gold silk. As gushing and hyperbolic as most published accounts were at the time, spectators agreed that no written description nor photograph could capture the richness of detail and splendor of what may have been the iconic summit of conspicuous consumption. Visions of the *durbar's* spectacle were presented to large audiences in India and the world, including black and white movie films made by several companies. Charles Urban, pioneer of the Kinemacolor process, returned to Britain with thousands of feet of colour film of the ceremonies. In an unprecedentedly long film – two and-a-half hours (16,000 feet) – three years before *The Birth of a Nation*, Urban showed his work in a stage setting with a Taj Mahal motif. Accompanied by a 48-piece orchestra, a chorus of 24, a fife and drum corps of 20, and three bagpipes, the film became one of the first major cinema hits as Londoners flocked to see it, and Urban became one of the first wealthy movie mughals.

Through it all, Lady Hardinge impressed the slew of visiting nobility with her calm, welcoming hospitality and her ability to handle any and all protocol issues which arose. Unflustered by the presence of the sovereigns – especially the demanding Queen – Winifred managed to meet all the expectations of both British India and the aristocrats visiting from home. At the State Ball, she wisely did not try to trump Lady Curzon's bejeweled "peacock" ensemble, choosing instead an elegant yet understated gown which showed off her several medals, and wearing her best tiara.

Winifred's decision not to try to be the centre of attention came out of her experience with the court at home. She was well aware that any attempt to upstage the Queen would be a dreadful mistake, one Her Majesty would not have forgiven. As it was, there was little chance that the vicereine would outshine the Queen, who came prepared to more than hold her own in terms of jewelry excess. In addition to her recently acquired Star of India badge, she also had the unique gems she had been given a few days earlier by the ladies of India – a large square of "historic" emeralds, engraved and set in diamonds, along with a necklace and pendant of emeralds set in diamond rosettes. That magnificence only enhanced the superb gems the Queen had brought with her. The "Cambridge emeralds" included a set of perfectly matched cabochon emeralds suspended in the 15 interlaced diamond circles of her tiara; a diamond and emerald necklace with two drops of uneven length, one a large pear-shaped emerald and the other a marquise diamond cut from the famous Cullinan; emerald and diamond earrings; two bracelets; an enormous emerald brooch; and an elaborate stomacher, also of emeralds and diamonds. When Queen Mary appeared in full regalia, she literally sparkled in the hot Indian sunshine or under the soft lights of a marble ballroom.

Whether *pro forma* or as a measured but heartfelt gesture the

King George V and Queen Mary at the Delhi Durbar in 1911. The Maharaja of Bikaner stands at the right. He would represent India at the Paris Peace Conferences in 1919.

King-Emperor and Queen-Empress, evidently delighted by the *durbar* and their Indian visit in general, rewarded Lord and Lady Hardinge for their role in its success by presenting them fulsome tokens of their royal esteem. The viceroy received the Chain of the Victorian Order from the King-Emperor, and the vicereine, a diamond and ruby pendant from the Queen-Empress, along with three large silver bowls with Hardinge's family crest, and silver-copper framed photos of the monarchs in their coronation robes. The many political threads woven into the tapestry of spectacles and ceremonies, bold and subtle, were aimed at bolstering Britain's Imperial image and rule, and at showcasing the monarchy.

Results were uneven. The King's announcements regarding Bengal's reunification and the new site for the capital were not universally welcomed. The fury of British merchants in Calcutta at the impending shrinkage of their access to the seats of power of the *Raj*, and business activity was reflected in the "HMG" "Hardinge Must Go" signs that appeared throughout the city. As three former viceroys, Curzon, Minto, and Lansdowne, attacked the proposed changes in the House of Lords, Hardinge found himself hard-pressed by the press at home and in India. Lady Hardinge also became a target for those waves of ire, despite her attempts to be pleasant to all, no matter their political views. All the outrage, however, had no palpable effect. The measures were implemented, leaving Hardinge and his admin-istration to suffer the fury of many Anglo-Indians after the monarchs sailed home on January 10, 1912. The King sliced close to the truth when he joked on the ship's deck awaiting its departure: "You seem very pleased, Charlie, to be getting rid of us!"

The King had made a special effort to correct the ceremonial blunder his entourage had made when he arrived by ordering an honour guard of Royal Marines to greet the viceroy when he accompanied the royals aboard the ship, followed by a salute from escorting British cruisers as the Hardinges' launch returned to shore. Basking in the glow of their sovereign's gratitude, and triumphant at the success of the great imperial spectacle they had overseen, the Hardinges were fortunately unable to see the trials and tragedies that awaited them in the coming years. Nor was it clear to any of those involved that the *Raj* had held its last *durbar*.

Piercing the Veil: Medical Care for Women

The basic purpose of various nations creating overseas empires was to favour the Mother Country economically and strategically through dominance, exploitation, trade and a fusion of cultures and interests that continues to be a source of puzzlement to historians. Britons in India for example did not see themselves as colonists in the way that others did in other the other major domains of the Empire. From the first arrival of British merchant adventurers in 1603, the goal was clear and simple: to enrich themselves and their masters in London. India was to serve as a source of wealth, and they were to go home rich. As the increasingly complex commercial ventures evolved into structures of governmental and military power, the Honourable East India Company managed to extend control over roughly half of the subcontinent by the early 19th century. As British influence in India expanded, so did the sense that Britain had "earned" India, and that responsibilities toward the subject peoples were limited to rendering justice, respecting and protecting their rights, and to "study their happiness." The status of women in India as indicated by such practices as *suttee*, female infanticide, early forced marriage and sexual intercourse, was seen by the overlords as clear evidence of the "barbarism" of Indian culture that supported British legitimacy as colonialists and imperialists.

As meandering as steps toward social reform in England in the early and mid-1800s were, the parallel pace in India was even more halting. Most senior British officials in India were reluctant to interfere with the intricate and vast workings of Indian society beyond what they felt was necessary to maintain the level of public safety and organization needed to support the systems of commerce, taxation, and governance that was called the *Raj*. Few of the British in India recognised a moral duty to improve the lives of the Indians, or to build the sophisticated infrastructure for an industrial state when many among the elites at home were not all that eager to do so in the Mother Country.

Although from the outset, India's British overseers created or transplanted such institutions as law courts and civic corporations, and copied specific ceremonies from home, such efforts were mainly aimed at keeping order, not to establish an imperial colony as such. In fact, many early British arrivals had "gone native," immersing themselves in Indian languages and culture, acquiring Indian wives or mistresses, and gaining an appreciation of Indian art and culture, from unique cuisine to even more unique sensuality. At the same time, the punishing heat, squalor, and devastating illnesses led the Company's men to feel themselves entitled to whatever pleasures and wealth they could acquire, since survival itself was a long-odds prospect. Bengal was the worst location in that respect, but in the early days of British colonization, chances of a Company clerk returning home were slim. In the 17th century, they were roughly one in six, and more than half of the Company's employees in Bengal died between 1705 and 1775.

Prior to 1885, the British government in India was officially tolerant and sometimes directly supportive of missionaries' efforts to bring Western medical care to the "natives," but overall, the *Raj* paid little attention to improving Indian women's health. The main foci of the British rulers were the health and well-being of the military and the European community. Illustrative of that hard reality was the fact that throughout most of the 19th century, the European medical community was comprised almost entirely of Indian Medical Service doctors and administrators. When, in 1882, the Viceroy, Lord Ripon, a Liberal reformist, attempted reforms aimed at increasing Indian participation in the areas of health, public works, and education, nearly all his efforts in the public health arena were thwarted by British officials. Even though it was becoming increasingly obvious that poor sanitary conditions caused disease, and that Europeans might contract infections from their servants, the British often failed – or refused – to recognize the links between improving the general health of Indians and their own welfare, and, indeed, survival.

The fact that the Europeans' death rates were lowest, and upper class Indians next, allowed British officials to maintain a fatalistic approach to public health issues. At the same time, growing awareness of microbes as a cause of disease reinforced the rulers' impulse to maintain distance between themselves and the ruled, socially and in the design of towns and cantonments. The only major concern of the British government in

India regarding Indian women's health was in regard to venereal disease since that was a serious problem in the Indian Army, and in British forces stationed in India. In 1805, the Honourable East India Company created "lock hospitals" at cantonments throughout India in which prostitutes suspected of having venereal diseases were confined and treated. Those peculiar institutions were officially closed in 1833, but reinstated in 1868 with the passage of the Contagious Diseases Act which mandated "regulation and inspection" of prostitutes at military cantonments. Although the Act was technically repealed in the 1880s, covert confinement of Indian women without due process to isolate British troops from venereal infection via Indian prostitutes continued in some cantonments.

While government concern for the health of Indian women in this case was incidental and aimed at reducing levels of infection and resultant costs of hospitalising British troops, the effect of the Contagious Diseases Act extended beyond the domain of the military. By allowing any European to declare any Indian woman a prostitute, which required her to submit to medical inspection, it meant that an Indian woman of any caste could be examined, and if found to be infected, confined. Beyond the resentments created by allowing even the lowest ranking European to label any Indian woman a social outcaste, it linked social respectability to medical diagnosis.

Even those vicereines who studiously avoided contact with the very poorest Indians were aware – however superficially – of the deplorable state of native health care, and felt some concern. In the Mother Country, from the mediaeval era to the mid-20th century, most British aristocratic women – especially those raised on large estates – were widely involved directly in caring for the poor, including some efforts to provide health care. Most vicereines were familiar with the "Lady Bountiful" role, a cliché based on the solid reality of an elegantly dressed and sweet-smelling grand lady from the nearby stately home sweeping into a tenant's cottage bearing baskets of food and clothing. Such aid, which allowed country gentry to act out their ideals of local voluntarism and Christian charity, also symbolised one form of *noblesse oblige*, and the elaborate feudal obligations and customs that embodied the web of hard labour on the land that underlay the privileged way of life in the upper tiers of the social hierarchy. In addition, a "lady's" ability to demonstrate a range of managerial skills and organize effectively was a hallmark of her upper-class status.

At the same time, however, those bent on serious reform saw elites' attempts to improve the public good in their locales as more symbol than substance, posturing in lieu of substantial reforms. Not only were such efforts limited in scope, but many saw them as merely a kindly mask over the elites' underlying objective of holding onto political power against the rising tides of populism and democracy. But even though providing private charity on the large estates was seen as women's – or more precisely – lady's work, it offered aristocratic ladies with first-hand views of the problems of the poor, especially the lack of sanitation, and marginal medical care. Up to the mid-1880s, most of the vicereines, as aristocrats raised or living in manor houses, were familiar with these personal and informal forms of charity, although some were also members of urban-based social reform organizations. In India, however, they found themselves in an alien and often hostile setting, facing a far wider and more complex range of familial, social, political, and ceremonial demands, and lacking even the most limited mechanisms of charity with which they were familiar at home.

Despite the grindingly slow pace of change, the wind freshened in fitful stages after the Napoleonic Wars. Some zealous British reformers saw India as fertile ground, a place where framing new laws could help create a society based on the "radical and evangelical" ideas often frustrated by the inertia of English society.[1] The increasing flow of European women to India also altered the relationship between Britons and Indians. The close relationships of the earlier *nabobs* and Indian women – either by marriage or as mistresses – faded away as Victorian morality and racism intruded themselves. The famed 'fishing fleet' – English women arriving in India seeking husbands – were shocked by the sensuality of Indian culture, and by many prospective husbands' attraction thereto. Their reports to friends and family reinforced strong beliefs at home and among many of the British in the subcontinent that Indian culture was inferior. Its art and mythology were graphically erotic, and its customs cruel and barbaric, like *suttee*, the ritual burning of widows, forced child marriage, and the *Thug* murder cult.

The sense of exaltation that followed, and which soared further after Britain's further ascent to the pinnacle of imperial power after Napoleon's fall, fed British self-confidence, and fuelled the resolve of many – but not all – among the British elites at home and in India to expose Indians to Western – i.e. Christian – values and beliefs and thereby create a better life for the native peoples over whom they ruled. That set loose a torrent of cultural imperialism, as well as moralising and evangelising. Even British women who were not missionaries saw it as their duty to bring Christianity and the benefits of Western culture to the "benighted natives" of India.

That climate of self-assuredness led 19th century British author Maud Diver to conclude that no woman – missionary or civilian – could live in India for any length of time without becoming drawn to advancing the welfare of the Indian people, especially by the commonality of all women's concern for the health and well-being of their families, and agonies and dangers of childbirth. Surely, Diver wrote, "...by reason of that common bond, a large measure of her love and interest must go out to the gentle, grey-eyed women whose…lives are too often crowded with very ugly realities."[2] The *memsahibs* who did endeavor to help Indian women were for the most part women who fell in love with the country and its people, or whose families had strong ties to India. Those who had been born in India and then married British officials were most likely to try to help; they were significantly attached to India, found it easier to accept the hardships, had better relationships with servants, and felt a responsibility to the local people they lived near.

These women were the exception, however. Most *memsahibs* focused on survival and mundane tasks at hand, on raising their children, helping their husbands' careers, and most importantly, coping with the heat, dust, insects, and predators, as well as the grinding boredom of daily existence. Women were also actively discouraged by their menfolk from any activity that might be perceived as outside social norms. The desire to conform to expected behaviour was aggravated by the impermanence of their living situations. Civil service wives usually moved around India frequently, so it was difficult to set in motion a long-term social program. The ever-present heart-tugging visions of "home" also weakened any inclination to believe that they had a real stake in India's future, let alone the betterment of its women. Many in the British community saw showing concern for the locals' welfare – missionaries excepted – as unacceptable behaviour for people so clearly superior to those they ruled. Beyond that, those trying to help Indian women often encountered apathy or outright resentment from those whom they sought to aid, along with the sturdy barriers of racial and religious prejudice and superstition. Even with those obstacles in clear view, some women made the effort, in the spirit of Diver's view that "… woman is the lever, the only infallible lever whereby sunken nations are upraised."[3] But it was also all too clear in a society based on strict social stratification and precedence that only action by leaders at the apex of the hierarchy had any real chance of stimulating interest and action on the scale required to bring adequate medical care to Indian women on any significant scale. It was not until 1885 that a vicereine – Hariot Dufferin – made this work "respectable" and gave urgency and momentum to the cause of improving medical care for Indian women.

Whatever impetus and visibility the wife of the Governor General or later, a vicereine, could offer in advancing these early efforts, there was a major difference between their work and achievements, and the labours of Englishwomen who lived in India for much longer periods, some nearly all their lives. The vicereine's stints there were limited to five years in most cases, far less than those of the missionaries, teachers, and female doctors, nurses and technicians who "came out" from England along with wives of Indian Civil Service officials, foresters, railway employees, etc.

Five years was also far less time than that spent by wives of British merchants and soldiers, many of whom bore burdens in India as heavy or greater than their menfolk. Many of the latter served as volunteers, committing themselves to "good works" for much longer periods of time and without the power and majesty of the government close at hand, or the recourse to luxury. It is hardly surprising that women labouring in those metaphorical vineyards frequently saw their activities as more substantive than those of transient figureheads. Beyond that was the sense of carrying out the larger mission as they saw it of bringing Christianity to the heathen.

The first soldiers in this battle were female missionaries whose involvement in medicine in India had begun a generation earlier in 1813, just after the Company lifted its ban on Christian missionaries working in India. It was a natural extension from caring for the natives' souls to caring for their earthly bodies, and from the 1830s onward, the London Missionary Society in South India included medical work as part of its evangelistic mission. The L.M.S. recognised that helping Indians medically, especially Indian women, gave them an entrée for spreading the gospel in the spirit of what later became known as "winning the hearts and minds." At the same time however, male missionaries' expectations that Western medical care would be welcomed by Hindus were confounded. Medical aid brought few converts to the church despite years of dedicated efforts to treat the sick, the opening of dispensaries in remote areas, and the introduction of the benefits of Western medical care to the locals. When missionaries' wives and daughters became more involved in medical mission work, it became clear that their efforts yielded more solid results. In helping to provide medical care in their "natural" role as nurses, the women made inroads into the hitherto forbidden area of native life, the zenanah, or women's quarters, which no man could enter however dire an illness might be or how urgent the need for medical assistance. That raised a new hope that Christian women's providing medical aid to Indian females would allow Europeans missionaries to increase their influence over the women in a household, and ultimately over their husbands and sons.

As a result, women missionaries became the leading edge of what missionary leaders hoped would be a medical and spiritual revolution. Implicit in those expectations was the assumption, based on initial contacts, that Indian women were unable to help themselves due to culturally determined attitudes. Consequently, Western women had to take the initiative in improving medical care, beginning with prenatal services, midwifery, and reducing infant mortality. Throughout the 1800's, European women faced many of the same dangers, and were statistically almost as likely to die during childbirth as were Indian women. Drawing on this common experience, the early female missionaries were able to draw attention to, and publicize in tracts that were read throughout England, Indian customs and traditions surrounding childbirth that directly conflicted with Christian beliefs. One missionary author, not herself a doctor, deemed indistinguishable the "unscientific'" practices and "un-Christian" customs of Bengali village midwives in the mid-19th century. Despite limited medical knowledge, and substantial cultural baggage of their own, the British women were shocked to discover how much tradition linked to birth was part of a wider cosmology of "heathen" beliefs and rituals. It therefore seemed impossible to institute Western medical care without also including a strong element of Christianity – science and religion being one in the eyes of the missionaries.

By the mid-1800s, thousands of socially conscious and religious women in England had taken up the cause. The first female medical missionaries went out to India in the 1850s, when the Zenanah Bible and Medical Mission began sending women missionaries, and later, female doctors, to work in the women's quarters of both Hindu and Muslim households, enabling cloistered Indian women to receive medical care forbidden when provided by male missionaries. One of many difficulties with providing this care was the dominant role of more senior inhabitants within the *zenanah*. Beyond the strict constraints imposed on younger women, in Hindu *zenanahs*, illness was viewed as the product of *karma*. That resulted in callousness toward suffering, and a disinclination to seek medical care from any source. If a husband chose to visit a hospital and describe his wife's symptoms, he might be given a bottle of medicine. In wealthy households, a male doctor might be sent for who could only prescribe for his patient without seeing her. Often high caste women refused to go to mission hospitals because of the proselytising integral to the care, and out of fear of losing caste by contacting foreigners. Low caste women also avoided seeking Western medical care, since they followed the lead of their high caste sisters. As a result, the only assistance during childbirth was provided by indigenous *dais* or country midwives, who were illiterate and ignorant of even basic sanitation, let alone physiology. The position of *dai* was often hereditary in a village, and the only training was that passed down from mother to daughter.

The suffering, death, and invalidism resulting from these practices were enormous and unchecked, except in those locales where missionaries introduced basic health techniques. The Delhi Female Medical Mission began its work in 1867, and in 1869, Clara Swain, the first fully qualified woman medical missionary, was sent to India by the American Methodist Episcopal Mission to open the first hospital dedicated to treating women and children.[4] Another medical pioneer, Elizabeth Bielby, spent most of her life in north India striving to "medicalise" childbirth. After learning basic medical skills from manuals, Bielby provided rudimentary medical care to women in various *zenanahs* for several years, then went to England on a furlough to acquire formal medical training, returning to India after receiving her degree. She inadvertently paved the way for creating the Dufferin Fund when she personally delivered a plea for assistance from the Maharani of Punna to Queen Victoria. During her meeting with the monarch, she offered details of horrors she witnessed during her years of Indian service. Bielby and other female doctors chose to work in India for reasons beyond their desire to provide medical care for Indian women. In a special paradox, lack of opportunities in Britain, including restrictive social attitudes, contrasted with the richer options for practicing in the Empire overseas, especially India.[5]

European female doctors were sorely needed for many years since Indian women moved very slowly into health care fields. Primarily through the efforts of Mary Scharleib, who had lived in India, and then obtained a medical degree in England, women, mostly Europeans, Eurasians, Parsis, and Indian Christians, were admitted to medical colleges in India, beginning with the Madras Medical College in 1875. A similar ethnic profile was visible in the medical colleges in Bombay, Calcutta, Agra, and Lahore that admitted women in the early 1880s. The Women's Christian Medical College, the first actual medical school for European women in India, opened at Ludhiana in the Punjab in 1894, and also offered training for Indian women as medical missionaries. But despite the expanding medical education for women, strong religious and caste prohibitions prevented all but a few high-caste Hindus or Muslim women from becoming doctors prior to 1914.[6] Despite the slight impetus provided by World War I, there were only about 150 female physicians in all of India by the late 1920s, and missions still provided more than half the hospital beds for women in the country.

Despite these efforts to train women doctors prior to 1885, for the most part missionary societies' women doctors remained the primary caregivers for Indian women. In the 1890s, about two-thirds of all female doctors in India – some 50 women – were missionary doctors – despite the Dufferin Fund's energetic attempts to recruit non-sectarian women doctors. Since the missionary efforts were steadfast in linking healing the physical body with Christian spirituality, and evangelising was a paramount element in their motivation and work, Indian women patients in mission clinics were suffused in religiosity while awaiting care from a doctor or nurse, including regular reminders of the importance of prayer to a Christian god as part of their treatment.

Whatever braking effect such evangelism had on their therapeutic impact, the female medical missionaries laid the foundations for improved medical aid for the women of India. Nor did their lack of formal medical education diminish the value of their work. Despite limited training and dependence on texts and common sense, dedicated missionaries were often able to ease the suffering of Indian women, and educate them in the basics of health care and sanitation. Missionary women also open gateways for expanding Western medical care as they provided service to the women who were confined in the *zenanahs* of local potentates. As the Indian princes saw the pain and suffering of childbirth reduced, and infant mortality lowered, they were impressed by Western medicine, especially when the life saved was that of a beloved wife or concubine, or a longed-for son and heir.

There was more than one contradiction in all that. First, the female missionaries' medical service to princely households made it easier when the vicereines began soliciting large donations from wealthy Indian overlords to support their projects to improve medical care for Indian women. Second, that earlier sowing of seeds led to wider acceptance of Western medicine that in turn gave impetus later to the growth of the Dufferin Fund, which the missionaries later came to resent as a competitor in providing female medical care in India.

The only area of female health other than venereal diseases in which the government showed any significant interest was midwifery. The British saw the practices of the *dais* as barbaric and primitive, and in fact, many were. In Indian folklore, midwives were portrayed as "wizened hags" who inflicted horrible and often unnecessary suffering on women in childbirth, and who accounted for the high infant mortality rate. As the symbol for India's regressive health care system, the *dais* became a target for reformers of all stripes. Although some civilian and missionary doctors made sporadic efforts to train *dais*,[7] the *Raj* paid little heed to Indian women's medical needs until the issue emerged as a part of an overall effort to impose a "progressive, humane West against a cruel and backward East."[8] That led to another paradox in the form of charges of "cultural imperialism" leveled by opponents of the Dufferin Fund's work as well as missionary medical efforts in a broader sense.

Although the British overlords felt some degree of responsibility for the health and well-being of their subjects, their official efforts were sporadic. After the Crimean War, when Florence Nightingale and her nurses established the need for improving not only the sanitation at military hospitals, but of upgrading public health in general, a greater interest in such matters arose in England, which gradually was exported to the Empire. "Sanitary commissions," what today would be called public health agencies, were established in the presidencies of Bengal, Bombay, and Madras by 1864, followed by similar organizations throughout British India by 1866–67.

These commissions had little money and limited authority, so they were not very successful at improving public health overall, despite the abiding concern by the British about their susceptibility to disease through contact with the "locals". Some saw the problems as intractable, given the contravening cultural beliefs. Although some Indians applauded their efforts, seeing the benefits of "medicalising" childbirth in terms of fewer dead infants, and women surviving difficult pregnancies at considerably higher rates than under the care of the *dais,* but most did not welcome such intrusions into long-standing cultural practices.

Enter the vicereine

In view of the increasing attention paid to childbirth and women's health throughout much of the world as part of the medical revolution of the mid- to-late 1800s, it is hardly surprising that it increasingly engaged the attention of the vicereines, whose charitable and social welfare efforts remained informal and loosely organised until the mid-1880s. Lady Canning's only real public interest in India was female education, a matter with which Queen Victoria also was concerned. Like many other Victorian women, they both understood the link between increased opportunities for female education and a general improvement in family life. But once the Mutiny erupted in 1857, the vicereine became involved in caring for its victims, particularly widows and orphans. Her letters to the Queen contained vivid detailed descriptions of horrors, especially the suffering of British women and children. Lady Canning's interest in medical care was limited to visiting wounded troops, and later to raising funds for British refugees displaced by the uprising. She evinced no interest in medical care for women, despite her friendship with Florence Nightingale, the revered "lady of the lamp" in the Crimean War.

The interests and works of vicereines who followed the martyred Charlotte Canning in the mid- to late 1800s are less well-known, and evidence of any contributions they made to female education or medical care is scant. Ladies Elgin, Lawrence, and Mayo are remembered primarily as adjuncts to their husbands' lives and careers, and not for any specific contributions they made to the common weal of India. Although more is known about Lady Lytton because of her husband's tumultuous and controversial tenure, there is little trace of her having initiated or supported any substantial social or educational efforts during her time in India.

Even if a particular vicereine had been so inclined, the first two decades following the 1857 uprising were not conducive to launching major social reforms, as an undercurrent of apprehension and alertness served to keep the focus of the British communities in India close at hand. Life within the virtual fortress of British society that emerged from the Great Mutiny, and especially the viceregal entourage, was heavily martial in flavour. Safety concerns made it that much easier for the *memsahibs* to stay within their own compounds, made to look as much as possible like "home" including cottage gardens, antimacassars, and other symbols and touchstones of stereotypical British country life. Excursions were limited to "safe" venues where one could be assured of a warm, even obsequious welcome, and exposure only to elements of Indian life deemed appropriate for British women of good breeding.

In that stable, and to some, stagnant environment, the vicereines of the mid- to later 1800s focused their energies on helping their husbands in traditional ways as social leaders, conveners and orchestrators of dinners, balls, and social events, and by overseeing the "appropriate" charitable endeavors, i.e., "doing good works." However, each vicereine was expected to show considerable political and diplomatic awareness and sensitivity, including some interest in "women's issues." Conversations with women missionaries, civil servants' wives, and the handful of female doctors would make them aware of the grim toll taken by customs of childbirth and the dearth of female medical assistance for nearly all Indian women. But, again, there is a scant and fragmentary record of their seeking to improve health care in any organised fashion. Although the facts were self-evident, even to British women kept isolated from natives, the full magnitude and consequences of the problems of women's health care were not fully appreciated. And beyond all that, the sheer size of India and its complexity bred a sense of helplessness to those surveying its problems and dilemmas.

While the women medical missionaries remained at the forefront in the struggle to improve women's health care in India, most British women there, whatever their concerns and good intentions, did not see the problem as one that required an organised effort, much less government involvement. Ultimately, it took Royal involvement and the appearance of a dedicated and charismatic leader to generate focused and substantial forward motion toward addressing what was clearly a nationwide problem.

That leader, Lady Hariot Dufferin, arrived in December 1884 as the new vicereine and quickly designed a careful and thorough approach to that cluster of problems, setting the pattern and the pace for future vicereines' involvement in social welfare by creating and heading a nationwide organization to provide female doctors and medical professionals for the women of India, and nurturing the expansion of its network of hospitals and dispensaries. Lady Dufferin's efforts were the result of a direct royal command from Queen Victoria, who even before she was named Queen Empress of India in 1877, was fascinated by the subcontinent

Hariot Dufferin, of all the vicereines, left the most lasting legacy to the promotion of social welfare among Indian women during British rule in India.

India. She eagerly awaited and read official dispatches and private letters that described in detail the lives of her Indian subjects as well as British officials. The Queen's interest in native women's health was initially stimulated by a letter from the Maharani of Punna, who had benefited from the services of Dr. Elizabeth Bielby, a professor of midwifery at the Lahore Medical School, and the first woman doctor in the Punjab. The Maharani had placed her handwritten entreaty to the Queen "to do something for our Indian daughters" in a locket, imploring Dr. Bielby to wear the locket until she could put the message directly into the Queen's hand, which the doctor did in 1882. Deeply touched by the Maharani's plea, and eager to demonstrate her concern for her Indian female subjects' welfare, the Queen summoned Dr. Mary Scharleib in 1883 to provide additional details of the medical situation of women in India. After hearing further stories of horrors suffered in childbirth and cultural barriers to treatment presented by male doctors, the Queen demanded action. "How can they tell me there is no need for medical women in India?" she asked Dr. Scharleib.

The Queen seized an opportunity for direct action when Lord Dufferin was named viceroy. In October, 1884, Lord and Lady Dufferin were invited to the traditional pre-departure "dine and sleep" visit to Windsor made by all viceroys and their wives. During a private interview, the Queen told Lady Dufferin of the urgent need to provide female medical professionals to serve Indian women and charged Hariot to take up this cause. Deeming "The welfare of Indian women…[a] subject…near to her heart" she urged Hariot to use her position as vicereine to develop a plan whereby the best available medical skill could be made available to the women of India while while "scrupulously respecting their own wishes and their own religion and even their own less sacred opinions and prejudices."[9]

The Queen chose well. The new vicereine was intelligent, charming, energetic, an experienced diplomatic wife, and a dedicated journal and letter writer. The Queen's charge gave her an immediate problem to study and propose a solution. Her correspondence and notes made after her visit with the monarch show that she almost immediately laid the foundations of what became the National Association for Supplying Female Medical Aid to the Women of India, which would be financially supported by the Countess of Dufferin's Fund. Lady Dufferin not only recognised the gravity of the situation, but also grasped the opportunity that the Queen's interest provided for keeping in regular contact on a subject of great personal interest. While corresponding with the Queen was always a principal duty of vicereines, Lady Dufferin knew that keeping the Queen abreast of progress on the specific issue of medical care for women would allow her to discreetly convey important information about her husband's perform-ance as viceroy, bypassing the Secretary of State. A prodigious, literate, and highly entertaining correspondent, Lady Dufferin wrote her first letters to the Queen during the voyage to India, in which she described a Canadian lady doctor going to India to work with a missionary couple.

In December 1884, after settling in at Government House in Calcutta, Lady Dufferin began learning all she could about medical care for women in India, as she soon found that despite the medical missionaries' best efforts, and the building of some hospitals, training schools and dispensaries for women, the overall picture remained grim. Horrified by further lurid details of practices used during childbirth, she concluded that if only the people

– that is, the men – of India realised there was a better, safer way for women to deliver babies they would support developing a medical delivery system for women. Keeping the Queen informed of her findings, the vicereine laid out her plan for addressing the Queen's challenge. A gifted strategic thinker, Lady Dufferin believed that an "association" to bring medical knowledge and relief to the women of India could succeed only if tightly focused, and more importantly, without any religious flavour. As her insistence on a strict non-sectarianism of her organization generated significant opposition and controversy, Lady Dufferin was forced to spend a great deal of time, energy, and political capital clarifying and defending her position.

Having spent years in the diplomatic world, the new vicereine fully grasped all the dimensions of her role, including the formal and informal power of her position, as well as her personal ability to gain support for her causes. As the Newcastle *Leader* later reported, Lady Dufferin attacked the project "With Irish impetuosity and Scots thoroughness combined..." quickly identifying British social and political principals and those Indian princes and leaders most able to assist her in the effort, well aware that many were doing it only to curry favour with the viceroy. She was well aware that she would need their financial as well as political support, and as opportunities presented themselves, she solicited pledges and donations as her "scheme" was developing.

Throughout the spring of 1885, Hariot talked to various people about her plan while laying foundation stones for hospitals and schools, and presiding over social events in Calcutta and Simla. Raising money at a garden fête to pay a missionary lady doctor to train some midwives only whetted her appetite for a broader effort. At the same time, she received unsolicited advice, primarily urgings that she concentrate on building hospitals and educating Indian students rather than recruiting female doctors from abroad. As useful as many of those suggestions were, Hariot felt strongly that what was needed was an organization that would do more and take a broader, national approach. She also had faith in the basic good and helpful nature of women: "There are so many idle women in India who would do something if they knew how or what," she wrote to the Queen. In stages, Hariot became confident that if she could find a way to bring them together in some sort of an association, they would be able to reach some solid objectives.

As one of the most aristocratic vicereines, and fully appreciative of the utility of pomp and circumstance in diplomatic settings, especially in India, Hariot Dufferin led the supremely comfortable and ostentatious lifestyle of the wife of the most powerful man in the British Empire. And yet she also was the first vicereine to gain personal insight into the poverty, squalor, and widespread disease throughout India by taking advantage of chances to learn about the "real" India during the annual viceregal tours. Whenever she could during the viceregal progresses, Hariot visited female schools, mission hospitals and dispensaries, and even leper asylums. Her visit to a *dai* class in Rawalpindi gave her an insight into the "unlearned" instruction of midwives, and the vast gaps in their knowledge of physiology and of basic medicine. The itinerary which was for the most part skewed to highlight only positive aspects of the local rulers could not mask the gap between the luxury of the princes' palaces and jewels, and the wretched conditions of their subjects, a contrast which spurred the vicereine to work all the harder on behalf of Indian women.

During her first visit to Simla in 1885, Lady Dufferin took the first public steps toward creating the organization she envisioned. She talked and wrote to many people including Indians, missionaries, and senior government officials and their wives, about the need for a national program to provide medical aid to the women of India. Her initiative was warmly welcomed – at least publicly – by all who heard of it. Walter Roper Lawrence, who served as Honorary Secretary of the Fund beginning in 1888, noted that Lady Dufferin's "great tact, and patience and ...constant energy..." won her broad support for the plan throughout British India.[10]

By June, Hariot was preparing her prospectus for the new organization, the National Association for Supplying Female Medical Aid to the Women of India, soon popularly known as the Countess of Dufferin's Fund – the organization which financially supported the National Association. In a letter to the Queen, Hariot laid out "the embryo" of her plan[11], which included soliciting reports from each province on efforts under way by female doctors. That proved to be a more complicated task than she envisioned as she found that more was being done to aid women than she and many others had thought. While encouraging, that did not diminish the enormity of the task ahead.

Her Prospectus set forth an Association under a Central Committee overseeing independent branches in Assam, Baluchistan, Bengal, Berar, Bihar and Orissa, Bombay, Burma, the Central Provinces, Madras, Mysore, Punjab, the North West Province (later the United Provinces), and the North West Frontier Province. The branches, while independent in their finances and operations, would adhere to the Association's guidelines, and would contribute a percentage of the funds they raised to the Central Committee. The Provincial Committees were to establish local committees to open a hospital or support an individual lady doctor or medical assistant, as their respective funding allowed. While addressing local problems by using existing resources and experience, these committees also contributed a portion of funds they raised to the Provincial Committees.

The Association's stated purpose was to raise and distribute funds to:

- provide medical tuition, including teaching and training women in India as doctors, hospital assistants, nurses, and midwives
- provide "medical relief" by establishing dispensaries and cottage hospitals under female supervision for treating women and children; by opening female wards under female supervision in existing hospitals and dispensaries; provide female medical officers and attendants for existing female wards; and found hospitals for women when funds or endowments became available
- improve the supply of trained female nurses, whether Indian, European or Eurasian, for women and children in hospitals and private houses

The Central Committee was to liaise between the provincial branches, work in regions of India lacking local or provincial associations, and interact with the princely state governments. Given the importance of the viceroy's relationship with the major rulers, Lady Dufferin assigned that responsibility to the Central Committee which she controlled, and the princes' sizable contributions and firm support of the Fund were in good part due to her initial contacts and aggressive personal lobbying. At the outset, large donations by the Nizam of Hyderabad and the Maharajahs of Jaipur, Ulwar, Rutlam, and Benares triggered a competition among the other princes as each sought to outdo his peers in assisting the viceroy's lady in her endeavors.

In addition to luring princely India into her web, Lady Dufferin also appointed luminaries from Anglo-Indian society to the Fund's Central Committee and Provincial Committees. To refute criticism that the Fund was a tool of British authority, Hariot shaded the truth by ascribing close ties and participation of government officials to India's "peculiar circumstances" and insisting that the Association "would not invite government interference." In fact, the list of patrons and patronesses mirrored the imperial hierarchy: the Queen Empress was Patron of the Association overall; Lord Dufferin (and succeeding viceroys) served as Patron in India, while Lady Dufferin (and all future vicereines) served as President of the Association and the Central Committee. Provincial governors and lieutenant governors were Vice Patrons, and their wives, Vice Patronesses. Other dignitaries and donors became Life Councillors, Life Members or ordinary members, depending upon their donations. Founding members of the Central Committee were C.P. Ilbert and Sir Steuart Bayley, members of the Viceroy's Council; A. Mackenzie, Home Secretary of the Government of India; General B. Simpson, M.D., Sanitary Commissioner with the Government of India; Maharajah Sir Jotendro Mohun Tagore; Syud Ahmed Khan, Bhadur, of Allyghur; and C.H. Moore, President, Bank of Bengal.

Major Harry Cooper, A.D.C. to the Viceroy was Honorary Secretary. *The Dufferins seated together with family and staff.* Politics were transparently evident in those choices, since Indian members of the Central Committee were members of the aristocracy with whom Lord Dufferin wanted to keep close ties, in part to thwart western-educated Indians attempts to wield nationalist sentiment a a political weapon.

As the only woman on the Committee, and its President, Lady Dufferin chaired all meetings, set agendas, and orchestrated its activities. Walter Roper Lawrence noted in his memoirs that his experience working with Lady Dufferin convinced him that "the ideal Council is a body of men presided over by a woman." However, men accustomed to heading organizations and presiding over meetings found it unsettling to work under the direction of a woman, even a vicereine. They were also shocked by the "dreadful facts" of Indian women's suffering, the human costs of superstition, ignorance, and the fearsome mortality rate among Indian children. Many had a sense of what lay behind the veils of *purdah*, but the Government of India had stood back from interfering with religion and customs, aside from outlawing *suttee*, suppressing banditry and terrorism, and attempting to raise the age of child marriage.

After putting a basic structure in place, in August of 1885, Lady Dufferin published the prospectus for the National Association for Providing Female Medical Aid to the Women of India. Interest in the vicereine's project was stirred by the Queen's agreeing to be Patron, widely reported in the Indian and British press, as was the monarch's donation of £100 and gold medals she proposed to award to the highest graduate of Indian Female Medical Schools. Victoria's blessing as Queen-Empress also gave the Association a certain cachet, and added substance to the image of her personal concern about the welfare of her "Indian daughters." The Queen's public support – and Hariot's role as wife of the viceroy – ensured a virtual torrent of positive publicity, with a full description of the Fund's prospectus published in Indian and British newspapers, as well as the *Journal of the National Indian Association*.

In addition to being the principal author of the Fund's prospectus, Hariot also wrote extensively about the Fund for newspapers or journals.[12] At the same time, she was also a tireless fundraiser, squeezing contributions from such diverse prospects as a rich Indian prince, a government official, and officers of the battalions assigned to provide security for the viceroy. Prior to the official publication of the Fund's Prospectus, Hariot wrote her mother that she should feel free to promote the scheme to potential donors in England and "When you come across people with loose cash, you may mention my scheme!"[13] She seized every opportunity to lobby wealthy and influential people, from state dinner and visits to maharajahs to *purdah* parties when she was alone with potentates' wives.

Hariot also found time to publish two books based on her detailed letters to her family: *My Canadian Journal* and *Our Viceregal Life in India* – both revealing her deep curiosity and appetite for adventure offered by her husband's diplomatic appointments. In the latter, she addressed some objections that critics had raised about her Fund, such as the fact that some Indian women did see medical men, that the Fund was an official arm of the government, and strictly non-sectarianism. She carefully countered each objection with her own data – or strong opinion, based on research. In her writings, Hariot made it clear that she understood the unique challenges of providing female medical aid to the women of India, especially the difficulties of making changes that might offend women's religious and personal sensibilities in a land divided by many dozens of languages, cultures, and the caste system. She pointed out that raising funds for medical tuition was the Fund's primary objective because the sooner well-trained native women entered the healing professions, the sooner Indian women's state of health would improve. While it would be necessary at first to bring English and American women doctors to India, in the long run only India could provide female doctors in sufficient numbers to permanently improve the medical care system for women. She saw the need to train native midwives as even more urgent, along with the training of nurses, since both were scarce throughout India.

Establishing dispensaries was another relatively "quick fix" proposed by the vicereine, who was well aware from the outset that her time in India was limited. Given the high cost of hospital beds and their use by the very sickest women, she saw dispensaries staffed by trained women as a way to stretch the Fund's limited monies. An additional benefit of that approach was that dispensaries' female medical officers got to know patients personally, making hospitalization less traumatic if required. Building and outfitting hospitals for women or establishing female wards in existing hospitals remained a primary goal, but the Fund's scarce resources in the provinces rarely allowed the creation of even a single ward, let alone a hospital. In recognition of that, a "where special funds or endowments are forthcoming" clause was added to the prospectus to help specify the goal of establishing such facilities.

Hariot also proposed a branch model for the Association to ensure that medical relief would be introduced into each province "in the way most pleasing and suitable to the conditions of its people."[14] Recognising some women due to maternal customs and traditions would not accept the medical relief being made available to them, Hariot waxed optimistic:"… if she can be made to understand that her own good health is necessary to the well-being of her house, and to the bodily strength of her children, I feel sure she will use her influence to forward our work."[15] But she also recognised that it would take a long time for Indian women to take up the professions of doctor or nurse, noting that it was only a quarter century since Florence Nightingale made nursing a "respectable" vocation for women in England. Hariot recognised – and took advantage of the fact – that even though there were significant health care career opportunities for English women, it would be many years before a sufficient number of doctors and nurses could be trained and sent out to India. The price tag on Hariot's lofty hopes was steep: it cost £500–600 in passage money, salary, and other expenses to bring an individual out to India – roughly equivalent to $60,000 in the early 21st century. Awareness of such pressures led Hariot on a constant search for money, including such typically British fund-raising events as an annual garden fête complete with a dog show, amateur dramatics, and fortune-tellers.

Whatever compromises she had to make, Hariot was not however, ready to abandon her position on non-sectarianism. That principle proved to be the most formidable barrier in her path. The Queen herself had stressed the need for this in their initial correspondence, and Hariot assured Victoria "…that I know the full importance of keeping the National Association quite unsectarian."[16] In her articles promoting the Fund, Hariot expressed her and the Central Committee's appreciation of missionary hospitals, dispensaries, doctors, and nurses significant efforts in improving medical care in India, but despite their obvious worth and selflessness, she made clear that the Fund could not, under any circumstances, employ them, or support their work financially. She held firm on the National Association's refusal to employ missionaries or provide hospital accommodation where medical treatment was combined with religious teaching. No officer of the Association was allowed "to exercise a missionary calling," nor would the Fund pay any expenses for medical missionaries.[17] Hariot asked the missionaries to view the Fund as a partner in their work, and promised that Fund activities would not hinder or interrupt their efforts. Expressing hope that they should work cooperatively, and without antagonism, she proposed that except in large towns where there was room for another medical establishment, or where a district or municipality raised funds to support a lady doctor, the Fund would not create any kind of competing effort. The vicereine's discounting competition in fundraising was naïve if not disingenuous. Clearly, some Indian rulers might divert a good portion if not all of their support for local missions to a program founded and favoured by the viceroy's wife.

Missionary journals quickly assailed the Fund's steadfast non-sectarianism, charging that Lady Dufferin's proscription against expressing religious beliefs was aimed directly at Christians, not Hindu or Muslim medical personnel employed by the Fund. The editor of the journal *Medical Missions at Home and Abroad* accused Lady Dufferin of requiring women providing health care in India under the Fund's auspices to remain "tongue-tied in the matter of their faith." That prohibition was, the editor insisted, a violation of their "natural" rights, and an affront to all Christians. Pointing out that the Association's provision of accommodations met religious and caste requirements of Indian medical personnel, the mission association asserted that the Association's *ipso facto* discrimination against Christians rendered hollow its non-sectarian stance.

Replying in a subsequent issue, Lady Dufferin began by stating her reluctance to engage in any controversy, but that the subject's gravity led her to respond. Taking offense ever so gently at the inference of the National Association's antagonism toward Christianity and its missionaries, she pointed out that all the Fund's officers were appointed on the same basis, just as members of the Indian Civil Service were. None were required to make any commitment or affirmation regarding faith, no "pledge was exacted" from any university or medical school student, nor were students and Association employees required to "abandon the most precious privilege of his (sic) faith." After rebutting other criticisms which she deemed "exaggerated and unfair, " the vicereine veered away from an extended argument regarding merits of secular versus missionary efforts, but restated her commitment to cooperating with medical missionaries as much as possible, including publicising their work in the Fund's annual reports. Noting that she had tried "in every possible way" to be friendly to many medical missionaries, she expressed the regret with a slight edge to it that she felt she had not been given the same consideration. Clearly annoyed at being singled out for "condemnation," Hariot concluded by noting again that her plan was merely following British Government guidelines for all officials in India.

The vicereine's letter generated an even stronger response from the mission journal. While admitting that Lady Dufferin had indeed established a "great scheme," the editor, in addressing her rebuttal word by word, conceded some possible misinterpretations, but finished by insisting once again that any aid that Lady Dufferin's scheme brought to suffering Indian women could not outweigh the damage done by preventing Christians from expressing their faith while engaged in medical work.

As the issue simmered on, the Fund continued to gain momentum. In 1886, Lady Dufferin claimed that it had raised roughly some three lakhs of rupees, which she estimated at about £23,000, of which the Central Committee controlled £12,000.[18] Progress in women's health care was also moving along parallel tracks. The Maharajah of Ulwar, for example, had started a dispensary under female supervision, and was providing two scholarships for women; plans for other dispensaries in princely states were in progress; female wards were promised by Lady Lyall for Agra College; a female ward in Delhi supervised by a lady doctor had been pledged; and several scholarships had been funded by princes – all with no involvement of the Central Committee or even the Branch Committees.

Hariot's long-range projects, beyond coordinating the overall work of the Fund, included assistance to poorer areas in India, where prospects of fund-raising were thin. The Association planned to aid the Agra Medical College and hopefully start a small model training school at Jubbulpore, entirely under female supervision, and under strict *purdah* in hopes of enticing young women "of good caste from the Independent States" to take up medical education. Other goals included promoting "sanitary" (public health) education in girls' schools, and publishing primers for women in the *zenanas* on topics like mothers' health, managing babies, the importance of fresh air, and what to do in case of minor accidents. Further costs emerged here since such publications had to be translated into several languages.

Since training midwives was another high priority of the Central Committee, as a stopgap, Lady Dufferin sought ways to keep *dais* from harming patients, In the driest of understatement, she observed that "when a midwife is so bad as to jump upon her patient by way of accelerating her recovery after her confinement, then training sufficient to teach [her] to leave the woman alone would be extremely desirable..."[19] In the meantime, the optimal strategy seemed to be an effort to convince midwives to do no active harm, with subsequent licensing of those who reached a level of professional competence. In the interim, the Central

Committee considered hiring two qualified midwives to visit various locations and educate women who showed interest in such work. Hariot concluded her 1886 report by noting that she and her colleagues had received broad encouragement for their plans, and a prediction of a "national movement" and a "feeling of kindness and good-will" because of the Association's work. She recognised that real progress would take years, but waxed sermonic with a lyrical imprecation that "we must begin it gently....tend it with patience and perseverance...each green leaf giving promise of a future abundant harvest."[20]

If, as many later judged it to be, the first three years of the Association's life were its most productive, that was primarily due to Lady Dufferin's single-minded dedication. Branch committees were established in the various provinces, and the Central Committee spent hundreds of hours working on ways to improve various aspects of medical care for women in India. Some of those plans, however, were ultimately scrapped due to lack of funds. One, a model training school for Indian women in medicine, was shelved despite continued efforts, but was revived 30 years later when the Lady Hardinge Medical College was founded.

Ever alert for fundraising opportunities, in December 1887 Hariot established a special fund to honour the Queen's Golden Jubilee which had been celebrated in London on June 20 and 21, a highlight of which had been the spectacle of Indian princes, "men of stately build and princely carriage", as Mark Twain noted, clad in their glittering ceremonial dress, paying their respects to the Queen-Empress and the Indian cavalry escorting the Queen to Westminster Abbey. The enthusiastic public reaction led Hariot to seek funds to celebrate the Queen's identifying the need for improved medical care for Indian women, including large sums from native princes and aristocrats, and smaller amounts from others in India and England, subscribed via Jubilee Cards specially designed for the occasion. Contributors' names were inscribed in a book presented to the Queen, with an introductory letter from Hariot as Lady President of the Dufferin Fund. Funds raised by these subscriptions were distributed to provincial committees throughout India, and also allocated to establishing endowment which Hariot hoped would put the Dufferin Fund on a solid financial footing for the foreseeable future.

In January 1888, Hariot wrote a summary report of the Association's first three years, noting that the three Annual Reports of the Fund so far had been "official and dull-looking" and included statistical data and lists of little interest to "only those already interested in the matter" and "to whom dreary returns of figures and facts are replete with life and meaning."[21] Hoping to generate wider interest in the Association, in this summary she broadly outlined the Fund's mission and activities and celebrated successes in meeting stated goals. On the surface of things, achievements seemed solid and prospects were bright. Her indefatigable fundraising had raised a small endowment of just under seven lakhs, with five and-a-half lakhs invested as a permanent endowment producing an annual income of some Rs 30,000. The Fund had provided building grants for building Dufferin Hospitals in Agra and Lahore, for salaries for medical women and nurses, and for annual scholarships for women students and probationer nurses studying in five established Indian medical schools which expanded their female classes. Beyond that, some 27 hospitals and dispensaries had been established, and a "Sanitary Primer" entitled *The Way to Health* had been published and distributed to public schools in Northern and Central India. Eleven medical women were working for the Association in India, five having come from the United Kingdom, while six were residents of India. The Fund's provincial organizations were focusing on building and outfitting hospitals in their own regions and finding and paying female medical personnel to staff them, or at least to staff women's wards in hospitals. Other efforts included establishing a training school for *dais*, funding translations of medical texts, and building an entire Female Department at the Agra Medical School.

In this report, as in all she did for the Association, Lady Dufferin sought to convince others of the worth of the cause to which she had dedicated her full efforts. Over the years, she had convinced many to support the Association through the leverage of being vicereine, her personal charm, and sometimes by straightforward intimidation. Her unique dedication and energy were of great value – and literally irreplaceable. After she left India, it quickly became clear that without her energy and on-site commitment the Fund could not maintain its previous headway. Even before she left, the Government of India was beginning to pick up the slack. From 1888 onward, all Dufferin Fund employees in its schools, hospitals and dispensaries were supervised by Indian Medical Service officers. This was in response to the Central Committee's request that the government to "recognize" the work of the Fund by having the Surgeon-General select "suitable" women as doctors, and chief medical authorities in each province "supervise, guide, and control" Association employees.[23] The government agreed under the provision that it was "distinctly understood that the employees of the Association are in now respect Government servants..." although "the government was not responsible for the pay or pension of Association employees,"[24] thus making the Fund at this point an extension of the government, rather than a private charity. As a result, its employees became the vanguard for the female medical service in India which was officially constituted in 1914. In the transition to government oversight, medical women were grouped in grades, corresponding to men in the Indian Medical Service: Registered Medical Women, Female Assistant Surgeons, and Female Hospital Assistants. Qualifications were equal for men and women, but Lady Dufferin proposed women receive slightly higher pay to attract them to medical work, since they had no pension scheme, nor expectation of regular salary increases. The Registered Medical Women were all Europeans at this time, while Indian women were studying and being registered at the other two grades.

Unhappily, Hariot's belief that she and her associates had made a good beginning, and that the National Association's efforts would be the basis for a broader system of female medical care was soon confounded. The direct connection with the government proved to be a two-edged sword. Eventually, as government appropriations kept the Fund's work alive, private donations dwindled. Although having the government inspect hospitals and oversee female doctors began under the best of intentions, experienced women doctors often found themselves serving under less-qualified, and often younger IMS civil surgeons. Female doctors were rarely allowed to perform surgery, taking the edge off of their skills, and reducing their status in the eyes of their patients. Not only were there were few opportunities for advancement, but male doctors often disrupted the carefully balanced system of *purdah* medicine established by the female doctors. The Central Committee's refusal to take a stand on such issues diminished the Fund's relevance and influence, while discontent increased among medical women in India.

When her husband announced in 1887 that he was stepping down as viceroy, Hariot was delighted at the prospect of returning to Europe, and being closer to her family, not to mention the enticement of living in Rome. Still, she longed for one more year to put her Fund on a more sound footing, despite her friendship with and confidence in the next vicereine, Lady Lansdowne. An obvious option was to maintain the connection by creating and heading an organization in Britain that would support the Fund's work there, allowing her to continue to have some influence on its programs and at the same time work on expanding its base of support. To that end, during a meeting of the Central Committee at Simla in March 1888, Hariot maneuvered an invitation to create a United Kingdom branch of the Dufferin Fund. She was also pleased to accept the Committee's request that she serve as Lady President of the UK branch for the first three years.

Lady Dufferin undertook this new challenge as she had in India, at full-steam, using her connections, charm, and energy wherever and whenever she could, including her royal contacts. Shortly after an initial meeting in late March, 1889, the Princess of Wales agreed to be Patron of the new organization, which was organised in branches corresponding to the provinces in India. Hariot then quickly assembled a 76-member General

Committee of worthies, including former viceroys, lieutenant governors, and other senior officials of the *Raj*, the Archbishop of York, the Lord Mayor of London, the Duke of Westminster, Lord Randolph Churchill, from the upper tiers of British society.[24]

While Hariot saw the UK branch as a way to continue work begun in India, she also realised that her continuing involvement would maintain pressure, however subtle or slight, on future vicereines who became the head of the Fund in India. She hoped that the UK branch would publicize the Fund's work more broadly at home, raise funds, and help select female doctors for Indian service. Through charity events and public appeals, the Committee in Britain raised passage money for medical women going to India, as well as "outfits." An innovation was the funding of scholarships at the London School of Medicine for women students who committed to work in India – something the Fund itself lacked funds for earlier. While in Italy, Lady Dufferin ceded the presidency to Lady Cavendish, but resumed that position in 1891, remaining Lady President for the rest of her life, dedicated to the work she had started, even as the Fund's resources and influence dwindled over the years.

The Dufferin Fund's activities and influence in India actually peaked in 1888, the year its founder departed. Although the Central Committee continued to exist, and was led by every succeeding vicereine, only a few demonstrated anything close to the level of passion and concern for women's health issues as did Hariot. The Central Committee soon ceased India-wide appeals for funds, accepting the argument that such efforts hampered provincial branches' attempts to raise money for local hospitals and dispensaries. The result was a shrinking endowment for the Central Committee and less money available for grants, despite assistance from the UK branch. Committee meetings became mere formalities, occurring only three times a year, in contrast with the almost weekly schedule under Hariot's tenure.

Real decision-making now lay in the hands of the vicereine as Lady President and the Honorary and Joint Secretaries, in consultation with the Director-General of the Indian Medical Service (IMS). Since each of those had other, more pressing duties in the government as tensions mounted on the Indian political scene and major wars erupted, members of the Central Committee felt less and less concerned with the Fund's work, and were content to continue to allocate small amounts flowing from the endowment at the annual meeting, and to publish the annual report. Despite some criticism of including the work of non-Association doctors and hospitals in its statistics, the Fund's annual reports provided a useful overview of the progress being made in medical aid to the women of India from all avenues, sectarian as well as missionary.

As the Fund's influence faded slowly under the decentralised model that evolved after 1888, the main efforts toward improving health care for women were made at local and regional levels. As long as the vicereines headed the national organization, people eager for status and prestige and connections to the highest levels of *Raj* society provided support for the Fund, allowing it to survive with government financial support. Nor were any of Hariot's successors eager to have the Fund end during their "reign." Most of them, as they looked for other ways to put their stamp on Indian affairs, continued to express interest in such health issues as nursing for "up country" Europeans, providing for maternal and child welfare, or female education. Until the last vicereine, Lady Mountbatten, arrived in 1943, few rose to the standards set by Lady Dufferin, either in finding new ways to address public health problems, energy, or raising funds.

During its half-century of existence, criticism of the National Association and, later, of similar social welfare organizations was muted, but it increased as the independence movement grew, and Indians assailed all aspects of British governance as part of the exclusionist rhetoric of nationalism. Such institutions as the Fund were now deemed as ways of destroying and weakening Indians' religions and culture. Naturally, Lady Dufferin saw any criticism of the Fund's work as unfair and unwarranted. How, after all, could anyone disparage attempts to improve medical care for women and children, even if they took place under the aegis of imperialism? Good works were good works. How could saving the women of India from unnecessary suffering, and even death be wrong? Those in the upper echelons of the *Raj* who often saw themselves as stewards of a future Indian nation believed that many of their policies and philanthropic efforts were progressive attempts to improve the lives of people who lacked the advantage of Western knowledge and culture.

In the wake of the *Raj*, some assailed the effect of the National Association on women's medical care in India, and on Indian society in a larger sense. Maneesha Lal, for example, saw the Dufferin Fund's creation, as having reinforced several deeply rooted British prejudices about race and gender in the colonies, and having helped relatively few women among India's huge population. She also faulted the Fund as perpetuating the myth of Queen Victoria's personal interest in the plight of her "Indian daughters," by citing again and again the story of the suffering Maharani's pleas. Lal wrote that by focusing on medical problems of India's upper-classes and higher castes, and especially *purdah-nashin* women, the Fund served only those who were strictly segregated by the custom, and not those at the many other levels of *purdah* practice linked to class, income, place of residence, form of religion, etc.[25] Except in extreme cases like epidemics or famine, therefore, Lal suggested, Western medicine had little real impact on the vast majority of Indians, male or female. Furthermore, the Fund's prominence until 1935 impeded other broader, more positive movements and concepts that might have had a greater and more positive effect, while its policies had a long-lasting impact on medical care for women. As a result, Lal concluded, the Fund's negative effects outweighed any positive impact it might have had.[26]

It is not easy to sort out the pros and cons of such arguments. Whether seen as appropriate revisionism of the glorification of imperialism, and items on a bill of particulars of the now fashionable general indictment of imperialism as a foul stain on the pages of history, or part of the savaging of the British and other imperial overlords that followed the dismantling of that particular world order, it nevertheless seems difficult to totally discount Lady Dufferin's efforts in establishing the National Association, or wholly wave aside the statistics. By 1888, several hundred thousand women were being treated, and by 1914 that number had risen to four million. Small numbers indeed compared with India's population at that time of more than 250 million, but obviously better than zero. Would it indeed have been better to have done nothing? Even if projecting current values back onto historical events is seen as acceptable, is it reasonable, given the values and prejudices of those times, to envision what alternative stratagems could have gained the support of the British elites in India? While it may seem to beg the question, one might argue that Lady Dufferin, a British aristocrat with a large family to care for, might, like previous vicereines, have focused primarily on her husband and children, served as figurehead of the high society of the *Raj*, and made the customary gestures of supporting "good works" in those areas deemed appropriate for a vicereine. Instead, she accepted the challenge from her sovereign, and set forces moving that relieved suffering on a much larger scale than anyone had previously done.

Whatever the credits and debits of the Dufferin Fund were on the balance sheet of history, it faded away slowly in the manner of the Cheshire cat. Registered under the Societies Registration Act of 1860, the Fund remained an official organization on paper until it was dissolved by the Indian legislature in 1957 when its remaining assets, debts, and liabilities were transferred to the Government of India. The Dufferin Fund finally vanished in 2002, when it was formally repealed during a clean up of various administrative laws. While there was no real opposition to the repeal, it triggered a discussion among members of India's parliament about the need for expanding medical aid for women and children, and the issue of establishing female wards under the direction of women superintendents in existing hospitals and dispensaries. One wonders what Lady Dufferin would have said about the fact that after 100 years, such matters were still being discussed heatedly and many women – particularly in poorer and rural areas of the country – still did not have the level of medical care she envisioned.

Whatever the actual effects the Dufferin Fund had for good or ill on women's health in India, Lady Dufferin reflected a model of social activism that remained in view in the viceregal establishments at varying levels and with mixed results throughout the tenure of the British *Raj*. Hariot's sense of duty, whatever the motives that drove it may have been, and whatever effects it had, was shared by thousands of British upper-class women as they and their husbands and sons served the monarchy and Empire. It is difficult if not impossible at this distance to imagine the milieu in which millions viewed Queen Victoria unquestioningly as an imperialist icon, and were moved by her oft-stated concern for her imperial subjects. Nor is there much residual reverence for the values that led women to support the Empire, at home, in female imperialist organizations, or in the far-flung realms thereof.[28] However naïve or dangerous it may be to take her, or any spokesperson for power and privilege, on their own terms, it seems clear enough that in establishing the National Association and lending her name to the Fund that supported its work, Lady Dufferin hoped to put things right and end what she saw was an enormous injustice, all the while following the tradition of aristocratic women in serving the less fortunate. In any event, after her reign, no vicereine was able to ignore social issues, and each looked for a way to contribute more than merely symbolic social leadership to a declining *Raj* – some more eagerly than others.

As she left India, Hariot felt that she had created a lasting legacy and that future vicereines would keep things going. She had, after all, received effusive tributes during her last few months to her efforts on behalf of Indian women, praise that almost eclipsed the *pro forma* accolades given her husband. During the Dufferins' final viceregal tour in the fall of 1888, Hariot received formal addresses, deputations, and gifts from local rulers and groups of both Indian and European women at every stop. Presentations followed a set agenda: each address was read out (often in more than one language) and Hariot made an appropriate reply. A copy was then given to her, usually in a silver or bejeweled casket, as a memento of the occasion. In Lahore, a group of men came representing both the men and women of the Punjab to thank her for her work on their behalf and to say good-bye. After presenting Hariot with an address of thanks and praise, they showed her a paper containing 25,000 signatures supporting the address, which would be bound and sent to her in London. Later in the day, Hariot received a second group of three gentlemen who came to represent the women of Gujranwalla and to offer their thanks. Before leaving, they asked if they might "walk around" her, to which she agreed, and later asked why. She was told that it was the custom to "walk round temples and other sacred things." When she related this story to Lord Dufferin, he replied lightly they never asked to walk around him.[28] Lady Dufferin's final and most impressive recognition came during the celebration of the Dufferins' reign at Town Hall in Calcutta just prior to their departure. Among the accolades being heaped upon the viceregal couple was the proposal that Lady Dufferin's portrait should be painted and hung in the Hall "...amongst all the Lieutenant Governors and *male* celebrities of the past! Is that not enough to turn my head?"[29] They may, arguably, be excused for overestimating the length of the shadow that they would cast on Indian history in the longer run, but in any event, hers proved to be considerably longer than his.

Lady Dufferin, of course, was being honoured as much for her charm and political skills as for her efforts in improving female medical care, for she had won many hearts as well as respect among the Anglo-Indians and the Indian aristocracy alike. Even within the broad standards of imperialist hyperbole, the outpouring of adulation seems unusual, even for a vicereine placed *ex officio* at the centre of attention. In journalistic accounts of the time, and judgments of historians alike, Hariot's blend of charm, noblesse oblige, and dignity and easy formality as the social leader of the *Raj*, created a glittering image that would only be outshown by Mary Curzon. Perhaps the most enduring tribute of all those came from the then-young journalist-poet Rudyard Kipling,[30] in the form of his Victorian lyric *Song of the Women:*

> How shall she know the worship we would do her?
>   The walls are high, and she is very far.
> How shall the woman's message reach unto her
>   Above the tumult of the packed bazaar?
>   Free wind of March, against the lattice blowing,
>   Bear thou our thanks, lest she depart unknowing.
>
> ...
>
> Haste, for our hearts are with thee, take no rest!
>   Loud-voiced ambassador, from sea to sea
> Proclaim the blessing, mainfold, confessed.
>   Of those in darkness by her hand set free.
>   Then very softly to her presence move,
>   And whisper: "Lady, lo, they know and love!"

In Hariot's footsteps

Lady Dufferin's greatest contribution to the *Raj* was not simply the creation of the National Association and its fundraising arm, the Dufferin Fund, or even the nationwide attention she brought to the problems related to women's health issues. More importantly, she established a pattern of behaviour for all of her successors. All post-Dufferin vicereines were actively involved – to a greater or lesser extent – in social welfare or health-related programs in a very public way, and they used their exalted position to create or expand those programs in which they had a personal interest. After Hariot, it was no longer enough for the vicereine to pay a quick visit to female wards and schools, cut ribbons, give out prizes, and receive deputations of Indian women for tea. While those activities remained an important part of the vicereine's public role, they were no longer sufficient to meet the standard set by the first "activist" vicereine. Each was named Lady President of the Dufferin Fund as soon as her husband was appointed viceroy, and knew instinctively that her success or lack thereof would be compared to that of Lady Dufferin. She also understood that her leadership would guarantee the continued participation of important persons in British-Indian society on the Fund's Central and Provincial Committees, as well as the continued support of royal and other distinguished patrons of the Fund back home.

None of her successors quite matched Lady Dufferin's level of enthusiasm for the Fund, but up until the late 1930s, all did their best to keep it going, with some actually seeking to restructure and streamline the organization and redirect some of its efforts, with varying degrees of success. There is little doubt that some of that pressure to maintain the Fund came from its founder's enduring passion for the cause of improving medical care for Indian women, which never waned. Throughout her long life, she wrote countless letters to the vicereines, the royal patrons, and the Secretaries of State for India about the progress of the UK branch of the Fund, encouraging them to keep the Fund's important work alive in India, even during the Boer War and World War I when war-related charities took precedence.

Whatever their family commitments and other interests, the post-Dufferin vicereines managed to keep the Fund in the public eye well into the 20th century, with some doing the bare minimum – providing nominal leadership by chairing the Central Committee (but leaving the bulk of the work to staff and other Committee members), and taking part in the cornerstone laying and opening of new hospitals or dispensaries. Others used the Fund presidency as the basis for related programs such as well-baby care and general health care for women, and made sincere attempts to publicize the other areas of medical need. Lady Dufferin's success at obtaining Queen Victoria's support as Patron of the Fund, and that of the Princess of Wales as a Vice Patroness gave her scheme the same level of respectability as similar charities in England. It also helped to ensure its longevity, since later queens and princesses also accepted the role of patroness or vice-patroness. No vicereine wanted to be the one who oversaw the demise of a fund with such important connections and visibility. And, as noted earlier, up until the very end, each vicereine also recognised the value of being able to communicate directly with the monarch or his consort. Providing regular reports on the Fund's progress and current activities was an excellent rationale for keeping in close contact with someone who had some influence over her husband's future – not to mention her own.

Lady Dufferin's distress at leaving her Fund was eased somewhat by the knowledge that her successor, Lady Maud Lansdowne, shared her commitment to the cause of female medical care and, more importantly, had the social and political skills necessary to manage the Fund's fundraising in the unique social milieu of British India. Her faith was not misplaced: Lady Lansdowne adroitly maintained the Fund's momentum, modifying its operations based on actual experiences gained during the initial years. Maud's years as president of the fund were not especially noteworthy in terms of programmatic innovation, but she would be remembered as an able administrator, conducting the Fund's affairs with courtesy and consideration, and publicising its progress by frequent visits to women's hospitals throughout India. By effecting such a smooth transition, Lady Lansdowne demonstrated that the Fund did not depend on its founder's presence in India, but that its work could be continued by successive vicereines. She strongly supported the creation of the Fund's UK branch and Lady Dufferin's continuing involvement including oversight of the recruitment and selection of women doctors for India, as well direct fundraising efforts.

While she supported the drive for better medical care for Indian women, Lady Lansdowne's primary interest was nursing, a passion she shared with the many Victorian women who were influenced by the work of Florence Nightingale in the Crimea. At the suggestion of Lord Roberts, Commander-in-Chief of the Indian Army, she became actively involved in improving nursing services for soldiers, and proved an effective advocate for better hospital and outpatient nursing. Her five years as head of the Dufferin Fund and her work with Lord Roberts also gave Lady Lansdowne organizational experience that would prove invaluable during World War I when she organised the Officers' Families Fund (OFF) to provide for the wives and dependents of army and naval officers. The OFF arranged for the loan of houses, negotiated special educational arrangements for children, arranged for needed medical assistance, and even provided clothing and general business advice to officers' families who found themselves in financial trouble due to "direct or indirect expenses that have unavoidably resulted from the war...." During the war, Lady Lansdowne also worked closely with volunteer medical societies such as Queen Alexandra's Imperial Nursing Service, having been both a close friend and a lady-in-waiting to Queen Alexandra for some years. As the war brought personal tragedy to her family, Lady Lansdowne dealt with it by helping other victims. After the death of her younger son Charles in October 1914, Lady Lansdowne opened and supervised a 54-bed military hospital at the family estate, Bowood. She also became a dedicated leader and supporter of the British Red Cross, serving on its council and as President of the Wiltshire Branch for many years.

Despite a large and growing family, the next vicereine, Constance Elgin, took a keen interest in the Dufferin Fund during the years 1894–98, and maintained a regular correspondence with the Queen about its work. Shortly after her arrival in Calcutta, she described a tour of the Eden Hospital for Women and Children: "It was a great pleasure to go over such a magnificent building, so large and airy and so comfortable...paved with marble which Dr. Joubert told me adds immensely to the healthiness of it. He took me over to the 'lying-in ward' where the patients are most tenderly cared for and the mothers made comfortable." The babies themselves ...all have delicately marked features, very small heads with a great deal of hair. They looked very much like a row of little wax dolls." Lady Elgin also took the opportunity to lobby the Queen on her husband's behalf, reassuring Her Majesty that "Lord Elgin is deeply interested and engrossed...in every detail of the work...and I beg to assure Your Majesty again that it will ever be our heart's desire to carry out Your Majesty's desires in every way."[31]

Lady Elgin kept up a steady stream of letters throughout her five years in India, telling the Queen all about new hospitals being designed and built, the progress of Indian female nursing students, and her inspections of existing Dufferin Hospital facilities. She never missed an opportunity to visit a Dufferin facility while on tour, reporting to the Queen that she had visited "...each Dufferin hospital we passed...at Quetta, Shikarpole, Moolitan, Lahore, Delhi, Cawnpore and Allahabad ("the best for the care of *purdah* women"), and have lain the foundation stone of a Dufferin Hospital to be built at Karachi...[which] promises to be a very complete institution."[32] Maintaining that royal connection paid off: when she learned that Lady Elgin was pregnant, Victoria offered to stand as godmother to the new baby boy, asking that he be called Victor Alexander, the male equivalent of her name – Victoria Alexandrina. The Elgins speedily accepted both the offer and the suggested name, and saw this demonstration of royal favour as a testament to Constance's work in India as well as her husband's.

Correspondence between Calcutta and London indicates that Lady Elgin – and even the Queen – had some concerns about an American vicereine's interest and ability to continue the Fund's work. Somewhat disappointed in the selection of Curzon as his successor, Elgin expressed his views to a member of his Council, Lt. General Henry Brackenbury. After commenting on Curzon's potential and possible obstacles to his success, Elgin noted that Constance and Dr. Franklin, the Fund's Honorary Secretary (who did much of the real work) were "a little despondent about the future of the Dufferin Fund" and were glad to hear that Brackenbury had spoken to Lady Curzon about its future. "I hope she will take enough interest in it to prevent its losing ground, for it is undoubtedly a valuable institution."[33]

Lady Elgin and her daughter prepare for a ride on their ponies in Simla.

The new vicereine held her first Central Committee meeting in mid-February 1899, despite being uneasy about her ability to lead the Fund, and keenly aware of the successes of her predecessors, and of the Queen's special interest in its work. She also knew that the success or failure of her leadership could well affect her husband's reputation with the monarch, and was therefore determined to keep the Fund functioning and effective. In the end, as so many other things intruded into her life, Lady Curzon was a little more than a figurehead Lady President, leaving most of the actual correspondence and management to Colonel Fenn, the Military Secretary to the Viceroy, and relying heavily on the rest of the Central

Committee for guidance. She shrewdly made sure she was visible at the appropriate times, meeting all public commitments related to the Fund, but she balanced those duties with her other, more political and social responsibilities. She wrote to her father that once Lent had begun "...I have less gaiety and more hospitals to occupy my time. So now you will begin to receive budgets about my good works." [34]

Despite the other distractions of her position and her near-obsession with producing a son and heir, Mary was determined to leave a legacy in India separate from her husband's and that of previous vicereines. Merely sustaining an organization organised by an earlier vicereine and led by every successive Lady Sahib wasn't enough. Given her own frail health during and after pregnancies, Lady Curzon quite naturally chose to focus on improving obstetric care. Shortly after Queen Victoria's death in 1901, Mary established the Victoria Memorial Scholarship Fund to train Indian women in Western methods of nursing and midwifery, and insofar as possible, provide "practical knowledge" to the infamous *dais* or indigenous midwives. The program was intended to be a stopgap measure until sufficient women doctors and nurses could be trained to oversee births in hospital settings, and thus seemed to be a reasonable adjunct to the aims of the Dufferin Fund. Like her predecessors, Mary was a charming and persistent fundraiser, and used her considerable charm to raise some £50,000 from princes and maharajahs to support her scholarship scheme, which eventually came under the Dufferin umbrella.

As with so much of the Curzon viceroyalty, controversy surrounds Mary's attempt to create an entirely new venture. Once the memorial scholarship program was firmly in place, she decided to extend her activities on behalf of better nursing by training nurses to serve British and European patients in "up-country" locations. She spent a great deal of time devising her plan, which she laid out at a meeting at Simla in 1903, having already personally consulted with leaders of all Indian states which would be affected by it. The nursing scheme was presented to and approved by Curzon's Council, and forwarded to St. John Broderick, the Secretary of State for India, a long-time admirer of the vicereine's, from whom she anticipated full support. In keeping with the nature of bureaucracy, Broderick and the home government made considerable changes in the original plan, and sent it back to be implemented just as Curzon's reign came to its sudden and dramatic end. As noted previously Lady Curzon's untimely death shortly after her return from India brought forth great outpourings of grief at the tragic loss of such a young and beautiful woman, and added to the myth of women as martyrs to India. Eulogised for her beauty, charm, and unswerving dedication to her husband's viceroyalty, even at the cost of her own health, Mary would be remembered mainly as the American vicereine, that is, renowned for who she was, but not for any contributions to India's social welfare.

It fell to the next vicereine, Lady Mary Minto, to create a new and more permanent nursing improvement scheme, an act that Curzon never forgave, believing that Lady Minto had usurped the idea and recognition rightly due his late wife. Lady Minto's version of the plan's genesis was straightforward: Before leaving England, a delegation from the Home Committee of the Up-Country Nursing Association for Europeans, which provided nurses for British civilians living in the region, approached her for assistance in expanding their work.

Even in the early 20th century, hospitals and nursing facilities were scarce in India, and British planters and other non-military personnel living in out-of-the-way places found it difficult to get trained nurses, let alone other Western medical care. A first attempt to solve this problem had been made by the wives of several senior British Indian officials who who pioneered the idea of providing trained Western nurses for Europeans in India, and established the Up-Country Association in 1892 in the Punjab and the United Provinces. Headquartered in Bareilly, the Association had enjoyed some success, but inconsistent funding prohibited its expansion to other areas of British India.

Having seen the success of the Dufferin Fund, and recognising the value of having the vice-queen of India as their leader and patron, the ladies asked Mary to help them create a wider organization to provide nurses for Europeans throughout British India – with the exception of Bombay, which already had a nursing association founded by Lady Ampthill. They proposed an entirely new organization, to be called the Lady Minto Indian Nursing Association (LMINA), which would recruit "suitable" trained nurses in England and make whatever arrangements were necessary to bring them to India and provide skilled nursing care for Europeans at "moderate" prices, the actual fee to be determined by the patient's income. Always eager for a new project – and flattered by the proposal that it bear her name – Lady Minto seized on this project as an opportunity to give substance to her Indian experience as she had done in Canada, and not incidentally, once again create a legacy separate from her husband's.

However eager she was to take on the nursing project, Lady Minto did not let her Dufferin responsibilities slide, actively supporting the Fund's current programs, including the Victoria Memorial Scholarships – always careful to give Lady Curzon full credit for its creation. Well aware of the animus Curzon bore her husband, and of his constant carping about Minto's incapacity as viceroy, Lady Minto also tried her best to separate her nursing scheme from the earlier version, hoping – in vain, as it turned out – to avoid incurring Curzon's personal animus.

Before responding to the request she had received in London, Mary and Sir James Dunlop-Smith, Private Secretary to the Viceroy, carefully reviewed the plan devised by Mary Curzon. It was, they concluded, a "hopeless muddle," and its structure had antagonised the heads of the existing nursing associations – which may have accounted for their entreaty to the incoming vicereine. Mary Curzon's proposed plan led Dunlop-Smith to comment that "Lady Minto is a most capable woman, but even she could never run this scheme as it is.[35]

Shortly after her arrival in 1905, Lady Minto took the Up-Country Nursing Association's draft plan, and moved boldly ahead. Unlike Mary Curzon, she had no doubts about her organizational, managerial, and political abilities. She was self-assured, an articulate writer, and a charming and persuasive advocate for any cause she undertook. Having reworked the initial proposal to her own satisfaction, she lobbied those who could make it a reality: her husband, the members of the Viceroy's Council, and the Lieutenant Governors, all of whom were supportive, and quickly agreed to provide living quarters in their areas for the Minto nurses. One cloud hung over the project: the lingering doubts in the minds of some about its origins when Mary Curzon's tragic death in 1906 led Lady Minto's critics to believe that she had merely commandeered and slightly altered a plan first proposed by the now-martyred Lady Curzon – a belief supported by articles in the British and Indian press written by a grieving and angry George Curzon and his supporters.[36]

Whatever its origins, Mary's enthusiasm and commitment to the project ensured that the Minto Association was soon active well beyond the UP boundaries. The Association sought to increase the number of European nurses in India (especially in northern India and Burma) and it more than met that goal, eventually opening centres in seven northern provinces, and two more in Burma. Most Minto patients were Europeans, although the services of Minto nurses were available to those Indians who preferred Western medical care – most often local rulers and their families. Minto sisters were recruited from England and other parts of the UK, and signed three- or five-year contracts, which in addition to their salary, provided full or partial passage to India and home, depending on the length of their contract. Later the Association was asked to provide nurses for both public and private hospitals, serving primarily as matrons and senior staff, with no say in the institution's management, even though they were responsible for the nursing staff and all nursing problems. The Association received an annual grant of Rs 35,000 from the Indian government, but depended primarily on membership subscriptions, augmented by fees paid for nursing work done.

By 1906, the nursing program was in full operation, and Lady Minto

turned her attention from organising to fundraising, issuing an appeal in both England and India for endowment funds to keep the organization financially sound, hoping to ensure its continuation after her departure. Like previous vicereines, she went where the money was, focusing on those who had the greatest incomes – the princes and other Indian aristocrats eager to help the Lady Sahib and gain favour with her husband. But Lady Minto's fundraising efforts went far beyond this usual approach. Because the Minto sisters served primarily Europeans, she sought support from the entire British-Indian community, including the military. The officers of the infamous 9th Lancers responded almost immediately to Mary's appeal, giving a total of Rs 2275. Surprised by their largesse, Mary asked Lord Douglas Compton, second in command of the Lancers, what had prompted such generosity. He replied that among the officers was a "rich but stingy" subaltern, who had been challenged by his brother officers to show his generosity, and offering to match any gift he might make. They were stunned and dismayed to find that the supposed miser had given Rs 500, but they kept their word and each matched the gift. Mary wrote in her journal that she felt "dreadfully sorry for the impecunious ones, but Lord Douglas says it will do them no harm as the cause is very deserving."[37]

The Mintos in a group pose while visiting the Begum of Bhopal.

Lady Minto really came into her own as a fundraiser with the huge "Minto Fancy Fête" she organised in January 1906 on the Calcutta Maidan. Fundraising events headed by the vicereine were not uncommon, but no one had ever undertaken something on this scale. The more usual approach was a garden party or a fun fair or ice cream social held on the lawn of the viceroy's residence, geared toward the upper reaches of Anglo-British society, with perhaps a sprinkling of maharajahs invited to provide local colour. Lady Minto, however, devised an event of a size and scope unlike any other in British India, although not quite on the scale of official *durbars* or royal visits. Aware that she would be criticised by British-Indian society for self-promotion if the event helped only her Association, Mary began by announcing that the proceeds would be split between her Association and local hospitals – which was greeted with skepticism by Calcutta society.

Confounding skeptics who had predicted failure and a lack of attendance, the fête was triumph, thanks to Lady Minto's attention to every detail and her perseverance in soliciting participants. She had modeled her fête on the tournaments held annually at Earl's Court in London, and pulled out all the stops to ensure its success, persuading the viceroy and the Commander-in-Chief to put on a full-scale military and naval tournament, complete with 10 massed bands, a trooping of the colour, artillery drives, mock battles, and even Highland games – a not-too-subtle nod to Minto's Scottish heritage. British-Indian society was amazed and thrilled at the novelties offered at the event – shooting galleries, fancy dress carnivals, and other side-shows. There were even some entertainments provided for Indian guests. The fête cleared a profit of some £25,000, and as promised, every hospital in Calcutta benefited from Mary's efforts.

In the end, the Minto Nursing Association was one of the most long-lasting legacies of any vicereine, although not quite on a par with the Dufferin Fund. As with the latter, each succeeding vicereine served as Lady President of the Minto Indian Nursing Association, but those who had a particular interest in nursing like Doreen Linlithgow, Eugenie Wavell, and Edwina Mountbatten were more directly involved in the Association's management and used their influence to help solve regional problems faced by the nurses. Although there were seldom more than 130 Minto nurses in India, the preference of Indians for English nurses slowly increased, and by World War II, when Indian doctors were regularly asking for Minto nurses for their hospitals, demand far outstripped supply.

Royal patronage also helped keep the Association alive. Queen Mary was Patron for 43 years, followed by Queen Elizabeth the Queen Mother. As with most charitable organizations, the LMINA's road was not always smooth, and there were the inevitable bureaucratic battles, particularly during World War II. In 1943, when the Association was squeezed out of its office in New Delhi when the Red Cross expanded its operations, Lady Wavell came to the rescue, providing an office on the viceregal estate, and arranging for the Association to share an office with the Dufferin Fund in Simla. She also arranged for Minto nurses to work in military hospitals whenever possible, and encouraged that effort over private patient nursing or work in Indian hospitals. The war also saw UK recruitment of nurses halted, primarily because war work took a higher priority and because nurses had many other career options once the war was over. The lure of service to the Empire was fading, and imminent independence portended at best an uncertain future for those charitable institutions established under the *Raj*.

Despite its excellent reputation and recognised value to Europeans in India, and to a lesser extent to Indians, the Minto Nursing Association did not survive past independence and partition. Just prior to the change in government, an Indian woman told Emma Wilson, the last Lady Superintendent of the Minto Nurses, that "...India would be foolish to let you Mintos go... because the Association sets a standard that Indians should aspire to."[38] In that spirit, the Association persevered, and by September 1947, Minto sisters were in the thick of the post-partition violence, working in refugee camps in Delhi and elsewhere, with salaries paid by the Association rather than the new government.

The Association itself was in chaos, since it depended on payment from individuals or hospitals for its survival, and little or no financial support was forthcoming. After partition, the Association's centres in the Punjab were eliminated, as was the governing Central Committee in India. Many of the Committee's British members had left for home, and Indian committee members were preoccupied with the many other social welfare problems facing the new nation.

Minto sisters had great difficulty getting to those who requested their services in major cities, and securing air transportation to reach Europeans in remote locations was nearly impossible. It became increasingly clear that no matter how much their services were valued, the Minto nurses were going to be a casualty of independence and partition. A November 1947 conference chaired by Lady Mountbatten formalised what everyone already knew: without the support of the new government the Association could no longer do its work. "The Association has fulfilled its purpose and should depart as an Association," was the official decision. Shortly afterward, with the full support of Lady Mountbatten and the agreement of Lady Violet Astor, Lady Minto's daughter, the Association was disbanded.

Mary Minto did not live to see the demise of her Association; she died in 1940, at the age of 82. Like Hariot Dufferin, she had maintained a life-long commitment to her Indian Association. Emma Wilson met Lady

Minto before she went out to India as a nurse in 1921: "She remains in my memory the most beautiful and gracious lady I ever met. Intensely interested in the work of her Association, she was until her death its inspiration. We Minto nurses felt that in her we had a friend."[39]

Winifred Hardinge faced different but no less daunting challenges when she took over the Dufferin Fund presidency in 1911. As more women entered the medical field in England, and to a more limited extent in India, the patriarchal structure and operation of the Dufferin Fund came under attack as being irrelevant and even antithetical to the changing medical environment. In 1907, a group of women doctors led by Dr. Annette Benson had formed the Association of Medical Women in India, (AMWI) which followed the lead of a similar organization created by activist women doctors in London who called attention to the problem of high infant mortality, and recommended expanded public health services such as inspecting school children for the most communicable diseases, and providing immunizations.

The Indian Association's journal offered a public forum for women doctors to express their discontent with the Dufferin Fund, and to lobby for an official women's medical service. In 1909, the AMWI Council had presented the Dufferin Fund's Central Committee with a set of demands including requiring the Secretary of the Dufferin Fund to be a "qualified medical woman," at least one medical woman be appointed to the Central Committee, and proposed establishing a female medical service with government support.

Lady Minto and the Committee "respectfully" considered all the Association's requests, but the only concession they made was to invite one of the deputation's members, Dr. Kathleen Vaughan, to join the Committee. At the same time, women doctors in England and India joined together in a UK branch of the AMWI, which gave the Association more influence and publicity for their lobbying efforts. After several meetings and considerable discussion, in 1910, Lord Morley, the SOSI, deftly shifted the responsibility to the government in India. In forwarding a request for a women's medical service, he noted that the "scheme did not seem entirely practical," and asked the government for their opinion, particularly on the issue of whether female medical aid in India was adequate or not – a not-so-subtle reflection on the work of the Dufferin Fund.

As the India Office and Government of India deliberated over these matters against the backdrop of rising tensions in Britain over women's suffrage, women doctors in both India and England sought better medical care for women with increasing fervor. It had been evident for some years that no matter how well-intentioned, the existing Dufferin Fund organization could not meet the enormous medical needs of Indian women.

Once again, press accounts of the Indian women's suffering in childbirth – complete with horrific details about the *dais* – fuelled the public debate in Britain and India.

The conflict fell right into Winfred Hardinge's lap. The Government of India rejected the initial proposals for a women's medical service, but finally agreed to support a service that would cost no more than a *lakh* and a half of rupees per year which would enable the hiring of 25 fully qualified lady doctors, a salary "ladder" ensuring steady advancement, and the establishment of a "provident" or retirement fund for the doctors. Lady Hardinge supported the new service as long as it remained under the umbrella of the Dufferin Fund, and wisely sought Lady Dufferin's assistance, urging her to communicate with the new Secretary of State for India, Lord Crewe, and give her support to that plan. Action was finally taken on the proposal in July 1910, when Crewe received a group of female doctors and other supporters. They were not seeking an exact counterpart of the IMS; rather they proposed a central organization that would control women's hospitals throughout India, staffed by women, in which locally educated and qualified women doctors would receive additional training in obstetrics and gynecology and then serve in smaller towns and villages.[40] Lord Crewe diplomatically indicated that while the proposal was under review by the Government of India, and although he sensed general agreement in principle, that "there might be some difference as to method."[41]

In standard bureaucratic form, the Indian government referred the proposal to the Dufferin Fund's Central Committee which discussed it at a meeting in January 1911, and promptly created a subcommittee to review the matter in detail, chaired by Lady Hardinge, who oversaw the debate and the flow of proposals and counterproposals from both India and England. In the end, the Government was reluctant to create any new organization that seemed to compete with the Dufferin Fund, even one that had the support of the founder and the current Lady President. Finally, in 1913, they agreed to pay a *lakh* and-a-half a year to the Fund to support a women's medical service, and asked the Fund's Central Committee to draw up a plan for that scheme. Their plan was adopted, and the Women's Medical Service was finally created in January 1914, but it remained under the aegis of the Dufferin Fund. Whatever their other differences of opinion, all involved agreed that the WMS owed its existence in large measure to Lady Hardinge's diplomatic leadership and consistent support.

As with most compromises, no one was entirely happy. In Britain, most medical women saw the new service as barely half-a-loaf. They felt the salaries to be inadequate, and there were disagreements about the level of required qualifications. Nor was AMWI entirely happy either because they had no real control over the new Service. The women appointed to it ran hospitals under provincial or local Dufferin Fund committees, making it impossible for the Central Committee to impose higher qualifications on the appointment of lady doctors even though they were the hiring authority, served as a court of appeals in employment issues, and held exclusive termination and assignment authority. On the other hand, the creation of the WMS increased the Committee's responsibility and activity, and indirectly prolonged the life of the Fund by increasing its influence on the new service's growth and development.[42] Despite all the negative views in Britain, forming the WMS guaranteed women doctors in India permanency of service, steady pay raises, a retirement fund, furloughs every three or four years, study leaves, the right to attend all hospital committees' meetings, and full professional control of the hospital.

As Lady President, Lady Hardinge became quite knowledgeable about medical issues, and recognised the continuing need for enhancing medical education for Indian women. Working with the Fund's Central Committee, she instigated the creation of a fully equipped and staffed medical college and hospital for women, along with a first class training school for nurses. Following the example of her predecessors, Lady Hardinge organised and directed the fundraising efforts, once again tapping the seemingly endless well of princely fortunes, raising some Rs. 15,00,000, with the expectation that the Government of India would provide the remaining money for the bricks and mortar and for on-going support. By early 1914, she was able to lay the foundation stone for the Medical College and Training School for Women at Delhi to be named for the Queen-Empress Mary. Sadly, she did not live to see its completion, and it fell to her husband to open the hospital, now named for the late vicereine, just prior to his departure from India. Lady Hardinge's untimely death in July 1914 elicited a huge outpouring of tributes in England and India, many of which expressed gratitude for her work on behalf of Indian women and children, including the establishment of the first "Children's Day" held throughout India to promote children's welfare, and the institution of zenanah wings in Dufferin hospitals. The Lady Hardinge Hospital and Medical College for Women still exists today, the legacy of her short and sad tenure as vicereine.[43]

By that time, with the Women's Medical Service well underway, and World War I the paramount concern throughout the Empire, Lady Chelmsford presided over a relatively static Dufferin Fund, as fundraising in both India and England faced stiff competition from war-related charities. She responded to declining revenues by proposing some streamlining of the Fund's operations – including those of the WMS – so that more money could be spent on direct services to patients rather than overhead and administration. She also instituted a system of independent inspection of

Dufferin facilities, changes to the format of Annual Reports, and kept the Fund in the public eye with a steady round of visits to Dufferin Hospitals. She laid a foundation stone for the Princess of Wales Hospital in Amritsar in 1916, opened or visited hospitals in Quetta, Karachi, Calcutta, Peshawar and Lahore, and made a special visit to the new Lady Hardinge College and Hospital in Delhi. Despite those efforts, the Fund's Annual Report for 1917 reported that there had been "little or no improvement" in the conditions of childbirth in India, despite the training offered by the Victoria Memorial Scholarships.

Undaunted, Lady Chelmsford sought to leave her mark on the by now traditional vicereinal issue of maternal and child welfare. Under the umbrella of the Dufferin Fund, she created the Lady Chelmsford All India League for Maternity and Child Welfare, which emphasised preventive health care, including prenatal care for women. The League had three primary activities: health "schools" to train a cadre of health "visitors" who would then disseminate information about basic health care and the importance of child vaccination; the establishment of child welfare centres where native women could come to receive information; and for the first time, a coordinated program of advertising and propaganda directed at women throughout India. These were not new ideas; Lady Chelmsford was transferring and modifying programs that had recently begun in England, primarily in response to the discovery that most young men entering the armed forces in WWI were in very poor physical condition. The Maternity and Child Welfare Act of 1918 prompted more attention to the health of children and young people, as well as the creation of women's hospitals, child welfare centres and "baby shows" throughout the United Kingdom. It seemed entirely appropriate that this new public policy emphasis should be exported to the Empire, and the vicereine was in the ideal spot to bring attention to it.

Lady Chelmsford and her successor, Lady Reading, found an ally in the Begum of Bhopal, Sultan Jahan, who ruled from 1901–1926. Bhopal had one of the first *purdah* hospitals under the direction of a female European doctor – the Lady Lansdowne Hospital, which had been opened in 1891 and was part of the Dufferin network. Sultan Jahan's greatest interest was education for women, but she was also an advocate for improving women's health care. She maintained women's hospitals and dispensaries in her state, and also introduced training programs for nurses, midwives, and health visitors, including the establishment of a Lady Minto Nursing School adjacent to the Lansdowne hospital in 1909. As one of the few women rulers, the Begum became a major force in maternal and child health, working with both Frances Chelmsford and her successor, Alice Reading.

In fact, despite almost constant ill-health, Lady Reading would make several major contributions to women's health care, and would be one of the most dedicated and hard-working vicereines. Although lacking formal leadership experience, Lady Reading had a keen intellect, a natural talent for organization and analysis, and was genuinely interested in finding a better way to improve medical care for Indian women and children. A quick review of the charitable landscape convinced her that some consolidation of the existing women's health organizations was essential – especially in terms of fundraising coordination. Her secretary, Yvonne Fitzroy[45] summed the situation up nicely in her diary, reporting after an early meeting of the Dufferin Fund's Executive Committee: it was "..a highly diverting Committee Meeting, during which all these efficient ladies gave way to the most unseemly passion. But from the point of view of getting things done, Committee Meetings in India are the despair of their President, even though they may contain some elements of humor."[45]

Taking the bull by the horns and overriding the contentious Committee, the vicereine announced the creation of the Lady Reading Women of India Fund, a broad-based appeal that would support a range of health services and facilities for women and children. In making the announcement, Lady Reading noted the need for care of Indian women and children, not only in childbirth and infancy but in every stage of development and need, and set an overarching goal of getting skilled medical aid to the poorest Indian women and children. Specifically, the Fund would assist the Hardinge Hospital and its medical education programs; create the Lady Reading Hospital for Indian Women and Children in Simla, staffed by women and specialising in eye and ear diseases, where nurses could be trained; and establish a nursing association for Indians along the lines of the Minto Association.

Sensitive to the reputation of the Dufferin Fund and its important patrons, Lady Reading proposed an affiliation with the Fund and its subsidiary organizations to avoid duplication of effort and any confusion about who was doing what. She also gave credit to her predecessors who "…with greater experience…I can claim, but hardly with more heartfelt interest…" inspired her efforts, and noted the progress made by those organizations started by earlier vicereines. The Dufferin Fund, the Minto Nursing Association, and the Chelmsford League continued for the time being to have their own Committees, although they began to move towards greater cooperation, setting up shared office space for all activities in Simla. However sensible her reorganization was, it was also clear that like vicereines before and after her, Lady Reading wanted to establish something that was entirely her own creation, and which would remain after her departure. Her Women of India Fund appeal was not designed to be permanent; indeed on her departure, she wryly commented that she was not leaving yet another organization to be maintained by the vicereine. That comment notwithstanding, Lady Reading understandably wanted to get public recognition for the work she did in India, and was not loathe to see her name emblazoned on buildings. When she discovered that one Dufferin Hospital had no nurses' quarters or sitting rooms, she quickly solicited funds from a neighboring maharajah to rectify the situation, with the condition that the new area be named the Lady Reading room.

Once the Women of India Fund was announced, money began to literally pour in for the proposed Simla hospital. With £20,000 in gifts from maharajahs and princes, Lady Reading was able to buy a house and grounds in Simla for the new hospital, which would also bear her name. Knowing how hard it was to raise funds for even the most worthy causes in England, she never ceased to marvel at the immense wealth of India. Whatever their motives for donating, there is no doubt that the generosity of the Indian princes and others enabled much if not all of the vicereines' charitable efforts, which in turn served as the foundation for the more democratic and organised welfare system that was created after independence.

Yvonne Fitzroy's diary offers a fascinating insight into how extensive Alice's charitable works were during her years in India, all the more amazing given her frail constitution and the fact that she underwent at least one operation for cancer during that time. In Yvonne's diary notes, sent privately to her parents, she was remarkably blunt about her views on the Readings' suitability for office – reflecting a not-too-subtle anti-Semitism – and the vicereine's sometimes imperious and cranky demeanor. Cautioning her parents not to share her letters or diary, Yvonne wrote: "B... has every reason to feel cattish about Their Exs and every single word I say will come straight back to them."[46] She reluctantly gave Her Ex credit for her considerable charitable work, reporting a rigorous schedule of visits to hospitals, infant welfare centres, orphanages, and old age hostels, and a seemingly endless round of meetings for the various charities under her purview. At the same time, Yvonne complained that she was "up to her eyes" in the All India fund, and that soon "....soon I shall think, speak, remember and dream of nothing in the world save what the Chelmsford girls used to call, 'Mother's Beastly Brown Babies.' Not the spirit for Empire Builders, you will admit but they have my sympathy."[47]

By 1924, three years in the vicereine's service had made Yvonne increasingly critical of nearly everything about Lady Reading – her insistence on formality on all occasions, her decorating and entertaining styles, even her bouts of illness which created more work for Yvonne – it seemed as though Alice could not put a foot right. Still she retained a grudging respect for Lady Reading's work on behalf of Indian women and children. The new hospital was completed within 10 months from the start of construction, an amazing achievement anywhere in India, but especially in Simla where the terrain made building so difficult. To be sure, Alice did not show quite the same attention to the project as the Dufferins had to the new Viceregal Lodge, but her intense interest in the hospital's design and outfitting was a source of some frustration to the builders and to her staff. "Opening Her Ex's hospital and saying good bye to Carey absorb all our energies. The lady descends on the Hospital daily and makes everyone's life a burden, but it must be admitted, she gets things done."[48]

The formal opening was an enormous celebration, with the viceroy praising his wife extravagantly, speeches by other worthies of British India, and a speech of thanks from the vicereine, who had arrived that morning with a birthday cake for the staff, and a rattle to be presented "with ceremony" to the first baby born there. Bright, airy and as up-to-date as possible, the new hospital was a significant addition to Simla's medical infrastructure. It also had the benefit of a personal endowment of Rs 5 lakhs from Lady Reading, a generous and unusual act for any vicereine. Her munificence was noted in the Simla paper: "...in the past many institutions have been started and erected...and then have been left by their founders without sufficient funds to ensure their future welfare." The Lady Reading Hospital still exists as do other health facilities bearing her name.

Lady Reading's other major legacy to Indian women was the establishment of "National Baby Week" throughout the country, an outgrowth of work started by the Chelmsford League. Baby Weeks were designed to educate Indian women, especially poor women, about how to raise children, emphasising the advantages of Western midwifery techniques, medical care, and childrearing methods. Early on, Lady Reading tried to include more Indians in both her social and charitable endeavors, an effort that generated both positive and negative comments from British-Indian society. As would be expected, she primarily included Indian aristocrats, such as the female rulers of native states, or wives, sisters, and daughters of other princes.

These connections were helpful in all her charitable works, but most especially in the establishment of the nationwide Baby Week program. By 1925, local and provincial Baby Weeks were providing exhibits, films, pamphlets, and demonstrations to help educate Indian women about how Western knowledge and medicine could prevent disease and help them raise healthier children. A National Baby Week Council composed of British-Indian and Indian worthies and chaired by the vicereine oversaw Baby Weeks throughout India. Under Alice's leadership, the number of Baby Week celebrations increased annually, each organised by a local committee, and there was a significant upturn in cooperation among various health and social agencies.

The largest and most elaborate Baby Week celebration was held in Delhi, on the *maidan* opposite the old Fort, set for January 1925 to coincide with the opening of the Legislative Assembly and the Council of State, because legislative support was essential to any real social progress, and the government was providing some grants to encourage health care efforts. At the opening ceremony, the platform party included the viceroy, municipal officers of Delhi, and a number of Indian representatives, "even the Swarajists" (those seeking self-rule for India), one of whom even proposed a vote of thanks to Alice for her efforts. Lady Reading replied with an impassioned speech about the importance of investing in children's welfare, urging anyone, "Indian or European" who thought that this effort was not needed to visit a city slum and see the problems for themselves. In her remarks, Alice noted that "the force was with us" and that an outpouring of public support over the past year had enabled great progress, despite those who had accused the organizers of "immoderate ambition." Women, she said have an "instinctive sympathy" for child welfare work, and in a nod to the emerging class of British feminists, reminded them that they "...too must surely recognize that emancipation is but the parent of service," and that greater opportunity also meant greater responsibility. The appalling statistics of infant mortality might seem remote from their daily lives, but they were in fact "...an indictment, not of a nation or a race, but of society." She also reminded her audience of their responsibilities: "interest and generosity alone, or both, are not enough…. If you are rich, then are you responsible for poorer humanity for the use of your riches; if you are wise, then are you responsible to the simple for the exercise of your wisdom; if you have leisure, then are you responsible to life itself for the uses to which you put that leisure. And if you are happy, prosperous, content – then, most of all, are you in your country's debt."[49] Those heartfelt and straightforward remarks clearly demonstrated her commitment to the cause, and were all the more remarkable because of her public image as a haughty and somewhat unapproachable vicereine.

Alice Reading left her successor a more structured and integrated charitable organization, but despite her best efforts at consolidated fundraising, she could not guarantee their financial solvency. Following what was by now a well-worn path for vicereines, Alice's successor Dorothy Irwin assumed leadership of the Dufferin Fund, which continued to oversee the Women's Medical Service, the Victoria Memorial Scholarships, and the Lady Chelmsford All-India League for Maternity and Child Welfare. In 1926, the Fund's 42nd Annual Report for 1926 highlighted the work of these charities, including the highly successful Baby Weeks, and provided important statistical data on the number of women served by Fund doctors, hospitals and dispensaries in the various provinces. Out of necessity, the Fund's Central Committee had begun to focus on administrative issues related to the WMS – recruiting and training women doctors and battling with the government over subsidies and regulations and policies which inhibited women's equal practice of medicine in India. The UK Branch continued to be headed by the redoubtable Lady Dufferin, still a force to be reckoned with in her late seventies. She enlisted all living former vicereines as Vice Patrons of the Fund, and held annual meetings of the UK branch at the India Office in London, one of which Lady Irwin attended before coming out to India.

By 1927, financial concerns of the WMS were the dominant issue facing the vicereine and her Committee as the Dufferin Fund's relevance and influence continued to wane. The reliance on government funding and oversight had turned out to be a mixed blessing. Private donors saw government support as replacing, not supplementing, their contributions, and the central government began to delegate the administration of health services. Without additional funds, any real expansion of women's medical services would be difficult, if not impossible. The existing government subsidy covered the pay of only 42 women doctors, plus the cost of the WMS Training Reserve and the Junior Branch of the WMS.

A request for an increase that would enable the hiring of eight more doctors was repeatedly rejected over the next few years, under the rationale that medical administration was not a function of the central government, but of provincial and local governments and the public at large. Lady Irwin used the Fund's provincial structure to approach local governments for salary support for WMS doctors in Dufferin hospitals, but without much success. "In nearly every province lack of funds and lack of interest have made it difficult for our doctors to carry on first class work," was the grim analysis offered in the 1927 Annual Report. Despite all that had been done since the Fund's inception in 1885, the fact remained that with few exceptions, local governments did not feel the same level of responsibility for medical aid for women and children as they did for men, and the private support which had enabled the Fund's early successes was no longer forthcoming. Even the formerly generous indigenous rulers began to reduce their contributions as the steady if uneven march to independence grew and they felt less pressure to assist the vicereine in her charitable projects.

In the face of stringincies, Lady Irwin did the best she could, seeing that the Fund's scarce resources were directed toward scholarships for women training as doctors and nurses and grants to female hospitals, and pursuing foundation funding for research on maternal and infant mortality. Even Lady Dufferin had to recognize the significant reduction in funds and interest in the Fund: in 1928 she reported that the UK branch had met only once in the previous year, and that the UK branch no longer recruited women doctors for India as WMS appointments went to women trained in India.

By 1929, those provinces which failed to provide part of the WMS salaries faced the prospect of having WMS personnel withdrawn from their area, and the Fund was able to provide only limited support for each of its charities: 40% for the Central Office, 35% for the Lady Chelmsford League,

35%, 15% to the Dufferin Fund, and a mere 10% for Victoria Memorial Scholarships.

The formidable Lady Willingdon was more than ready to take on the challenges facing the Dufferin Fund in 1931. Marie's powerful personality overshadowed her quieter husband. Her single-minded – some said obstructionist – approach to any task was legendary, whether it was advising Lutyens on the construction of the new capital, redecorating official residences, or organising and fundraising on behalf of various charities. Even her detractors were in awe of her ability to get things done. During the First World War, she had established several hospitals for soldiers (these too outfitted in her signature colour, mauve, even down to the blankets on the beds), and the Women's Branch of the War Relief Fund. She also created the Bombay Presidency Women's Council, which provided free milk, parenting advice, and day care for Indian women throughout the Presidency. As vicereine, she maintained an intense interest on maternal and child health and female education, and was tireless in her fundraising efforts for the Dufferin Fund and related organizations. Her obituary in the *Times* diplomatically described the dread of government officials as the vicereine came at them "...with long subscription lists...[but] recognised her singleness of purpose." Any organization she chose to support was bound to succeed, but only if things were done her way. Her social welfare activities while vicereine were significant, but were eclipsed by her obsession with redoing the Viceroy's House and supporting her husband, whose age was beginning to affect his ability to govern.

There are few mentions of the Dufferin Fund in the records of the vicereines after the 1935 Jubilee year, with the exception of annual Fund meetings chaired by Edwina Mountbatten in 1947 and 1948, just before departing India. Although the Fund continued to exist on paper until 2002, when the Indian legislature formally dissolved it, and transferred its few remaining assets to the government, the late 1930s and the 1940s saw a shift in focus from maternal and child health to war-related relief efforts. Another significant change was the increased involvement of both Indian men and women in the vicereines' charitable and public health efforts. Nevertheless, the a time when women's roles were rapidly evolving throughout the world, the model of an "activist" vicereine set by Hariot Dufferin remained relevant – perhaps more so than in the past. Each of the last three vicereines had more freedom of action and more opportunities to serve than her 19th and early 20th century predecessors, and no longer had to restrict their activities to women's health matters, although obstetrics, prenatal care, and children's health remained paramount. These latter-day vicereines expanded their interests to broader public health concerns, and worked diligently to involve the emerging Indian leadership in their causes.

Doreen Linlithgow's legacy was, for example, an effort to eradicate tuberculosis, which was widespread throughout India. In Peshawar alone, some 60,000 cases were reported in one year, most of which were blamed on the *purdah* tradition, the all-enveloping *burkahs* worn by women providing the ideal conditions for microbial incubation. Lady Linlithgow played a pivotal role in the creation of the Tuberculosis Association of India (TAI), personally issuing an appeal in 1937 for funds to begin a nationwide program of education and treatment. The Rs 10 million raised through this appeal along with funds given to the King George V Thanksgiving Fund enabled the TAI to open its doors and start regional and provincial TB clinics. Despite her hard work, Lady Linlithgow realised that, as with the Dufferin Fund, the efforts made by the TAI seemed to be a drop in the bucket: by 1946 there were only about 6,000 beds available for the estimated 2.5 million TB patients, roughly 500,000 of whom died each year. Several TB sanatoria and hospitals in India were named in the vice-reine's honour, and she retained a life-long interest in TB treatment after her return to England.

As World War II began, Lady Linlithgow turned her attention toward encouraging women's involvement in war relief activities. A book called "Queen Mary's Book of India" was published in 1943 to raise funds for the India Comforts Fund, in which the vicereine outlined the need for Indian women to become engaged in what was by now a worldwide conflagration. Once aware that India itself was threatened, Indian women in large numbers began to join the various women's services: the newly created Women's Auxiliary Corps, the Auxiliary Nursing Service – which trained over 1,000 nurses in its first six months of existence – and the Women's Voluntary Service (WVS), which at the government's request took over all matters concerning Indian evacuees, war widows, and abandoned wives. Lady Linlithgow also worked with the Director-General of the Indian Medical Services to raise the standards of the Indian Military Nursing Service[50] so that it was nearly on the same footing as the Queen Alexandra Imperial Military Nursing Service India.

In 1942, the vicereine had established the Silver Trinket Fund, appealing to Indian women to donate their silver "trinkets" to aid the war effort, raising some eight *lakhs* by October of that year. The funds were spent on blood-drying and transfusion plants, bacteriological units, mobile canteens, ambulances, mobile hospitals for bombed areas in Britain, and helped provide buses and cars for the use of convalescent troops and YWCA war service. The Silver Trinket Fund also provided £10,000 toward the establishment of an Indian Ward in the Seamen's Hospital at Greenwich.

When the Linlithgows left India in 1943, it fell to the last two vicereines, Eugenie Wavell and Edwina Mountbatten, to continue and expand her war

relief efforts. Both encouraged Indian women to join the Red Cross, the St. John Ambulance Brigade, and the Women's Volunteer Service. As noted before, since both of their husbands were serving military men before becoming viceroy – Wavell as Commander-in-Chief India under Lord Linlithgow, and Mountbatten as Supreme Commander South East Asia Command – Eugenie and Edwina were already heavily involved in war relief efforts before becoming vicereine.

Lady Wavell's particular concern was the welfare of wounded troops, and one of her first acts as vicereine was to set up a program that provided personal care items to soldiers. She and her daughters also set an example for other British women in India by working in military hospitals throughout the war. Her lack of aristocratic background did not affect her ability to be an effective vicereine, and it may in fact have contributed to her capacity to work well with Indian and British women throughout the war. Eugenie was more approachable than her predecessor, with a warm and charming personality, and had more in common with the military and civilian British-Indians whose presence had been tolerated, but not particularly enjoyed, by earlier, more aristocratic vicereines.

Nonetheless, Lady Wavell did share her predecessors' understanding of the power of her position to get things done, as she led an effort to establish an expanded system of hospitals and dispensaries, and called a

1944 conference of governor's wives to review WVS and Red Cross activities throughout India. And although the war overshadowed almost every other aspect of the viceroyalty, Lady Wavell still took every opportunity to learn more about the more traditional concerns of vicereines – the state of female education and general public health – visiting schools, infant welfare centres, canteens, and hospitals when she accompanied her husband on tour. She publicly supported improved public health services throughout India, highlighting the problem of infant mortality and the "crying need" for better prenatal care, properly trained midwives, and more and better baby clinics.

As she watched the demands for self-government escalate, Lady Wavell recognised that the time for British leadership in Indian public health policy – as in so much else – was coming to an end. She engaged Indian women in her work much more than past vicereines, and corresponded with Indian women leaders such as Cornelia Sorabji, the renowned lawyer and activist, about how to get more Indian women into the health professions. "Indian women must do their part if the health of their country is to be improved," she wrote to Cornelia, seeking advice on how Indian women "of good education" could be encouraged to enter the profession.[51] When the Wavells were removed from the viceroyalty hastily and rather unceremoniously, if she felt any bitterness, Lady Wavell did not convey it to her successor or to anyone else publicly. Lady Mountbatten, already famous in her own right as well as the wife of a senior military commander who was also a second cousin of the King-Emperor, was widely known throughout the Empire for her work with the Red Cross and as Lady Superintendent of the St. John Ambulance Brigade. Experienced in organizational politics, supremely confident in her own abilities, and seemingly tireless, Edwina was more than equipped to take up the vicereine's by-now traditional banner of social welfare. Her socialist political views and liberal attitude toward people of other races were viewed by most of British-Indian society as highly suspect, but "Lady Louis" (as she was generally known) could not have cared less about their approval. Becoming vicereine was a challenge, but unlike her immediate predecessors, she was used to being in the public eye, as an exceptionally talented public speaker and quite skilled at using the press to advance any cause she championed.

Social welfare work would, in fact, be one of the things Lady Mountbatten enjoyed most about her brief reign, along with her behind-the-scenes efforts to effect wider social and political change. She had already earned high praise for her Red Cross work on behalf of British prisoners of war, particularly in Java and Sumatra, and her work for civilian relief in Malaya. Mountbatten reported that in 1945 Lady Louis actually arrived in some locations before his troops were well-established, and once she had seen the grim conditions in the camps, she badgered generals, air marshals, and admirals into doing whatever was necessary to get the prisoners evacuated as quickly as possible. Lady Mountbatten also made countless visits to military hospitals treating officers and IORs (Indian Other Ranks), making detailed notes on patient care and recommendations for improvements at each stop, including lists of items in short supply, the number and quality of the nursing staff, even such relatively minor information as how out-of-date the magazines were. She was not reluctant to pass on her recommendations to her husband and others in power, in some cases indicating which branch of the service should run a particular hospital. Each of her typed reports ended with a list of the people she had met, hospital personnel and patients she had seen, those to whom thank you notes should be sent, and an ACTION NECESSARY list.[52]

In an odd twist of fate, the last vicereine would turn out to be the most influential since Hariot Dufferin, and would leave even more beloved by the Indian people. Lady Mountbatten initially was reluctant to come to India, preferring to remain in England, continue her war relief work, and settle in to what she hoped would be a quiet post-war existence. She had gained enormous respect and recognition for her war work – already receiving medals from both the American and Belgian Red Cross organizations for her service – and was often asked for her advice on a host of welfare issues. But despite being a "modern woman" in every sense of that term, Lady Mountbatten, like all those vicereines before her, never seriously considered not sharing the viceroyalty. Instead, she looked for ways to continue the work she believed in so strongly, and strove to strike a balance between the established viceregal formality and the need to make meaningful contacts and connections with the Indian elites who would soon rule the subcontinent – most of whom in years past would not have entered the vicereine's social or political orbit, let alone her inner circle.

Even before she left England, Lady Mountbatten was anticipating how she could get involved in good works, seeking information about the voluntary and missionary societies in India, and receiving suggestions for action and the names of influential women who could help from Isobel Cripps and Stella Reading (the second Lady Reading), among others. Once in India, she moved rapidly, meeting with leading women who could offer guidance, including an old friend of her mother's, Mrs. Sarojini Naidu, a poet and Congress Party politician, and Mrs. Pandit, Nehru's sister. Edwina literally hit the ground running, as during her first weeks in India, she met with the heads of the YWCA, the Women's Voluntary Service, the Red Cross, and the Human Rights Commission, as well as Lady Rama Rao, the President of the All-India Women's Conference and Miss Wilson, head of the Minto Nursing Association. She sought out Dr. Bhimrao Ambedkar, who came to talk with her on behalf of the Scheduled Castes, the "untouchables,"[53] while quickly learning all she could about the complex of charities she now led, meeting with the heads of all the Dufferin Fund charities, visiting hospitals, dispensaries and clinics throughout the subcontinent, and chairing endless meetings, searching for ways these organizations could continue in a soon-to-be independent India. Edwina also made sure that her husband and other people of influence knew what she was learning about the state of social welfare in India, issuing regular "bulletins" to her daughters and husband, her colleagues at St. John Ambulance and the Red Cross, and even to her mother-in-law, who could be relied on to show them to the King and Queen.

India's sectarian strife, Edwina wrote, was "artificially engineered…and the result of previous policies, missed opportunities and mistakes made on all sides." She believed that India's problems were economic and social rather than religious or political, and that the key to a peaceful transition was to improve overall living conditions, educational standards, employment opportunities, and health. Illiteracy was rampant, large numbers of women were still dying in childbirth, and infant mortality rates were very high: 62 out of every 1,000 died in the first weeks of life, and 430 out of every thousand died before they reached the age of five. Nurses were desperately underpaid, nursing standards were lax or non-existent, and Indian women were still reluctant to enter the nursing profession, or even to take on ordinary volunteer work.[54]

Lady Mountbatten's gloomy assessment of the current situation made it seem as though the work of previous vicereines and other dedicated souls who had laboured so hard for so long had literally been a drop in the bucket, but she was not dissuaded by the discouraging outlook. Instead she began a concentrated campaign to educate and engage those whom she expected to lead these efforts in the coming months and years, skillfully using the power of her office as vicereine.

When her husband held his first meeting of British Residents, Lady Mountbatten gave a tea party for their wives, leading the conversation to a discussion of welfare and medical services in India. She was stunned to learn that some of these women who had spent years in India knew almost nothing about the conditions she described. "Lack of knowledge and parochial viewpoint and Anti-Indian feeling of many appalling even now," she wrote in her diary that night.[55] When Mountbatten met with the Provincial Governors a few days later, his wife organised a two-day long meeting of their wives. She introduced them to the leaders of government departments responsible for industry, health, food and public works, and brought in senior officers of the medical and nursing services, both civil and military, as well as representatives of the Red Cross, St. John Ambulance,

The Mountbattens, the last and most regal of the Viceroys, photographed as they had taken office in the Durbar Hall in March 1947.

the Guides, the WVS, and the YWCA – the first time the leaders of so many organizations concerned with social welfare had been brought together. Under the vicereine's determined leadership, the group identified ways they could cooperate and reduce, if not eliminate, duplications of effort.

It was just the beginning, Edwina announced. In a few months, she planned to bring together all the Indian-sponsored welfare organizations, an ambitious yet obvious approach to the myriad of social welfare issues facing the country, and one that required the political power of the vicereine to make it possible. Some said Lady Mountbatten was merely making friends with the wives of political leaders in order to increase Mountbatten's influence on their husbands on the important issues inherent in the upcoming transfer of power, and like every other vicereine, Edwina was well aware that her friendships with the wives, and sisters of leading Indian politicians could be useful to her husband, but that was not her primary goal. She was primarily interested in getting influential women – both British-Indian and Indian – to begin to understand the changes that were bound to come with the transfer and to start looking forward to ways they could contribute in the new social and political environment. As vicereine, Edwina also set an example for British-Indian women who led charitable organizations throughout India by taking every opportunity to pass on the leadership of her own charities. She refused to preside at meetings of organizations where she was Lady President or Patroness, preferring instead to work behind the scenes and let Indian members of the Executive Committees preside. "… I insist on bringing more and more Indians to those committees and letting the limelight shine on them," she wrote to Stella Reading, with whom she was working on a Red Cross appeal for both India and Palestine.[56]

As the months to independence were counted down, Lady Louis tried to tie up some of the loose ends of the more than 60 years' charitable work done by her predecessors. She visited hospitals and public health facilities all over India which bore their names – Ripon, Dufferin, Irwin, Hardinge, Reading, Linlithgow, Wavell, and Willingdon – urging Indian medical leaders to continue providing what services they could once the British left. She held meetings of the Dufferin Fund and oversaw the dissolution of the Minto Nursing Association, making the difficult decisions demanded by the impending end of the British *Raj*. Edwina believed that the most useful service she could perform prior to the transfer of power was to convince the leaders of medical and social welfare organizations all across the subcontinent to work together toward creating national teams of experts which would be ready to take over these important responsibilities when the British left.

Throughout the hot Delhi summer of 1947, she met almost continuously with leaders of volunteer organizations and government agencies, introducing people of like interest to one another, poring over pages of limp and smudged documents to find out exactly who had what responsibility and where there were areas of possible cooperation. She worked tirelessly with organizations to arrange for the transfer of assets, staff and income, and with help from her by-now close friend Nehru, was instrumental in passing the Nurses Council bill which established standards for nursing care.

The months after independence brought ghastly violence to many parts of India – shops and houses burned, women raped, mosques and temples burned to the ground – as millions of Hindus and Muslims fled to what they hoped would be safer ground, Hindus to India and Muslims to Pakistan. Lady Mountbatten – now the wife of the Governor General, no longer vicereine – made personal visits to hospitals where the victims of sectarian violence were being treated. As she had during the war, she aggressively took on the refugee issue, making dangerous trips to the worst areas of conflict in the Northwest Frontier Province and the Punjab to see for herself the results of Hindu-Muslim violence: "...the devastation is like the Blitz at its worst...it all seems so senseless and yet nothing seems to stop them," she wrote.[57] Once again, Edwina took the initiative: just 11 days after the handover, she toured East and West Punjab, seeing for herself the squalid conditions in which refugees were living, and the dearth of basic medical care and supplies, inadequate public sanitation and clean water, lack of temporary housing, and the inability of refugees to find new, safe homes, not to mention the problem of employment for displaced persons. Unconcerned with her personal safety, the last vicereine left an indelible image in the minds of those who saw her – that of a British woman who cared deeply about their welfare, and who brought hope to a nearly impossible situation. Cool and collected when others were gasping in the heat, the seemingly indefatigable Lady Louis brought an atmosphere of calm to a volatile situation, however briefly, and epitomised the qualities of the British *memsahibs* which passed into legend.

When violence broke out later in Delhi, the vicereine made arrangements to protect the families of those Muslims who worked at Government House, arranging for some 5000 people to be brought into the relative safety of the compound. She instituted rationing for everyone who worked in Government House in an effort to ensure sufficient food for those under her care, noting that "Pammie ...has become quite keen on SPAM."[58] Edwina became Chairman of the Relief Committee overseeing the procurement and distribution of medical supplies, food, clothing, and water for the refugees in the hundreds of camps springing up all over the country. The emergency offered Lady Mountbatten another chance to advance her scheme for cooperation among social service agencies; she set up her own coordination council, the United Council for Relief and Welfare, working with Rajkumari Amrit Kaur, the Minister of Health. As she had during the war, Edwina kept a gruelling schedule, her 18-hour days including endless committee meetings and visits to refugee camps and hospitals to see conditions for herself and make sure supplies were getting to those in most urgent need. She traveled to the worst areas of rioting, heedless of the danger of attack or infection, to meet with military and government officials, and established a Finance Subcommittee composed of prominent Indians to oversee the funds coming in from the Red Cross and similar organizations. In the midst of this tremendous workload, whenever she could find time, she made personal visits to encourage her team of Indian women volunteers.

As the violence continued, both Mountbattens were overwhelmed by the demands on their time, and the increasing pressures to make significant progress in their respective areas before they left in 1948. After the Mountbattens made a brief visit to England in November 1947 to attend the wedding of Princess Elizabeth and Prince Philip, Edwina and her Council was given joint responsibility for the refugee problem with the Indian government. Throughout December and January, she traveled again to the Punjab, set up the Missing Persons Office in Delhi to help people reconnect families separated during the rioting, and worked with the Ministry of Health to help civilians who had been gravely wounded, losing limbs, eyesight, or speech. Her Council also had taken responsibility for identifying and returning women who had been abducted and taken far away from their homes, a problem complicated by religious constraints and the reluctance of some women to return, either because the preferred their new lives, or from the shame of what had happened to them. She may have no longer been vicereine, but in her final months, Edwina set a record of service and action unparalleled since the days of Hariot Dufferin.

While Lady Mountbatten oversaw the final transition – and in some cases, the demise – of the vicereines' programs for improving public health, interest and concern for the people of India did not end with her departure in 1948. She visited the subcontinent almost every year between 1950 and her death in 1960 – the only vicereine who ever returned to India after her reign. Her visits were usually in conjunction with her work for the St. John Ambulance Brigade or the Red Cross, and allowed her to visit old friends in India, including India's first president, Jawaharlal Nehru, with whom she maintained a close, some said intimate, friendship. After her sudden death in February 1960, the Edwina Mountbatten Memorial Fund and the Edwina Mountbatten Trust were established in India and the UK respectively to raise funds for the causes she had championed. In the best tradition of the vicereines, the Fund Committee in India was comprised primarily of wealthy maharajahs and princes, while the Queen's husband, Prince Philip, was Patron of the Trust in England, and donations were forthcoming from other British and European royals. The goal was to raise £1,000,000 to support Edwina's favourite charities, principally those in the less developed nations of the Commonwealth. Interestingly, the appeal was more successful in India than in the UK, a testament to the enduring generosity – and still relatively unlimited resources – of Indian aristocrats. Some 50 years after her death, the Edwina Mountbatten Trust continues to fund efforts to help children through the Save the Children Organization and to expand the work of the Order of St John.

Taking a longer view, it seems unlikely that Lady Dufferin foresaw the end results of the effort she began in 1885, and the complicated web of charitable activities that would flow from her initial plans. She did live long enough to see some of the results of formal government involvement with the Fund, which confirmed her belief that in the long run, the *Raj* would have to play a primary role in providing for Indian women's health care. Like many Britons, she believed firmly in the supremacy of the *Raj,* and its responsibility to expand British influence, culture, and education to people in the Empire.

The question of whether the vicereines' efforts to improve Indian medical care had any real and long-lasting effect or were simply another example of British colonial paternalism remains open. There is no doubt that from their exalted positions they were able to influence Indian aristocrats and government officials on health-related issues, and that their programs – and aggressive fundraising – made possible many hospitals, dispensaries, and infant welfare centres that would not otherwise have been established, enabling millions of women to receive care that would otherwise not have been available to them. Given India's enormous population, the number of patients served – some four million in one year, at the most – would seem to have barely scratched the surface. Despite relatively low patient numbers, there is no doubt that without the direct involvement of the vicereines, many medical care issues would not have received the attention they did under the *Raj.* Whatever their rationale for being involved – aristocratic tradition, a sense of duty, the need to create a more meaningful role for themselves, politics, or a genuine desire to help – the story of the vicereines does demonstrate their desire to make a real difference in India, and to leave a legacy, most visible in the number of hospitals, colleges, and other institutions bearing their names.

In any event, the woman who began it all in 1885 had a long and productive life of public service. Until her death in 1936, Lady Dufferin endured great happiness and deep sorrow, including the loss of her husband and all four of her sons. When the Dufferin Fund celebrated its 50th anniversary in 1935, Hariot was 92, but still energetic and articulate enough to give an address at the India Office to mark the Jubilee. In its fiftieth anniversary report published in 1935 – for which Lady Dufferin wrote a foreword – the Association counted as its greatest success the manner in which its work had opened the eyes of Indians to the suffering of their women, and the ability to mount a nationwide effort to confront the problem. Giving full credit to "thousands of young Indian women who [had] given themselves freely to the service of their country as doctors, nurses, and midwives," the authors credited the Fund with having been the impetus for improving medical care for all Indians. Although the Fund had not lived up to the vision she had for it in 1885, Lady Dufferin continued to promote medical care for Indian women and the Fund's golden anniversary offered a final chance to honour her for her lifelong devotion to the cause. Queen Mary's congratulatory letter noted that:

> [despite]...a long life, which has not been without many sorrows, it must be an abiding satisfaction...to think that this enduring monument...still flourishes in India and may perhaps play a not unimportant part in binding together British and Indian interests in the years that are to come.[59]

Similar praise came from the viceroy, Lord Willingdon, reporting to Lady Dufferin on the Jubilee meeting of the Dufferin Fund in India that: "It was a complete success; people came from all over." The messages from the founder and their majesties were "...received with the greatest enthusiasm. You may well be gratified that the great work which you initiated here, which has done so much for countless women in India still flourishes and that there are many local workers to carry it on in India." Lady Dufferin even managed to write a letter to the Maharajah of Tagore, complimenting him on remarks he made on the radio regarding the Fund's Jubilee celebration in Calcutta. The Maharajah noted in his diary that "The grand old lady has written in her shakey hand...[and] is still deeply interested in the womanhood of India." [61]

Perhaps not the worst of epitaphs...

8

The Captains And Vice-Queens Depart

As each vicereine faced the end of her Indian tenure, her perspective on the experience as an ordeal or adventure – and for the most part, a mix – was shaped by her and her husband's perception of how much he had succeeded or failed as viceroy. The following précis of a viceroy's stint, written in 1909, sums up how many Indians saw the proconsuls' impact on Indian affairs in practical terms:

> He comes [to India] and wants to do good, but is surrounded by English who pull him by the tailcoat whenever he approaches what they consider a dangerous subject...Usually he swims with the official stream, saves what he can out of his enormous salary, shoots tigers and amuses himself with viceregal tours and visits to native princes, spending half his years away from native India in the Himalayas, giving balls and entertainments to Anglo-Indian ladies. The last year, he is already defunct, so he packs up and goes home satisfied that he's done no worse than his predecessors.[1]

Most vicereines would probably have challenged that somewhat simplistic and less than charitable perception on the grounds that it failed to reflect all the energy that the viceregal couple expended in fulfilling their duties, and ignored the affection they felt for India and its people. In some cases, such a *defensa* would have been disingenuous, although the evidence suggests that each vicereine truly believed that she had had a significant effect on the country. While the early vicereines' contributions were less publicly visible than those of the late 19th and 20th centuries, even they recognised that their function went beyond that of a figurehead in rituals, and social leadership, even if most of their service was limited to the British-Indian sphere, with an occasional foray into educating Indian females or providing them with medical care. Clearly, once Hariot Dufferin set the pattern for service to indigenous women, vicereines found themselves virtually obliged to continue and extend her model of involvement. Most worked hard at doing just that, and their diaries and letters contravene the traditional view of the vicereine as a "great ornamental" whose days were spent lying on a chaise lounge under a *punkah*, looking down her lorgnette at her social inferiors, or presiding at balls, dinners, or other grand occasions.

In view of that, it is tempting to ascribe those efforts to social norms regarding aristocratic women's service to underlings, or a search by women in an age of subjugation and tight limits on their options for a solid purpose in their lives, as a way to establish or reinforce their sense of self-worth beyond serving as a helpmeet to their powerful husbands. At the same time, it is clear that that some vicereines eagerly looked forward to going home, some soon after arrival in India, and others later, after enduring the climate, the battering of unending social demands, and constant concern for children and family half-a-world away.

As suggested earlier, however, others were reluctant to give up the public acclaim, pomp, and luxury, and expressed strong regrets at leaving India. They not only enjoyed the power and influence that came with being vicereine, but came to appreciate and admire India and its people. As one *memsahib* wrote, India "found its way into [their] bones," and they retained an active interest in Indian affairs for the rest of their lives. Even vicereines initially reluctant to "go out" found something fascinating about the region – the beauty of the landscape, people, exotic cultures, or the chance to improve the health and quality of life of women. And over time, the uneven workings of memory served to blur the more unpleasant aspects of their "reign" – the suffocating heat and humidity, dust, arduous travels, numbingly dreary official social events, and omnipresent threats of assassination – and bring into sharper focus the romantic vision of a glorious reign, which for most was the grandest experience of their lives.

Although the viceroyalty was a five-year appointment, many viceroys did not complete their full term of office. Several negotiated an early exit with the home government, which made them "lame ducks" during the final months of their tenure. They usually cited family concerns in seeking an early departure, but sometimes party politics or a change in government came to bear. Lord Northbrook, for example, apparently sought replacement to extract his son from the "clutches" of an older woman with whom he had become entangled in Simla. Lord Lytton resigned after a Liberal election win, as did Ripon, who resigned to allow the Liberal government to appoint his successor before an imminent Conservative election victory. Lord Dufferin's request to be relieved in 1888 came as a surprise. And while he publicly expressed a desire to be closer to his teen-aged sons, in fact the socially dynamic Dufferin found British-Indian society rather dull, and longed for the sophisticated European ambience of his earlier diplomatic assignments. While "not a man to despise the pomps of power," Dufferin found that eventually even the grandiose ceremonial aspects of the viceroyalty began to pale. "It is," he wrote, "an odd thing to say, but dullness is certainly the characteristic of an Indian Viceroy's existence."[2] Although his successor, Lord Lansdowne, stayed for his full term, he and Lady Lansdowne were more eager to get home than almost any other viceregal team, in good part due to the fact that they had come directly to India from the Governor Generalship of Canada. "Hallelujah!" Lansdowne wrote, realising that there were only two more months to go.[3] When, halfway through his term, Lord Hardinge suffered the tragic loss of both his wife, Winifred, and his elder son in 1914, he soldiered on, even agreeing to the wartime government's request that he extend his term by six months. Lord Chelmsford on the other hand, was "encouraged" to leave India when the government felt a stronger hand was needed to deal with the rising independence movement.

Despite Alice Reading's chronic and sometimes severe health problems, she and her husband would gladly have stayed on. "Her Ex don't want to leave, no, not she," wrote Yvonne Fitzroy in 1924. "She frankly admits ten years of it would not be too much for her."[4] Dorothy Irwin fully expected to count the months until she could leave India, but as her departure approached, she felt the onset of a great affection for the country and its people which made her much sadder at the prospect of leaving than she had ever expected to be. Still, no viceregal couple was more reluctant to leave India than the Willingdons. After 20 years of red carpet pomp and ceremony in Canada and India, Lady Willingdon found it difficult to go home and give up her queenly status, and even becoming a marchioness failed to ease that pain.

On the other hand, the longest-serving viceregal couple, the Linlithgows, were happy to return home, even though it was to a Britain worn down by the war, for they had been heavily battered by political struggles over Indian independence and the problems of an India also beset by military pressures, and in the end, a great famine in Bengal. As they prepared to leave in 1943, Linlithgow's successor, Field Marshal Lord Wavell, was already on hand as Commander-in-Chief India. In 1947, however, the Attlee government gave the latter only a month's notice that he was being replaced by Mountbatten, whose supreme self-confidence buffered him against the shocks of presiding over the steepest plunge in Britain's imperial fortunes since the loss of the American colonies. The Mountbattens' easy manner and glamour attracted worldwide media attention while their obvious concern for the future of an independent India earned the couple tremendous public affection, and cheering crowds lined their path as they drove to the airport for their final flight home.

The timing and manner of other vicereines' leaving India, and the welcomes they received at home usually hinged on politics, with two salient exceptions, Mary Louisa Elgin and Julia Mayo, both of whom lost their husbands in India and returned home to receive fulsome praise for their bravery in the face of tragedy. Although several of their successors did not enjoy so effusive a welcome, once they left India, criticism of the vicereines was generally muted and confined to the gossip circles of British India. Their role and service was recognised,, but almost always in relationship to their husband's reign. Viceroys on the other hand, generally received glowing public tributes for their Indian service, honours from the monarch including upgrades in the peerage, or new official posts. Such praise and advancement was viewed in official circles as more or less *pro forma*, especially since the accolades *sometimes* directly contrasted with views expressed privately among British elites. On the other hand, those leaving India under something of a cloud naturally affected how their wives felt about the viceregal experience, and especially the ending of it, perhaps most notably Lytton, pilloried in the press and denounced by politicians at home as a war-monger in Afghanistan and a spendthrift, indolent, and morally lax proconsul. Similarly, although Ripon was praised by Indian leaders for his liberal policies, he was widely condemned in Britain as a "traitor...who surrendered white interests for...a maudlin and misplaced sentimentalism."[5] Arguably the saddest of all was Lord Curzon, who, seething at losing his battle with Kitchener, and openly disdainful of his successor, returned to Victoria Station with his wife and family to find not a single government official was present to welcome him home. A further insult was the government's denial of the customary earldom given to viceroys which only increased Curzon's fury. The final grand slight rendered a viceroy, Wavell's summary removal in 1947, while not entirely unexpected, was due to post-war military and political machinations. While his hasty ouster was softened slightly by an earldom, that honour was overshadowed by his being succeeded by the most glamorous senior British commander of World War II.

However dark or sunny the circumstances of a viceroy's departure, his wife had to accept them, and move on to the next chapter of their lives. As with so much of the business of the *Raj*, their leaving involved an elaborate series of carefully proscribed rituals and ceremonies, including farewell dinners, public and private receptions, lengthy speeches, honours given and received, and finally, embarkation for home when the principals were emotionally and physically exhausted. Sometimes, the vicereines were more sensitive than their husbands to how great the change would be. When the Dufferins hosted a dinner party at Viceregal Lodge prior to their departure in 1888, Lady Dufferin, intent on impressing upon her husband that "...never more will he sit upon a throne and perform regal ceremonies" proclaimed the event to be "our last great function anywhere." Dufferin, eager to be away, did not mind.[6]

The departure of the Dufferins in 1888 exemplified the complicated ritual that surrounded all viceregal couples right up until the end. The Dufferins' sequence of exit events began in Simla in September, with a reception given by the local Freemasons at the Town Hall, where, along with their daughters, the Dufferins were met at the door by men wearing Masonic aprons, sashes, white cloaks, black cloaks, red tunics, stars, crosses, medallions, orders, and emblems of all kinds. The evening's events included the presentation of a Masonic jewel to the vicereine, and dancing until midnight, after which the viceregal family departed in a stately procession with the Masons singing and sending them off with three cheers.[7] Lady Dufferin had earlier received a unique personal honour before leaving Simla, when the Persian Consul-General came from Bombay to present her with the Order of the Sun. The viceroy and his entire staff were in attendance, in full dress uniform as the Consul-General presented the vicereine with a letter from the Shah announcing that the Order of the Sun of the Sublime Empire was designed specially for ladies of high rank, and that the Shah had conferred it upon Her Excellency so that "she might adorn her virtuous breast therewith and remain under the protection of the Gracious God." The Consul-General also made a short speech in Persian to which Mortimer Durand, the Foreign Secretary of India[8], replied, also in Persian. The following day, the viceroy returned the courtesy, presenting the Consul-General with a handsome gold medal and making a very long speech in Persian thanking the Shah once again for the honour bestowed upon his wife.[9]

Posing for group photographs was always a dominant activity in viceregal life, and especially so when the viceroy and vicereine prepared to take their leave. Leaving each viceregal residence for the last time required a series of pictures: the viceregal couple with staff alone; with ladies alone; with servants; and finally encircled by the brilliantly uniformed lancers of the viceroy's bodyguard. Each picture was carefully staged, the viceroy and vicereine seated in the middle on chairs atop a luxurious carpet, with the other participants either seated alongside the couple or standing behind them, arranged in order of rank and importance

Other essential ceremonies prior to leaving were chapter meetings of the Star of India and the Order of the Indian Empire, with the viceroy investing new members and bidding a formal farewell as Grand Master of both orders. The Dufferin's last such investiture in Simla began with a dinner party, to which several "native gentlemen" were invited – unusual because most Indians were reluctant to dine with Westerners, due to dietary restrictions of their religion or caste. As several hundred more guests entered to watch the investiture along with those assembled for dinner, the assemblage filled the ballroom on both sides, the men in full military, official or evening dress, and women wearing their most elegant ball gowns, and festooned with jewelry. The investitures for both orders were similar, but required the viceroy to change from the robes of one Grand Master to another between the two ceremonies. Once both were concluded, the procession left the room to remove their robes, while guests dispersed into the drawing room and elsewhere for refreshments.[10] It may now appear to have been all a bit too much, but few attending at the time thought so.

In any event, the Dufferins' exit from India was thought to be particularly intricate. Their departing Simla for the annual fall viceregal tour of the major princely states was followed by departure ceremonies in Calcutta, a brief stop in London to see family and friends, and eventually, something in the way of a retracing of steps, to the British Embassy in Rome. Lady Dufferin, who had become quite skilled at organising moves over the years, spent most of each morning prior to her departure from Simla overseeing the details of the impending move, including organization of her wardrobe. She also sorted out mementos, some of which went to the family home, others to their temporary London residence, and some to various charities. With her bent for organization, Hariot placed items destined for those locations in each corner of her room which she designated as Clandeboye, London, Rome and Calcutta. As the corners filled up, she moved the "heaps" to corresponding corners of the large ballroom, from whence they could be packed and sent. After several days of concentrated effort, she finished a job which most women of her class might have done once or twice in their lives, but which she had done many times – four times a year in India alone – and with Dufferin continuing his diplomatic career, she saw no end in sight to the cycle. "Photographs alone become a cargo in a very short time," she lamented.[11]

On a bright clear day in November, after saying goodbye to friends and staff whom they would not see again when they reached Calcutta, the Dufferins left Simla for their last fall tour. Although the spectacle was splendid enough, with mounted troops and military bands in full dress escorting their carriages to the edge of town, the drive to the railway station at Umballa was gruelling and uncomfortable. Not only were they bounced and shaken for 11 hours, but there were disruptions as well: three men unsuccessfully tried to stop the viceroy's carriage by lying across the road in order to give him a petition; a policeman fell off his horse, and a carriage in the procession – not the viceroy's – was upset. To cap it off, the Dufferin girls' horses collapsed from exhaustion, and the search for replacements added to the delay. At last they reached Umballa and gratefully settled down in their railway carriages for the night, ready to begin the final tour in the morning.

Over the following month, the Dufferins moved back and forth across India on the viceregal train, paying farewell visits to government officials and princes in Lahore, Patiala, Agra, and Dacca. Fêted and honoured at each stop, they attended *durbars*, dinners, and receptions. Lady Dufferin remained actively involved in Dufferin Fund work throughout that grand processional, opening or visiting Dufferin Hospitals along the route and receiving tributes and awards from various groups for her efforts. Their final trip through India continued to offer fascinating sights and events, as when in Patiala they attended the wedding of the *rajah*, now one of the senior potentates, who had been a young boy when they arrived in India.

The Dufferins were met at the station by an elegant gold and silver carriage, and passed through crowds of natives, elephant carriages, troops, silver sedan chairs, and finally through an arch to an elaborate camp prepared especially for the occasion. The viceroy and his family had their own camp, each member of the family with a separate tent, while another camp nearby had been arranged for the other government officials and European visitors. Like all such temporary dwellings, the viceregal camp was meticulously organised and beautifully landscaped with a coloured gravel garden in the centre which included pots of flowering and fragrant plants and fountains to provide the cooling sound of running water during the heat of the day. Each tent had been extravagantly furnished by the maharajah, including warm blankets and even furs for the chilly mornings and evenings. The wedding celebrations included a *durbar*, during which the maharajah sat on a magnificent green and gold throne while other gilt furniture, some even wrapped in gold chains, was provided for all participants. Dressed in a satin costume of white and gold, topped by a pale green turban enhanced by a superb fringe of diamonds all around and a large feathered plume in front, the maharajah opened the *durbar* by announcing that in honour of his wedding he was going to build a hospital for women and provide Rs 10,000 annually to operate it – a gesture designed to please the vicereine. In his reply, Dufferin thanked the maharajah for his generosity, and also expressed his gratitude that the princes had agreed to contribute troops to a Frontier Defence Force. The day ended with a state dinner for some 200 people, held in the *durbar* hall which was now illuminated by some 4,000 candles.[13]

The farewell tour continued with a stop in Agra, where once again Lady Dufferin was entertained by the ruling prince and laid a foundation stone for a new lying-in hospital which has been paid for by the Dufferin Fund. "A *shamiana*, and a dais, a hanging stone, a hammer, a trowel, and a speech, all as usual," she noted in her diary.[13]

Late in November, the Dufferins received a solid reminder of the imminent transition when they left the viceroy's train so that it could go to Bombay to meet the Lansdownes. This reduction in viceregal pomp was quickly forgotten in the wake of the tremendous reception they received on arriving in Calcutta. The station had been elaborately decorated, and two large mounted guards of honour waited to accompany them on the drive to Government House through streets thronged with cheering natives. But the warm welcome failed to relieve Lady Dufferin's sadness as she gazed at the nearly empty rooms which they now occupied in the viceregal residence

– the viceroy's private quarters having been prepared and set aside for the new occupants. A bit of the Dufferins' gloom at leaving India's "heavenly sunshine" for the winter fogs of London was lifted when their sons Fred and Archie arrived to accompany their parents on the voyage home.

The pace of events intensified as their departure date neared, peaking the day before the Lansdownes arrived as the Dufferins received farewell deputations from Indians, in groups and individually, hosted a garden party for several hundred, and ended the day with a Dufferin Fund Central Committee meeting, Lady Dufferin's last official act as vicereine. On December 13, she wrote "D has laid down his great burden and we are now Viceroy and Vicereine by courtesy only."[14]

When the Lansdownes had arrived at Government House with flags flying, bands playing, and guards of honour stationed on the lawn, the Dufferins had awaited their successors atop the red-carpeted marble steps, watching as the viceroy's bodyguard and other mounted escorts preceded the Lansdownes' carriage, which stopped precisely at the midpoint of the grand marble staircase. After they were escorted up the steps and greeted warmly by the Dufferins, the two men went into the throne room for another brief ceremony, while Hariot served Maud tea in the drawing room. That evening Dufferin gave a men-only dinner for Lansdowne in the huge ballroom, while the two vicereines and the wives of senior members of the government dined separately. Lady Dufferin had planned the evening's events with great care to make sure that the Lansdownes' entry into their new home was memorable and pleasant – in stark contrast to the rather dreary welcome she and Dufferin had received from the Ripons. With her customary attention to detail, she made sure that Lady Lansdowne had a proper introduction to upper tier British-Indian women, providing the incoming vicereine with detailed information about each guest, and making personal introductions to ease her elevation to her new role.

The details of viceregal hospitality aside, the Lansdownes' arrival in Calcutta highlighted the Dufferins' reduced status. On Sunday, as the Lansdownes went with full viceregal panoply to services at the cathedral, the Dufferins rode "humbly in a two-horse shay" to the smaller parish church. But whatever her feelings about her decline in status, Hariot was cordial and friendly to her successor, taking her to visit Calcutta's zoological gardens on Sunday evening while the new viceroy and his predecessor discussed matters of state. The Dufferins' last melancholy gathering with their staff the night before their departure began with Lansdowne's official swearing-in in the Council Chamber, and appropriate speeches and obeisances from senior officials and polite bows all around. Then, Hariot wrote: "…we put on our bonnets and went downstairs to have an 'Historic group' photograph," marking the beginning of a new viceregal "reign."

That official ceremony was followed by the most difficult time, the personal farewells to friends and colleagues, which brought Hariot and the others nearly to tears, after which the Dufferins descended the great marble steps of Government House for the last time, "...shaking hands all the way, and followed by hearty cheers from those we left behind." Now Lord and Lady Lansdowne accompanied the Dufferins to the station, in a reversal of the of the Lansdownes' arrival procession, with the same glitter and military pomp on display as they drove through crowds of onlookers and beneath arches which had displayed "Welcomes" to be seen by the arriving Lansdownes, and now featured such legends as "Sorry to Part" and "Safe Home" on the other side for to the Dufferins to view.

As with any public spectacle, and especially one in an authoritarian regime, many saw the outpouring as something less than genuine. A rumour circulated that the public displays of affection were stage-managed behind the scenes by the viceroy himself in a desperate attempt to appear more beloved of Indians than his liberal predecessor, Lord Ripon. Others surmised that he was jealous of the very genuine praise and accolades being offered to his wife, seen by many in India and at home as much more popular than her husband. Purportedly, the Calcutta tribute was arranged by the conservative Indian Association, along with some supporters of the departing viceroy in the Muslim community, and "encouraged" by His Excellency, who contacted two Congress Party leaders, W.C. Bonnerjee and Manmohun Ghose, to assure that the farewell surpassed his predecessor's.[15]

Hariot noted in her diary that she and Lord Dufferin were "still wearing the disguise of Viceregal personages" as they left Calcutta, so they enjoyed the comforts of a special train and the guards of honour accompanying them. During the two-and-a-half day trip west they were greeted by old friends at various stations along the route, and welcomed at the Bombay Station by the Queen's son, the Duke of Connaught, and a large party of government officials. Once again, flags and banners filled the railway terminal's main ticket area in a vast, heavily and garishly decorated hall, where, amid marble pillars, carved capitals, and galleries, Dufferin was honoured by officials of the city of Bombay. Afterwards, the viceregal couple was entertained at a large dinner party at the Lieutenant Governor's residence at Malabar Point, and then by a play in town, both events staged as benefits for the Dufferin Fund, which pleased Lady Dufferin greatly. Further farewell festivities included a presentation to Lady Dufferin by a group of *purdah* women of a sandalwood box and two bags containing signatures of Indian women of many races and religions in appreciation for her non-sectarian efforts to improve women's health. When Lord Dufferin asked to address the ladies, his wife noted that it "caused a great flutter in the dovecote," but in the end, the ladies decided that inasmuch as the former viceroy was leaving the country the next day, no real harm could come of the meeting, and agreed. The final days in Bombay were a flurry marked by Dufferin Fund meetings and hospital visits for Lady Dufferin, the laying of a school foundation stone, an afternoon harbour cruise, and finally another male-only banquet honouring Lord Dufferin at the Byculla Club.

After the Dufferins passed through the streets of Bombay on December 14, they participated in the formal farewell ceremony under a magnificently decorated pavilion erected on the Apollo Bunder, from which launches shuttled travelers to and from ships in the harbour. Lady Dufferin watched this last viceregal ceremonial with mixed feelings, realising that these were the final public salutes, guards of honour, and escorts, and that a quieter and somewhat less public life would now begin. However, that anticipated decline in pomp was relative, since their subsequent tour of duty at the British embassy in Rome, one of the premier diplomatic appointments in the Empire, also involved elaborate protocol and ceremony, even if well short of viceroyalty. Whatever the new assignment meant to Lady Dufferin, it fell well short of the splendors she witnessed and perquisites she enjoyed as vicereine, and allowed no chance for her to replicate the self-fulfilling efforts that arguably put a greater lasting stamp on India than those of her husband.

Although Lady Dufferin's departure rituals were more elaborate than most vicereines', especially in respect to the volume of personal tributes, the Dufferins' leave-taking experiences represented the overall level of ceremony and social and official functions surrounding viceregal transfers of power during the high *Raj* of the late 19th and early 20th century. Later vicereines were sent off with much the same level of extravagance and formality, with each event following detailed printed regulations and schedules carefully framed to assure that departing and arriving viceroys received as balanced a share of recognition as possible.

Ironically, the carefully prepared procedures were most blatantly ignored by George Curzon, the viceroy otherwise most obsessed with protocol and ceremony. When he prepared to leave, Curzon, with an eye on his political future in Britain, and always eager to mix with royalty, managed to stay in the country long enough for him and his wife to welcome the Prince and Princess of Wales in Bombay as the latter started their Indian tour. After that, the Curzons were to remain in the city to greet the incoming viceroy and his wife, Lord and Lady Minto, who were to host the royals during their processional across India. In a fit of pique because of the circumstances of his resignation and the fact that he had been refused the honour of staying long enough to accompany the Prince and Princess on their tour, Curzon welcomed the royal couple with all due grace and ceremony, then bombarded the Mintos with insults and slights both in public and privately. The barrages began even before Minto arrived when George, notified of his successor, asked rhetorically: "Isn't that the gentleman who jumps hedges?" – a reference to Minto having spent six years in his youth racing horses under his Cambridge name, "Mr. Rolly."[16] As the new viceroy was about to land, Curzon cancelled the official dockside reception at the Apollo Bunder, and remained out of sight as the Mintos reached Government House, leaving a very embarrassed Lady Curzon to offer as cordial a welcome as possible in that awkward situation. When Curzon finally appeared in a shooting jacket and house slippers, sauntering into the drawing room as his wife was serving tea, it would have been seen as a studied affront under any circumstances, but especially from someone widely known to be so particular about appropriate costume and demeanor. Both Mintos were furious, and Lord Minto adjudged: "The observance of these customs and courtesies…[was] entirely and inexcusably absent."[17]

Lady Minto's indignation at Curzon's rudeness was overshadowed by duties related to attending the royal visitors. This was, after all, the first royal tour of India since Edward VII's trip some 30 years before, and the first visit of a royal princess. Having quite literally grown up in Windsor Castle and regularly taken tea with the Queen and her children, Lady Minto was not intimidated in the least at the prospect of escorting the Prince and Princess around India. The royal visit enabled the new vicereine to earn high marks from British-Indian society by quickly adapting to her new role and easily managing the required royal protocol, even joining the Princess atop elephants as they toured the princely states.

In the end, Mary Minto's reign as vicereine mirrored Hariot Dufferin's in many ways: both developed a deep interest and love of the region and were eager to experience the "real India," seeking adventure and accepting inconvenience and even real danger with good humour and *sang froid*. The parallels extended to their departures, as both women were genuinely sad at the prospect of leaving India. Many British-Indians felt that the Mintos surpassed even the Dufferins in popularity, and that they were losing real friends as their reign came to an end. Tears and linen hankies were widely visible in the crowd when Lord and Lady Minto and their daughter Eileen descended the marble staircase at Government House in Calcutta for the last time. The vicereine kept her composure initially, but finally teared up when they reached the station. "I tried to feel as stoney as possible," she wrote, "but tearful eyes, the pressure of the hand, and a 'God bless you' are enough to upset one."[18] The crowd at Government House included many Indians close to the Mintos, the Maharajahs of Gwalior, Kashmir,

Bikaner, Benares, and Jodhpur among many others. Caught in the press of leave-takers, it took the Mintos nearly 20 minutes to make their way down the steps, literally fighting their way through the throng. At the bottom of the steps, Lady Minto curtseyed to the Hardinges, stepped into the carriage and departed with very mixed feelings – wrenching sorrow eased only by the prospect of returning home. Their passage through the gates for the last time as the band played "Auld Lang Syne," and to the station along boulevards gaily decorated with bunting and flags and thronged with cheering crowds led Mary to write later that: "A wonderful chapter in our lives is ended." After the final viceregal train trip and more farewells in Bombay, they embarked for home on the Royal Indian Marine steamer *Dufferin*. Mary wrote wistfully of the beauty of the evening as they sailed out of the harbour: "Nature seemed to understand our mood and I could not have wished to bid a more perfect farewell to the shores of India. The East has cast her magic spell around us, and nothing can ever fascinate me quite in the same way again."[19] But like all the other vicereines except Edwina Mountbatten, she never returned.

Lady Minto's successors did not enjoy the same celebratory exit from the viceregal throne. As noted previously, fate denied Winifred Hardinge the experience of a formal viceregal departure at all. Exhausted by three years in India and traumatised by the assassination attempt on her husband in 1912, Lady Hardinge went to England in the spring of 1914 for a rest, where she died unexpectedly in July after a short illness. Hardinge was devastated; the loss of his partner of 24 years was a heavy blow, eased only slightly by the presence and sympathy of their 14-year old daughter, Diamond, who had remained with her father in India. Both Hardinge sons were with Winifred when she died, but with no provision for viceregal home leave, her husband was unable to attend her funeral, which only deepened his grief.

Although Hardinge was eager to pass the proverbial baton to the Chelmsfords in 1916, and well-disposed to ease the transition, Lady Hardinge's death deprived the new vicereine of the advantages of both the formal and informal introduction to her duties usually provided by her predecessor. Whether or not due to that lack of orientation, Lady Chelmsford proved an unpopular vicereine, and was seen by many British-Indians as rather dull. The death of their eldest son Frederick in 1917 while serving in Mesopotamia overshadowed the last years of the Chelmsfords' viceroyalty, and by 1921, they were both eager to leave, partly due to almost continuous unrest throughout India and Central Asia, and partly due to a general perception that Chelmsford had lost the confidence of the home government. Beyond a great deal of negative press for both the viceroy and vicereine, Chelmsford was elevated only to viscount, not the customary

post-viceregal earldom, nor did he receive the coveted Order of the Garter. While those slights left Lady Chelmsford embittered, she was never able to leave the prestige of being a vicereine behind. During her long widowhood in Italy, she insisted upon being known as "La Contessa d'India."[20]

Alice Reading spent her last year in India slowly recovering from an operation for cancer which kept her from taking part in many ceremonial functions, but did not diminish her desire to stay longer in India. While Reading expressed his regret at leaving India "with all its weighty problems" in a letter to the King, he admitted that he was looking forward to going home again for Alice's sake, "...although I think she will regret leaving even more than I."[21] Alice's expression of that sentiment to Dorothy Irwin on her arrival was reinforced by the way she husbanded her energy in hopes of enjoying the final months of her stint as vice-queen, including generating some highly positive coverage in the press – which some said was organised by her husband and not reflective of how she was viewed by British-Indian society.

As noted earlier, Dorothy Irwin, once the most reluctant of vicereines, expected to be "skipping down the steps" when it came time for her to leave India. But as with so many others, she and her husband both felt some sadness at leaving "this tremendous office" and "vivid Indian scene."[22] Her sense of regret was fuelled to a great extent by her deep

The Irwins at Simla with the Maharaja of Patiala. Having dreaded her time in India, Dorothy Irwin was sad to leave the sub-continent.

involvement in the details of the construction and decoration of Viceroy's House in New Delhi, and the thought of not living in the mansion exacerbated her unhappiness at leaving. There were some notable variations in the Irwin's leave-taking ceremonies when, after welcoming the Willingdons in Bombay, the couple departed aboard the liner *Viceroy of India*. As warships in the harbour boomed out a 31-gun salute and a military band played "God Save the King" in the customary manner, a flight of airplanes appeared to waggle their wings in farewell. And another and more significant symbol of India's transition was the presence of Mahatma Gandhi at both the Irwins' departure and the Willingdons' arrival rituals, frail and scantily clad in contrast to the Indian potentates, but far more imposing for all that.

No one was more glum when she left India than Marie Willingdon. Not only did she adore the trappings and powers of vicereinealty, but the Willingdons' many years of Indian service brought them much closer to the region than most viceregal couples, and unlike the others, they planned to return annually once their "reign" ended. Their road to the pinnacle had not been smooth or even. In 1921, Willingdon was so widely viewed as Chelmsford's successor that he received well over a thousand letters of congratulation. When it was announced that Lord Reading was to be the new viceroy, both Willingdons were deeply disappointed, and publicly embarrassed, Marie visibly far more than her husband. Sir Harcourt Butler, another disappointed candidate, used the plural deliberately when he wrote: "I think the Ws feel very much that they were not viceroy. I doubt if they would have done although they are good workers and figureheads. She is too imperious."[23] Delay and disappointment sharpened the edge of her ambition to the point where she became the subject of amusement in Britain and India when she finally ascended unto the heights. After setting the highest standard among vicereines for raw energy and involvement in details, she found the prospect of descent as gloomy as ascent had been giddy. Toward the end, Marie found the prospect of turning viceregal power over to the Linlithgows almost unbearable. "He longs to get home," wrote Butler. "She dreads it."[24] The sense of loss transcended the end of power and pomp. The Willingdons had made more real friends than earlier viceroys among Indian rulers and the rising intelligentsia, all of whom would now be left behind. While Willingdon, who became a marquess as a reward for his long years of service, enjoyed retirement for only a half-decade, Lady Willingdon lived on until 1960, expending her considerable energies in support of various of charities.

Lady Willingdon's blunt description as she left India of her husband's successor, Lord Linlithgow, as "too pompous" was all the more ironic given her having presided over perhaps the most tightly controlled and formalistic of viceregal courts. Although World War II did not significantly diminish the ceremonial duties of the vicereine, Lady Linlithgow deftly struck a more even balance between casual, comfortable family life and the obligatory pomp which served to reasonably satisfy most British-Indians as the social fabric of the *Raj* rapidly unraveled over the next few years. By the time the Linlithgows left, they had come as close to becoming an institution as any viceregal couple, in part due to the onset of hostilities that extended Linlithgow's tenure, but also because Lady Linlithgow found much about India fascinating. But both were more than ready to go home when the time came. Wartime exigencies made their departure, like the Wavells in the wake of the conflict, a pale facsimile of the ornate leave-takings of their predecessors, in good part because they were by airplane. Both Doreen and "Hopie" received mixed reviews for their service in India during the longest viceregal stint, and arguably the most difficult conditions under which any viceroy served, including the greatest civil unrest, wartime disruption, and prospect of invasion in the history of the *Raj*, as well as one of the most severe famines.

The Wavells' difficult viceregal service during the war was followed by two equally trying years of riots, mutinies, and the complex political battles associated with creating two large independent nations, and attempting to transfer power to them in as orderly a manner as possible. As Wavell struggled to form an interim government, he found himself in the jaws of a vice between Muslims and Hindus in India, as well political factions in Britain. However, when he had been appointed in 1943, Wavell had understood from Churchill, whom he knew disliked him personally, that he might not serve the customary five years, and would very likely leave when the war ended. While the announcement of his departure should not have been too great a shock, especially since Wavell had asked when it was likely that he should come home, Labour Prime Minister Clement Attlee's offering the viceroyalty to Lord Louis Mountbatten in December 1946 while Wavell was in London was an unkind cut. However studied that injury, the Prime Minister added a gratuitous insult by leaving Wavell in the dark. Rather than letting the viceroy know that his move was part of a proposed "Breakdown Plan" for the new government, Attlee sent Wavell on his way with a terse letter of dismissal that sketchily acknowledged the latter's service. As a result, Mountbatten felt that even though Wavell was scheduled to receive an earldom, he had been badly treated by the government, and characteristically, Mountbatten let Attlee know his feelings. The new viceroy also added some personal support to the campaign for Wavell's receiving the earldom, and when they reached India, both he and Lady Mountbatten publicly displayed their regard and respect for the Wavells, who had been given barely a month to prepare for departure. After the Mountbattens' state entry into Delhi riding in an open landau, not atop an elephant like earlier viceregal couples, they arrived at Viceroy's House on March 22, 1947 and were escorted up the red-carpeted marble steps where the Wavells awaited. Mountbatten bowed, and Edwina curtsied, as protocol required, but also as a demonstration of their personal respect for the man who would still be viceroy until he left Delhi the next day, and who had given much hard service in the face of high odds and many misfortunes during World War II.

Despite her original misgivings, when her time to leave came, Edwina was devastated, perhaps as much by separation from Nehru as from India. She even welcomed the staggering heat of Delhi in June. "The heat increases...the hot wind has commenced and scorching dust storms are upon us. But I love Delhi even like this and India and the Indians and my heart aches at the thought of leaving them so soon."[25] By the time the Mountbattens left India, now as Governor General and wife, not viceroy and vicereine, they had become beloved icons to masses of Indians, akin to national heroes. The image of the last viceroy and vicereine and their daughters sitting on the ground beside Gandhi's funeral pyre came to symbolize an eleventh hour change in British official attitudes toward India and its people.

In her last days as vicereine, Lady Mountbatten kept up a punishing schedule – hosting official dinners and receptions, opening exhibitions, and receiving and entertaining newly appointed foreign ambassadors – in addition to wrapping up her own work and personal correspondence. Two days before the transfer of power, the Mountbattens flew to Karachi to bring official greetings from the King to a new member of the Common-wealth. They were greeted with the news that security services reported a possible assassination attempt on Pakistan's new Governor General Mohammed Jinnah, during the next day's State procession. Undeterred, the Mountbattens insisted that the events go ahead as scheduled, and that evening were guests at a state dinner and a reception for some 1,500 of Pakistan's leading citizens. The next morning, the Mountbattens drove to the Assembly in an open Rolls-Royce lent by a maharajah, and made the trip back with no incident. "Thank God I have brought you back alive," Jinnah said to Mountbatten as they drove through the gates.[26]

The actual transfer of power took place at midnight on August 14, 1947, the date of August 15 having been declared inauspicious by Indian astrologers. The following day, the Mountbattens took part in yet another swearing-in ceremony in the Durbar Hall of a soon-to-be-renamed Viceroy's House, this time as Governor-General of a newly independent nation. For the last time, a British woman donned a formal gown and all her jewels and decorations and sat upon the golden throne of the vicereine.

Like her many predecessors through the years who had faced fear of assassination, Lady Mountbatten remained composed as the loud "pop" of a flashbulb shattered the ceremonial quiet. Some in the audience feared that it was a bomb, but the last vicereine remained calmly in place, showing no concern for her personal safety. After the ceremony, when the couple entered a horse-drawn carriage for the drive to the Council Chamber, the crowds along the route were enormous, and had to be physically moved back by the guard of honour so that the Mountbattens could leave their coach. The day ended with a state banquet, speeches and a reception for 3,000 guests in the State rooms of the building now known as Government House. For the last time, a British viceroy and his wife entertained people who had been their subjects in the sprawling mansion, and illuminated gardens.

Months later, the schedule for the departing Governor General and his wife was no less complicated than that for the viceroys. Mountbatten determined that he and his wife should visit India's states and provinces to say good-bye, and Edwina squeezed in visits to hospitals, dispensaries, sanitoria, and other medical and welfare organizations at each stop. The travelling itself was hard on her; driving along twisty roads made her carsick and her neuralgia was made worse by flights in unpressurised aircraft. In one week, she flew to Baroda with Mountbatten to say good-bye to the maharajah; visited a camp in Kurukshetra in 115 degree heat where crowds of refugees surged toward her to bid her farewell; held a meeting on the rescue and repatriation of abducted women; received an address from a municipal council; and held a farewell reception for the personal staff. Despite her attempts to steal some time for rest, Edwina was slowly being worn down by the non-stop pressures of her welfare work and the endless public appearances and social events honouring the Mountbattens for their service. Insomniac, she took medicine for sleeplessness and for relief for her blinding headaches, made even worse by the heat. In May, Nehru, now Prime Minister, accepted the Mountbatten's invitation to join them at Simla and Mashobra. Edwina luxuriated in the time she and Nehru had together, talking quietly for hours, cementing the unique bond between them that existed until her death.

Lady Mountbatten counted down the days until her departure with sadness, while her husband filled his days drafting endless memoranda advising his successors on a host of issues: relations within the Commonwealth, the future of the princely states – even the need for cabinet ministers to take regular vacations and the importance of installing air conditioning in the offices of senior public officials. The response in India to the last viceroy's political and administrative decisions and recommendations, however, were not universally popular in India or at home. But by

Lord Louis and Edwina Mountbatten depart the Viceroy's House in New Delhi for the last time in 1948.

displaying openness to social change and working on behalf of the suffering amid the great upheaval of partition, the Mountbattens earned affection and respect throughout the subcontinent, much of it visible in emotional public and private departure ceremonies, and tributes offered even while massive communal rioting and slaughter swept the region. At a banquet prior to their departure in 1948, Jawaharlal Nehru summed up the feelings of millions of Indians and Pakistanis for Edwina. "Wherever you have gone you have brought solace, hope and encouragement. Is it surprising therefore that the people of India should love you?"[27] Edwina could not hold back her tears at his speech, nor at her husband's and it was clear to all attending that her sorrow at leaving India was genuine and heartfelt. She did better at concealing her emotions during the reception for 7,000 people which followed the banquet, in the final display of vicereinal hauteur.

Edwina's private parting from Nehru was more emotional. During an early morning visit on the day they departed, Edwina had given Nehru one of her most treasured possessions, a small 18th century French box of gold and enamel, as well as a valuable emerald ring, and a silver St. Christopher medal, however odd such a gift might seem to be to a non-Christian. Nehru also received more traditional gifts from the Mountbattens – their photographs and a silver box, on which, Nehru later told Edwina, his name had been misspelled. He had given her an ancient Indian coin on a bracelet, a box of mangoes, and a copy of his autobiography – meant to be read on the airplane trip home.

Unique among the final pre-departure ceremonies was a tribute from the Delhi municipality, as, for the first time since the attempt on Hardinge's life in 1912, a viceroy – albeit now only Governor General – and his wife drove along the Chandni Chowk, the old highway in Delhi, to receive the address. Progressing through huge crowds to the open space by the Jumna River where Gandhi's pyre had been built, the Mountbattens were surrounded by tens of thousands of wildly cheering Indians, with an equal number pressing to get into the site, matched by huge enthusiastic throngs lining the streets the next day as they drove to the airport, accompanied by the new Indian head of state, Chakravarthi Rajagopalachari, three guards of honour, and all of the cabinet and the diplomatic corps. While such large crowds along parade routes were not unusual in India, this outpouring of affection and gratitude was unlike any of those previously directed at departing rulers and their wives. It was not about curiosity, or deference to power, but a display of affection and respect for two people who had made a special and longstanding impression on India as a whole and the lives of the Indian people.

The irony of why that had come so late in the day was lost in the furor of criticism that greeted the Mountbattens when they returned home. Many critics assailed his flamboyance and his imperious administrative style, while others viewed him as a virtual traitor for handing the empire's "jewel in the crown" to people whom they judged unfit to govern themselves. Despite all that, Lady Mountbatten received many accolades for her humanitarian work during the last days of the *Raj*, in good part due to her wartime work in Britain and Southeast Asia. Unlike the first vicereine, Charlotte Canning, whose early death served as a warning to all European women brave enough to come to India, the last vicereine would be remembered for her work on behalf of the Indian people and for her assaults on social and racial barriers in the late twilight of the *Raj*.

Again, it may seem that for all their efforts and sacrifices, the vicereines were, like their husbands, little more than tinsel proconsuls whose works have over time proved to be, as Longfellow warned, "footprints on the sands of time." No postage stamps, coins, or currency bore their visage, nor have any commemorative stamps been issued in their honour in the British Commonwealth, India, or Pakistan. With over a half-century between past since that wan sunset, it has become fashionable to wax critical of the "Poona colonels" and the imperiousness of the *Raj*, tinged by the especially refined hauteur of British elites that can still set nerves on edge.

Fashion has, of course, had its way in the crafting of history as much as any other facet of human activity. But the saga of the vicereines, however thin and pathetic as it may seem through lenses ground in hindsight, stands as something more than a small monument to the spirit of women caught up in elaborate and very durable webs of power and culture. Even the most feeble and timid among them strove to do good works and put their stamp on the flow of history, and while some facets of their experiences seem trivial or bizarre, or merely interesting tidbits of *Zeitgeist*, there is a solid layer of sterner stuff running beneath the gilt and glitter which warrants somewhat more attention than it has received since the fading of the *Raj*, or than it is likely to receive even now in the after-swirls of the wake of imperialism, when tempers have not yet cooled.

Notes

Introduction

1. MacMillan, Margaret, *Women of the Raj*

Chapter 1

1. As Julia Bush, in *Edwardian Ladies and Imperial Power* (London" Leicester University Press. 2000) noted, from 1857 onward, "India required suitably noble viceroys to represent its Empress," p. 36.
2. Lord Northbrook, Viceroy from 1872–1876 was a widower.
3. Quoted in Bence-Jones, p. 1.
4. Morris, *Stones of Empire*, p. 76.The daughter of Edith and Robert Lytton, Emily became a Theosophist and a firm supporter of Indian independence.
5. Bence-Jones, *The Viceroys of India*, p. 229
6. For a contemporaneous view of that dilemma, see A. J. Herbertson and O. J. R. Howarth, eds., The Oxford Survey of the British Empire (Oxford: Clarendon Press, 1914), pp. 209–214.
7. MS Eur F118/95, 96: Corr w/Montague and Lloyd George
8. Morgan, *Edwina Mountbatten*, p. 376
9. Mountbatten was awarded an earldom after the transfer of power in 1947.
10. Morgan, p. 378.
11. Moseley, *Last Days of the British Raj*, p. 90
12. Despite a gift of £3000 from his father-in-law which prevented Curzon from having to request an advance on his viceregal salary, immediately after arriving in India, Lady Curzon had to ask her father for an additional $5,500 to pay Lord Elgin for the stables.
13. Mrs. Verney's duties began even before leaving London, when the new vicereine insisted that she accompany her and her daughters on shopping trips. The Chelmsford daughters also proved to be a trial on the trip out, outweighing the comfort Mrs. Verney took in travelling with a military escort.
14. Lady Canning became close friends with Sir Colin Campbell, Commander in Chief of the Indian Army who freely discussed military matters with her. He also showed her letters and telegrams which made her privy to the highest levels of the decision-making process.
15. The sisters' double wedding in 1869 was the social event of the London season. Albertha's marriage was annulled (at her petition) in 1883, while Maude remained happily married until her husband's death in 1927.
16. Hardinge, *Loyal to Three Kings*, p. 18.
17. Fowler, *Below the Peacock Fan*, p. 255.
18. Nicolson,, *Mary Curzon*, p. 109
19. Fitzroy, Sir Almeric, *Memoirs*, p. 335
20. Lyall, p. 60
21. The IOCI was given only to women and limited to British Princesses, wives or female relatives of Indian princes, and wives or female relatives of the viceroy, the Governor General of

Madras, Governor of Bengal, Secretary of State for India, or Commander in Chief in India. The insignia had to be returned to the Secretary of the Central Chancery of Orders of Knighthood upon the vicereine's death. No appointments were made to this order after August 14, 1947.

22. Reading paprs, OIOC, Mss Eur F 237/5
23. Antrim files, PRONI, MIC 615/A/1
24. Reading papers, MSS Eur 103/A
25. Quoted in Fowler, p. 105
26. Until 1924, there was no provision for home leave for the Viceroy. The vicereine could, and often did, return to England to rest, marry off daughters, or check on family estates.
27. Nicolson, *Mary Curzon,* p. 111
28. Butler, p. 27
29. Nicolson, *Mary Curzon,* p. 112.
30. Willingdon papers, OIOC, Mss Eur F 237/21
31. Birkenhead, p. 174.
32. Butler, p. 28.
33. Ibid p. 27
34. Ibid
35. The cost of such tight security was high; Lord Willingdon cited the expense of using 16,000 troops to guard the route between Calcutta and Delhi as a rationale for shifting to air travel.

Chapter 2

1. Howes, Peter, *Viceregal Establishments in India,* 1949, New Delhi, The Governor-General's Press
2. Owen, *Lord Cromer,* p. 63
3. Morris, Jan, *Stones of Empire,* p. 67
4. Ibid.
5. Morris, p. 68
6. Morris,
7. Owen, *Lord Cromer,* p. 63.
8. Bence-Jones, *Viceroys of India,* p. 172.
9. Ibid., p. 47
10. Quoted in Fowler, p. 113.
11. Lady Dalhousie had died of seasickness during a voyage home to recover her health.
12. Allen, *Burning Plain,* p. 50
13. Royal Archives, VIC/M59/12
14. Surtees, *Charlotte Canning,* p. 17
15. Dufferin, *Our Viceregal Life in India, p. 286*
16. *Reading papers, OIOC MSS Eur 103/A*
17. Surtees, p. 206
18. Morris and Winchester, p. 40
19. Quoted in Bence-Jones, *The Viceroys of India,* p. 160.
20. Catchcal.com, copyrighted 1999–2004
21. Morris and Winchester, p. 68.
22. Ibid.
23. Bence-Jones, *Viceroys of India,* p. 71.
24. Curzon papers: Mss Eur F 306/43
25. Sir Hugh Gough, accompanied by the Governor General, Lord Ellenborough defeated the local army of Gwalior in December 1843.
26. Quoted in Bence-Jones, *The Viceroys of India,* p. 168.
27. Royal Archives VIC/M59/12
28. Birkenhead, p. 179
29. Birkenhead, p. 180.
30. Nicolson, p. 123.
31. Ferguson, p. 183.
32. Blunt, *India Under Ripon,* p. 334.
33. Quoted in Bence-Jones, *The Viceroys of India,* p. 57.
34. Bence-Jones, *Palaces of the Raj,* p. 139
35. Royal Archives VIC/M59/12
36. Quoted in Bence-Jones, *The Viceroys of India,* p. 143.
37. Quoted by William Dalrymple, "Surrey in Tibet," in *Travel Intelligence*
38. Nicolson, *Mary Curzon,* p. 123.
39. Bence-Jones, *Palaces of the Raj,* p. 142.
40. Nicolson, p. 124.
41. Butler, p. 28
42. Glendevon, p. 69
43. Morgan, p. 421.

44. Ibid, p. 392.
45. Ibid, p. 422.
46. Bence-Jones, *Viceroys of India*, p. 215.
47. In an odd juxtaposition, Emily was devoted Theosophist, and a firm supporter of Indian independence, even as her husband designed the new imperial capital. It was, she said, the last place in the world where "little nobodies can come and play at being kings and queens."
48. Lutyens, *The Lyttons in India*, p. 106
49. Morris, *Stones of Empire*, p. 80.
50. Bence-Jones, *The Viceroys of India*, p. 253
51. Bence-Jones, *Palaces of the Raj,* p. 203.
52. Quoted in Bence-Jones' *Viceroys of India*, p. 272.
53. Lutyens, *Edwin Lutyens*, p. 323
54. Ibid.
55. Ibid, p. 434
56. Ibid, p. 443
57. Fowler, p. 384.

Chapter 3

1. Pottinger, p. 16
2. The assassin was a Pathan named Sher Ali, a former member of the Punjab mounted police, who had been convicted of murder.
3. Baring assumed the titles of 1st Viscount Baring of Lee and 2nd Baron Northbrook on the death of his father in September 1866. He was named 1st Earl of Northbrook in 1876 in recognition of his service as viceroy.
4. Father of the future viceroy, Lord Irwin, later the first Earl Halifax.
5. Quoted in Fowler, p. 229
6. Ibid, 230
7. Ibid
8. Lady Ripon was known in her family as "Hat," based on her initials, Henrietta Anne Theodosia.
9. Nicolson, *Helen's Tower*, p. 144
10. Nelly married Ronald Craufurd Munro-Ferguson, MP, later Viscount Novar, in 1889; Victoria married twice: first in 1894 to the 5th Baron Plunket of Newton and after his death married Col. Francis Powell Braithwaite; Hermione never married.
11. Evelyn's daughter Dorothy married Harold MacMillan a future Prime Minister, while their son Charles, married Adele Astaire, sister of the movie star Fred Astaire.
12. Just five years later, Beatrix would make an equally good match, marrying Henry de la Poer Beresford, 6th Marquess of Waterford
13. After Constance's death in 1909, Elgin would marry again and father yet one more son, born in 1917, five months after his father's death.
14. OIOC, Elgin papers, MSS Eur 230
15. Quoted in Fowler, p. 265
16. Ibid, p. 274
17. Curzon had recently been named Lord Warden of the Cinque Ports, and Walmer Castle was the Warden's residence
18. Ibid p. 297
19. OIOC, Dunlop-Smith papers, Mss Eur F166/26
20. General Sir George Barrow wrote to Curzon before he arrived that: Kitchener and the secretaries run the government, Lady Minto runs the patronage. HE runs the stables.
21. OIOC, Dunlop-Smith papers, Mss Eur F 166/26
22. Ibid, Mss Eur F 166/15
23. When he died, Alington left Edward a set of waistcoat buttons the King had admired, and £100 to Queen Alexandra.
24. Winifred's nickname, which family and close friends used all her life.
25. Cambridge University Library, Hardinge papers 127
26. Hardinge later served as King Edward VIII's private secretary until his abdication.
27. Metcalfe, later Sir Aubrey, continued his service in India and became Foreign Secretary in the Government of India in the 1930s.
28. Verney, p. 47
29. Ibid, p. 189
30. Butler, p. 41
31. Montgomery-Hyde, p. 41
32. Butler, p. 65
33. Birkenhead, p. 186
34. Ibid, p. 90
35. Irwin's reserve even extended to his closest personal relations. After his elevation to the

earldom, he always insisted that his daughter-in-law Ruth address him as "Lord Halifax." "I am certainly not going to become "Popsy" or any other silly nickname," he said, "and since I often have to talk to her for her own good, it would be highly inconvenient for her to call me Edward." (Birkenhead, p. 501)

36. The couple were intimates of George VI and Queen Elizabeth, and Dorothy tried in vain to get the King to intervene and prevent her husband's appointment as U.S. Ambassador, believing that his political career would be damaged if he left the country.
37. Birkenhead, p. 543
38. OIOC, Willingdon papers, Mss Eur F237
39. Trench, p. 23
40. Prime Minister Stanley Baldwin offered Linlithgow his choice of the viceroyalty or the cabinet post of SOSI, hoping that he would choose the latter, where Baldwin felt he would be more useful. When Linlithgow elected to go to India, Baldwin was forced to name the Marquess of Zetland as SOSI.
41. Her maternal grandfather, Sir Ernest Cassel was the 1st Baron Mount Temple, and a close confidant of King Edward VII. Edwina's father could claim Lord Melbourne, Victoria's prime minister and the 7th Earl of Shaftsbury as distant relations.
42. Edwina did have second thoughts about her actions when she learned that the King and Queen refused to send their daughters out of the country.
43. Quoted in Morgan, p. 112.
44. These were the" black sheep" Vanderbilts: Cornelius Vanderbilt III ("Neily") had been disinherited by his father when he married Grace Wilson and remained estranged from his parents for most of his life, reconciling with his mother some 27 years after his father's death..
45. He arranged for his elder daughter Patricia to inherit his earldom as the 2nd Countess Mountbatten of Burma.
46. Ibid, p. 378.

Chapter 4

1. Minto papers, Bodleian Library, Ms Eng Hist c. 466/2; a draft of *India, Minto and Morley*, with a note, "not used."
2. Lansdowne papers, OIOC, MSS Eur D 558/4 – corr w/ SoS Cross 1891
3. Mathilde Kschessinska, a beautiful seventeen-year-old ballet dancer.
4. Cowles, p. 32.
5. Ibid.
6. Rose, p. 63.
7. Ibid.
8. Quoted in Rose, p. 65.
9. Ibid.
10. Rose, p. 67
11. Butler, p. 75
12. Fitzroy diaries, OIOC, E312/11, A, B, and C.
13. Morgan, p. 111
14. Ibid. 110
15. Morgan, p. 111

Chapter 5

1. Quoted in Masters, *Great Hostesses*.
2. Hickman, p. 272.
3. MacMillan, p. 48.
4. Ibid.
5. Appointments to both orders ceased after Indian independence. Queen Elizabeth II is the only surviving member of both orders.
6. Lady Lansdowne was later made a Companion of Honour for her work with the Red Cross during WWI.
7. Morgan, p. 383.
8. Ibid, p. 388.
9. Buckle, p. 34
10. Denholm, p. 161
11. Quoted in Bence-Jones, p. 125
12. Whatever the vicereine's personal preference, the staff generally used the term "Her Ex" in informal conversation, sometimes respectfully, sometimes not.
13. Birkenhead, p. 176.
14. In 1916, Chelmsford's MilSec, Ralph Verney, was paid £1,200/year, plus a house for his family.
15. Charles was killed in 1914; Violet later married Lord Astor of Hever.
16. Prinsep's family had connections with the HEIC; he himself was educated at Hailybury and was destined for the ICS.

17. Quoted in Buck, p. 96
18. Buchan, p. 216
19. Butler, p. 30 (K stands for Knight)
20. Lutyens, p. 40.
21. MacMillan, p. 50.
22. The change made by the Linlithgows was relatively minor: the guests who were to be brought forward for conversation were identified before the event, and thus somewhat forewarned.
23. The viceroy's band was drawn primarily from British units serving in India. They (and their families) lived on the viceregal estates. The band had a full mess with a billiard room, bar, tennis courts and dining room. They played at state occasions, banquets, dinners, dances, concerts, etc., and moved with the viceroy to Simla. Disbanded in 1942.
24. *Illustrated London News*, September 18, 1869
25. Minto papers, OIOC
26. Sultan Kaikhusrau Jahan who ruled Bhopal from 1901–1926 was an advocate for women's emancipation. She was the first president of the All India Conference on Education and first Chancellor of the Muslim University of Aligarh.
27. Fitzroy diaries, OIOC, E 312 (9)
28. Eileen ultimately married her Simla acting partner, Lord Francis Scott, with whom she emigrated to Kenya after World War I.
29. Lutyens, p. 46
30. Fowler, p. 267
31. Woodyat, p. 52
32. Nicolson, *Helen's Tower*, p. 145
33. Bence-Jones, p. 141
34. Quoted in Bence-Jones, p. 145
35. Gopal, p. 177
36. Quoted in Nicolson, p. 116
37. Bradley, p. 57.
38. Quoted in Fowler, p. 268
39. Buchan, p. 236
40. Gilbert, p. 23
41. The explorer Sven Hedin noted the difference between the two Marys: "She [Lady Curzon] was of no blood. She was always playing la grande dame, not *being* it like Lady Minto." Quoted in Gilbert, p. 47.
42. Irving p. 20
43. Reed, p. 182.
44. Kincaid, p. 284.
45. Traces of this tradition have been maintained on India's Republic Day, when the President drives in the former viceregal carriage, under a similar silken-fringed umbrella along the Central Vista in Delhi.
46. Ibid., p. 277
47. Quoted in Fowler, p. 384.
48. Morgan, p. 388
49. Ibid
50. Morgan, p. 422
51. Volhasen, p. 292

Chapter 6

1. Morris, *Spectacle of Empire*, p. 11
2. Cannadine, *Ornamentalism*, p. 18
3. Ibid.
4. Cannadine, *Ornamentalism*, p. 44
5. (*Durbar* from the Persian *darbar*, a court or levee, referred to a council for administering affairs of state, as in *durbars* of native rulers, in some Indian units, or grand ceremonial gatherings.)
6. Fowler, p. 193
7. Metcalfe, *Ideologies of the Raj*, p. 77
8. Buckle, *Letters of Queen Victoria*, p. 463
9. Ibid.
10. Fowler, p. 194
11. Lutyens, *The Lyttons in India*, p. 74
12. Fowler, p. 201
13. Fowler, p. 207
14. Quoted in Nicolson, p. 103
15. Ibid, p. 105
16. Quoted in Fowler, p. 281
17. Menpes, Mortimer, *The Durbar*, p. 9

18. Quoted in Fowler, p. 294
19. Ibid, p. 286
20. Ibid, p. 287
21. Ibid, p. 287
22. The peacock dress, minus its emeralds, can now be seen at Kedleston Hall, the Curzon family seat.
23. Nicolson, p. 167
24. Fowler, p. 290
25. Nicolson, p. 167
26. Ibid, p. 168
27. Quoted in Fowler, p. 292
28. Ibid.
29. Rose, *King George V*, p. 132.
30. Ibid, p. 133.

Chapter 7

1. Rose, p. 134
2. Irving, *Lutyens, Baker and Delhi*, p. 12
1. Hutchins, *Illusion of Permanence*
2. Quoted in Lind, *The Compassionate Memsahibs*, p. 34.
3. Ibid, p. 35.
4. Arnold, David, "Western Medicine in an Indian Environment," in *The New Cambridge History of India: Science, Technology and Medicine in Colonial India*, p. 87.
5. This open discrimination also significantly aided the recruitment of lady doctors by the Dufferin Fund.
6. Arnold, p. 88.
7. Midwife training was begun in Madras in 1854, and was slowly extended throughout the country.
8. Arnold, p. 90.
9. Quoted in the Prospectus of the Dufferin Fund, published 1885.
10. Lawrence, Walter Roper, *The India We Served*, p. 110.
11. Letter from HD to QV, June 14, 1885
12. E.g. her article in the April 1886 issue of the *Asiatic Quarterly Review* describing the Fund's first year activities and plans for the coming year
13. Dufferin, Hariot, *Our Viceregal Life in India*, p. 163.
14. "The National Association for Supplying Female Medical Aid to the Women of India,' in the *Asiatic Quarterly Review*, April, 1886, p. 265.
15. Ibid, p. 266.
16. Royal Archives, VIC/N43/26
17. *Asiatic Quarterly Review*, p. 269.
18. Closer to £30,000, or about $3 million early 21st century dollars.
19. *Asiatic Quarterly Review*, p. 272.
20. Ibid, p. 274.
21. Dufferin and Ava, Hariot, "A Report of Three Years Work of the National Association for Supplying Female Medical Aid to the Women of India," p. 2
22. Dufferin and Ava, p. 6
23. Ibid, p. 7.
24. It is interesting to note that the UK General Committee included both men and women. No woman, other than the vicereine, was a member of the Fund's Central Committee in India until the appointment of Dr. Kathleen Vaughn in 1909.
25. Lal, Maneesha, "The Politics of Gender and Medicine in Colonial India: The Countess of Dufferin's Fund, 1885–1888," *Bulletin of the History of Medicine*, Spring 1994: pp. 29–66
26. Ibid, p. 65.
27. Two of the Queen's daughters helped organize female imperialist organizations, and the women who led them often had close ties to the monarchy. (Bush, p. 68.)
28. Dufferin and Ava, *Our Viceregal Life in India*, Vol. 2, p. 320
29. Ibid., p. 273.
30. Kipling's family had been 'taken up' by the Dufferins during their time in India and young Rudyard was enchanted by Hariot.
31. Royal Archives, VIC/N49/98
32. Royal Archives, VIC/N49/136
33. Elgin files, OIOC, Mss Eur F 84 33/a
34. Curzon Papers, OIOC, Mss Eur F 306/43
35. Dunlop Smith papers, Mss Eur F166/26
36. Despite entreaties from mutual friends, Curzon never forgave Lady Minto, refusing to speak to her when their paths crossed, and rudely ignoring an invitation to her daughter's wedding sent at the urging of Lord Cromer.

37. Minto, Mary, *India, Minto and Morley,* p. 107
38. Wilson, C.A., *"Never in Poona,"* unpublished memoirs of C. A. Wilson, OIOC, Mss Eur C251
39. Wilson, Emma, *Gone with the Raj,* p. 16
40. Lady Hardinge advocated strongly for the creation of the WMS.
41. Balfour, Margaret and Young, Ruth, *The Work of Medical Women in India,* p. 47
42. The ties between the WMS and the Dufferin Fund were further strengthened by creating the post of Medical Secretary for the Fund which was held by a member of the WMS, a role later expanded to Chief Medical officer of the WMS and Joint Secretary of the Fund.
43. After her death, Sir Harcourt Butler became President of the Dufferin Fund and its associated charities until the arrival of Frances Chelmsford in 1916.
44. Yvonne was the daughter of Sir Almeric Fitzroy, Knight Clerk of the Privy Council
45. OIOC, Fitroy diaries and correspondence, E 312/1
46. Ibid.
47. Ibid.
48. Ibid
49. Fitzroy correspondence and diaries, OIOC E 312 9(b)
50. The IMNS had been established in 1926.
51. Wavell-Sorabji letters, OIOC, Mss Eur F 165/130
52. Mountbatten papers, MB1/P92, Tours, 1945
53. Himself a member of that caste, Ambedkar was later the first Minister of Law and helped shape India's constitution.
54. Morgan, p. 387
55. Ibid.
56. Mountbatten papers, MB1/Q61: Corr w/Stella Reading
57. Morgan, p. 391
58. Ibid, p. 408.
59. Dufferin papers, PRONI, N4/V4
60. Ibid.

Chapter 8

1. Blunt, p. 48.
2. Gopal, p. 176
3. Quoted in Bence-Jones, *Viceroys of India,* p. 158.
4. Ibid, p. 240.
5. Anglo-Indians never forgave Ripon for his "surrender" of white interests, and his statue, erected in Calcutta in 1915, was paid for entirely by Indians, without any Anglo-Indian subscription.
6. Bence-Jones, p. 307
7. Dufferin, *Our Viceregal Life in India, Vol.II,* p. 299.
8. In 1893, Durand negotiated the frontier between British India and Afghanistan, called the Durand Line, now the official border between Afghanistan and Pakistan.
9. Dufferin, p. 318.
10. Ibid.
11. Ibid, p. 319.
12. Later that night, Nelly Dufferin's tent went up in flames (probably from the fireplace, although arson was suspected); Nelly and her maid barely escaped, both losing all their clothes in the blaze.
13. Dufferin, Vol. 2. p. 331.
14. Ibid., p. 341
15. Gopal, p. 174. Gopal says that this accusation would have been "unbelievable" of any viceroy in the 19th century except Dufferin.
16. After Curzon departed, a general serving in India told him that "Kitchener and the secretaries run the government, Lady Minto, the patronage, and HE runs the stables."
17. Quoted in Fowler, p. 303.
18. From Mary Minto's journal, quoted in Buchan, *Lord Minto: a Memoir,* p. 329
19. Ibid.
20. Bence-Jones, *The Viceroys of India,* p. 229.
21. Reading papers, OIOC, Eur Mss E 238
22. Birkenhead, p. 307
23. Quoted in Bence-Jones, *The Viceroys of India,* p. 264.
24. Ibid., p. 265.
25. Morgan, p. 422.
26. Ibid, p. 403.
27. Quoted in Bence-Jones, *Viceroys of India,* p. 314

Short biographies

Charlotte Stuart Canning, 1817–1861, Vicereine, 1856–1861
Born Paris, March 3, 1817, daughter of Sir Charles Stuart (later Lord Stuart de Rothsay) then ambassador to France, and Elizabeth Yorke, third daughter of Earl of Hardwicke. Extensive aristocratic and royal connections: granddaughter of two earls (Bute and Hardwicke), and wife of another; named for Queen Charlotte, George III's wife; served as Lady-in-Waiting to Queen Victoria. Married September 5, 1835; no children. Charlotte's detailed letters to Queen Victoria during the 1857 uprising conveyed a unique personal perspective of that conflict; also known for her superb watercolours and sketches of India. Died of malaria November 18, 1861. Known as the first renowned female "martyr of British India." Her grave and memorial at Barrackpore have remained under guard since Independence.

Mary Louisa Lambton Elgin, 1819–1898, Vicereine, 1862–1863
Born 1819, daughter of the Earl of Durham and Lady Louisa Elizabeth, eldest daughter of 2nd Earl Grey. Married 8th Earl of Elgin on November 2, 1846, after the death of his first wife. Children: Victor Alexander (1849), Robert (1851, died 1853); Charles (1853, died 1863); Frederick (1854); Louisa (1856). Accompanied Elgin during his tour as Governor General of Canada. In 1863, she learned of the death of her son, Charles, in England, which was followed by that of her husband in India. Mary Louisa returned to London to oversee the family estate until her son Victor Alexander, the 19th earl (and later viceroy) came of age. Died in Scotland on March 9, 1898.

Harriette Catherine Hamilton Lawrence, 1819–1917, Vicereine 1864–1869
Born County Meath, Ireland, daughter of Richard Hamilton, a rector, and Catherine Tipping, distant relatives of the Hamiltons who were later ennobled as Dufferin. Married August 26, 1841. Children: John Hamilton (1846), Henry Arnold (1848), Charles Napier, (1855), Herbert Alexander (1861), Catherine Letitia (Kate), Harriette Emily (1863), Alice Margaret, Mary Emma, Edith (d. 1861), Maude Agnes; two other children died in infancy One of only two vicereines who lived in India before becoming vicereine, and the only other vicereine than Charlotte Canning who experienced the Indian Mutiny. Died December 28, 1917.

Blanche Julia Wyndham Mayo, 1827–1918, Vicereine 1869–1872
Born East Riding England, 1827, fourth daughter, first Baron Leconfield and Mary Fanny Blunt, daughter of the Rev. William Blunt. Married October 31, 1848; children: Dermot Robert (1851); Maurice Archibald (1853); Algernon (1854); Terrance Theobald (1865); Florence Blanche Madeline (1861); Eva Constance Aline, (1863); another daughter born before Dermot died in infancy. Remembered chiefly for dignified behaviour following her husband's assassination in 1872. Later served Queen Victoria as an Extra Lady of the Bedchamber, 1874–1901. Died January 31, 1918.

Edith Villiers Lytton, CI, VA, 1841–1936, Vicereine 1876–1880
Born September 15, 1841, one of twin daughters of the Hon. Edward Villiers (brother of Lord Clarendon) and Elizabeth Liddell, daughter of Lord Ravensworth. Married October 4, 1864; children: Edward

Rowland John, (1865; died 1871); Henry Meredith Edward, 1872; died 1874); Victor Alexander George (2nd Earl) (1876); Neville Stephen (1879); Elizabeth Edith, (1867); Constance Georgina (1869); Emily (1874). Her major social concern in India was female education. First vicereine to attend a major public ceremony, the Imperial Assemblage, 1877. After her husband's death, her financial problems were eased by appointment as Lady of the Bedchamber to Queen Victoria and later Queen Alexandra. Died September 12, 1936.

Henrietta Anne Theodosia Vyner Ripon, CI, 1828–1907, Vicereine 1880–1884
Born 1828, West Riding, Yorkshire, daughter of Captain Henry Vyner and granddaughter of Earl de Grey, her husband's great uncle; married April 8, 1851; children: Oliver (1852); daughter Mary (1857, died 1858); her husband's principal political advisor and supporter throughout his career, actively aided his imposing liberal policies in India. In later life, actively supported the Liberal party and several children's welfare organizations in West Riding. Died February 28, 1907. Served as Lady of the Bedchamber to Queen Victoria, 1872–1874.

Hariot Georgina Hamilton Dufferin, CI, VA, DBE, 1843–1936, Vicereine 1884–1888
Born County Down, Ireland, February 5, 1843, eldest daughter of Captain Archibald. Rowan-Hamilton, of Killyleagh Castle, distantly related to the Dufferins. Married October 23, 1862; children: Archibald James (1863–1900); Terence John Temple (1866–1918); Ian Basil Gwaine Temple (1870–1917); Frederick Temple (1875–1930); Helen Hermione (1863); Hermione Catherine Helen (1869); Victoria Alexandrina (1873). Much admired by British and Indians for her major women and children's health efforts, esp. the Dufferin Fund, which she actively supported interest until her death. A prolific and lucid correspondent and author, her books on her time in India and Canada are among the most detailed accounts of viceregal experiences. Died October 25, 1936.

Maud Evelyn Hamilton Lansdowne, CI, VA, GBE, 1850–1932, Vicereine 1888–1894
Born December 17, 1850, youngest of seven daughters and seven sons of the Duke of Abercorn; married November 8, 1869; children: Henry (1872); Charles (1874); Evelyn Mary (1870); Beatrice Frances (1877). Most aristocratic of all the vicereines: daughter of a duke; married a marquess (as did her sister); one daughter married a duke, the other a marquis; son Charles married Lady Violet Minto. Renowned political hostess; succeeded Hariot Dufferin in both Canada and India. Post-India social work included creating the Officers Family Fund in the Boer War, and active service with Queen Alexandra's Nursing Corps, British Red Cross ,and St. John Ambulance Brigade; Lady of the Bedchamber to Queen Alexandra. Died October 21, 1932.

Constance Mary Carnegie Elgin, CI, 1851–1909, Vicereine 1894–1899
Born 1851, daughter of Sir James Carnegie, 6th Bt, and 9th Earl of Southesk; married November 9, 1876; children: Edward James (1881); Robert (1882); Alexander (1884); David (1888); John (1892); Victor Alexander (1897); Elizabeth Mary (1877); Christian Augusta (1879); Constance (1880); Marjorie (1885–1901) Rachel Catherine (1890). Weakened health, childbirth complications, and family issues limited her effectiveness in India; attempts to promote the Dufferin Fund described in correspondence with Queen Victoria. Died September 24, 1909.

Mary Leiter Curzon, CI, Kaisar-i-Hind Gold, 1870–1906, Vicereine 1898–1905
Born Chicago, Illinois, May 27, 1870, daughter of Levi and Mary Theresa Carver Leiter. Married April 22, 1895; children: Mary Irene (1896); Cynthia Blanche (1898); Alexandra Naldera (1904). The only American vicereine, her epithet "perfect" due to her youth, beauty, and her impressive appearance and conduct at the 1903 Durbar. Established Victoria Memorial Scholarships for nurses and laid ground-work for the Minto Nursing Association. Died July 18, 1906 from heart failure shortly after returning to England.

Mary Grey Minto, CI, DStJ, 1858–1940, Vicereine 1905–1910
Born (1858) and raised at St. James's Palace; daughter of General Sir Charles Grey and Caroline Eliza, VA, daughter of Sir Thomas Harvie Farquhar. Especially close to the monarchy since father was private secretary to Prince Albert and later Queen Victoria. Married July 28, 1883; children: Victor Gilbert (1891); Gavin William Esmond (1895–1917); Eileen Nina (1884); Ruby Florence (1886); Violet Mary (1889). In India, established the Lady Minto Nursing Association. Like Hariot Dufferin and Maud Lansdowne, was wife of the Governor General of Canada. Wrote a book about her Canadian experience, and later, *India, Minto and Morley*, a brief for her husband's dominant role in the Morley-Minto reforms of 1909. Post-India, promoted the Minto Nursing Association, served as Extra Lady of the Bedchamber to Queen Mary; died July 14, 1940.

Winifred Sturt Hardinge, CI, Kaisar-i-Hind Gold, 1868–1914, Vicereine, 1911–1914
Born 1868 in Dorset, daughter of 1st Baron Alington; married April 17, 1890; children: Edward (1892–1917); Alexander (1894); Diamond (1900); coordinated efforts leading to the Women's Medical

Service in India; helped establish first medical college for women in India (later named in her honour). Honoured by King and Parliament for her bravery during the assassination attempt of 1912; died unexpectedly on July 14, 1914 while in England for a rest from the Indian climate.

Frances Charlotte Guest Chelmsford, CI, GBE, 1869–1957, Vicereine 1916–1921
Born 1869; eldest daughter, 1st Baron Wimborne and Cornelia Henrietta Maria, Duke of Marlborough's eldest daughter; married July 27, 1894; children: Frederick Ivor (1896–1917); Andrew Charles Gerald (1903); Joan Frances (1895); Anne Molyneux (1898); Bridget Mary (1900); Margaret St. Clair Sidney (1911). Received GBE for war relief work. Lived in Italy after her husband's death in 1933; known as "La Contessa d'India." Died September 24, 1957.

Alice Edith Reading, CI, GBE, Kaisar-i-Hind Gold, 1866–1930, Vicereine 1921–1926
Born in London, 1866, daughter of Albert Cohen, a prosperous merchant. Married December 8, 1887; one son: Gerald Rufus Isaacs (1889). The only Jewish vicereine, and one of the most active in social welfare; despite operations for cancer and slow recovery, founded the Women of India Fund to coordinate existing social welfare organizations' fundraising and established the Lady Reading Hospital at Simla. Alice's health declined after she left India, and she died on January 30, 1930.

Dorothy Evelyn Augusta Onslow Irwin, CI, DCVO, JP, DGStJ, 1885–1976, Vicereine 1926–1929
Born 1885 Clandon, Surrey, younger daughter of 4th Earl of Onslow and Florence Coulston Gardner, elder daughter, 3rd Baron Gardner; married September 21, 1909; children: Charles Ingram (1912); Peter Courtenay (1916–1942); Richard Frederick Wood (1920); twin girls born July 1910: Mary Agnes (died August 1910); Anne Dorothy. Social work efforts in India included fundraising and administration of Dufferin Fund, Women's Medical Service,and All-India Education League; oversaw final details of building of Viceroy's House in New Delhi. Post-India experiences included accompanying Lord Irwin/Halifax during his ambassadorship in Washington D.C. during WWII. Died 1976.
George Goschen, 2nd Viscount Goschen of Hawkshurst served as viceroy and acting Governor General of India 1929 -1931

Margaret Evelyn Gathorne-Hardy, CI, LGStJ, Kaisar-i-Hind Gold
Youngest daughter of the 1st Earl of Cranbrook; married January 26, 1893; children: George Joachim (1893–1916); Phyllis Evelyn (1895); Cecily Winifred (1899). Died July 11, 1943.

Marie Brassey Willingdon, CI, DBE, GBE, DJStJ, Kaisar-i-Hind Gold, Order of the League of Mercy, 1875–1960, Vicereine 1931–1936
Born 1875 in Sussex, daughter 2nd Earl Brassey and Lady Idina Mary Nevill, lst Marquess of Abergavenny's daughter; married July 20, 1892: children: Gerard Frederick (killed in WWI, 1916); Inigo Brassey (1899). Like Harriette Lawrence, lived in India prior to becoming vicereine. Charming, energetic, and controversial, and best known for garish changes to Viceroy's House, and obsession with the colour mauve, she was devoted to India, and devoted extensive effort to the welfare of the Indian people and war relief. . Died, January 30, 1960.

Doreen Maud Milner Linlithgow CI (1936), DGStJ, Kaisar-i-Hind Gold, 1886–1965, Vicereine 1936–1943
Born in Yorkshire, May 20, 1886, second daughter of Sir Frederick George Milner, 7th Bt, and Adeline Gertrude Denison, daughter of William Beckett. Married April 11, 1919; children: twin sons, Charlie and John (1912); daughters Anne (1914 – twin sister died); Joan (1915); Doreen (1920). Active in public health matters, especially tuberculosis treatment and prevention. Established Tuberculosis Association of India (TAI), and made personal appeal in 1937 for funds to support nationwide program of education and treatment, and open regional and provincial TB clinics. Encouraged Edward Lutyens to remove Lady Willingdon's to "infelicitous additions" to the interior and gardens of the Viceroy's House in New Delhi. Died August 2, 1965, from injuries in a car wreck near Hopetoun.

Eugenie Wavell, CI, 1887–1987, Vicereine 1943–1947
Born in London, the daughter of Col. John Owen Quirk, and Eugenie O'Brien; married 1915; children: Archibald John (1916); Pamela (1918); Felicity (1920); Joan (1923). Wife of a career soldier and wartime vicereine; focused her energies on the Red Cross, St. John Ambulance Brigade, and other war relief efforts in India, including hospital work with her daughters. Returned to England in 1947; died 1987.

Edwina Cynthia Annette Ashley Mountbatten, CI, CBE, GBE, DCVO, GCStJ, 1901–1960, Vicereine 1947 (then wife of the Governor General of India, 1947–48)
Elder daughter of 2nd Baron Mount Temple and Amalia Mary Maud Cassel, the only child of Sir Ernest Cassel; married July 18, 1922; children: Patricia (1924); Pamela (1929). Internationally famed for her war relief work when she went to India, she earned further respect and admiration for working with refugees, freed prisoners-of-war and victims of massive rioting in post-Independence India and

Pakistan; oversaw dismantling of the Minto Nursing Association, and transfer of leadership of charitable organizations from British to Indian women. Died February 21, 1960.

Honours awarded to various vicereines

CI	Lady of the Imperial Order of the Crown of India
CBE	Commander of the Order of the British Empire
DBE	Dame Commander of the Order of the British Empire
GBE	Dame Grand Cross of the Order of the British Empire
DCVO	Dame Commander of the Royal Victorian Order
VA	Royal Order of Victoria and Albert
DStJ	Dame of Grace of the Order of St. John of Jerusalem
GCStJ	Baliff Grand Cross of the Order of St. John of Jerusalem

Kaisar-i-Hind   Instituted in 1900 to reward public service in India; Gold (1st Class)awarded by the Sovereign on the recommendation of the Secretary of State for India; silver (2nd Class) awarded by the Viceroy of India

Some commonalities

Three predeceased their husbands (Canning, Hardinge and Reading)
Two lived in India prior to being vicereine (Lawrence and Willingdon)
Five (Dufferin, Lansdowne, Irwin, Willingdon, Wavell) lost sons in WWI or WWII
Four served as ladies-in-waiting to the monarch before or after India (Canning, Lytton, Lansdowne, Minto)
Three lived into their nineties (Lytton, Dufferin, Minto)
Two viceregal families intermarried (Minto daughter to Lansdowne son)
Three had close personal ties with the royal family (Minto, Irwin, Mountbatten)

PICTURE SOURCES

The authors and publisher wish to express their thanks to the following sources of illustrative material and/or permission to reproduce it.
The Bridgeman Art Library, The British Library, The Maharaja Ganga Singhji Trust, Lallgarh Palace, Bikaner, India and Topham Picturepoint

Acknowledgements

Many people contributed to, and helped make this book possible. Our thanks to Texas A&M University's Department of History which funded Roger's faculty development leave in 2001–2002. Special thanks also to departmental colleagues Drs. Julia Blackwelder, Quince Adams and Jim Rosenheim, all of whom offered research direction and moral support. Gratitude is also due to Dr. Herb Richardson, Director, and Mr. Don Bugh, Executive Associate Director of the Texas Transportation Institute who made it possible for Penny to do research in the United Kingdom and remain a part-time employee at the Institute. Professor David Cannadine, currently the Whitney J. Oates Senior Research Scholar at Princeton University, provided thoughtful and most helpful comments on an early draft of the manuscript, and his wise counsel as the project moved forward. Sandra Tucker, associate professor at the Evans Library at Texas A&M was an invaluable resource for online and interlibrary loan information. Laura Nowlin's editing and proofreading expertise helped ensure clarity and accuracy.

We are grateful for the permission of Her Majesty Queen Elizabeth II to make use of material from the Royal Archives. We also appreciate of the assistance provided by the staffs at the archives where the primary source material was located: the British Library's Oriental and India Office Collection (now the South Asia, Pacific and Africa Collection); Miss Pamela Clark and the staff at the Royal Archives, Windsor Castle; the National Library of Scotland; the Public Record Office of Northern Ireland; the National Library of Ireland; the Borthwick Institute of Historical Research, York University; the Bodleian Library and the Indian Institute, Oxford University; Cambridge University; the Mountbatten Archives at Southampton University; the Public Record Office, County Durham; the Public Record Office, Kew; Rice University, Houston, Texas; Hopetoun House; the Indian Army Museum, Colne, Lancashire; and the Bowood Estate.

A long-term project such as this necessarily engages the interest of many friends and colleagues, and we are grateful for their encouragement. Our children, Eric Beaumont, Anne Beaumont, Katherine and Gregory Mason deserve special mention for their love and understanding.

Index of names